HAMLYN ALL COLOUR
BOOK OF DIY AND HOME IMPROVEMENTS

HAMLYN ALL COLOUR
BOOK OF DIY AND HOME IMPROVEMENTS

TED SMART

CONTENTS

Introduction   7

PART 1: EXTERIOR

CONCRETE *Brian Daniels*

Concrete types, aggregates, and admixtures	10
Tools and techniques	12
Mixing, estimating quantities, storing	14
Formwork and foundations	17
Project 1: Laying a garden path	18
Project 2: Laying foundations for a wall	20
Project 3: Laying a damp-proof floor for a workshop	21
Repairing a broken path edge	21

BRICKS, BLOCKS & RENDERING *Brian Daniels*

Brick and concrete-block types and sizes	22
Tools and techniques	25
Bonds and piers	26
Bricklaying technique	28
Project 1: Building a brick wall	29
Jointing and pointing	30
Project 2: Building a pierced-screen wall	31
Repointing brickwork	32
Repairs to rendering	32
Tyrolean rendering	33

PAVING, PATIOS & STEPS *Brian Daniels*

Planning	34
Project 1: Laying a patio	36
Using stone and concrete paving	37
Concrete blocks, crazy paving, and brick paving	38
Laying concrete paving blocks	38
Brick paving patterns	39
Project 2: Building garden steps	40

ROOFING REPAIRS *Brian Daniels*

Roof structures	42
Roof access: ladders and scaffold towers	44
Slates and tiles	46
Repairing ridges	47
Repairing hips and valleys	48
Repairing flashing	50
Repairing chimneys	51
Gutters	52
Project: Re-tiling a window bay	54
Re-felting a flat roof	55

EXTERIOR TIMBER *Mike Lawrence*

Protection and preservation	56
Tools and techniques	58
Fascias and soffits	58
Bargeboards	59
Windows	59
Doors and frames	60
Wall cladding	60
Project 1: Building a lean-to	62
Fences and gates	64
Project 2: Building a shed	64

EXTERIOR DECORATING *John Sanders*

When to do it	68
Types of surface	68
Types of decorating materials	69
Preparing wood and metal	70
Painting technique	71
Painting rendering	73

MAINTENANCE CHECKLIST *Mike Trier*

Symptoms, causes, and cures of common problems inside and outside the house	74

This edition first published in 1989
as the *Home Handyman* by The Hamlyn
Publishing Group Limited
part of Reed International Books
Michelin House, 81 Fulham Road
London SW3 6RB

Reprinted 1990

Copyright © 1982 Hennerwood Publications Limited

ISBN 0 600 56360 X

Produced by Mandarin Offset
Printed and bound in Hong Kong

PART 2: INTERIOR

PLUMBING *Stuart Burrell*

Domestic water and waste systems	78
Pipework and fittings	78
Tools and techniques	81
Project: Fitting a double-bowl sink unit	84
Plumbing in a new cistern	86
Installing a shower	87
Burst and frozen pipes	89
Changing washers	89

CENTRAL HEATING *Stuart Burrell*

Designs and control systems	90
Changing a valve	93
Maintenance	94
Changing the pump	95

ELECTRICITY *Mike Lawrence*

Principles	96
Fuses	98
Domestic systems	98
Tools and techniques	102
Project 1: Converting a single socket into a double	107
Project 2: Power to outbuildings	108
Project 3: Wiring up an instantaneous shower	109
Project 4: Installing a wall light	111

INTERNAL WALLS *Robert Tattersall*

Wall types	112
Removing a load-bearing wall	114
Building a partition	116
Wall and ceiling fixings	120

CARPENTRY *David Fisher*

Wood types	122
Tools and techniques	124
Joints	130
Finishes	134
Door furniture	136

INSULATION *Mike Lawrence*

Draughtproofing	139
Roofs	140
Attics and lofts	141
Flat roofs	142
Walls	142
Floors	143
Windows and doors	143
Ventilation	144
Plumbing	145

INTERIOR DECORATING *Ann Lamacraft*

Colour	148
Equipment	150
Painting	152
Decorative paint finishes	156
Wallcoverings	160
Wallpaper and vinyl	163
Plastic laminates	166
Wallboards	169
Ceramic tiles	170
Floor coverings	174
Floorboard finishes	179

Glossary	183
Index	186

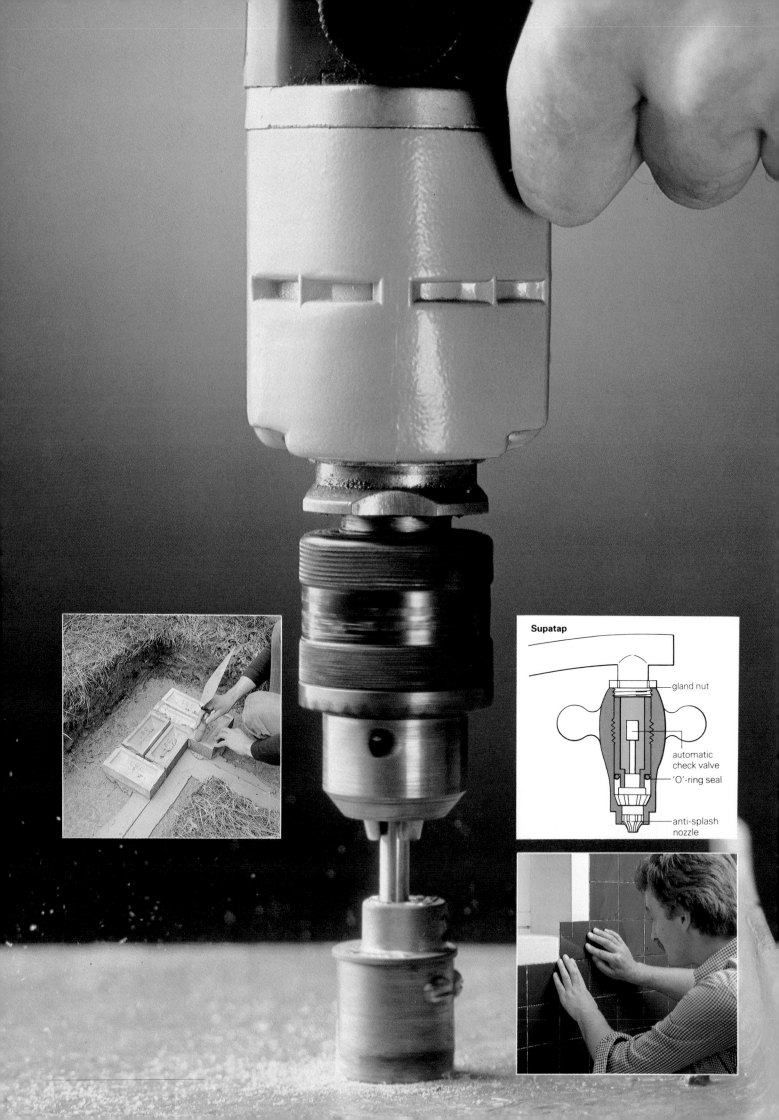

Supatap

gland nut

automatic
check valve

'O'-ring seal

anti-splash
nozzle

INTRODUCTION

Today more people than ever rely on their own knowledge and practical skills to carry out new work, repairs, and maintenance in and around the home. This book is designed to show you how to acquire that knowledge and exercise those skills.

People become involved in DIY work for a variety of reasons. No doubt the chance to save money is one of the most important. But this has rarely if ever been the only reason – and in any case the increasing use of mass-production methods in the home-improvement field has created a situation where it is often cheaper for the handyman to buy certain items than to make them himself. On the other hand, many people are attracted by the crafts element of DIY – the pleasure of designing and making something, of putting one's own, individual stamp on a piece of work. A third reason is the widely held conviction that much household repair and building work done by professionals nowadays is not only over-priced but too often of a standard that many a home handyman could improve on if he had the know-how.

There are whole areas of home-improvement and repair work that until a few years ago do-it-yourselfers tended to avoid but which today are well within the competence of the more enthusiastic handyman. Domestic plumbing is a striking example of this. The use of copper and plastic piping and fittings has made the cutting and joining of pipework a simple matter; equally important for the handyman is the fact that such fittings are now readily obtainable not only at builders' merchants (where do-it-yourselfers have only recently begun to feel welcome) but also at the High Street DIY stores.

Industry was slow to respond to the DIY revolution. But today easy-to-use materials (paints and other coatings, adhesives, plastics of all kinds), easy-to-use tools (especially power tools), and easy-to-assemble kits (such as base units for fitted kitchens) are widely available and are often remarkably cheap. More recently we have seen the rise of specialised shops that hire out equipment that is essential for certain home-improvement work but that it would be quite uneconomic for the handyman to buy for just one particular project.

The experienced home handyman knows that two of the keys to successful DIY work are, first, knowing which jobs or parts of jobs he can tackle and which he would better leave to professionals; and, second, knowing which things he can build entirely himself and which he should assemble from bought-in components. This book will help you to acquire that kind of basic know-how. It shows in word and picture how to plan and carry out a host of major and minor construction, repair, and maintenance jobs in the house and garden. The many techniques and projects are illustrated in vivid step-by-step photo sequences and drawings, and any potential problems (from technical pitfalls to safety matters and building regulations) are clearly spelt out. Finally, the book aims to make DIY not only a useful but also a satisfying hobby for beginner and enthusiast alike.

PART 1
EXTERIOR

This section deals with the outside of the house and outbuildings, paving for the garden, and the gates, fences, walls, and other boundaries to the property. It features large and small items of maintenance and repair, general improvements to the appearance of the outside of the house, and a whole range of projects – from building a brick or pierced-screen-block wall to re-felting a roof.

Concrete 10–21
Brick, Blocks & Rendering 22–33
Paving, Patios & Steps 34–41
Roofing Repairs 42–55
Exterior Timber 56–67
Exterior Decorating 68–73

CONCRETE

Concrete is one of the most basic of building materials. In its freshly mixed state it can be used for foundations, floorings, garage drives, paths, and steps. As factory-made pre-cast products, it can be used to lay a patio or build a garage.

Concrete is not the most beautiful of materials, and it does tend to stain and look dirty rather than mellow and soften with age. But if appearance is critical, there are many things that can be done to improve its looks. You can, for instance, add colouring agents to the mix; you can produce an interesting texture on the surface; or you can expose the natural stones in the concrete. In the garden, you can also introduce other materials such as bricks and timber to complement your concrete and add warmth of colour.

What is concrete?
The basis of concrete is cement, which when mixed with water acts as a glue to bind the other constituents together. To provide strength and bulk, crushed stone or gravel (coarse aggregate) and sand (fine aggregate) are added to the mix. The cement and water paste coats the particles of aggregate and, when it sets, binds them together into a dense mass. By varying the proportions of cement and aggregates, concrete of various strengths can be produced to suit different applications. (Mortars and renderings, incidentally, are concrete mixes without the coarse aggregate.)

Freshly mixed concrete can be moulded. It begins to set one to two hours after mixing. After about seven days it will have gained about half its ultimate strength, and at 28 days it will have reached about 85 per cent.

How to buy concrete
You can buy concrete in various forms. If you need large amounts – a minimum of three cubic metres (which weighs seven tonnes!) – you could buy ready-mixed concrete. This would be delivered to your house in a mixer truck and tipped probably just off the road. You would then have to transport it yourself by wheelbarrow to the job. Smaller ready-mixed quantities are also available but at a higher cost.

At the other end of the scale, you can buy various-sized bags of dry-mix, which contains all the ingredients for concrete except water. Dry-mix is more expensive than buying the individual ingredients and mixing them yourself, but it is more convenient to use.

Between these two extremes falls the majority of concreting jobs, for which it is most appropriate to buy bags of cement and aggregates and to proportion and mix them yourself, either with a shovel or using a power mixer.

Cement
Ordinary Portland cement is suitable for practically all concrete projects that the home handyman is likely to tackle. It is made in accordance with a British Standard, and should be exactly the same no matter which manufacturer's name is on the bag.

Ordinary Portland cement is sold in 50kg (110lb) bags and is available from all builders' merchants and most garden centres. For special applications, there are a number of other types of cement; these are more expensive but could occasionally be worthwhile.

Rapid-hardening Portland cement gains strength more quickly than Ordinary Portland, but its strength at 28 days is roughly the same. Because the reaction between the water and cement proceeds more rapidly, however, more heat is given out during the initial stages. So if you are obliged to lay concrete during the winter months, consider using rapid-hardening Portland cement. It will still need protecting from frost, but for a shorter time.

Sulphate-resisting Portland cement is used to improve the resistance of concrete and mortars to attack from sulphates, which are contained in some soils and can be troublesome particularly when there is ground water present. Sulphates, too, are present in some degree in clay bricks, but will not be a problem unless the bricks become saturated and remain wet for long periods. Under these conditions the sulphate salts soak into the mortar, where they react with the cement and cause the joints to expand. It takes about a year for attack to become noticeable.

Free-standing walls and retaining walls backed by soil are particularly vulnerable to such attack, and for these structures you should use bricks of special quality which have a low soluble-salt content. If you use second-hand bricks, and you are not sure what type they are, use mortar made with sulphate-resisting Portland cement.

White and coloured cements. White Portland cement is available in 25kg (55lb) bags as well as the normal 50kg (110lb) size. Tints can be achieved by adding dry powder colours to the concrete mix in its dry state before the water is added. Particular care is required in proportioning and mixing materials to ensure that the colour of your concrete is even and consistent from batch to batch. If you are matching a colour, remember that the concrete will look darker when wet than when dry. Colours, too, will fade over the years. When using coloured pigments, white Portland cement is often used instead of the grey Ordinary Port-

1

2

3

land cement because the colours will come up brighter.

Masonry cement can be used for mortars, and is particularly suitable for the weaker mortars used with concrete bricks and blocks where strength is not important. It contains a proportion of inert filler material and a plasticiser so that, without using lime, a smooth mortar mix is produced.

Aggregates

Two types of aggregate are needed for cement. The coarse aggregate, which adds body to the concrete, may be either crushed rock or gravel; both are suitable. They are graded by the supplier into different sizes, and the 20mm (¾in) size, which is used for foundations and ground slabs, is the most common. For thin concrete sections, such as paths of 75mm (3in) thickness or less, 10mm (⅜in) sized aggregate would be more appropriate.

To fill the spaces between the pieces of gravel or rock so as to produce dense concrete, fine aggregate is also needed in the mix. For concrete, the fine aggregate is coarse, gritty sand known as sharp or concreting sand. Fine sand, known as soft or bricklayer's sand, is used only for mortars and renderings.

Combined aggregates, which contain both the coarse and fine material mixed together, are perhaps the easiest to deal with. You need to order, stockpile, and mix only one material instead of two. But beware, some aggregates have too high a proportion of fine particles and have to be mixed with extra coarse.

Concrete ingredients 1 Ballast of fine and coarse aggregate; 2 Aggregate suitable for thin concrete sections; 3 Bricklayer's sand for mortars and renderings; 4 Ordinary Portland cement; 5 Cement with red toner; 6 Cement with green toner.

material. However, beware of any confusion of terms with your supplier. The term should imply a material that has been graded and mixed in the right proportions. This is best for concrete work. Avoid 'as-dug' ballast, which may contain too much fine material. In particular, do not use unwashed 'as-dug' ballast, which may contain soil and other impurities.

Admixtures

Admixtures are used to modify the properties of concrete in some way, perhaps to delay the set or to make it more workable. They are available from builders' merchants in the form of liquids, powders, or pastes which are added to the concrete during mixing.

There is a strong body of opinion that reckons admixtures should be avoided by the amateur, who will have enough on his hands to proportion and mix the basic ingredients of concrete correctly, without this extra complication.

Certainly, Ordinary Portland cement, mixed properly, is suitable for the majority of jobs without any extras. Occasionally, however, the use of an admixture can make the work easier. You must be scrupulous, though, about following the manufacturer's instructions on storage, dosing and mixing.

Retarders reduce the initial rate of reaction between the cement and water, and so delay the setting of the concrete. It is possible to delay the set for several hours, during which time you could place, compact, and finish the concrete in a more leisurely fashion than normal. When the set does start, hardening will proceed at the normal rate.

This admixture really comes into its own with ready-mixed concrete, where

Bag your own aggregate
Aggregates can often be bought in plastic bags if only small amounts are needed. It is worth taking a few heavy duty plastic bags to your garden centre or builders' merchant to investigate; and be prepared to fill the bags yourself. Fill the bags only about half full, otherwise you will have great difficulty in lifting them and they will very likely burst.

Skin protection
Some skins are sensitive to cement and contact can cause rashes and irritation. Always wash off cement immediately it gets on hands and arms; if your skin is sensitive, wear rubber gloves.

you could well be faced with a sufficiently large volume to make its use justified. If you anticipate difficulty in handling the volume of ready-mixed concrete you require, ask your supplier for a special grade containing a retarder. The admixture will be incorporated as part of a controlled mixing process.

Accelerators increase the initial rate of reaction and accelerate the setting and early strength development of the concrete. More heat is given out in the early stages of setting, which can be used to advantage in freezing weather. Accelerators may cause problems in large batches of concrete if the work is not completed in a short time.

Water-reducing agents, known as plasticisers, increase the workability of the concrete, or permit concrete to be made with usual workability but with less than usual water; this results in an increase in strength.

Air-entraining agents are used to form minute bubbles of air in the cement paste which increase the concrete's impermeability, durability, and particularly its frost resistance. They are especially useful where concrete may come into contact with de-icing salts, as on a driveway.

Tools & Techniques

You will probably already have many of the tools needed for concreting; others you can make for yourself out of scrap timber. If you do have to buy any items, it is worth buying the best quality you can afford. Concrete is a very demanding material as far as equipment is concerned – it is heavy and can strain and buckle wheelbarrows, and it will corrode light-aluminium parts of tools. Whatever the tools, though, they must all be cleaned thoroughly after use. Hardened concrete on spades and shovels only adds unnecessary weight.

Tools required are as follows:

A **steel tape measure** for setting out – a 15m (50ft) tape is long enough for most purposes.

A **builder's level** about 900mm (3ft) long, and with at least two bubble tubes set at right-angles to each other so that you can check for vertical as well as horizontal accuracy.

A **shovel** and a **spade**; a shovel has greater capacity and is far better than a spade for moving aggregates and for mixing concrete, but a spade is necessary for removing topsoil and digging foundation trenches.

An ordinary **garden rake** is useful for the initial spreading of concrete when laying a slab.

Your garden roller will come in handy for compacting soil and hardcore to form a base for concrete. A light roller for lawns, however, may not be heavy enough; instead you could make **a rammer**. Cast a block of concrete in a cardboard box and insert a broom

handle or a length of steel tube into the fresh concrete. Leave it as long as possible to set and harden before use – ideally a full 28 days.

You will need a **wheelbarrow** to transport concrete or aggregates. A light garden barrow will not be strong enough to cope with much of this kind of work – it may buckle the frame or wheel if you overload it. If you have a lot of material to move, hire or buy a heavy-duty steel barrow.

Basic carpentry tools, such as a general purpose **saw** and a **claw hammer**, will be needed to make the formwork to contain and mould the concrete.

Plastic buckets can be used to measure out materials, but look for those with strong handles. You will need two, one of which should be kept exclusively for cement and should remain dry. If you intend to carry concrete in buckets to the job, it is worth buying heavy-duty rubber or galvanised steel buckets with sturdy handles.

To finish the concrete, you will need a soft **brush** or a harder **broom** and a **wooden float**, **steel float**, or **steel trowel**, depending on the surface you require.

Tools you can make
A **builder's square** (which is, in fact, a triangle) is invaluable for ensuring that the corners of a slab or patio are square when setting out. You can make one from three pieces of straight, scrap timber screwed together. The three pieces should form a triangle the length of whose sides is in a 3:4:5 ratio. These proportions ensure that one of the angles is a right-angle. The square can be made to any size provided you maintain the proportions. A convenient size has sides 600, 800, and 1000mm (23½, 31½, and 39½in) long.

A levelling aid, known as a T-shaped **boning rod**, is useful. You will need three rods, all of exactly the same height. Use two pieces of timber for each one. The leg of the 'T' should be about 1200mm (4ft) long and the cross-piece about 600mm (2ft). Screw the cross-piece to the top of the leg, making

Equipment for working with concrete
1 Builder's barrow of heavy-duty steel;
2 Spade for digging trenches; 3 Shovel for moving aggregates; 4 Garden fork for removing topsoil; 5 Plastic bucket with strong steel handle; 6 Builder's square; 7 Claw hammer, 8 15m (50ft) steel tape; 9 Builder's level; 10 Boning rods, used for establishing levels during setting out; 11 Home-made tamping beam to compact concrete; 12 Stiff broom for texturing surface of fresh concrete; 13 Carpenter's saw for making formwork; 14 Steel trowel; 15 Wooden float; 16 Steel float.

Long-range levels
To establish levels over long distances, a technique using a hosepipe and water is very accurate. An ordinary garden hosepipe is suitable, but stick a short length of transparent plastic tubing in both ends of the hose. Hammer a peg into the ground and tie one end of the hose to it, making sure that this end of the pipe is at the required level. Hammer a peg where you want to set the next level and tie the other end of the hosepipe to it. Fill the hosepipe with water. Let it flow out at the other end to make sure that all the air is expelled. Water finds its own level so, when the water at the correctly levelled end of the pipe is at the top, gradually lower the other end until the water is at the top of this end as well. This top is now at the level you need and you can put in another peg to the required height.

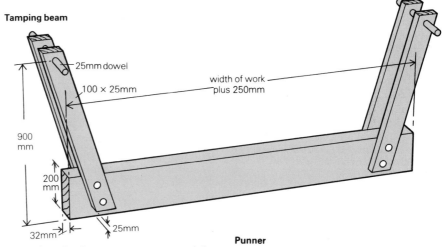

Tamping beam
25mm dowel
100 × 25mm
width of work plus 250mm
900 mm
200 mm
32mm
25mm

sure that it forms an accurate right-angle.

A proper **mixing platform** will keep soil out of the mix and enable you to shovel off the concrete without wastage. For a solid job, make the platform out of 10mm (⅜in) external-quality plywood about 900mm (3ft) square. Nail battens or offcuts underneath to raise it off the ground.

To compact concrete, you will need a **punner** (for concrete in a foundation trench) and a **tamping beam** (for a concrete slab). You can make a punner by nailing together a few pieces of timber to form a pad about 300 × 200mm (12 × 8in) square and about 75mm (3in) thick. Drill a hole in it large enough to take a broom handle, and cross-nail this to keep it firm. A tamping beam is simply a length of straight timber about 300mm (12in) longer than the width of the formwork. For small slabs, 100 × 50mm (4 × 2in) section timber is suitable; for larger slabs such as a garage drive use 150 × 50mm (6 × 2in) timber. The beam will be much easier to use if you fit handle-bars at each end, so that you can operate it standing up rather than in a crouching position.

Punner

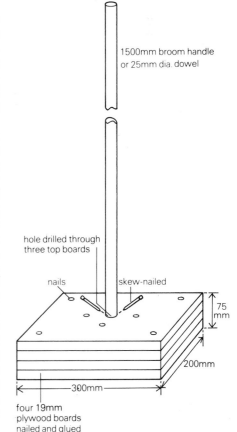

1500mm broom handle or 25mm dia. dowel
hole drilled through three top boards
nails
skew-nailed
75 mm
200mm
300mm
four 19mm plywood boards nailed and glued

Mixing, Estimating & Storage

The first job, whether it is to work out the number of paving slabs you need or to determine the volume of concrete required, is to calculate in square metres the area involved.

For rectangles, it is easy; multiply the length by the width. For triangular shapes, it is half the length of the base times the height. You can work out irregular shapes with straight sides as a combination of rectangles and triangles. For a very irregular area, draw it out to scale and then, to the same scale, draw 1m squares over it. You can then estimate the area by counting the squares and averaging-out part squares.

Having calculated the area in square metres, all you do to find the volume is to multiply the area by the depth of the concrete, which will be in decimals of a metre. The result is in cubic metres.

Say, for example, you wish to build a patio 6m (20ft) long and 3m (10ft) wide. The area of the concrete is $6 \times 3m = 18m^2$ The depth of the slab is to be 100mm or 0.1m. The volume of concrete is $18 \times 0.1m = 1.8m^3$.

Always allow a margin for wastage, rounding up volumes to the nearest half or whole cubic metre. With units such as bags of cement, paving slabs, concrete blocks, allow 10% to the nearest

Ready-mixed concrete being delivered. A simple chute has been made to direct the concrete to the exact spot.

whole unit on the number you estimate. It is much better to have one or two blocks left over at the end of the day than to be one short so that you cannot finish the job completely.

Ready-mixed concrete
If you need a volume of three cubic metres or more, then you should consider using ready-mixed concrete. If you need slightly less than this amount, ask around to see if any of your neighbours need concrete and will buy the remainder from you.

With ready-mixed concrete it is vital to be prepared for when the truck arrives; if you keep the driver waiting too long, you may be charged extra. Decide where best the concrete can be tipped. This should obviously be as near to the job as possible, but the truck is about 2.5m (8ft) wide and 3.5m (11½ft) high and so it cannot manoeuvre easily into a tight drive. Generally the driver will leave the road to discharge his load only if there is a suitable area of hardstanding for him to drive on to. But you may be able to build a rough timber chute to carry the concrete from the mixer to the site.

Put down a plastic sheet to receive the concrete. This will make cleaning up much easier afterwards. Round up as many wheelbarrows, shovels, and friends to help as you can muster. Three cubic metres takes a lot of effort

to transport. Make the route for wheelbarrows as easy and safe as possible. Fix strong, well-supported planks of wood to form ramps down steps. Do not fill barrows too full at first until you have had time to get used to the weight; once a barrow starts to tip, it takes a lot of strength to get it level again and you could end up with a barrow-load of concrete in your flower bed.

To find suppliers in your area, look in *Yellow Pages* under 'Concrete: ready-mixed'. Prices vary, so get more than one quotation. The supplier will need to know how much concrete you require in cubic metres, when you need it, what you need if for, and how you propose to handle it on delivery. He can then determine an appropriate mix and the cost. When you place an order, find out what is the latest cancellation time. If it rains, your gang of helpers may disappear, and you will need to delay delivery.

Mixing your own: choosing the mix
If the job is too small to justify ready-mixed concrete, or you prefer to do the work in stages over several week-ends, you will have to buy the ingredients and mix your own. The first thing is to decide what mix proportions to use, so that you can estimate what volume of each material you need.

For normal concrete work around the house, however, only two basic mixes need be considered.

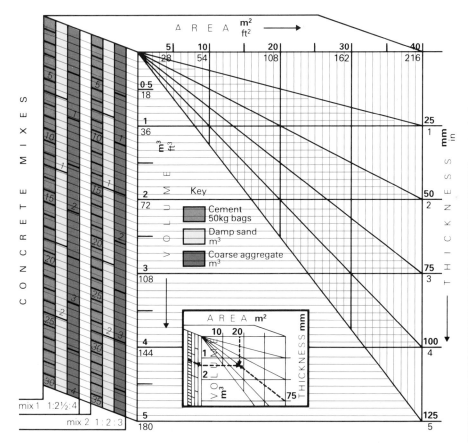

To find the proportions of cement and aggregate needed for either mix one or two, read along the diagonal line from the value of the required thickness of the layer (on the right-hand axis) to the point where it intersects with the vertical line extending down from the value of the area to be covered. The volume and proportions are obtained by reading to the left along the horizontal line.

Avoid concrete stains
Take care not to splash fresh concrete on to aluminium door and window frames. Aluminium is susceptible to alkalis and will be permanently stained if the concrete remains in contact with it.

Remove concrete waste
Concrete can set under water. You will never clean concrete off a spade merely by letting it soak overnight in a bucket of water. And never flush waste concrete down a drain. It will harden and may cause a blockage.

Making a smoother mix
A common practice when mixing concrete is to add a few squirts of washing-up liquid to the bucket of water. This acts as a 'wetting agent', enabling the water to mix more readily with the dry materials to produce a smoother mix.

Boot test for concrete
A simple way to check whether you have added enough water and the concrete is of the correct workability is the 'boot test'. The concrete should be capable of being moulded, yet be stiff enough to retain an impression. Tread the heel of your boot into the mix: the impression left in the concrete should be close textured and quite identifiable. If it appears crumbly, the mix is too dry; if cement slurry oozes into the depression, the mix is too wet. Adjust either with more water or more dry material.

Concrete Mix 1 is an all-purpose mix suitable for general concrete work such as foundation and floor slabs. Proportions by volume are 1:2½:4. Using a bucket to measure out ingredients, this gives: 1 bucket of cement to 2½ of damp sand to 4 of coarse aggregate.

Because the fine particles fill the spaces between the bigger particles, the volume of concrete will not be 1 + 2½ + 4 = 7½ buckets, as you might expect, but is, in fact, about 5 buckets.

For 1m³ (one cubic metre) of Mix 1 concrete you need 6 bags of cement, 0.5m³ of damp sand and 0.8m³ of coarse aggregate.

With combined aggregates, the proportions for Mix 1 concrete are 1:5. Using a bucket to measure out the ingredients, this represents 1 bucket of cement to 5 of combined aggregates. The yield is about five buckets of concrete. For 1m³ of Mix 1 concrete you need 6 bags of cement and 1m³ of combined aggregates.

Concrete Mix 2 is stronger and more suited to thin sections such as slabs of 75mm (3in) thickness or less. Proportions by volume are 1:2:3. This represents 1 bucket of cement to 2 of damp sand to 3 of coarse aggregate. The yield is about 4 buckets of concrete.

For 1m³ of Mix 2 concrete you need 7 bags of cement, 0.5m³ of damp sand and 0.75m³ of coarse aggregate.

Using combined aggregates, the proportions required for Mix 2 concrete are 1:3¾. This represents 1 bucket of cement to 3¾ buckets of combined aggregates. The yield is about 3¾ buckets of concrete.

For 1m³ of Mix 2 concrete you need 7 bags of cement and 1m³ of combined aggregates.

Sand is almost always supplied damp, and the proportions given for both Mix 1 and Mix 2 are calculated on this basis. If the sand is dry – really dry throughout and not just on the surface – reduce the amount of sand at each mixing by about half a bucket in both cases.

Mixing your own: buying materials
Using the example of a slab for a patio (see 'Mixing, Estimating & Storage', page 14), the slab is 100mm (4in) thick and Mix 1 is, therefore, appropriate.

So, for 1m³ of Mix 1 concrete, you would need 6 bags of cement, 0.5m³ of damp sand and 0.8m³ of coarse aggregate. For the 1.8m³, which we calculated as the volume of the concrete slab, you would need:

1.8 × 6 = 10.8 bags of cement
1.8 × 0.5 = 0.9m³ sand
1.8 × 0.8 = 1.44m³ coarse aggregate.

Adding on 10% extra to the cement, and rounding up to the nearest whole bag, you will need 12 bags of cement. Rounding up the quantities of aggregates to the next half or whole cubic metre, you will need 1m³ of sand and 1.5m³ of coarse aggregate.

Dry-mix concrete
For small jobs, dry-mix concrete can be bought in bags up to 50kg (110lb), which makes about 0.02m³ of concrete.

Two grades of dry-mix are normally on sale, which correspond to Mix 1 and Mix 2 concrete. One is a general-purpose mix and the other is for thin sections or where you want a fine finish.

In addition to the convenience of having all the materials needed in just one bag, dry-mix means little wastage at the end of the job. Savings on wastage help offset the higher initial cost.

Technique

Hand-mixing

It is essential to mix up all the ingredients in the dry state (*see 1, below*) before you add water. This also applies when you are using dry-mix, since the contents may have separated out during handling. Empty out the whole bag and mix thoroughly first before adding the water.

Measure out the individual materials into a heap using a separate bucket, which can be kept dry, for cement. Tap the bucket of cement a few times with the shovel and re-fill it to the brim.

Mix thoroughly until the whole pile is uniform in colour and there are no light streaks of cement (*see 1, below*). Then form a crater in the pile (2) and add water sparingly. Shovel dry material from the sides into the crater (3) until the water is absorbed and then turn the whole pile over a few times. Continue mixing in this way until the concrete is uniform and workable (4) – stodgy rather than runny.

Staining of paths and driveways can be prevented by mixing on a plastic tray or on plywood.

Power mixing

To take the hard work out of mixing the concrete yourself, you can buy or hire different kinds of power mixer. Some consist of these mixers simply of a mixing drum on a trolley which is turned by rolling the trolley up and down. Another type is powered by an ordinary electric drill, which is connected to a gearbox at the back of the machine. Then there is a range of somewhat larger mixers, driven by either petrol or electric motors, that have a detachable drum to simplify storage and maintenance and make them easier to store. Stands are generally available, too, so you can mount the mixer at the correct height for discharging directly into a wheel-barrow. Alternatively, you may find it easier to wheel the mixer to the job to discharge the concrete.

If you have a lot of concrete to mix, it may be worth hiring a diesel-powered mixer – the type you see on most building sites – which can produce about $0.08m^3$ of concrete in one mix. But if you hire any power equipment, make sure you are given a demonstration and an instruction sheet so that you understand exactly how the controls work – there may be occasions when you need to turn the machine off in a hurry! Be ready to start the job as soon as the machine is delivered. It will be costing you money while it is standing idle on site.

To mix concrete to the right consistency in a power mixer, add half the coarse aggregate and half the water first; then add all the sand. Mix for a minute or two, then add all the cement and the remainder of the coarse aggregate. Finally, add just as much water as you need to obtain a workable mix. When you have worked out how much water you need for one mix, make a mark on the water bucket as a guide for re-filling. Most beginners add too much water. The concrete should fall off the mixer blades cleanly without being too sloppy.

Do not leave the mixer empty for too long. During a lunch break, leave it running and add the coarse aggregate and water for the next batch. This will keep the drum and blades clean. To clean the mixer at the end of the day, again put in a few shovelsful of coarse aggregate and some water, and leave it running for a while before emptying. All the cement must be removed.

Like all machinery, mixers can be dangerous if misused. Always stop the mixer before putting anything – a shovel and particularly your hand – into the drum.

Storage of materials

The paper bags in which cement is sold are not waterproof and, if stored on the ground, they will absorb moisture and the cement will start to set. The best way to store cement is undercover in a garage or shed. Make a platform from planks of wood placed on bricks and stack the bags of cement flat on them. If cement must be stored outdoors, stack the bags on a slatted platform away from the ground so that air can circulate; and cover them with a plastic sheet, weighted or tied down to stop it being lifted by the wind.

If a bag has been partly used, the remaining cement can be stored for a while by placing the bag into a stout plastic bag and sealing the top tightly.

All bags of cement, no matter how well stored, will eventually set by absorbing moisture from the atmosphere. It is advisable, therefore, to plan carefully and buy only enough bags of cement for the job in hand.

If you buy coarse and fine aggregates separately they must be kept separate during storage. Use planks of wood to form storage bays.

Pile the aggregates on an area of hardstanding – ideally concrete, otherwise plywood or hardboard or, if nothing else, plastic sheeting. This will make shovelling it up much easier than if it were on bare earth, it minimises wastage and avoids contaminating the fine aggregate with soil.

Try to keep the sand covered, otherwise leaves and litter will blow on to the heap and will be troublesome to remove. Uncovered sand, too, is particularly tempting to small children, and you could well find yourself mixing someone's favourite doll or toy car into your concrete.

Formwork & Foundations

For slabs, paths, and patios laid on the ground, you will have to make timber formwork to retain and mould the fresh concrete. The sides of the formwork must be substantial. Use straight timber about 25mm (1in) thick. Set the side forms on edge, the top edge being at the level of the finished slab. It is obviously easier if the forms are the same width as the slab is thick, otherwise you will have to recess them into the ground. Hold the side forms in place with pegs, to which the forms are nailed. The peg-tops must be below the top of the formwork.

Use your builder's square to ensure that the corners are square, and make the butt joints fit tight, otherwise cement will seep through and your slab will have ragged corners.

When you lay a path or patio, you must slope the concrete very slightly to allow rainwater to drain away. So set one side of the formwork lower than the other to allow for the slope. To check the fall, place a straight edge across the formwork and use a spirit level half a bubble out of true.

Placing and compacting

Build up foundations by putting the concrete in the trench in layers about 200mm (8in) thick, and compact each layer thoroughly with a punner. This will expel air trapped in the mix and give a strong, dense concrete.

For slabs, put the concrete into the formwork, working it into the corners, and spread it evenly with a rake to a level just above the tops of the forms.

This excess will allow for settlement.

Compact the slab with your tamping beam using a rhythmic chopping action. Lift the beam and drop it down again a few times then change to a sawing action, which will level high spots and fill low spots as you move the beam along the tops of the forms. Continue tamping until the concrete is flush with the tops of the formwork.

Finishing and curing

A wide variety of finishes can be given to the surface of the concrete. Which you choose will be governed by your own personal preferences, and the use to which the concreted area will serve. For a garage drive, the fairly rough texture left by the tamping beam would be appropriate. For a workshop floor, a smoother texture obtained with a wooden float – used with a wide sweeping action – would be easier to keep clean.

You can create a lightly textured finish, suitable for a garden path, by brushing the freshly compacted concrete with a soft broom. If the path slopes along its length, use a stiff garden broom for a deeper texture to give even greater slip resistance.

A more decorative finish can be obtained by exposing the pieces of stone or gravel in the concrete. Finish the slab with a soft brush, wait for an hour or so until the concrete has begun to harden and the stones will not be dislodged, then lightly water the surface and carefully brush away the cement slurry. Repeat until the stones are revealed just proud of the surface.

Fresh concrete must be cured after it has been laid. This is to prevent it from drying out too quickly, both to maintain sufficient water in the concrete to allow the setting to continue and also to prevent thermal cracking. Curing can be carried out simply by sprinkling the surface with water from a watering can to keep it damp for three or four days. An easier method is to lay a plastic sheet over the concrete to prevent the mix-water from evaporating.

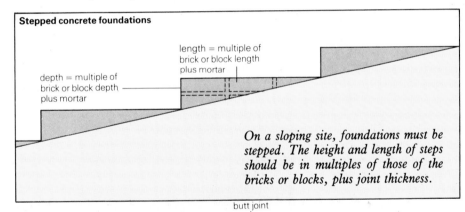

Stepped concrete foundations

length = multiple of brick or block length plus mortar

depth = multiple of brick or block depth plus mortar

On a sloping site, foundations must be stepped. The height and length of steps should be in multiples of those of the bricks or blocks, plus joint thickness.

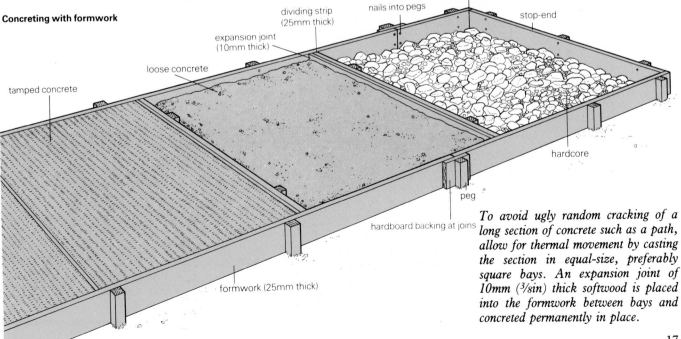

Concreting with formwork

tamped concrete

loose concrete

expansion joint (10mm thick)

dividing strip (25mm thick)

nails into pegs

butt joint

stop-end

hardcore

peg

hardboard backing at joins

formwork (25mm thick)

To avoid ugly random cracking of a long section of concrete such as a path, allow for thermal movement by casting the section in equal-size, preferably square bays. An expansion joint of 10mm (3/8in) thick softwood is placed into the formwork between bays and concreted permanently in place.

17

Project 1

Laying a garden path

Although paths, these days, are more often laid with paving slabs or bricks (see pages 35 and 38–9), a path of solid concrete, laid in situ, can have advantages if properly built: there are no joints, as there are with paving slabs, which need to be pointed; the path can be made to 'flow' more naturally around curved shapes in the garden; it can, of course, be tailor-made to fit awkward areas without any intricate cutting of slabs; and the material lends itself to a greater variety of colours and surface textures than many other commonly used pavings.

The first task is to establish the line of the path on the ground and to remove grass and topsoil and any obstructive plant roots along its length. Mark the edges of the path with lines and pegs before digging (*see picture* 1). Levels can be taken from a datum peg hammered into the soil beside the path (2).

The concrete for the path should be 75mm (3in) thick, so remove enough topsoil to allow for this. Dig out any soft areas and fill them with a hardcore of broken bricks and rubble.

Use T-shaped boning rods (see centre drawing, opposite page) to obtain the final levels. First drive in a peg at each end of the path (3) – the tops should be at the finished level of the path. Place a boning rod on top of each peg and get someone to hold these in place. Drive a peg in the ground in an intermediate position along the path and place a third boning rod. Then sight along the three rods from one end. All three should be in line; if not, adjust the height of the intermediate peg until they are. Any number of pegs can be driven in, depending on the length of the path. The pegs act as guides, enabling you to trim the base – to 75mm (3in) below peg-top level – until you have a level and even surface on which to lay the concrete. If you use

this method, your 75mm (3in) thick path should not end up 100mm (4in) in some areas and perhaps only 50mm (2in) in others.

If you want the path to curve, mark out the shape with a piece of string tied to a peg at one end and a stick at the other (see top drawing, opposite page). Draw a smooth arc on the ground with the stick. Adjust both the position of the peg and the length of the string until the curve is exactly right.

Set up the timber side forms (4) following the string lines. Then drive pegs into the ground along the outside of the forms at about 1m (3¼ft) intervals to keep the forms in place. For a long path, you will have to butt the side-forms together; back up the joints with a piece of hardboard and place a retaining peg at this position. Paint the timber with a mould oil (5) to prevent the concrete sticking to it.

Set the side forms so that the finished path will slope from one side to the other to enable rainwater to drain off quickly. The amount of fall depends on the width of the path. For a 1.5m (5ft) wide path, set one form 25mm (1in) lower than that on the other side. Use a timber straight-edge to span between the forms, the lower end of which should be packed up on a 25mm (1in) thick offcut. Place your spirit level on the straight-edge and adjust the side forms until it is horizontal. When the formwork is set at the correct levels, fix it in position by nailing through into the support pegs.

If your soil is of soft clay, you will need to remove 150mm (6in) of topsoil, replacing it with 75mm of hardcore, which should be rolled and well-compacted (6) along the full length of the path. 'Blind' the hardcore with tamped-down sand (7).

Concrete expands and contracts slightly with temperature changes, and with large areas or long lengths of concrete expansion joints should be

formed to allow for this movement without cracks forming. A slab cast in one piece should not be more than 3m (10ft) in either direction. Nor should the length be more than twice the width. To avoid these critical sizes, you will have to divide up the slab into a number of sections.

For your path, divide up its length into equal-sized bays and mark on the side forms the positions of the strips. A good expansion joint can be made with a softwood board of the same width and depth as the slab and 10mm (⅜in) thick. Cut it to length so that it slots neatly between the forms, to the correct level, and back it up temporarily with a strip of formwork timber and a couple of pegs to support it (8). Concrete right up to the joint. Then concrete the next bay almost to the back of the joint, remove the pegs and temporary support strip, and again concrete tight up to the joint. The expansion joint should be left permanently in position (10).

Mix 2 concrete (see page 15) is appropriate for the path. Mix up enough to complete a full bay and place it within an hour of mixing. Spread and rake the concrete to a level a little above the tops of the forms, then compact it with a home-made tamping beam (9) and finish it by drawing a soft brush gently across the surface.

If the path runs close to a wall or building for all or part of its length, so that you cannot use a two-man tamping beam (see bottom drawing, opposite page) across the forms in the normal way, lay the concrete using what is known as the alternate-bay method. Fix forms across the width of the path to make stop-ends at joint positions. Then lay concrete in alternate bays, tamping the concrete with the beam resting on the stop-ends instead of the side forms. Remove the stop-end timber and fill in the remaining bays with concrete.

5

6

7

Marking a curve for a path

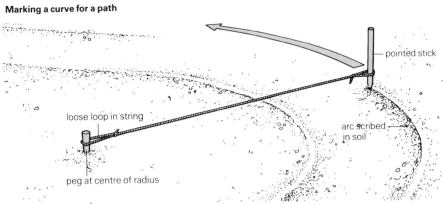

pointed stick

loose loop in string

arc scribed in soil

peg at centre of radius

Boning rods

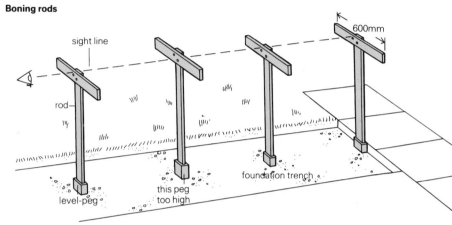

600mm

sight line

rod

level-peg

this peg too high

foundation trench

Using a tamping beam

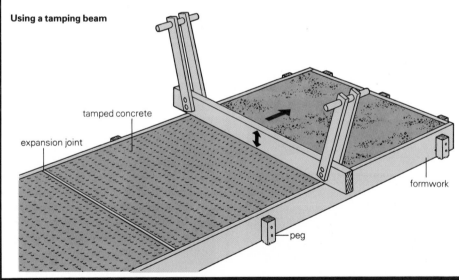

tamped concrete

expansion joint

formwork

peg

8

9

10

Surface finishes for concrete 1 Use a soft brush to produce a light-textured, non-slip finish. If the path is built on a slope, use a stiffer brush to make deeper grooves in the surface. 2 A wood float, used with a semi-circular wrist movement, gives a smooth but slightly open finish. 3 With practice, a steel float can give a very smooth, close finish. 4 For an exposed aggregate finish, first lightly brush the concrete. Then, when it has hardened slightly, brush and water gently until the aggregate particles stand slightly proud of the surface.

Project 2

A wall foundation

Foundations serve to transmit the weight of walls to levels of firm ground which are capable of carrying the loads without settlement and are below the level susceptible to movement due to frost.

All walls need sound foundations. Soil conditions vary considerably in Britain, however, and so hard and fast rules cannot be given for foundation depths and widths. Shrinkable clay subsoils are particularly troublesome because of the degree of seasonal movement to which they are subject. For all but simple, low garden walls and light building structures it is advisable to seek professional advice. If in doubt, talk to your local building inspector, who will know the subsoil conditions locally and may be able to make recommendations.

As a general guide, the width of the foundation trench should be at least twice the width of the wall.

For a half-brick-thick wall, the foundation should be about 300mm (12in) wide and 150mm (6in) thick in a trench 350mm (14in) deep. For a full-brick-thick wall, lay a foundation strip 500mm (20in) wide and 250mm (10in) thick in a trench about 500mm (20in) deep. If you have not reached firm soil at the level of the underside of the foundation, keep digging until you do and fill the extra depth with hardcore, which must then be well-compacted.

First clear the area of topsoil. Set out the trenches using pegs and strings close to the ground (see 1, below). Check with a builder's square to make sure that the corners are square. Then set up profile boards straddling the centre lines of the walls and stretch string between to indicate trench width.

When the trenches have been excavated (2) to about the right level, drive pegs into the trench bottoms to a level at which the peg tops indicate the required thickness of concrete. Check the levels of the peg

tops with a straight-edge and spirit level (3) to ensure that they are all at the same height. Trim the trench bottoms using the pegs as a guide.

If the ground slopes, step the foundations (see upper drawing, page 17), so that you can course-in when you begin to build.

Mix the concrete (Mix 1 will be appropriate) and place it in the trench, compacting it with a tamper (4) or punner to the level of the peg tops. Finish by patting it with the back of a spade to make a reasonably flat surface.

When the concrete has hardened sufficiently, stretch a string from the profile boards to indicate the outside edge of the wall. Using a level or plumb line, transfer the line of the string to the surface of a thin layer of mortar, onto which you will be laying the bottom course of bricks or blocks. You are now able to lay the first brick or block at one end or corner of the wall. Since it is the first, lay and level it very accurately as it will form a guide for all the others (see page 29).

Project 3

Laying a damp-proof slab for a small workshop floor

A thoroughly dry concrete floor is necessary in a workshop where tools and equipment are to be stored. So, to keep damp out, lay a damp-proof plastic membrane before you lay the concrete slab.

Prepare the base for the slab in the normal way, compacting the soil and filling any soft areas with hardcore. Then spread a layer of sand over the base. On top of the sand, lay a sheet of 1000-gauge plastic sheeting (see photograph at left), which you can buy from a builders' merchant, allowing plenty of overlap round the edges of the slab. If you need to use more than one sheet, make sure to overlap the joints between the sheets with a double fold at least 150mm (6in) wide.

Make and fix formwork, and place and compact the concrete to form the slab on top of the membrane. Take particular care to ensure that the membrane is not torn or damaged.

Curving formwork

To enable the sides of formwork to bend more easily round a curve – for a bend in a concrete path, for example – make saw cuts into the timber, to about half its thickness, on the outside edge. Use extra pegs to hold the curved section of the formwork in place.

Alternatively, you can use strips of exterior-quality hardboard to form the sides of the formwork. These will bend more easily around curved shapes. You will need quite a number of pegs to make sure that the hardboard is held firmly in position. The drawback is that hardboard will not stand up to energetic use of a tamping beam.

Guard against damp

If paths and patios are to be located hard up to a wall, they must be laid a minimum of two courses of brickwork below the level of the damp-proof course in the wall. However, it is better practice to keep hard surfaces back from the wall altogether, leaving a narrow margin that can be filled with soil for planting or with pebbles and gravel.

Rainwater dripping from the eaves and gutter might otherwise splash back from the paving and saturate the bottom few courses of brickwork. This would encourage lichen growth on the brickwork and, in the winter, could lead to frost-damaged bricks.

Lifting cement bags

A 50kg (110lb) bag of cement is an awkward shape to carry, so get someone to help you lift it. If you bring a bag home in your car, lay a plastic sheet on the boot floor first. Some cement always seems to find its way out of the bag; and if the bag splits when you are manoeuvring it out you will not waste too much.

Repairing broken edges of paths

If the edge of your path or concrete drive has been damaged and has cracked and broken away, a neat repair can easily be made with the aid of PVA (polyvinyl acetate) adhesive.

First break away any remaining weak sections of the edge with a bolster chisel and club hammer, at the same time clearing away any broken concrete pieces (see 1, below). If the broken section of edging extends to the entire depth of the concrete, you will need to provide a firm base for the fresh concrete by putting well-compacted hardcore under the damaged area. If the underlying soil is soft, dig it out and increase the depth of hardcore.

Place a straight piece of timber formwork along the edge of the concrete slab, overlapping the damaged area on both sides, and hammer pegs into the ground behind the timber to hold it in position (2). Both timber and pegs should be flush with the surface of the existing concrete. Prime the edge of the damaged concrete (3) with the PVA adhesive, following the manufacturer's instructions, and allow to dry. Prepare a sand/cement mortar using 1 part cement to 3 or 4 parts of coarse sand, and adding PVA adhesive to the mixing water; the mix should be rather drier than usual. Then paint the damaged edges with more adhesive and, while these are still tacky, trowel in the mortar and tamp it down (4). Smooth and level the new concrete and finish it to match the surface of the rest of the path. Remember to protect the repaired area until the mortar has had time to dry and harden.

BRICKS, BLOCKS & RENDERING

Bricks can be used for both horizontal and vertical surfaces – for paths and patios as well as for walls. Their handy size, too, is appropriate for small projects such as barbecues and plant containers, as well as for bigger jobs such as house extensions and garages. They are extremely flexible in use and attractive in appearance. For many jobs, however, concrete blocks offer advantages. They are often cheaper and, because they are bigger, speed of construction is quicker. Unless you buy facing blocks, however, you will need to paint or render your concrete blockwork to achieve a good appearance and make it weather resistant.

Variety in bricks
Clay bricks, one of the oldest manufactured products, are nowadays made with the aid of high-speed technology; a variety of processes is used to deal with the characteristics of the different clays found in Britain. Almost half the bricks produced in this country are made from fletton clay, which contains a proportion of fuel oil. They virtually fire themselves, only a small amount of coal dust being added to the kiln during the firing process. The result is a very economical, low-cost product.

A large proportion of bricks is made by what is known as the wire-cut process. A fairly stiff mix of clay is extruded through a die like a rectangular column of toothpaste and is sliced into bricks by taut wires.

A more traditional method, still common in south-east England, is the soft-mud process. Water is added to the clay, which is pushed into moulds and tipped out to form a type called stock bricks, which get their name from the raised piece of metal that holds the mould in place.

Not all bricks are made from clay. There are calcium silicate bricks, often known as sand-limes or flint-limes, which are made from a mixture of lime and silica sand. The ingredients are reacted with steam under pressure in an autoclave – a sort of giant pressure cooker. The finished product is smooth and ranges from white to buff in colour, so that it is often used for interior, light-reflecting brickwork. Different textures and coloured pigments can be added during manufacture to produce quite a wide range of bricks.

Then there are concrete bricks, which are quite common in some parts of the country. These are made in a mould, in the same way as precast concrete, and are available in a wide variety of colours and finishes.

Calcium silicate and concrete bricks can be used for just as wide a range of purposes as can clay bricks.

Selection of bricks
The large number of different bricks available can make selection confusing, but it is well worth taking some time and trouble to find the right brick for the job you have in mind. It could prove a costly mistake to choose solely on the basis of price. The fletton brick, for example, is durable and entirely appropriate for general walling, but it should

not be used for garden projects where it is likely to become saturated with rainwater and groundwater. In particular, you should avoid using it for paving, steps, retaining walls backed with soil, and the tops of free-standing walls. During the winter, water in the brick will freeze and the brick face is likely to crumble, a process known as spalling.

Bricks are classed in three varieties:
Common bricks are quite simply bricks that do not have an attractive appearance. They are used where they will be out of sight, or where they are to be painted or rendered.
Facing bricks are specially made or selected for their good looks. There is a vast range from which to choose, and considerable variation in price, too, from the lower-cost flettons to very expensive hand-made bricks.
Engineering bricks are made for special applications where very high strength, durability, and imperviousness are important. In the past they were used for lining sewers and as a damp-proof course in walling; it is, however, unlikely that the do-it-yourselfer will have a use for them.

In addition to varieties, bricks are also classed in three qualities:
Interior quality, as the name suggests, are suitable only for interior use, as, for instance, for partitions which are to be

plastered. Bricks are not manufactured to this quality; they are simply rejected commons or facings. Lightweight concrete blocks have nowadays largely superseded interior-quality bricks.

Ordinary quality The majority of bricks available are of ordinary quality. They are durable in normal situations but, for any severely exposed part of a structure, they must be protected by copings and other means to prevent them from becoming saturated.

Special quality bricks are durable even in the most exposed situations, where they may become saturated and frozen in winter. They are the best general-purpose bricks since they can be used for virtually any application – for paving and dwarf walls, for steps and other features, as well as for general walling where, generally, they have an attractive appearance.

Common bricks may be offered in all three qualities and facings in ordinary and special qualities.

The durability of calcium silicate and concrete bricks is related directly to strength. For example, calcium silicates are available as load-bearing, facing, and common in six strength classes, from the strongest in Class 7 down to Class 2. A minimum of Class 4 is required for earth-retaining walls and for sills and copings; a minimum of Class 3 is required for free-standing walls; and Class 2 is satisfactory for general walling above damp-proof course level.

The classification system for calcium silicate and concrete bricks is perhaps a little complex for the home handyman. As with all bricks, it is always advisable to seek guidance from the manufacturer on the suitability of a particular brick for the job you have in mind.

Frogs and holes

Bricks may be solid or perforated with holes or have frogs (shallow depressions in the bed face). Wire-cut bricks generally have holes, whereas pressed or moulded bricks have frogs. These are introduced to ensure that the bricks are evenly fired throughout and also to reduce weight. They have no bearing on the performance of the brick or its strength, but they do, to some extent, dictate how the bricks are laid.

For general walling, bricklayers often lay 'frogs down' because the mortar goes further. It is advisable, though, for the do-it-yourselfer to lay 'frogs up' to ensure that the frogs are filled with mortar and the wall is solid and strong. Using special quality bricks, you can lay 'frogs down' for paving. Bricks with holes can be laid only on edge for paving instead of on their bed faces, and so you will need quite a number extra per square metre.

Sizes of bricks

Nowadays, bricks are produced to metric dimensions and, while they are still very close in size to the old imperial-sized brick, you will need to thicken up the joints slightly when matching to existing, older brickwork.

The standard metric size is 215mm (8½in) long, 102.5mm (4in) wide and 65mm (2½in) deep. For calculation and design purposes, the practice is to allow for the thickness of a joint on all these dimensions. The nominal size, known in the trade as the format size, which allows for a 10mm (⅜in) joint, is 225 × 112.5 × 75mm (9 × 4⅜ × 3in). There is also a range of bricks in what is known as modular sizes. Format sizes for these are

$300 \times 100 \times 100$mm ($12 \times 4 \times 4$in)
$300 \times 100 \times 75$mm ($12 \times 4 \times 3$in)
$200 \times 100 \times 100$mm ($8 \times 4 \times 4$in)
$200 \times 100 \times 75$mm ($8 \times 4 \times 3$in)

Modular brickwork looks quite different from traditional brickwork because of the different proportions of the bricks. Individual bricks do vary in size and not all are strictly rectangular.

Brick and block types 1, 2 Clay bricks with one face keyed; 3 Extruded-clay brick; 4 Fletton common brick; 5 Calcium silicate brick; 6 Concrete walling block; 7 Clay air bricks; 8, 9 Clay facing bricks; 10 Clay multi-colour stock facing bricks; 11 Concrete paving block; 12 Hand-made clay facing brick; 13 Extruded-clay facing bricks; 14 Yellowy-buff clay facing bricks; 15 Facing bricks with close-textured surface; 16 Concrete block; 17 Calcium silicate facing brick; 18 Concrete block with halving joint; 19 Plinth stretcher; 20 Purpose-made special; 21 Double-bullnose brick forming an external angle.

Special-shape bricks
In addition to the standard rectangular shape, bricks are made to special shapes for particular purposes. There is a wide variety of 'specials', including copings, plinths, bullnosed bricks with rounded corners, and angled bricks that are useful (for instance) for angled, projecting brickwork under a bay window. Special-shaped bricks, however, cost much more than standard bricks and may have to be ordered much earlier than the rest.

Choosing and buying bricks
Generally, new brickwork for the house and garden must be chosen to match or harmonise with existing brickwork. Certainly, for home extensions, new should look well against the old. If your house is modern, you should have little difficulty. With older properties, see if you can find a loose brick and take it to a merchant to identify and, if possible, match it; some builders' merchants offer a special brick-matching service. Building Centres in many cities have representative ranges of bricks on show

to enable one to compare samples. London is particularly well-served with the Brick Advisory Centre at the Building Centre, where there are some 800 different bricks permanently on show. Often, however, the best approach is to choose a multi-coloured brick, perhaps a red multi or a light multi, the overall tone of which is made up of many subtle colours.

To calculate how many bricks, you will need, draw up your plans in metric measurements and scale off the sizes of the brickwork elements. A half-brick-thick wall in stretcher bond (that is, with the long side visible) will require about 60 bricks per square metre of walling. A full-brick-thick wall will need about twice as many. Allow 10 per cent or so for wastage and cutting.

The price of bricks varies according to how many you order. The price per brick for, say, 500 will be much higher than for a lorry load of 5,000 or 6,000 because of the handling and transport costs involved.

Concrete blocks
Concrete blocks are available in a range of types and a variety of finishes. Dense-concrete plain-wall blocks are suitable for virtually any structural use. They are weather-resistant and may be left in their natural state ('fair-faced' as the trade calls it) if appearance is not too important. They can, however, look attractive if painted.

Lightweight, load-bearing, plain wall blocks are also suitable for most structural applications, and they are easier to handle and to cut than the dense-concrete type. They are not generally weather resistant and so will probably need to be rendered or coated with a protective finish if used externally.

If you wish to build a block wall outdoors and do not intend to render or paint it, choose facing blocks, which are available in many different colours and textures, including exposed-aggregate and split-faced finishes.

For use in the garden, as for garden walls and carports, screen wall blocks are appropriate. They are made of

dense concrete pierced through to form a decorative pattern. They are quite attractive but have become something of a visual cliche in suburban gardens.

Sizes of blocks
The most commonly available size of block is 450 × 225mm (18 × 9in), and this can be used alongside standard brickwork for bonding purposes. All types of block are made to this size, in thicknesses from 63mm to 225mm (2½ to 9in). Most manufacturers also produce modular blocks measuring 400 × 200mm (16 × 8in), in thicknesses up to 200mm (8in).

Storing bricks and blocks
On delivery, bricks should be stacked on a level area of hardstanding or on scaffold planks to keep them away from damp soil. Stack the majority of bricks on edge, but arrange those at the side to slope inwards so that there is no danger of them falling off.

Cover the brick stack with a plastic sheet to keep the rain off. Saturated bricks are difficult to lay because they cannot exert the suction required and so will tend to float on the mortar bed. They are also more likely to give rise to the powdery white deposits you sometimes see on new brickwork. Bricks contain soluble salts and when water dries out of a saturated brick, these salts are brought to the surface and deposited as a white powder known as efflorescence. It is harmless and will eventually disappear, but it is best avoided altogether by keeping the bricks dry before laying them; during construction cover the partly finished brickwork with a plastic sheet at the end of each working day.

Concrete blocks should be stored in dry conditions for at least a week before use. Stack them clear of the ground on planks of wood. Place them on edge, leaving spaces between them to allow air to circulate. The stack will be more stable if you put alternate layers at right-angles. Cover the stack with a plastic sheet tied down to prevent rainwater from splashing under the edges.

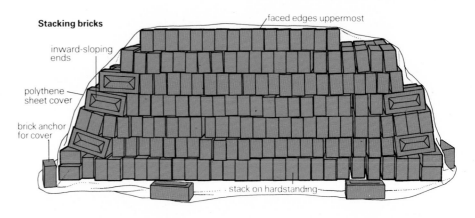

Stacking bricks
faced edges uppermost
inward-sloping ends
polythene sheet cover
brick anchor for cover
stack on hardstanding

Tools & Techniques

There are only a few essential tools needed for bricklaying and blocklaying, and some you can make yourself.

Tools to buy

A **bricklayers' trowel** with a blade size of about 250mm (10in) from tip to base of handle. Smaller sizes are available but, in the long run, it is worth getting used to a full-sized trowel. The blade will have one straight edge, for scooping up mortar, and a slightly curved edge, for cutting and cleaning up bricks. Left- and right-handed versions are available. For finishing joints, a small **pointing trowel** is useful.

To cut bricks and blocks, you will need a **bolster chisel**, a cold chisel with a 100mm (4in) wide blade; and a **club hammer**, a small hammer with a head weighing about 2kg (4½lb). Plastic shields are available for bolster chisels to protect your hand.

To ensure that your brick- and block-work is level and vertical, you need a **builder's level** 800 to 900mm (32 to 36in) long, and incorporating both horizontal and vertical bubble tubes.

You will need a **steel tape measure** 15m (49ft) long. To measure out materials for mortar, you will need two **buckets**, one exclusively for cement, which can be kept dry.

Tools to make

A **gauge rod**, which is used to ensure that brick courses are rising evenly. This is made from a straight piece of scrap timber at least as long as the height of your wall. Mark the rod with shallow saw cuts every 75mm (3in) – a brick depth plus a 10mm (⅜in) joint.

A **builder's square** is essential for ensuring that the corners of your work are square.

You will also need a **line and pegs** to stretch between corners to ensure the work is level. You can buy these or improvise by attaching fine string to two large galvanised nails.

For mixing mortar, make a **mixing board** out of scrap plywood.

Bricklayer's tools **1** *Gauge rod with mark every 75mm (3in);* **2** *Hawk to carry mortar;* **3** *Pointing trowel;* **4** *Bricklayer's trowel;* **5** *Builder's level;* **6** *Club hammer;* **7** *Repointing chisel;* **8, 9** *Bolster chisels;* **10, 11** *Steel pins and line.*

Bonding with bricks

The strength of a wall and much of its visual appeal lie in the way in which bricks are bonded. Essentially, bonding is a matter of ensuring that the vertical joints (perpends) in one course are overlapped by bricks in the course above and below it.

Many different bonding patterns have evolved over the centuries of brick usage. The simplest and most commonly used today is stretcher bond: the bricks are laid lengthwise with only their stretcher (long-side) faces visible. The wall is therefore half a brick thick. Stretcher bond is suitable for the majority of projects the do-it-yourselfer is likely to tackle – for the external leaves of cavity brickwork, for low garden walls, and for small buildings such as garages. Piers, which provide lateral strength and stability, are essential; check with your local building inspector

on the dimensions and spacing of these. It is necessary to cut bricks to bond only in the piers, at openings, and at the ends of walls.

For more substantial, full-brick-thick walls, there are many other, more decorative bonding patterns, which consist of various combinations of stretchers and headers (the end faces of a brick). All involve much more cutting of bricks, including the making of closers (bricks cut lengthwise), and they require greater skill in bricklaying.

English bond, for instance, consists of alternate rows of stretchers and headers. Flemish bond has stretchers and headers alternating in every course. It is more decorative than English bond but is not quite so strong. In addition, there are garden-wall varieties of these bonds (the term is misleading because these patterns are used for buildings as often as for free-standing garden walls). Eng-

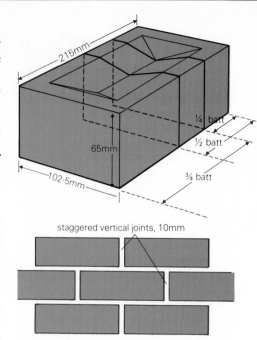

staggered vertical joints, 10mm

lish garden-wall bond consists of three courses of stretchers, then a course of headers, and so on. Flemish garden-wall bond has a course of stretchers and then a course of alternate headers and stretchers.

Piers

In normal, fairly sheltered locations and using 450 × 225mm (18 × 9in) blocks laid in stretcher bond, you can build up to four courses high using 100mm (4in) thick blocks, seven courses using 150mm (6in) blocks, and nine courses with 225mm (9in) blocks. For walls above these heights, and in windy locations, you will have to build piers to provide additional support. They

Right If making a wall with piers or complex bonds, practise by 'dry-laying' the first few courses. 1 (main picture) Stretcher bond first course used to locate the corner and pier. 2 Second course in stretcher bond: note bonding at the pier. 3, 4 Setting out first and second courses in Flemish bond. 5 Splitting a brick to make a closer.

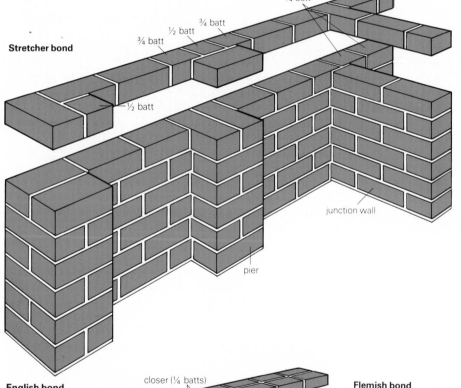

Stretcher bond

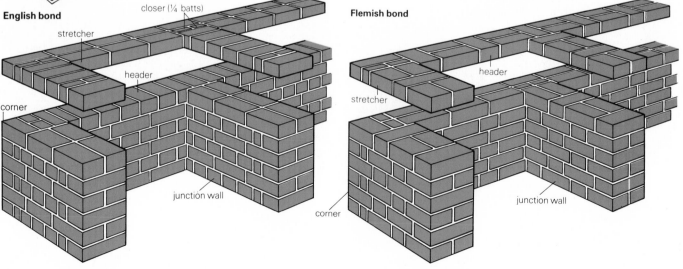

English bond

Flemish bond

should be at least twice the thickness of the wall and spaced at intervals of not more than twice the wall height. Block walls of 100mm (4in) thick blocks should have piers spaced at not more than 2.5m (8ft) intervals.

Mortars for bricks and blocks

Mortar acts as a gap-filling glue. It must not be too strong a glue, however, because any settlement cracks in the wall should take place within the joints rather than in the bricks or blocks, which would thereby be damaged.

For brickwork below ground level, use a mortar mix of 1 part of Ordinary Portland cement to 3 parts of sand. A general-purpose mortar mix for most other work is 1 part of Ordinary Portland cement to 1 part of hydrated lime to 6 parts of builder's sand. The lime is added to the mix to improve its workability and to make laying easier. You can mix up a largish batch of lime and sand first (known as 'coarse stuff'), and this will last all day. Then mix mortar, adding cement to a small amount of coarse stuff, to make up enough to last for one to two hours. Mix the cement into a slurry with water before adding to the coarse stuff, otherwise you will get concentrations of cement in the mix. After one to two hours, depending on how warm the weather is, any unused mortar that has begun to set must be discarded; do not add more water in an attempt to re-mix.

Instead of lime and Ordinary Portland cement, you can use masonry cement and builder's sand. A general-purpose mix is 1 part masonry cement to 5 parts builder's sand. This mix is particularly recommended for concrete blocks and bricks and for calcium silicate bricks, where it is important to use a weaker mortar. Never use a plain Ordinary Portland cement and sand mortar mix with these materials.

Dry-mix mortar is available from most DIY shops and builders' merchants and, for small amounts of brick- or blocklaying, it is better than buying the ingredients separately and mixing your own. Make sure that you buy a *bricklaying* mix and not a straight sand and cement mix.

Bonding with blocks

Blocks are normally laid in stretcher bond, overlapping those in the course below by half a block length. You can buy half blocks to avoid having to cut them at piers, ends of walls, and door and window openings. However, corners should be bonded in. If the thickness of the block is the same as half the block length, you will have no difficulty. With thinner blocks you will have to

Technique

Bricklaying technique

Handling the trowel correctly is the key to good bricklaying. At first concentrate on the proper sequence of operations and on accuracy, and let speed develop naturally. Saw off a slice of mortar with the trowel, slightly rounding the back of the slice to form a fat sausage. Then, with a sweeping action, lift the mortar on to the trowel; it should load the trowel completely. Place the mortar slice by holding the trowel above the brickwork and rolling off the mortar, pulling the trowel back sharply as you do so. Form a fairly even bed about

12.5mm (½in) thick by flattening the mortar with the trowel point. Position a brick, tapping it with the handle-end of the trowel to bed it firmly. Butter the end of the next brick to form a perpendicular joint, again about 12.5mm (½in) thick, and place it in position. Tap the end of the brick to adjust the thickness of the joint, and then the top to bed the brick into the mortar. Mortar will be squeezed out of the joints as the bricks are laid. Scoop it off with the trowel as you work to prevent the brick faces from being stained with cement. Make frequent checks with a spirit level and a gauge rod to ensure that the brickwork is plumb and level.

cut the block lengthwise to form closers in order to maintain the bond.

There is a number of alternative arrangments to stretcher bond which, to some extent, reduce the amount of cutting involved. You can, for example, use quarter or third bond, which can be continued around corners but will still entail some cutting at the ends of the wall and at openings. To save cutting blocks altogether, you can build square piers at the corners and lay blocks in stretcher bond between them (using some half blocks). The wall and pier should be bonded together by means of expanded-metal ties laid across the joint.

Decorative screen wall blocks are laid one above the other in stack bond.

Strictly speaking, this is not a bond at all and horizontal reinforcement (by means of thin strips of expanded metal) may be needed.

Cutting bricks and blocks

Bricks cut across their width are known as batts; there are quarter, half, and three-quarter batts, and to keep down costs you should always aim to get two half batts or a quarter and a three-quarter batt from one whole brick. Bricks cut lengthwise into two thin halves are known as closers.

It takes a good deal of skill to cut bricks by striking them with the cutting edge of the trowel, as bricklayers do. Here is a method suitable for the do-it-yourselfer. Place the brick on a sand

Project 1

Building a brick wall
All walls need sound foundations, and building the footings must be the first job (see 'A wall foundation', page 20). Then proceed as follows.

Stretch a line between the profile boards to indicate the outside edges of the wall and the corners. Then, under the string, lay a thin bed of mortar at each corner or end of the wall. The line indicated by the string must now be transferred to the mortar on top of the foundations. You can use either a plumb bob or a spirit level (*see* 1, *below*). Place the spirit level upright against the string and, when the bubble indicates that the level is vertical, make a mark in the mortar at the foot of the level. Make a similar mark a little distance away from the first one and join up with a straightedge. At corners, (2) draw an intersecting line at right-angles using the same technique.
When the line indicated

by the string guide has been transferred to a line drawn in the mortar, you will be ready for bricklaying. Lay mortar at a corner or at one end and position the first brick accurately. Build up the corners and ends of the wall (3) what will be to two courses above ground level; the top course should be laid with frogs downwards or have a thin layer of mortar (4) to provide a level surface on which to lay the damp-proof course. Check frequently with the gauge rod, the level, and the builder's square to ensure that the brickwork is rising evenly and accurately. Then stretch a line between successive courses and infill between the brickwork at corners and ends.
Lay the damp-proof membrane (5), rolling it out from a corner in each direction. Smooth it down with a trowel and lay a mortar bed on top. Again, build up the corners and ends to three or four courses, checking the

right-angle with a builder's square (6), and in-fill between using a string line as a guide.
Garden walls half a brick in thickness can be built in stretcher bond to a height of about 1m (3¼ft), but they must be supported by 225mm (9in) square piers at intervals of about 2m (6½ft). A full-brick thickness is needed for walls higher than this, which allows a choice of bond patterns.
Tops of free-standing walls should be protected with a coping to prevent rainwater from saturating the bricks. You will often see a top course of bricks laid on end – a 'soldier course', as it is called. But these do not provide a really adequate coping because they do not overhang the wall and are not weathered with a sloping top to throw rainwater clear. Special shaped coping bricks or precast-concrete copings are more effective. They should be laid on a damp-proof membrane.

Recessed joints
Do not attempt to make recessed joints, especially with bricks with holes. If too much mortar was raked out, rainwater could seep through and fill up the holes in the bricks, which could lead to problems, during freezing weather.

Format sizes
Designing and setting out using the format size of a brick (brick size plus a joint thickness) can be used as the basis of calculation for most purposes. However, for openings in brickwork, the size of the opening will be in multiples of the brick format size *plus* an extra joint thickness. Piers of brickwork between openings will be in multiples of the format size *minus* a joint thickness.

Efflorescence
If efflorescence appears on your brickwork, do not wash it off with water as the salts will dissolve and be re-absorbed into the brickwork. Scrape or brush it off with a stiff brush or buy a proprietary staining treatment.

bed. With a steel rule, measure the particular batt required and score all the faces of the brick with a sharp nail. Cut a groove along the score-line all round with a bolster chisel and club hammer and, placing the bolster on the long face of the brick, strike with a firm blow. A clean break should result.

Lightweight concrete blocks can be cut in a similar way to bricks, using a bolster and club hammer. Some blocks are made with slots at half and quarter points to make cutting easier. Autoclaved aerated blocks are easiest to cut as they can simply be sawn to shape using an ordinary handsaw.

Jointing and pointing

The joint between bricks can be finished off as bricklaying proceeds (jointing) or they can be raked out to a depth of 12.5mm (½in) or so and finished later with fresh mortar (pointing). Jointing is more common because

1 To form a struck joint (here using black mortar), first fill the vertical joints and finish them to a V-shape. 2 Then point the horizontal joints, each with a slight slope and projecting lower edge. 3 Run the point of your trowel along a straight edge to trim excess mortar and complete the job.

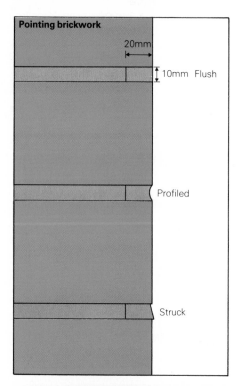

Pointing brickwork

20mm

10mm Flush

Profiled

Struck

it is quicker, and with practice quite a neat joint can be achieved. Pointing is normally used only when a coloured mortar is being used or you want to shape the face of the mortar – to give it a special 'joint profile', to use the jargon of the trade.

The joint finish is largely determined by the type of brick. With a smooth brick you can make a *flush* joint. Use a small pointing trowel or wait until the mortar has begun to set, then rub it over with a coarse rag.

A simple *profiled* joint can be made using a stick or a piece of wooden dowel rod (traditionally an old bucket handle was used). Before the mortar is too dry, shape the vertical joints first over an area of about a square metre, and then do the horizontal joints. A sharper profiled joint can be made using a pointing trowel to form what is called a *struck* joint. Run the straight edge of the trowel at a slight angle under the bricks in the course above so that a slight slope

is formed, which allows rainwater to run off easily.

If you are matching existing, older brickwork, you must match the existing joint shape and colour as well as the bricks themselves. In this case, pointing should be more successful. Rake out the joints as you build and later point them with a matching mortar, taking particular care with the shape of the joint. To match mortar, experiment with dyes and different coloured sands, pointing up small unobtrusive areas and allowing them to dry before comparing. Be sure to label each trial area with the mortar recipe to ensure that you can reproduce the most successful one.

Brick-cutting gauge

If you have many bricks to cut, you can make a cutting gauge from a rectangular piece of plywood, about 300mm (1ft) long and 100m (4in) wide, and a short timber batten. Place the batten on the plywood at right angles to the long sides. On one side of it measure out the length of a half batt, 107.5mm (4¼in), and, after nailing the batten into position, cut the plywood to size. On the other side of the batten, measure out the length of a three-quarter batt, 161.25mm (6⅜in), and again cut the plywood.

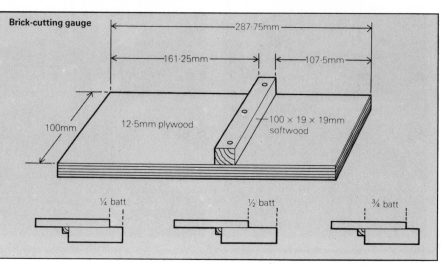

Brick-cutting gauge

287·75mm

161·25mm

107·5mm

100mm

12·5mm plywood

100 × 19 × 19mm softwood

¼ batt   ½ batt   ¾ batt

Project 2

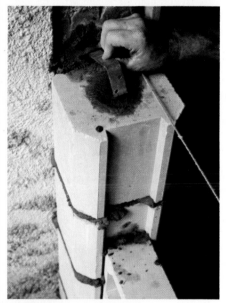

Building a concrete-block screen wall

Concrete screen-wall blocks, which are available in many different patterns from garden centres and builders' merchants, are useful because, while they can form an effective barrier, they also help to contribute light and airy feeling in the garden.

Screen-wall blocks are laid in stack bond (one directly above the other), and they need support at a maximum of 3m (10ft) intervals with piers of bricks or ready-made concrete pilaster blocks (they may also need horizontal reinforcment with strips of expanded metal across the joints). The strength of the individual screen blocks varies, depending on their design, so you should consult the manufacturer's leaflet to determine the correct pier spacing and reinforcement.

To build a screen wall you must start with the piers. Because of the pattern, the blocks cannot be cut and so the spacing between the piers must exactly equal a given number of blocks plus the joints between them. For boundary walls over 1.8m (6ft) high, the piers will need reinforcing vertically with 50 × 50mm (2 × 2in) steel angle, which is bedded into the foundation and rises vertically through the hollow centre of each pilaster block. Check the manufacturer's recommendations for fixing. You must also reinforce a gate if it is attached to the piers. Specially made pier or pilaster blocks are hollow, and they have a channel on one or more faces to receive the sides of the screen wall blocks. Concrete is poured into the hollow centres of the pilaster blocks as they are built up to form a solid column. If you are using brick piers instead of pilaster blocks, wire mesh should be built into the brick joints and should project outwards so that it can also be bedded into joints between blocks. This ties the screen wall into the supporting piers.

Bed the first pilaster on mortar and check it carefully to make sure it is vertical and in line. Then bed the first pilaster at the other end of the wall. Fill the pilasters with a fluid concrete mix and build up three courses or so at each end, filling again with concrete, which should be well compacted with a rod. Check that the pilasters are in line and are vertical. You can then start to lay the screen-wall blocks. Spread a bed of mortar on the top of the foundation and into the recess in the lowest pilaster. Place the first block into position, pushing it well into the recess in the pilaster and tapping it carefully to bed it firmly. Repeat at the other end of the wall. After checking for accuracy, stretch a string line between the two blocks to form a guide for in-filling with the remaining blocks.

To form the vertical joints between blocks, the side of a block already laid must be spread with mortar and the next block butted up to it. Take care to keep mortar off the faces of blocks – dried mortar smears will look unsightly.

Walls should not be built to a height of more than five courses at a time. If you wish to build higher, leave the wall for 24 hours before continuing.

Joints should be pointed, either course by course, or at the end of a section of walling, using a small pointing trowel. They can be finished with a slight concave profile using a stick. When the mortar has begun to dry, any that has strayed onto the block faces can be scrubbed off with a wire brush. Newly built blockwork should be covered with a plastic sheet to protect it from the weather, particularly frost, while the mortar sets.

When the wall is the right height, finish it at the top with specially-made coping slabs, and place a pilaster cap at the tops of pilasters.

Repointing brickwork

Mortar joints in brickwork inevitably crumble in time on exposed walls; chimneys are particularly vulnerable. The old mortar must be raked out to a depth of 12.5mm (½in) or so and the joint made waterproof with new mortar. If you are patching an area of wall, you must match the new mortar colour and profile to that of the existing mortar. If you are repointing the whole wall, mortar colour is not so critical and you can choose a different profile. It is better, however, to match that of the rest of the house.

Use a chisel and a club hammer to knock out the old mortar, first from vertical joints, and then from horizontal joints. Work on an area of about a square metre at a time. Brush down completed sections to remove dust and then soak the brickwork so that it will not absorb moisture from the new mortar too quickly. Do not prepare too much mortar: mix up enough for an hour or so's work, using a mortar mix of 1 part Ordinary Portland cement to 1 part hydrated lime to 6 parts builder's sand. Press the mortar into the joints, doing the vertical joints first. For most joints, finish flush with the brickwork. For struck joints, slope the mortar as you work. For illustration of different pointing shapes, see page 30.

To form a flush joint, rub it with a rough rag along the joint when the mortar has begun to set, and, later, brush off mortar crumbs. To make a slightly concave joint – known in the trade as a profiled joint – use a stick or a rounded piece of metal rod. The struck joint is the most difficult. During re-pointing, the mortar is sloped with a trowel. It should project slightly over the brick below and tuck slightly under that above. A straight-edge is then placed along the horizontal joints and the mortar projection is straightened and cleaned up by running either the pointing trowel or what bricklayers call a frenchman along the straight-edge. A frenchman can be made by heating the blade of a kitchen knife and bending the end into a right-angle.

Rendering

Rendering has been used for hundreds of years, initially to plug gaps, to keep out draughts, and to weather-proof walls. The decorative possibilities, however, soon became apparent and finishes such as pargetting and later stucco became popular. Stucco was used in the 18th and 19th centuries as a render to cover rough brick and stone in order to lend an appearance of smooth coursed and carved stone.

Nowadays practically all renderings are based on Portland cement but there is a wide variety of techniques used to give many attractive finishes. These include roughcast (also known as wet-dash and, in Scotland, harling), in which the final coat, containing a proportion of coarse aggregate, is thrown on to the wall and is left untrowelled. Dry-dash (otherwise known as pebble-dash) is a technique in which small, clean pebbles are thrown on to a freshly applied render coat and left exposed. A more recent finish is Tyrolean, produced by a hand-operated machine, which flicks mortar on to a render coat. Textured finishes can be created with a trowel when applying the final coat.

For the most part, however, you need a high degree of skill to apply these finishes, and you should not undertake them lightly. It is best to call in a professional plasterer if appearance is critical and the areas involved are large.

The do-it-yourselfer, though, can tackle repairs and perhaps even apply a Tyrolean finish to a concrete-block garage.

Repairs to rendering

Defective rendering tends to flake away from the backing wall in patches, and it may be loose for quite a distance around the obvious signs of damage. Test it for soundness by tapping it with your knuckles. A shallow sound indicates that the rendering is loose. Weak render must first be chipped away from the wall to expose the backing of brickwork or blockwork. Leave the edges of sound rendering square or, if you can, under-cut them slightly with a chisel. Use a wire brush to clean out dust and loose pieces of rendering still adhering within the area to be patched. Rake out mortar joints between bricks or blocks to improve the key for the render.

If the existing rendering is quite thick, it is best to build up the patch in the same manner as the original was applied. First apply an undercoat about 12.5mm (½in) thick using a 1:1:6 mix of cement/lime/sand or, with masonry cement, 1:5 of cement to sand. Renderings should be stiffer than mortars used for brick or blocklaying, so add water very sparingly until the mix is just workable. Trowel the undercoat into the patch, working it well into joints; you may find a small pointing trowel best for this work.

When the first coat has partly set, scratch the surface to provide a key for the next coat, then leave it for a few

Repairs to rendering 1 First chip away all loose render from the brickwork. Undercut the edges of the sound rendering and rake out the mortar joints to further improve the key. 2 Using a trowel or (as here) a wooden float, apply an undercoat of render, working it well into the mortar joints and beneath the undercut edges. 3 Score the undercoat to make a key for the finishing coat. 4 When the undercoat has set, apply the finishing coat, scraping off the excess with a straight-edge to make a flat surface. 5 Smooth off the new render with a wooden float. The repair can be painted when the new render is dry.

days to harden. Apply the second coat using the same mix. This coat should be thinner than the first. Work the mortar well into the edges of the existing rendering, leaving it slightly proud of the surface. Then scrape off the excess with a straight edge, preferably a steel rule, to leave a level surface flush with the surround. To improve bonding a PVA building adhesive can be added to the rendering mix.

Rendering concrete blockwork

Concrete facing blocks require no protective finish. Dense-concrete plain wall blocks, too, are weatherproof but their appearance may not be very attractive. Open-textured and lightweight blocks require an applied finish to make them weatherproof as well as to improve their appearance.

Tyrolean rendering is the easiest finish to apply. It has a neat textured appearance coupled with good weather resistance. Another advantage is that the dry ingredients are bought ready-mixed in bags, so you do not have to worry about the proportions. Various colours are available. Machines to apply it can be hired from hire shops and many builders' merchants.

The Tyrolean rendering can be applied directly to the blockwork, but you will find that a more successful finish can be achieved by first rubbing a thick slurry of sand and cement into the blockwork to fill its somewhat open surface texture and the joints. The slurry consists of 1 part of Ordinary Portland cement to 2 parts of fine sand. Mix the ingredients dry and then add water until a fluid but not too runny slurry is obtained.

Dampen the blockwork and, using a soft hand brush, apply the mix along the wall. Go back to the beginning and work the mix into the blockwork with a pad of rough sacking in a regular sweeping action. Then leave the wall for a few days covered with plastic sheeting to

A Tyrolean finish is achieved with a hand applicator that is turned by hand and flicks mortar onto the surface of the wall.

allow the mix to cure.

As an alternative, the blockwork can be given an undercoat of the Tyrolean mixture, which should be brushed in thoroughly to fill the open texture. This method has the advantage of giving an undercoat of the same colour as the finish and thus more even and denser in colour.

The finish should be applied by machine in three applications. The first application should produce a speckled appearance with individual specks evenly distributed.

For successive applications change the angle of the machine to the wall, which will help to produce an even build-up of mortar. Keep the machine moving at a constant distance from the wall to avoid concentrating mortar in particular areas.

Allow each application to dry so that the wall regains its suction before applying the next coat. The drying time will vary greatly according to the weather – on a hot, dry day, for instance, the finish can be applied fairly quickly.

You can leave the rendering with the deeper as-sprayed finish or, for a slightly softer appearance, lightly rub it down with a rubber-faced float. After completing the application, a fine mist spray from a hosepipe will help the finish harden, but do not use too much pressure or drench the wall.

PAVING, PATIOS & STEPS

Paved areas and hard surfaces fulfil important practical needs around the house and garden. No matter how small the property, there will always be a need for a well-designed patio and for paths that enable you to reach the front and back doors, washing line, and garden shed without trampling over wet grass. There is also the visual or design aspect to be considered since the materials and layout of paved areas will influence the appearance of the garden.

Think carefully about where you site a patio. Butting it up to the back of the house is the conventional but not necessarily the best location. It should get plenty of sun, be sheltered from the wind, and offer a reasonable amount of privacy. As far as appearance is concerned, it is generally more successful if the patio merges smoothly with the rest of the garden. You can soften its hard edges with raised and planted walls, for instance, and with steps and paths that lead the eye to lawns and shrubs.

If the garden has different levels, exploit these to add interest to the garden rather than flattening them out with level areas of paving. In particular, paths are visually tedious if they run in a straight line from one point to another – from the back door to the garden shed, for example. Straightness draws too

34

much attention to the path and divides up the garden into bits and pieces.

The first thing is to plan the patio and paths on paper, drawing the garden to scale and marking fixed features such as manholes and mature trees, which must be incorporated into the design. With a new garden, it is advisable, too, to obtain an idea of the existing levels so that you can draw sections through the garden and work out the height needed for steps and retaining walls.

A paved area adjacent to a house wall must be at least two courses below the level of the damp-proof course. This, therefore, should form the datum or fixed level that you can use as a reference point to work out the degree of slope across the garden.

With the outline design drawn up, the next stage is to consider materials both from the practical viewpoint and with some regard to how they will look together and with the house. There is a wide range of paving materials available but the use of too many different types, particularly in a small garden, will look fussy. A sound approach is to select materials similar to those used in the construction of your house, such as bricks, concrete, and stone; this will help to unify the house and garden.

There is a wealth of paving materials to choose from, but it is worth taking care in selection and design, if you intend to use different materials together.

Far left *The charm of natural brick is enhanced by changes in level and the mixture of plant, water and hard surfaces. The overhanging shrubs help to soften the edges and make the patio an integral part of the garden.*

Below *Geometrical patterns and spiky plants complement each other on this modern rooftop patio. A similar effect could be achieved in a town garden.*

Project 1

Laying a patio

Laying concrete slabs is quite an easy operation. You need a firm and level base on which to work, so the first step is to prepare the ground. Dig down deep enough to bring the finished patio to the level you require – the level being marked by pegs (see drawing at right). The pegs then act as a guide to enable you to trim the sub-soil. Allow for a slight slope across the paved area to drain rainwater away from the house. If the ground is firm, you need dig out only the softer areas and replace the soil there with well-compacted hardcore. On soft clay soils, however, it is advisable to roll or firmly compact a 100mm (4in) thick layer of hardcore over the whole area, finishing it with a 50mm (2in) layer of sharp sand to fill in large gaps.

Mark out the edges of the patio with pegs and string to ensure that the edges of the slabs make straight lines – individual slabs vary slightly in size – and use a builder's square to make sure that your corners form right-angles.

Begin bedding slabs in at one corner. You can lay a mortar bed under the whole of the slab; or you can lay five pads of mortar about 50mm (2in) high, one under each corner and one in the middle of the slab; or you can lay, side by side, three 'sausages' of mortar the same length as each slab – but in this case you must make sure that the mortar sausages lie parallel to the direction of fall to help drainage of water beneath the patio (see photograph 1). Mortar used should be a 1 to 4 mix of cement and sand. Tap down each slab with a wooden mallet or with a hammer on a piece of softwood: treat the slabs gently to avoid breaking them (2). Level each slab against its neighbour and against your wooden peg reference points (which should, of course, be removed progressively as work proceeds); or use a

long plank with a perfectly straight edge to level the slabs right across the patio (3). Leave 12.5mm (½in) wide joints between slabs and, to ensure that joint spacing is consistent, insert wooden spacers, which will prevent adjacent slabs closing up (see drawing below).

Joints can be filled in various ways. You can, for instance, mix a cement/ sand slurry and pour it into the joints. Or you can mix the cement and sand dry (the sand needs to be very dry) and brush the dry mix into the gaps; then you sprinkle the joints with a watering can fitted with a fine rose. Generally, the most manageable method is to mix up a very stiff mortar and press it firmly into the joints with the edge of a pointing trowel. You can finish the joint with a rounded stick to achieve a recessed profile. After completing the paving, do not walk on the slabs for at least three days, taking particular care to avoid corners. The edge of the patio can butt up to a lawn or to a flower border (4). If the patio is bounded by a wall at the bottom of the slope, leave a small gap between slabs and wall (5), filling the gap with pebbles to help drainage.

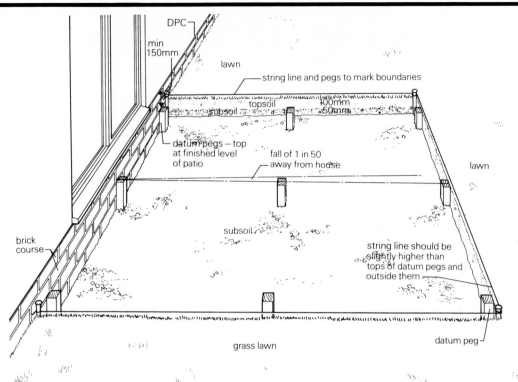

DPC
min 150mm
lawn
string line and pegs to mark boundaries
topsoil 100mm
subsoil 50mm
datum pegs – top at finished level of patio
fall of 1 in 50 away from house
lawn
brick course
subsoil
string line should be slightly higher than tops of datum pegs and outside them
grass lawn
datum peg

1

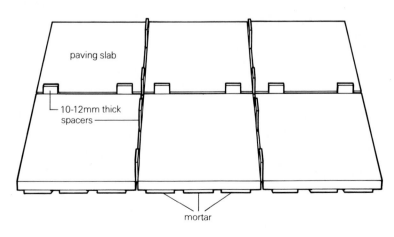

paving slab
10-12mm thick spacers
mortar

Stone

New stone for paving is nowadays expensive and is not as readily available as other materials. Suitable stone includes granite, which is very hard and durable; limestone, which varies in durability but is more mellow in appearance, with colours such as buff, cream and brown; and sandstone, which varies in colour from red, pink, and buff to green.

It is possible to buy second-hand stone slabs from merchants and garden centres or, better still, from demolition contractors; they should be much cheaper if you buy them from the last named. Second-hand stone will probably not be of a standard thickness; allow for this when bedding the slabs.

Cutting stone slabs is difficult, and it is generally better to work with the shapes you have, in-filling any gaps with bricks or cobbles. The slabs are very heavy and, to avoid uneven settlement on soft ground, it is advisable to remove the topsoil and replace it with well-compacted hardcore. On top, lay a sand bed 50 to 100 mm (2 to 4in) thick in which to bed the slabs, moving them from side to side to seat them firmly. Joints between slabs can either be left open or filled with sand; or you can brush in soil, in which you can grow alpines and other small plants.

Concrete

For large areas of hardstanding or long paths, consider laying concrete in situ and finishing it either with an exposed aggregate finish or with a brushed texture. For techniques for laying in situ concrete, see page 37. Concrete paving slabs are more expensive than in situ concrete, but are generally easier to lay. They are available in a wide range of colours, textures, shapes, and sizes, from most garden centres and builders' merchants.

The least expensive slabs are the cast concrete type, which are about 50mm (2in) thick. These are suitable for most paving provided only light loads are to be carried. They require some care in bedding, particularly when you are tapping them into position, as they are brittle and may crack. Much stronger are the hydraulically pressed concrete flags, which are generally about 38mm (1½in) thick.

Both cast and hydraulically pressed slabs can be obtained in a number of finishes. These range from a fairly smooth surface, which nevertheless has some slip resistance; a riven surface that has the appearance of split stone; textured finishes in which the crushed stone aggregate in the concrete is exposed; and various patterned surfaces that simulate the effect of brick paving and tiles. Colours, too, vary considerably, from slate greys to quite bright reds and greens. It is generally better to underplay the contrasts in colour and to mix only closely matching colours. This has a more subtle effect, though bolder colours can be used in small areas for accent. Colours fade somewhat over the years, and slabs in shady areas tend to mellow with lichen growth.

Sizes of slabs run from 675 × 450mm (26½ × 18in) to 225mm (9in) square, the most popular size being 450mm (18in) square. This is not too heavy to lift and lay, and is of an appropriate scale to fit in with gardens large and small. Most manufacturers produce leaflets showing the range of shapes and sizes of their slabs and various patterns in which they may be laid. With some of the more complex shapes such as hexagons it is advisable to study recommended patterns and colour combinations before ordering.

Concrete blocks
A recently introduced paving material to this country, although it has been used for many years in continental Europe, is the concrete block, which is now available in Britain in many colours and a variety of shapes. The rectangular blocks are 200 × 100 × 65mm (8 × 4 × 2½in) in size. They are laid on a bed of sand and tightly butt-jointed so that they interlock. After they have

Above Concrete paving blocks are available in many different colours and shapes, some fitting like a jig-saw. *Left* Laying a paving-block area: *1* Sharp sand is screeded to form a level bed. *2* Place blocks against each other in the chosen pattern. *3* The blocks can be cut easily and accurately with a hydraulic stone splitter. *4* Bed blocks in with a plate vibrator.

been positioned, sand is spread over the paving and a plate vibrator (available from hire shops) is used to bed them firmly. Rectangular blocks are usually laid in a herringbone pattern, which means that some blocks need to be cut along the edges.

The area also needs to be enclosed by a formwork of some kind to ensure that the blocks do not spread. Properly laid, concrete paving blocks are suitable for heavy loads and may, for example, be used for a garage drive as well as for a patio or other paved area.

Cutting concrete slabs and blocks
To cut concrete slabs, mark the line of the cut by scribing a line with a sharp point against a straightedge. Then lay the slab on a bed of soft sand, making

Brick paving patterns

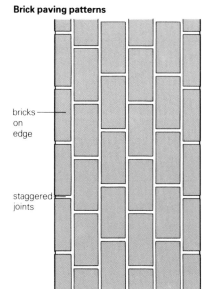

bricks on edge

staggered joints

Stretcher

Herringbone

Above and left The rich colours and textures of clay paving bricks are delightful. Right Bricks, like concrete paving blocks, can be laid in a variety of patterns. The cross-section at the bottom shows a path on a sand bed flanked by edging bricks bedded in mortar.

The first thing to do is to sort out the larger pieces with straight edges and to lay a number of these to give you a straight line along the edges of the path or patio. Then you can infill with the smaller, irregular pieces in the middle. However, a more informal approach can also be attractive. This can be achieved by laying the paving with a deliberately ragged edge, over which trailing plants can grow. Whichever method you adopt, first lay the broken pieces loose, fitting them together in attractive combinations of shape and colour, before you begin to fix them in their mortar bed.

Bricks

Bricks are among the most versatile of paving materials. There is an enormous range of colours and the small unit size is particularly well suited to the smaller garden. They can match the bricks used for the house and serve visually to link the house and garden.

Two sorts of brick are available for garden paving. You can use standard-sized bricks which are frost resistant and generally, therefore, will need to be of 'special quality'. Alternatively, you can buy specially made paving bricks, which are usually thinner in section but are very hard and dense.

Standard bricks can be laid flat on their bedding faces or, more traditionally, you can lay them on edge (but this uses more bricks). Perforated bricks, of course, must be laid on edge. There are many bonding patterns to choose (see drawings), from the simple stretcher bond to the more decorative basket weave and diagonal herringbone.

sure that it is evenly supported and there are no voids underneath. Using the bolster and club hammer, cut a groove all the way round the slab, including the edges; alternatively, you can use a masonry-cutting disc fitted to a circular saw. Then break the slab by laying it face down over a timber batten along the groove and tapping the waste end gently with the club hammer.

Concrete blocks can be cut to size in a similar way, but they are much harder and denser than slabs and the pieces to be cut are much smaller. If you have many blocks to cut it will pay you to hire a block cutter.

Crazy paving

Both natural stone and concrete slabs can often be bought from local councils in random broken and cracked pieces, which are suitable for crazy paving. Again, a firm base is required for laying, and it is generally advisable to lay the broken pieces of slab onto a continuous mortar bed rather than onto mortar pads; the pieces are often triangular in shape and the mortar pad method would not provide sufficient stability for these.

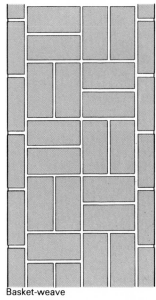

Basket-weave

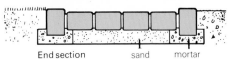

End section   sand   mortar

Project 2

Side view

patio

concrete paving slabs

soil

hardcore blinded with sharp sand

concrete walling-unit risers

concrete strip foundation

Front view

concrete slab

concrete screed

concrete strip foundation

mortar

soil

hardcore

soil

Garden Steps

Steps can be blended successfully into their surroundings by choosing a building material used elsewhere in the garden and by following the contours of the ground. The most important general principle is to ensure that the scale of the steps is compatible with the scale of the garden as a whole. In this example, precast concrete paving slabs, as used for a patio nearby, form the treads of the steps; to complement them, risers are built with blocks of reproduction dry-stone walling. The blocks are quick to lay and, because each incorporates false joints and appears to be made up of eight or nine modestly sized stones, they are of a scale suitable for a small garden.

To build the steps, the first job is carried out on paper. Draw out cross-sections from front and sides to determine the number of steps you need for a given height of riser and depth of tread, so as to fit the overall space available (see drawing above left). In this example the height of each step is made up of the height of a walling block and a mortar joint plus the thickness of a slab tread and a mortar joint. Remember to allow for small details, such as making the treads overhang the risers at both front and sides; this improves the appearance of the steps.

The first stage of construction is to build strip foundations on each side of the steps on which to lay the walling blocks. To economise on materials, foundations are formed in sections, each section rising by the same amount as each step. To fix the top of each foundation section, hammer timber pegs into the ground (picture 1) and level them by means of a spirit level set on a straight-edge. The foundation trench for each step can then be excavated to the required depth.

To form stop-ends to each section of the foundations, place timber planks across the width of the steps (2) and adjust them for level so that they align exactly with the relevant peg tops. Rough battens, all cut to the same length, are fixed between the planks to maintain the correct spacing.

Concrete for the step foundations is placed and tamped (3) to form level strips on which to lay the walling blocks. When the strip foundations have been completed (4) the stop-end boards can be removed.

Begin construction of the steps at the bottom of the flight. Lay a mortar bed on top of the foundation and carefully position the first block (5), using a string line as a guide for alignment. Subsequent block risers are supported on the back edges of the tread slabs forming the step below. Each side wall is built of blocks carried back to the stop-end that will support the next step. The area within the block walls is then partly filled with hardcore blinded with sand, and topped with a layer of concrete (6). The concrete must be thoroughly tamped (7) until it is flush with the tops of the blocks. When this concrete base has begun to harden, lay mortar (8) on both the concrete and the tops of the blocks to receive the slabs of the next step.

Set the slabs to overhang the block walls by about 50mm (2in) all round and tap them to the correct level (9) using the handle of a club hammer. Slabs should be laid at a slight angle, falling by about 6mm (¼in) in every 300mm (1ft) to the front or side to allow rainwater to drain off.

The final step takes shape. Note (10) the way in which the top of each strip foundation aligns with the top of the slab of the step below. This alignment must be exact or it will be difficult to set the blocks and slabs at the correct level; fine adjustments can be made by varying the thickness of the mortar layer supporting the slabs.

ROOFING REPAIRS

Because the roof is out of sight it is generally out of mind, and so it receives very little attention until it starts to fail. Yet the roof is the first line of defence against the elements: it will not last for ever and neglect will hasten its decline. New pitched roofing and major roof repairs such as re-tiling are not jobs for the do-it-yourselfer, but there are many simple repair and maintenance jobs that can be undertaken provided proper safety precautions are followed.

Pitched roofs

Older pitched roofs are generally covered with clay tiles and slates while, on houses built since the last war, concrete roof tiles are more common. Nowadays, the majority of new pitched roofs are covered with synthetic slates, or concrete tiles, many of which are given the appearance of the more traditional tiling materials such as slate and clay.

Re-roofing is now a major building activity; it is estimated that there are almost eight million pre-1939 houses in Britain, many of which have slated and clay-tiled roofs that are reaching the end of their useful lives. Clay tiles are laminar (layered) in structure. Water can enter the layers so that, if there is a

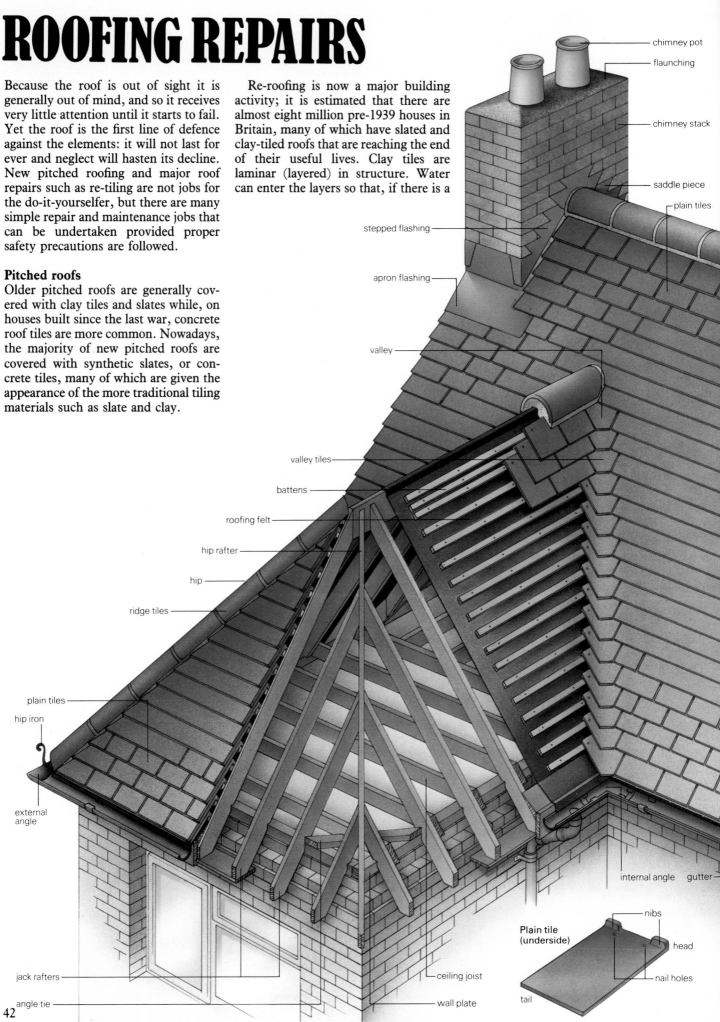

chimney pot

flaunching

chimney stack

stepped flashing

saddle piece

plain tiles

apron flashing

valley

valley tiles

battens

roofing felt

hip rafter

hip

ridge tiles

plain tiles

hip iron

external angle

internal angle   gutter

jack rafters

angle tie

ceiling joist

wall plate

nibs

head

Plain tile (underside)

nail holes

tail

frost, the surface may crumble, a process called spalling. Underburnt clay tiles from between the wars are particularly susceptible and many are now failing. Slate is also laminar in structure and many existing slated roofs were originally fixed with ungalvanised nails, which have rusted away and no longer hold the slates in place.

While you can replace the odd tile or replace one or two missing slates, these are often symptoms of more general trouble. It is advisable to get a pro-fessional roofing contractor to give your roof a thorough check-up. By patching small areas that have obviously failed, you may be putting off only briefly the moment when a complete new roof is necessary, and your efforts up a ladder will have been wasted.

Long-term neglect of your roof can result in decay and movement of the rafters, which in turn will loosen the slates and tiles. Consequently, rain will get into the loft and will eventually rot the ceiling joists and damage ceilings.

Missing slates and broken tiles are obvious warnings; more subtle signs are tile fragments that fall into the roof space and the gutters.

There are several methods of surface-coating old roof coverings which are designed to seal cracks and keep out water. However, the roof is always subject to slight movement which can cause the coating to crack, and it is not always obvious where the cracking has occurred. On the other hand, if the coating seals the roof too effectively, the circulation of air within the roof space will be considerably reduced and condensation could result. Often, too, the appearance of the roof is marred; and, if you wish to sell your house, this serves to draw attention to a defect.

It is better in the long run to opt for a new roof. The cost depends on the complexity of the roof, on the new roof covering you select, and, of course, on the area involved. Look in *Yellow Pages* for roofing contractors; select ones that are members of the National Federation of Roofing Contractors and enquire

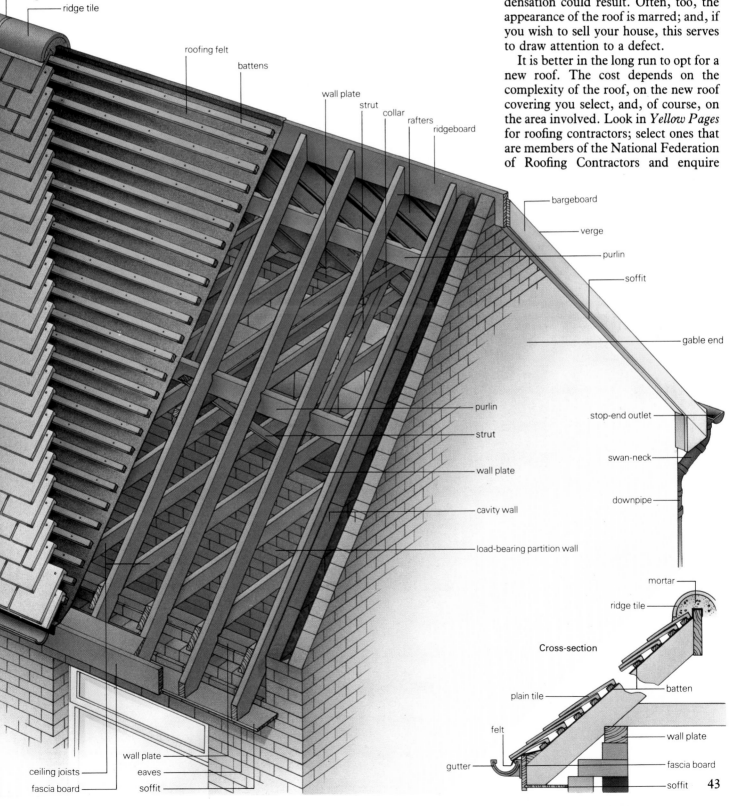

what guarantees they offer. Or ask around and find a satisfied customer to recommend a contractor. Always get at least three estimates before choosing a contractor.

You can replace an old slate roof with either new or second-hand slates, and a clay plain-tile roof with new plain tiles. But concrete tiles and lightweight synthetic slates are more economical, and therefore nowadays more common as re-roofing materials. The harsh colours that people still associate with concrete roof tiles have largely been superseded by softer, more sympathetic colours. There is a wide range available and, in consultation with your roofing contractor, it is worth taking some trouble to select a profile and colour that suits the style of your house and fits in with other roofs in the neighbourhood. Roofs have an important functional job in keeping the weather out, but they also significantly affect the appearance of your property. You will increase its value if the new roof harmonises with the rest of the house rather than sticks out like a sore thumb.

Access to the roof
Safe access is the first priority in tackling any roofing job; do not be tempted to take short-cuts – it could be your life that is at risk. If you have any doubts about safety, call in a professional. A **ladder** should extend at least two rungs above the eaves. Do not stand on the upper rungs because you must have something to hold on to; about the fourth rung from the top is the highest safe position. With an extending type allow at least a two-rung overlap on a 4m (13ft) long ladder and a three-rung overlap on a 5m (16ft) ladder. When selecting the length of a ladder, remember that the distance from the foot of the ladder to the wall should be about a quarter of the ladder height.

If your gutters are of plastic, use a ladder stay to hold the ladder away from the wall so that it does not rest on the gutter, otherwise the gutter might break or the ladder slip.

Right Safe means of access are vital for working at height. If the ladder needs to be placed across a window area (1) lash a stout batten to the top of the ladder. At the eaves use a special stay (2) to keep the ladder clear of plastic guttering. To prevent the ladder sliding on a gutter, tie a rung to a screw-eye fixed to the fascia (3), or take advantage of an open window (4). Always secure the foot of the ladder (5). A scaffold tower (6 and left) fitted with lockable castors (6a) provides a large, stable platform. For work on the roof, use a special roof ladder (7).

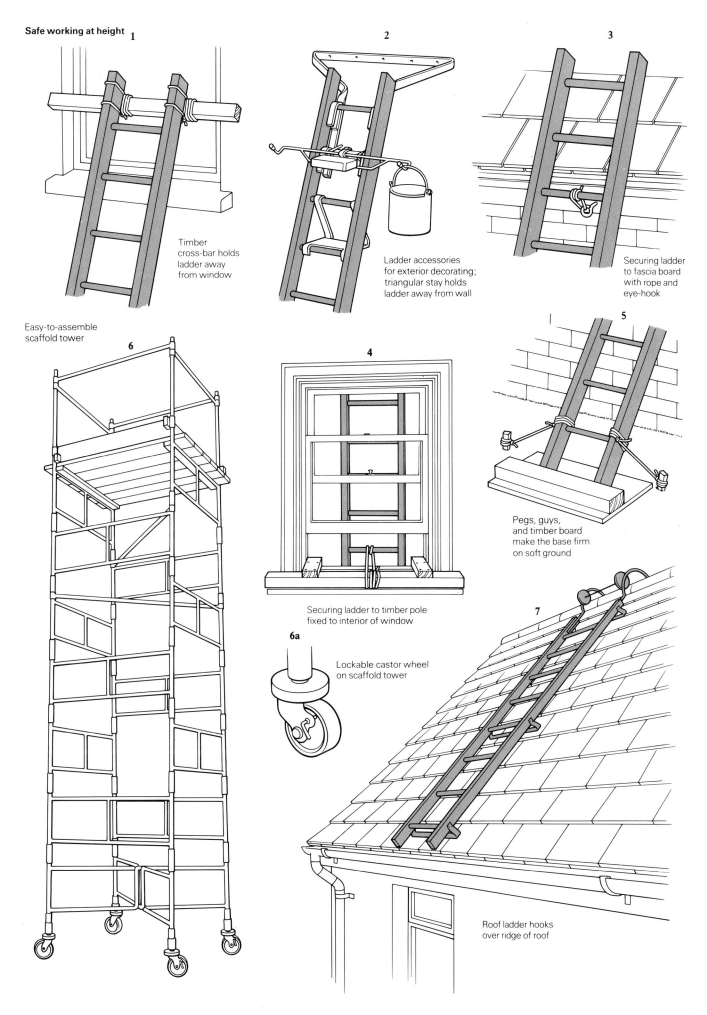

Safe working at height 1

Timber cross-bar holds ladder away from window

2

Ladder accessories for exterior decorating; triangular stay holds ladder away from wall

3

Securing ladder to fascia board with rope and eye-hook

Easy-to-assemble scaffold tower

6

4

Securing ladder to timber pole fixed to interior of window

6a

Lockable castor wheel on scaffold tower

5

Pegs, guys, and timber board make the base firm on soft ground

7

Roof ladder hooks over ridge of roof

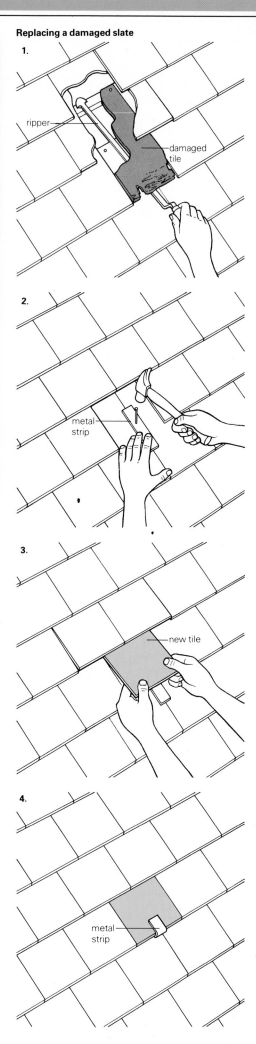

To secure the ladder at the base, tie or wedge it to pegs driven into the ground, and wedge it level on uneven ground; on hardstanding, place a heavy weight, such as a sandbag, at the foot to secure it. It is always advisable to secure the ladder at the top as well; tie it to a stout ring bolt fixed to the eaves to stop it sliding sideways.

Use a **scaffold tower** where a ladder would be unsafe or inconvenient – when working on chimney stacks, for example, where you need a working platform. These can be hired from hire shops or from some builders' merchants, in heights up to about 10m (33ft). Check on the manufacturer's recommendations on safe working heights and other safety features before you take it home.

Various fittings are available for the base of the tower: castors so that on level ground you can move it easily; square base plates for a fixed location; and special leg attachments that allow you to level the tower on uneven ground. Many towers, too, have outriggers to stabilise the base.

Over a height of about 3.5m (12ft) the top of the tower should be secured to the wall, preferably to ring bolts fixed to the soffit.

A **roof ladder** is essential once you reach roof level and wish to ascend the

Above Slipping or broken slates may be due to rusted fixing nails or to delamination caused by frost action, which may eventually affect the whole roof. **Right** *To repair the odd broken slate, remove the old nails with a slater's ripper (1). Then slide out the damaged slate, and nail a strip of sheet metal through the gap between the slates below and into a batten (2). Insert the new slate (3), and bend up the metal strip to secure it (4).*

pitch. These span from the gutter to hook firmly over the ridge. You can buy or hire roof ladders, which have wheels at one end to enable you to push it up the roof slope without damaging the tiles. When in place, the ladder is turned over so that it hooks over the ridge.

Do not be tempted to crawl on the slates or tiles; apart from the serious safety hazard, you may damage more tiles than you climbed up to repair in the first place.

Jobs for the handyman
Apart from a completely new roof, which is a job for the professional, there are many maintenance and repair jobs that can be carried out. Ridge tiles are vulnerable parts of a roof, being subject to wind uplift and crumbling of the mortar bed. Defective ridges can be

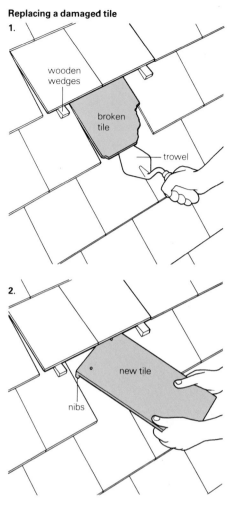

Replacing a damaged tile

1.

wooden wedges

broken tile

trowel

2.

new tile

nibs

replaced and loose ridges re-bedded and pointed. Mortar fillets at abutment walls can be re-made, and chimney pots can also be re-bedded. Then there is the most common maintenance job of all on the roof – unblocking gutters and downpipes that have clogged with leaves. All of these jobs have one thing in common; they require that you have safe access to the roof.

Fixing a slipping or damaged slate
Slates slip usually because the two nails that hold them in place have corroded or the end of the slate, as a result of wind up-lift, has broken at the nail holes. This may indicate more extensive problems but, to solve the immediate difficulty, the odd loose slate may be fixed back in place using a metal clip made from lead, aluminium, or copper, about 25mm (1in) wide and 225mm (9in) long.

Remove the old slate. Nail the metal strip through the gap between the pair of slates beneath using a galvanised nail fixed into a tiling batten. Replace the slate, keeping it flat and easing it under the row above and, when in position, bend the projecting end of the metal up and over the slate to clip it in place.

To remove a broken slate that is still held in position by the nails, you will have to buy or hire a slate ripper to cut

Above Underfired clay tiles (common on houses built in the 1920s and 1930s) are very susceptible to frost damage; the long-term solution must be to re-tile the roof.
Right To replace the odd broken tile, carefully raise the bottom of the tiles above and insert wedges to support them (1). Not all tiles are nailed; if you are lucky, you will be able to use a trowel to unhook the nibs of the broken tile from the batten and replace it (2) with a new one.

the nails. This has a long, flat blade with a sharp hook at the end. Slide the ripper under the slates above and hook it round each nail in turn. A sharp pull should cut the nail. Slide out the damaged slate, fix a clip with nails, and fit a new slate in place.

To repair larger areas of damaged slates, strip off the old ones and start replacing new slates from the bottom using galvanised nails. Do not drive the nails firmly home. Work upwards until you reach the final row, which fits under the existing slates and for which, again, clips will be necessary.

Repairs to clay tiles
Plain tiles, which are common on older houses, generally have small projections (nibs) that hook over the tiling batten to fix them in place. Depending on the roof pitch, they are nailed only every

fourth or fifth course. A broken tile can be replaced fairly easily by lifting the edges of the tiles above with a trowel, wedging them up and, again using the trowel, lifting the nibs of the broken tile over the batten and sliding it clear. If the tile is nailed, use a slate ripper to break these before you pull the tile out. Fix a new tile by reversing the process and hooking the nibs over the batten.

Repairs to the ridge
The ridge at the top of a slated or tiled roof generally finished with rounded or angled ridge tiles bedded in mortar. The mortar joints between ridge tiles are liable to crack, perhaps as a result of slight settlement of the roof, and water penetration hastens the deterioration so that eventually the ridge tiles become loose. If this happens, wind can lift a tile and blow it off.

You can rake out the joints and re-point the ridge; but for a sounder job it is best to remove all the ridge tiles, chip off the old bedding mortar, and fix the tiles afresh. If one or two of your ridge tiles are broken or cracked, a local roofing contractor with probably have a stock of second-hand tiles and he may be able to match yours in colour and pattern. The alternative is to replace all the tiles.

When re-fitting ridges or fixing new

1.

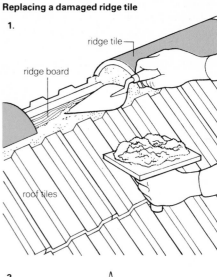

2.

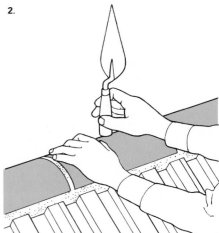

3.

ones, soak all the tiles in water to reduce the risk of the new bedding mortar shrinking and cracking. The mortar used should be a mix of 1 part cement to 3 parts fine sharp sand. Apply the bedding mortar and squeeze the ridge tile down on top of it so that the mortar begins to ooze out. It can then be neatly struck off and the join pointed.

With deep-profiled tiles, such as the traditional pantile, there is quite a large gap between the hollow of the tile and the base of the ridge. This should not be filled up solid with mortar because a large amount such as this might shrink and crack. Instead, mortar in slips of broken tile or purpose-made dentil slips, available from builders' merchants, to help fill the gap. For similar reasons, tile slips are also needed at the eaves and, with plain tiles, at the verge.

Repairs to hips

Hip tiles, which cover the angle formed by the intersection of two pitches, are bedded in the same way as ridges, except that a hip iron is screwed to the base of the hip rafter to stop the tiles sliding down. When bedding hip tiles, place the bottom hip on the roof and mark and cut it off so that the end follows the line of the eaves on both sides. Having bedded the first hip, stretch a string alongside it to the top of

Above Ridge tiles, which may be square or 'half-round' in section, are likely to be blown off the roof if the mortar jointing and bedding have been allowed to deteriorate badly. **Right** *To fix a new ridge tile, clean off all the old crumbling mortar (1) and apply a new mortar bed. Press the tile down on top (2), tapping it level. Then strike off the excess mortar (3) to form a neat joint. If the mortar bed between the topmost roof tile and the ridge tile is more than a couple of inches deep, pack the mortar with bits of broken tile.*

the hip rafter to act as a guide for bedding the remainder in a straight line. Where bold-profile tiles have been used for the roof proper, use dentil slips to pack out the deep mortar bedding under the hip tiles.

Sealing verges

Dampness in gable walls can be the result of water penetrating the verge as a result of cracked and missing mortar. You can seal fine cracks with a proprietary mastic or, if the mortar has deteriorated too badly, you should chip it off and repoint the verge.

Fitting underfelt

Nowadays all slated and tiled roofs have felt below the slate or tile to keep out windblown snow and to conduct any

condensed moisture from beneath the tiles to the gutter. The underfelt is secured to the tops of the rafters and is taken over the ends of the rafters to overhang the gutter. The tiling battens are nailed on top of the underfelt in order to hold it in place.

Many older roofs, however, are not felted, so driven snow and draughts can penetrate. When the time comes for the roof to be stripped and re-tiled, this is obviously the best occasion to fix underfelt. However, as a stop-gap measure, you can cut strips of underfelt to fit in between the rafters rather than on top of them. The strips should run from ridge to eaves and should be slightly wider than the spaces between rafters so that they will sag a little in the middle. Staple each side of the felt to thin battens and then pin the battens to the sides of the rafters close to the tiles. At the eaves, push the felt through under the tiles if you can, so that it projects over the gutter. How successful you will be depends on the detailing at the eaves, which can vary quite a lot. Before you start the job, take a look at the eaves to ensure that the job is practical.

Repairs to valley gutters

Valley gutters, usually formed of lead or zinc, slope down at the inside angle formed by the intersection of two roof pitches. In time the gutters may crack and corrode, allowing water to seep into the roof. Simple cracks can be sealed using a proprietary bituminous mastic to a thickness of about 1.5mm (¹⁄₁₆in) and overlapping the cracks by about 50mm (2in) on each side. To reinforce the repair, the mastic should be covered with metal foil or thin roofing felt, with the edges well sealed in the mastic.

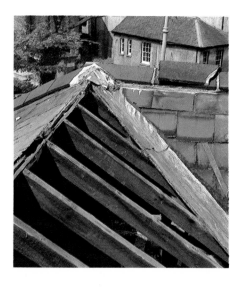

Above A badly deteriorated roof in the process of being stripped, repaired, and re-tiled. Note the corroded valley gutter and damaged ridge. **Below** *Re-roofing in progress, using interlocking concrete roof tiles. The tilers have installed new underfelt over the rafters and under the new battens; the roof of a house of this age would not originally have been felted.*

Then cover this with a further 1.5mm (¹⁄₁₆in) layer of mastic. To be sure that no fine cracks have been missed, after the main repairs have been completed coat the whole length of gutter with a liquid bitumen made for the job from builders' merchants.

If the valley is beyond repair, a new one must be fitted, which, depending on the age and design of your roof, may be a job you should leave to a professional. If you decide to have a go yourself, tiles or slates alongside the gutter must be stripped and the old gutter removed. Check the supporting timbers and packing fillets to make sure that they are still sound and have not begun to rot, and remove old protruding nail heads.

Sheet zinc is normally used to re-line valley gutters as it is light and easy to bend. Alternatively, three layers of good quality roofing felt may be used, the first layer being nailed down and subsequent layers fixed with felt adhesive. Trim the end of the zinc or felt to form a turnover at the eaves to direct water into the gutter.

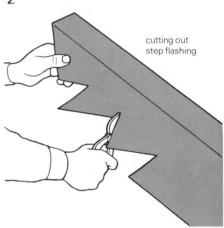

1.

soakers

2.

cutting out
step flashing

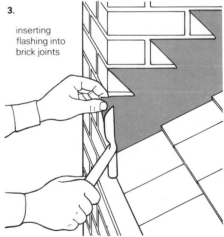

3.

inserting
flashing into
brick joints

Repairs to flashings

Flashings are basically strips of water-proof materials used to cover the line where a roof meets a vertical surface, such as a wall or chimney. Lead is the traditional material for this purpose because it is easy to bend and shape; but it is so expensive nowadays that bituminous felt is often used instead.

Cracks in flashings may be tackled in a manner similar to that described for repairing valley gutters. If a flashing is turned up against a wall and dressed into a mortar joint in the brickwork, the mortar may deteriorate, allowing the flashing to come away from the wall. Repair is simply a matter of raking out the joint, wedging the flashing back in place if it is still sound, and repointing.

Straight, horizontal flashings, such as those that cover the junction of a lean-to roof with a wall, are fairly easy to repair or renew. Remove the old flashing and clean up the brickwork and tiles with a wire brush. If there is one, repair the triangular mortar fillet, which serves as packing between wall and roof, with new mortar. Then form a new flashing using a proprietary sealing tape. Various types are available, some surfaced with aluminium foil and others with grey plastic to resemble lead. Follow

Above Lead or zinc flashing eventually corrodes and the mortar joints into which it was dressed will crumble, allowing it to come away from the chimney wall. Right To make repairs, carefully remove the old soakers (which go under the tiles and are turned up the chimney wall) and the cover or side flashing (1), and use them as templates to cut new pieces to shape (2). Refit the soakers and cover flashing, turning the top of the flashing 'steps' into raked out joints in the brickwork (3); hold the flashing with wedges while repointing.

the manufacturer's instructions carefully, particularly regarding the use of a primer, which is necessary in some circumstances. Then peel off the backing paper and stick the tape in position.

Alternatively, you can use bituminous felt, which should be sealed onto the tiles with mastic to stop it curling, or lead; both of these must be dressed into a mortar joint in the brickwork. Rake out a joint, bend the felt or lead to form a flange about 25mm (1in) wide, and wedge it into place; then carefully bend and tap down the lower half over the tiles. Finish by repointing.

Stepped flashings down the pitch of a roof at an abutment wall or alongside a chimney are not so straightforward.

Details around chimneys are particularly complicated, with an apron flashing at the front, a back gutter, stepped flashings down the sides and, perhaps, soakers (small pieces of lead, copper, zinc, or bituminous felt that are used to weatherproof junctions). It is best to get a contractor to carry out this work.

Mortar fillets for abutment walls

Sometimes where a pitched roof meets an abutment wall, instead of a stepped flashing, a mortar fillet is used to seal the junction. This is quite common where the party walls of terraced houses are built up through the roof to act as fire-breaks. Over the years, the fillet may crack away from the wall and allow water to penetrate.

Weak and crumbling mortar should be chipped away and the fillet repaired with fresh mortar. The crack between the fillet and the wall can then be sealed with a proprietary mastic.

Repairs to chimneys

No work on a chimney should be attempted until a proper working platform has been erected; a ladder or roof ladder really is not adequate because you will need both hands free to tackle any chimney repair, and you may have to lift quite heavy weights such as chimney pots. With proper safety precautions, you can repoint the chimney brickwork using the techniques described on page 32, and you can set about replacing damaged chimney pots and the flaunching (the mortar in which these are set). Major chimney repairs are work for a professional.

Flaunching that is not too badly cracked may be repaired with a mastic sealer. For a more permanent repair, and to replace a cracked chimney pot, chip off the old flaunching and trowel on new mortar. Before you begin, however, cover the fireplace openings in the rooms below in case you cause falls of soot. Remove the flaunching with a bolster and club hammer and take care not to damage any sound chimney pots. When the brickwork at the top of the stack is exposed, rake out the joints and wet the bricks ready to receive the new mortar. Use a mortar mix of 1 part cement to 3 parts sharp sand. Trowel on the mortar to about 63mm (2½in) thick around the pots, and curve it down smoothly to about 12.5mm (½in) at the edges of the chimney stack.

If the chimney is no longer being used, the top of each pot can be closed off with a section of half-round ridge tile bedded in a mortar flaunching. The tile will keep out rain but will allow air to circulate and prevent condensation inside the flue.

Problems arising from crumbling mortar are common on older roofs. Slate or tile roof coverings are always subject to slight movement due to wind, and roof timbers will sag over the years. This movement causes mortar joints, beds, and fillets to crack and this, in turn, lays them open to frost damage. **Above** *A typical example of a deteriorated mortar fillet at the junction of a slate roof with an abutment wall.* **Below** *Cracked flaunching, the mortar bed into which chimney pots are embedded. Provided the roof timbers and brickwork are sound, repairs to flaunching are basically a matter of chipping off the old mortar and replacing it with new.*

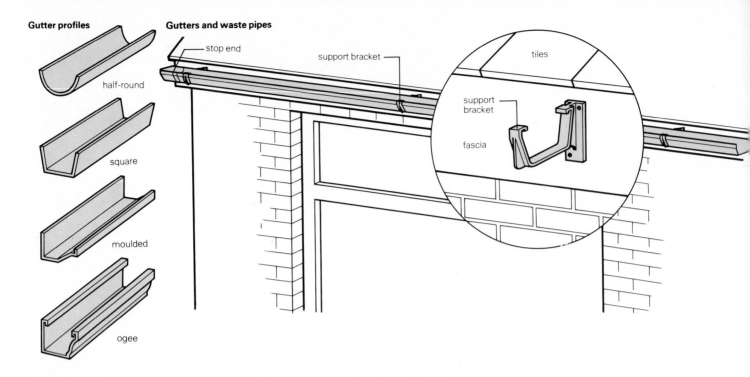

Gutter profiles

half-round

square

moulded

ogee

Gutters and waste pipes

stop end

support bracket

tiles

support bracket

fascia

Gutter maintenance

Gutters should be inspected at least once a year, ideally in early winter when dead leaves have stopped blowing about but before the hard frosts set in. Blocked gutters, a simple job to rectify, can cause quite serious problems if they are neglected. For example, water pouring over the gutter instead of down it can cascade on to paving below and splash back to saturate the bottom few courses of bricks. Frost can spall and crumble saturated bricks.

So clean out the gutters as part of your annual maintenance programme. Use a small trowel or make a curved wooden scraper to fit inside the gutter and scoop out the muddy mixture of leaves, paper, and other debris.

Check the state of the rainwater pipes by flushing down the gutters to see if the water drains away. It is quite likely that the swan-neck pipe at the top of the downpipe, where there are overhanging eaves, is also blocked. You can try rodding it clear but you may have to dismantle it (with a modern PVC system of guttering this is easy). Take the blocked section to ground level to clear it in safety.

While cleaning the gutters take the opportunity to seal any leaking joints with a mastic; with cast-iron gutters, check that there is no corrosion. If you need to fit a new length of cast-iron gutter, make an accurate drawing of the existing profile or take a section of gutter to a builders' merchant to get an exact match. To take off a section of gutter, first remove the bolt holding the sections together. At best you will have to use penetrating oil to ease the bolt; at worst you will have to saw off the bolt.

Access to gutters

One of the few disadvantages of plastic guttering is that it is not rigid enough to support the weight of a ladder. Probably the best answer is to buy a specially designed ladder stay (see drawing 2 on page 45) to keep the top of the ladder away from the eaves. Another, cheaper way is to make up a length of filler block out of scraps of timber to prevent the gutter deforming.

Fitting new gutters

When fitting new plastic guttering, lubricate the sliding joints with ordinary washing up liquid to avoid damaging sealing gaskets.

Take care in lifting off the damaged section as it will be heavy and unwieldy. Scrape the old jointing compound off the end of the remaining gutter and clean it ready to receive the new putty.

If you need to cut cast-iron guttering, turn it upside down and saw through from the bottom – it will be more stable this way round. Then drill a hole so that you can bolt it into place. A standard length will, of course, already have its bolt hole.

Paint the new section before fitting it on – it is easier to coat all sides while it is still on your bench. Paint the end of the existing gutter too, where the new putty is to be applied; putty sticks better to new paint. Form the joint using metal-window putty, pressing the new gutter into it firmly until it begins to squeeze out. Then line up the holes and fit a new bolt to fix the new and old

sections together. Do not over-tighten.

Sometimes asbestos-cement gutters are fitted as an alternative to cast-iron ones. While they do not suffer from corrosion or rot, they do become brittle with age and can easily be damaged. Half-round guttering, 100mm (4in) wide, is most common for houses, but other types, such as ogee guttering, of this width are also made. New sections of asbestos-cement guttering are sold in 2m (6½ft) lengths. Sections are fitted in the same way as cast-iron ones, using a non-hardening mastic to form the joints and a galvanised nut and bolt to hold the lengths together; again, do not over-tighten. If you wish to paint asbestos-cement guttering to enhance its appearance, you must first apply an alkali-resistant primer, as oil-based paints will otherwise flake off after a time.

If you need to replace the complete guttering system, PVC guttering secured with snap clips, and incorporating ready-bonded neoprene pads, is easiest to fit. It is light to handle and requires no painting. Various widths and lengths are available. To help you to choose, study manufacturers' literature, which you can probably pick up from a builders' merchant, select a system suitable for your home, and decide on the fittings required. In determining gutter lengths, remember to allow for overlaps where spigots fit into sockets.

Fascia boards and barge boards

While inspecting or working on gutters, it is advisable to look at the fascia boards. If the boards are rotten, screws holding the gutter brackets may loosen and sections of gutter come away. To replace a fascia, see page 58.

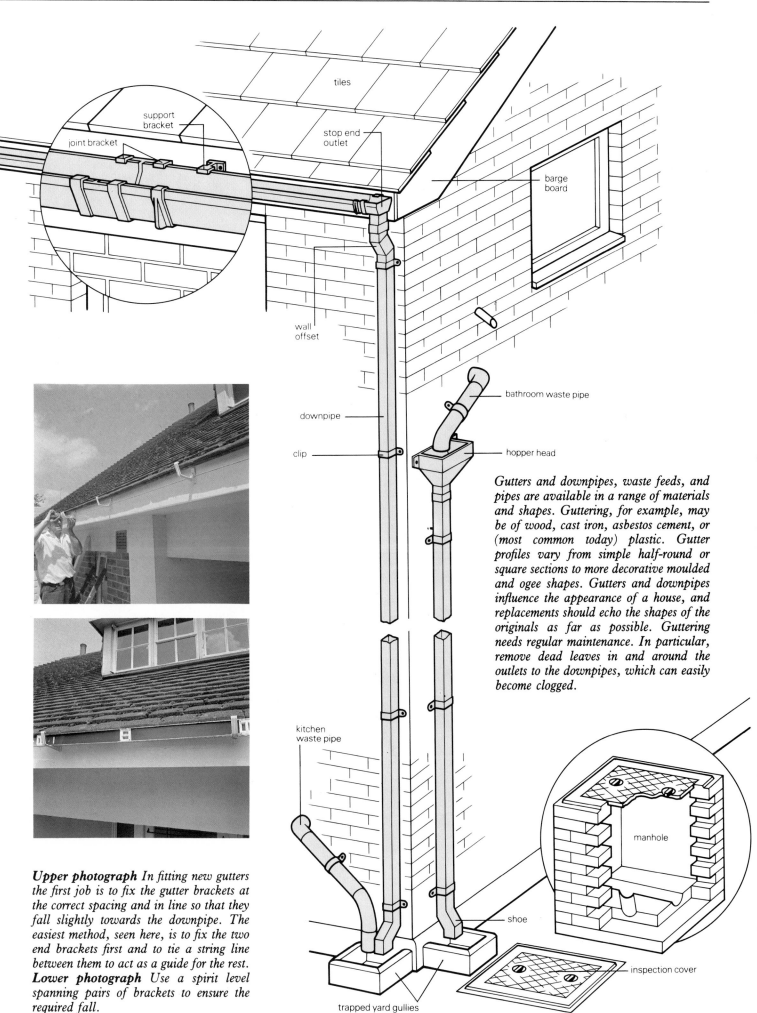

tiles

support
bracket

joint bracket

stop end
outlet

barge
board

wall
offset

bathroom waste pipe

downpipe

hopper head

clip

Gutters and downpipes, waste feeds, and pipes are available in a range of materials and shapes. Guttering, for example, may be of wood, cast iron, asbestos cement, or (most common today) plastic. Gutter profiles vary from simple half-round or square sections to more decorative moulded and ogee shapes. Gutters and downpipes influence the appearance of a house, and replacements should echo the shapes of the originals as far as possible. Guttering needs regular maintenance. In particular, remove dead leaves in and around the outlets to the downpipes, which can easily become clogged.

kitchen
waste pipe

manhole

shoe

inspection cover

trapped yard gullies

Upper photograph In fitting new gutters the first job is to fix the gutter brackets at the correct spacing and in line so that they fall slightly towards the downpipe. The easiest method, seen here, is to fix the two end brackets first and to tie a string line between them to act as a guide for the rest. **Lower photograph** Use a spirit level spanning pairs of brackets to ensure the required fall.

Project 1

Re-tiling a bay

Vertical tiles hanging between ground- and first-floor bay windows are a common decorative feature of suburban houses built in the 1920s and 1930s. Like those on the roof, these tiles are subject to deterioration over the years. Slipped and broken tiles are particularly visible on such a prominent feature as a bay and will spoil the appearance of the property. Replacement is not such a problem as for roofs: access is easier, and the bay is in any case closer to the ground. You will find the work simpler if you hire a tower scaffold.

Generally, 265 × 165mm (10½ × 6½in) plain tiles are used for vertical cladding; there are also ornamental tiles available of a similar size. In this particular example, concrete plain tiles were used; but there is a considerable range of colours available, so you should be able to match your roof tiles.

When the old tiles and battens have been stripped off the bay, the first job is to mark out a gauge stick (1), a straight, narrow piece of wood that is used to ensure that each new course of tiles is laid to the correct bond. The lines marked on the gauge represent the widths of one tile and one and a half tiles. Now nail roofing felt to the underlying brick over the entire area to be tiled; then using a tape measure (2) mark on the felt the spacing of the battens to which the tiles will be nailed; the battens are nailed at 114mm (4½in) centres. You can mark the interval at each end of bay, then use chalked string snapped on to the felt to indicate the line of each batten. The battens, 38 × 19mm (1½ × ¾in) in section, are nailed through the felt into the brickwork. The positions of the bottom batten and eave undercourse batten are established (3) by temporarily positioning normal and undercourse tiles as a guide.

With all the battens in position, use the tile gauge to mark on them one tile and one and a half tile widths (4) to make sure that the bond of one tile on top of another is maintained.

At the external angles formed by the bay cut the undercourse tiles by scoring and pincering them to form mitres (5). This is necessary because the undercourse features a sprocket (that is, the undercourse tiles lean at a greater angle than those of the other courses; for the latter, use external-angle tiles, which obviate the need for cutting). Before fixing the undercourse, dress lead or zinc soakers (6) around the mitred corner to cover the joint. Where the bay runs into the walls of the house, position more lead soakers to cover the tiles, then cover the soakers with side flashings, which are fixed and pointed into the wall brickwork. Now score and cut the tiles (7) so that they make a good, neat fit. Continue tiling until the job is completed (8), nailing each tile with two 38mm (1½in) aluminium alloy nails into its batten.

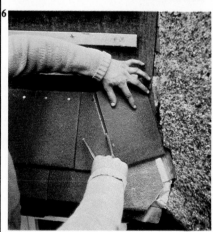

Flat-roof repairs

Older flat roofs may be finished with asphalt. This is melted on site from solid blocks and spread to a thickness of about 19mm (¾in). Cracked asphalt may be sealed with bituminous mastic applied with a small trowel. For extra strength, sandwich glass-fibre between layers of mastic. To ensure that any fine cracks have not been overlooked, brush a bitumen-latex emulsion over the whole roof after the larger cracks have been repaired.

Sheds and workshop roofs may be finished with one or more layers of bituminous felt. If this becomes damaged, it is best to strip it completely and replace it with new felt. The heavier the felt used, the longer will it last; but in any event it is desirable to use at least two and preferably three layers of felt, as shown in the drawings below.

To re-cover a shed roof, use wide strips of felt laid along its length. Start with the eaves, laying the first strip so that it overlaps the eaves and verges by about 25mm (1in). Nail along the top edge of the strip using large-headed, galvanised nails. Fold the corners and nail through two thicknesses of felt, and then nail up the sides and along the bottom. The next strip should overlap the first by about 75mm (3in), and the area to be overlapped should first be painted with a bitumen sealer. Last of all, fit a 300mm (12in) wide strip to lie astride the ridge.

If your shed has a pitched roof of 30° or more you can use felt slates, which are available in strips of four tiles. These are fixed in a similar way to ordinary felt, with broad-headed galvanised felting nails, the bottom of one strip overlapping the top of the one below. More substantial buildings, such as garages and house extensions, are generally covered in two or three layers of roofing felt bonded together and topped with a layer of granite chippings to reflect sunlight.

The most common cause of failure is blistering and cracking of the felt. Repairs may be carried out using bituminous mastic, which is trowelled into the crack. The mastic is then covered with a bandage of glass-fibre, the edges of which must be sealed down, and a futher layer of mastic applied.

Corrugated roofs

Lean-to structures, such as conservatories and garages, may be roofed with corrugated sheeting of clear plastic, or of asbestos-cement or aluminium alloy. Plastic sheets – PVC or the stronger glass-fibre-reinforced polyester – are easily cut with a padsaw and fixed by drilling holes in the tops of the corrugations and screwing through into the purlins. Specially moulded foam-plastic strips are also available to fit under the sheets at the eaves. Sheets come in various sizes, so consult manufacturers' literature to work out what type of sheet is required.

Asbestos-cement sheets will become brittle and porous after a while. They can be waterproofed with two coats of liquid-bitumen proofing after lichen and moss have been removed with a fungicide. Cracks can be repaired with a mastic sandwich. For a longer-lasting repair, a new sheet of asbestos-cement can easily be fitted. Fixing holes should be made through the tops of corrugations to coincide with the positions of the roof joists. Use galvanised screw nails incorporating soft rubber washers to make the fixing.

When you are inspecting or working on a roof of corrugated sheeting, you must not walk or kneel on the sheets. A board should first be placed across the roof, and positioned over the roof joists for maximum support.

Stages in refelting a flat roof 1 Remove old felt and galvanised clout nails. 2 Fix wooden drip rails and fillet. 3 Nail down first felt layer. 4 Stick down second layer with special adhesive. 5a, b Fixing felt at gutter edge. 6a, b Fixing felt at other edges.

Re-felting a flat roof

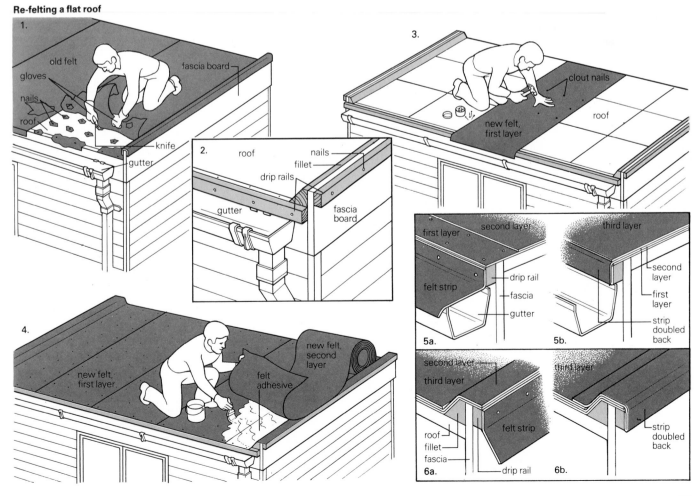

55

EXTERIOR TIMBER

Although most of the timber used in house-building is concealed within the structure, a certain amount is traditionally used on the house exterior. It is, therefore, constantly exposed to the weather and also to attack by certain plants and animals, and unless the wood used is naturally durable or is protected in some way it will soon deteriorate. Furthermore, wood is a popular material for building garden fences, gates, outbuildings, and a host of other structures. To find out just how much wood there is to look after on and around your home, take a short tour around the the property. Here is what you might expect to find.

Starting at roof level, the guttering will be fixed to wooden **fascia boards**, which are nailed to the ends of the **rafters** of both pitched and flat roofs. The fascia boards may be flush with the house wall surface, or the house may have overhanging box eaves. In this case you will also find a horizontal board, called a **soffit**, fixed between the fascia board and the wall. Because guttering is usually attached close to the surface of the fascia board, decoration and repair work is difficult to carry out unless the guttering is removed; many fascia boards tend, therefore, to be neglected and in very poor condition – indeed, you may find that they have deteriorated to the point where the gutter fixings are no longer safe.

At the triangular end of a main, gable, or dormer roof, the ends of the ridge board, the roof **purlins** (horizontal battens that support the rafters), and the tile battens, on to which the tiles are hooked, are protected by **barge boards**. As with fascias, they may be almost flush with the house wall, or there may be an overhang fitted with soffit boards. Once again, such timbers are often neglected and in poor condition, yet if

Timber features of house and garden

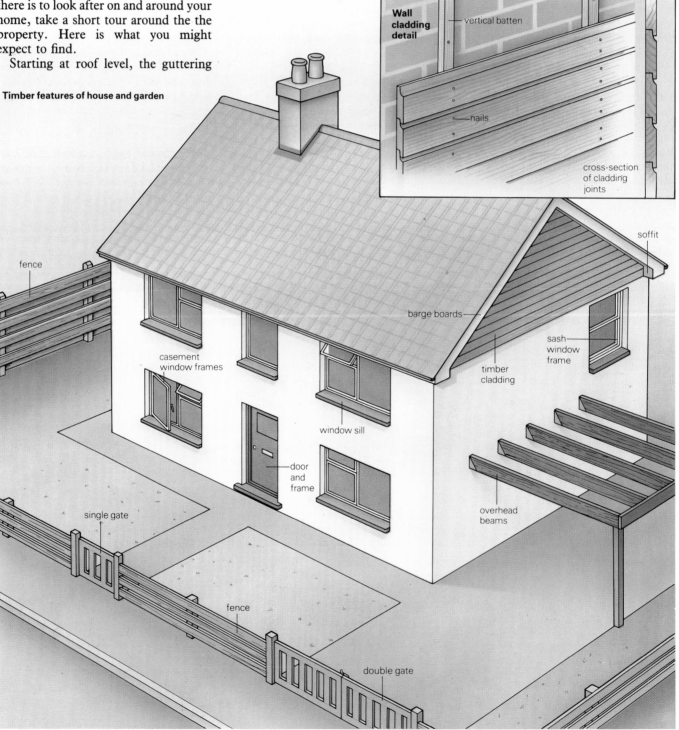

Wall cladding detail
- vertical batten
- nails
- cross-section of cladding joints

fence

casement window frames

door and frame

single gate

fence

double gate

window sill

barge boards

soffit

sash window frame

timber cladding

overhead beams

they are allowed to deteriorate, damp may begin to attack the roof timbers behind, with potentially very serious and expensive consequences.

Your home may have part or all of the exterior walls covered with **timber cladding** – lengths of tongued-and-grooved timber with a shaped profile – that forms an attractive wall finish when it is in good condition, but an eyesore when it is not. The cladding usually runs horizontally, and is nailed at intervals to vertical wooden battens fixed to the surface of the wall beneath. Because it is completely exposed to the weather, timber cladding is notoriously difficult to maintain in good condition.

Naturally, your home will have its share of doors and windows, more often than not with timber frames and sills. Because there are joints in these, there are plenty of opportunities for the weather to penetrate and cause decay. Deteriorating putty also allows water to get into the wood. You may also have bay windows and porches, all containing a fair share of exposed woodwork.

Away from the house you will probably have a number of timber outbuildings – a shed, greenhouse, summerhouse, perhaps a timber garage – and other wooden structures such as vegetable cold frames, sand pits, or children's climbing apparatus. And linking house and garden there may be a lean-to conservatory, a canopy, and covered ways of timber construction. Last of all, your property may be bounded by wooden fences and gates, which are at risk not only from the weather but also from ground moisture. It all adds up to quite a burden of care and maintenance.

Protection and preservation
There are two inter-related solutions to the problem of caring for exterior woodwork. The first is to protect its surface as much as possible from moisture and, to a lesser extent, sunlight. The second is to give it a second line of defence by treating it with chemical preservatives, which, if properly applied, will prevent attacks by wood-destroying fungi and wood-boring insects.

So far as the first point is concerned, the object is to combine careful construction with good surface protection. By assembling frame joints carefully and fixing structural woodwork sensibly, moisture traps can be avoided and the risk of rot greatly reduced. Then, by ensuring that the wood surface is sealed all round with a decorative and protective coating, we can hope to ward off the damaging effects of water and sunlight. The parts of structural timber most prone to attack are end grain and

hidden areas. So, for example, the butt (end grain to end grain) joint between adjacent lengths of fascia board will open up as the wood contracts in warm weather, allowing water to penetrate as soon as it rains. With timber cladding, the inward-facing surface of the boards is often not treated, and so moisture can easily enter the wood, causing excessive movement and, eventually, rot that will force the paint off the outer face from within. On window frames, the expansion and contraction breaks paint films and allows water to enter the frame joints, while defective putty encourages water to seep along the glazing bars. So the importance of regular and thorough exterior decoration becomes obvious; once paint films begin to crack and flake off, rot can gain a foothold.

The use of preservatives to treat and protect structural timber is now becoming more widespread. Much factory-produced joinery – door and window frames, for example – is now pre-treated with a wood preservative before being primed. It is possible to buy timber for home constructional use that has been factory-treated with preservative – most large timber merchants stock it. And a growing range of preservative products is now available to the do-it-yourselfer.

In the case of these DIY products, it is important to choose the right one for the job. Tar-oil preservatives such as creosote are used mainly for woodwork such as fences and outhouses. They are cheap and easy to apply by brush or spray, but they have a strong and

Coloured wood preservatives are easy to apply, need little maintenance, and remain effective for several years.

persistent smell and cannot easily be over-painted unless well weathered. Water-borne preservatives, by contrast, contain salts toxic to fungi and insects, have no smell, and can be over-painted when completely dry. Organic-solvent types contain similar compounds in a solvent (usually white spirit) and penetrate dry wood more quickly than water-borne types. They, too, can be over-painted when dry, unless they contain an additional water-repellent ingredient. The latter type is intended for treating cladding, fences, and outbuildings that will be left in a natural finish, and some contain pigments to enhance the colour of the wood. Lastly, emulsion types have the consistency of mayonnaise and can be applied thickly to the wood surface, thereby giving a much heavier dose of fungicide than is possible with other products. They are especially useful for treating the hidden faces of timber areas such as fascias and barge boards.

In general, preservative must be applied liberally to all surfaces of the timber. Ideally the wood should actually be immersed in a shallow trough and weighted down for at least 15 minutes to give the preservative time to penetrate thoroughly to a depth of a few millimetres. Remember that preservatives should be applied *after* joints have been cut and holes drilled but before assembly or construction.

Tools & Techniques

You will need a modest selection of everyday woodworking tools to carry out repair and restoration work on the exterior timber of your house. These should include the following:

Measuring and marking tools: a steel tape, a trysquare, sliding bevel (for matching angles other than 90°), and a spirit level.

Cutting tools: a hand saw, a tenon saw, and perhaps also a coping saw for cutting curves and holes.

Shaping tools: at least three chisels of different blade widths – say 6, 12, and 19mm (¼, ½, and ¾in) – a smoothing plane, and one or more abrasive tools such as Surforms and rasps.

Drilling tools: a power drill (which can also drive accessories such as saws and sanders if you have them), a bradawl, a hand drill (useful for working away from power points and up ladders), and perhaps a carpenter's brace for making large holes.

Joining tools: a claw hammer, several screwdrivers, and a nail punch.

Miscellaneous tools: a pair of pincers, an adjustable wrench, a cold chisel or small crowbar.

Obviously, for elaborate constructional projects you may need all the resources of a carpenter's workshop, but the above selection will enable you to carry out most of the repairs covered here. You will also need ladders and scaffold towers (see pages 44–5).

Patching damaged wood

Your inspection of the exterior woodwork may have uncovered wholesale decay, which will necessitate the complete removal of the affected timber. Often, however, rot is localised and it is possible to chop out the damaged area, patch it with exterior filler, or replace the area with new wood and then paint or otherwise protect the entire component thoroughly to guard against further attacks. The aim of such repairs is disguise and strength, and for this reason cuts at each side of rotten sections are made at an angle. So, for example, a section of rotten sill is cut away in a wedge shape, narrower at the bottom than at the top, so that when the new piece is fitted the whole is as strong as it was before. On a garage door, rot in one corner is cut out by sawing up the grain at an upward diagonal from the door edge. On planking, damaged wood is removed by making saw cuts at 45° to the face edge instead of at 90°, so that the new section can be skew-nailed or screwed into place.

Fixings are an important element of outdoor repair work, too. When fixing wood to wood, driving nails carelessly can split the wood, allowing water to penetrate. Near the edges of boards pre-drill holes if possible, and use screws rather than nails for fixing any work that you may need to remove or dismantle in the foreseeable future. Fixings into masonry must be made securely; masonry nails are useful for rough fixing, but they can split the wood, and for fixings carrying a load there is no substitute for using wall plugs or wall anchors, set deep into the masonry.

Fascias and soffits

If your fascias and soffits show only localised signs of rot, you may be able to chisel away the rotten wood and patch the area with an exterior-quality filler. However, you will make a better job and save yourself a lot of future maintenance by taking down the guttering and removing the fascias and soffits altogether. Decayed sections can then be cut away more carefully and new wood fitted, or if necessary the boards can be completely replaced.

The first job is to take down the guttering and to remove the fixing brackets, if used. The type known as ogee guttering, which has a straight back plate, is screwed direct to the fascia, and you may have to saw through the screws with a hacksaw blade if you cannot unscrew them. Gutter brackets are screwed to the fascia or, if made of iron, to the rafter ends.

Now prise off the fascia and soffit board (or boards, if several lengths have been used) with a cold chisel or crowbar, and pull out all nails. If the joist and rafter ends or soffit bearers are rotten, screw new wood securely to them to form fixing points for the fascia board, and daub the wood liberally with preservative. Clean up good timber, filling nail holes and other damage with exterior-quality filler, and treat it

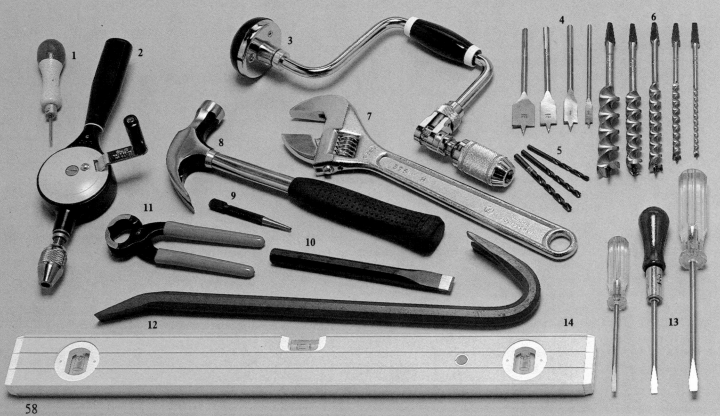

thoroughly with water-borne or organic-solvent preservative. Then, when the preservative is thoroughly dry, apply a primer, undercoat, and one topcoat on all surfaces, paying particular attention to end grain.

Now offer up the soffit board to the underside of the rafters or soffit bearers, and mark on it the centre of the last bearer it reaches. Take it down and make a 45° mitred cut across the board at this point. Offer it up again, and nail it in place so that the inside edge is pressed firmly against the wall. Mitre the end of the next length of soffit, and nail it so that the mitred joins meet neatly at the centre of the bearer. Punch in nail heads, fill, and prime.

Add the fascia panels in a similar fashion, driving one nail into the rafter end and the other into the edge of the soffit. Cut mitred joints as before, and punch in and fill all nail heads. Finally, apply a top coat of paint over the complete system. It is now ready for the guttering to be refixed.

Barge boards

The job of repairing and replacing barge boards follows similar lines to those described for fascias. Again, basically sound timber can be re-used, but it should first be stripped and treated with preservative. Both sound and new wood should be thoroughly primed and painted before being installed.

Use the old barge boards as templates for cutting the new ones, and particularly for matching the angle at which the boards meet at the roof ridge, and for the tailpiece that fills the gap where the lower end of the barge board meets the fascia panel at the corner of the roof. If there are soffits behind the barge boards, remove and repair or replace these first.

Windows

Window frames need more (and more-frequent) maintenance than most other exterior woodwork. Perhaps the commonest problems are caused by rot attacking window sills and the lower parts of opening casements and sliding sashes, and by faulty putty allowing water to penetrate the glazing bars. If the rot is not extensive, patching may be possible, but a badly damaged window is best replaced completely.

Crumbling putty should be raked out of the rebates all round each pane with an old chisel or a glazier's hacking knife, and the exposed wood allowed to dry out before being treated with preservative, primed, and painted. New putty should then be bedded in all round, smoothed off at an angle of 45° to the glass, and left to harden for 14 days before being primed and painted over. To ensure a good seal between

Tools used in installing or maintaining exterior timber 1 Bradawl; 2 Hand drill; 3 Brace; 4 Spade bits (used with 2); 5 Twist drills (used with 2); 6 Auger bits (used with 3); 7 Adjustable spanner; 8 Claw hammer; 9 Nail punch; 10 Cold chisel; 11 Pincers; 12 Crowbar; 13 Screwdrivers; 14 Spirit level; 15 Panel saw; 16 Tenon saw; 17 Bevel-edge chisels; 18 Sliding bevel; 19 Try square; 20 Steel tape; 21 Smoothing plane; 22 Wood rasp; 23 Surform planes.

putty and glass – the source of the trouble in the first place – run a moist finger over the putty edge immediately after bevelling it, and when painting carry the paint film on to the glass by about 3mm (⅛in). Check the condition of all your windows at least once a year, and retouch any flaking paint between major redecorations to minimise the risk of rot.

Rotting sills that are too decayed to patch should have the rotten sections cut out with saw and chisel. Make the saw cuts at an angle to the edge of the sill so that the section removed is wedge-shaped. Then cut a new piece of wood, slightly thicker and wider than the sill, to match the cut-out and tap it into place. It should be a tight fit, but it can be glued too if necessary. The plug is planed down to match the profile of the sill, and finally it is sanded, primed, and painted.

The joints on hinged casements often begin to open up, causing the casement itself to sag and allowing water to penetrate the joints. If this has happened, remove the affected casement from the frame and gently wedge it on the workbench until all its corners are right angles once more. You can tighten up loose joints by driving small glued hardwood wedges into the mortises, or by recessing L-shaped metal repair brackets into the surface of the frame at each corner. The brackets can then be covered with wood filler and over-painted. Do these jobs before attending to any putty repairs that may be necessary.

Doors and door frames

Exterior doors, like windows, are particularly prone to rot, and may sag on their hinges or bind in their frames. The frames themselves may also rot, particularly at the sill and at the bottom of the stiles.

Frame and sill repairs are comparatively easy to carry out. In the case of frames, rotten sections, usually at or close to ground level, can be cut away and replaced by matching sections, while rotten sills can be prised out and replaced with new wood – either a machined section or a tailor-made sill of hardwood.

To repair a rotten frame, make a cut at an angle of 45° through the frame, prise out the rotten section, and cut a piece of new wood to match, with a 45° angle at the upper end. Treat it with preservative, ideally standing the wood in a tin of the chemical overnight to allow thorough penetration of the end grain, and then screw and plug it into place. Fill the butt joint, then prime and paint.

To replace a rotten sill, prise it away from the bottom of the side frames, cutting through tenons first if they were employed in the original construction. Then cut the new sill section to the required length, sloping the tip and front with a plane and cutting out a drip channel on the underside, preferably with a routing tool. Hold the new sill in place, and mark where it has to be cut to fit round the existing frame members. Cut out these recesses, check for fit and treat the sill underside liberally with linseed oil before driving the sill into place with a mallet. If necessary, secure the sill by driving cut nails through it into the masonry below, punching in and filling the nail heads. Oil the top and front of the sill.

Rotten sections of the door itself can be cut away and replaced with new wood. If the rot extends right across the foot of the door, cut away a strip of the bottom rail and replace it with a batten cut to the same width and glued and screwed to the sound part of the rail. Countersink the screws deeply if necessary. If the rot has extended up one corner of the door, cut away the damaged wood by making one saw cut up from the bottom of the door, along the grain line, and another upwards from the door edge to meet the first line. Cut a new piece of wood to match that removed, and glue and dowel-joint it into place. Fill the joints, then prime and paint.

Weatherboards are added to the lower face of exterior doors to throw rainwater away from the sill. They should be removed if rotten, and replaced with new ones – standard machined sections are available from timber merchants. A new weatherboard must be shaped at each end to allow it to clear the frame, and should be preservative-treated, primed, and painted before being screwed into position.

Doors that stick within their frames may have collected a great many coats of paint, the thickness of which is causing the door to bind against the frame. If this is the case, remove the door and plane the binding edge until it clears the frame by 3mm (⅛in). Prime, paint, and re-hang. Another cause of sticking is expansion due to moisture absorption through the unpainted top and bottom edges of the door. Again, planing, followed by priming and painting of the door edge, top, and bottom should cure the problem.

Warped doors often lose their shape because of moisture getting into the timber through unpainted top or bottom edges. It may be possible to correct the warp, but unless it is a valuable door and worth the lengthy treatment required to put it right, you will do better in the long run to fit a new door. Doors are sold in several standard sizes; if your door opening is slightly different, you can plane down the next largest size, add narrow hardwood battens to the top or bottom to gain extra height, or have a door made to size.

Wall cladding

Timber cladding on exterior walls is usually run horizontally, and nailed to vertical timber battens that are fixed to the masonry beneath (if the cladding is vertical, the battens run horizontally). The timber is usually tongued and grooved so that, despite the inevitable shrinkage, it remains draught-proof and weather-proof.

It is the inevitable swelling and shrinking, caused by changes in the moisture content of the wood during cycles of wet and dry weather, that cause paint films to crack and flake, and open up joints, allowing rot to gain a foothold. It is also frequently the case that such cladding is put up before being primed and painted or sealed; once in place the visible face is decorated, but the rest of it can absorb moisture and harbour rot unseen until too late.

Small areas of rotten wood can often be chiselled out and patched, but generally you will be faced with replacing substantial sections. Since individual planks are usually nailed through their faces to the battens beneath, you should be able to punch the nails through to free the affected plank. If the ends of the cladding are accessible, you will then be able to slide the plank horizon-

Installing timber wall-cladding 1 Fix a horizontal batten at the base of the area. 2 Instal vertical battens at 1m (3¼ft) intervals. 3 Lay the first plank against battens. 4 Drive nails in near the top edge of the plank. 5 Instal remaining planks. 6 Punch in and fill nail heads.

tally out of its groove; otherwise you will have to saw through the tongue along one side of the board and prise it out. A new piece, treated with preservative and primed and painted on all surfaces, can then be either slotted into place from the edge of the clad area, or pinned in after the inner part of the tongue has been removed.

At the same time, check the condition of the wall battens; unless they are sound replace them with treated wood. Use galvanised nails to fix the cladding to the battens, and punch in the nail heads; then fill, prime, and paint.

If your cladding is in such bad condition that complete replacement is the only solution, consider the following. Even if you treat the new wood with preservative and put it up perfectly, you will still have to paint it regularly, and it will not last for ever. It will also cost you quite a lot of money. But there is an alternative that costs little more to install, is maintenance-free, and lasts for years. This is plastic cladding.

Most types consist of thin, interlocking PVC extrusions, although one or two are planks of cellular construction, or multi-plank units. They are attached to battens in much the same way as timber cladding, but use special clips rather than nails, and each system includes finishing strips for top edges and sides. The system can cope with internal or external corners, and the planks can be easily cut to cope with obstacles or other irregularities. The only maintenance such a system needs is an occasional wash-down with detergent. The main objection to such cladding is that many people do not see the point of having cladding unless it is of timber.

Linked woodwork

Many 'add-on' structures such as carports, verandas, and covered ways are built with timber frames and lean-to or flat roofs, either covered with roofing felt or with translucent roofing materials. The sides may be solid panels, glazed areas, or open structures – simple posts set in the ground and supporting the roof. All these timbers are prone to rot and decay, and those in contact with the ground particularly so.

Repair work to rotten timber on structures of this sort is generally fairly straightforward. Posts and rails can be cut out, with the structure temporarily supported by props and struts as necessary, and new preservative-treated wood added, using the same sort of patching techniques already described for doors, windows, and other exterior timber. Where posts sunk into concrete are involved, it is well worth considering replacing the timber with a galvanised metal post instead. To retain the look of timber, the post can be boxed in with planking.

There are two particular problem areas with lean-to structures of this sort. The first concerns glazed roofs, where the glass is supported by slim glazing bars. These glazing bars are notoriously prone to decay, and it is almost impossible to repair them without stripping the entire roof. Metal repair plates will effect a temporary repair, but in time you will have to replace them. When you do so, ensure that all new wood is thoroughly treated with preservative, and that joints are a tight fit and are sealed with non-setting mastic to discourage water penetration. Do not paint them; you are only storing up trouble for yourself for the future. Instead, treat them with a preservative stain that will enhance the appearance of the wood, will not flake or peel, and needs re-applying, with the minimum of preparation, only every three to four years.

The second major problem with lean-to structures is making a water-tight join where the structure meets the house wall. Its roof usually abuts the building at a wall plate screwed to the house wall, and it is at this point that water running down the house wall is most likely to penetrate. The most effective solution is to put in a proper flashing strip, which should be tucked into a chase cut in the house wall immediately above the wall plate, and should extend out over the lean-to roof surface by at least 100mm (4in). The chase can be cut in the mortar course immediately above the wall plate, and the flashing is then mortared into it. You can use a proprietary flashing strip for this. In the case of translucent

Project 1

Building simple lean-to structures

Whatever type of structure you intend to build, you must follow sound building practice. Briefly, this means that posts supporting the roof must be of adequate strength and must be built on adequate footings, and should if necessary incorporate a damp-proof course linked to that in the house wall; roofs must be of a suitable pitch, adequately covered and weatherproofed where they are attached to the house wall, and supported on wall plates fixed securely.

For the simplest lean-to structure, such as a carport or a canopy over a patio, these requirements can be met by using 100mm (4in) square posts set in concrete to a depth of at least 600mm (2ft). Wall plates supporting the rafters should be of 100 × 50mm (4 × 2in), while the maximum span for the rafters themselves depends on the weight of the roof covering and the rafter size. For a lightweight roof covering, a 75 × 50mm (3 × 2in) section rafter can span up to 2.3m (just under 8ft), a 100 × 50mm (4 × 2in) one up to 3.1m (about 10ft).

The wall plate at the house wall should be fixed with expanding wall bolts set into holes drilled in the bricks themselves, not in the mortar. Rafters are notched with a 'birdsmouth' cut to fit over this wall plate and over the horizontal bearer at the outer edge of the roof. The latter may be simply supported on vertical posts, or it may rest on a masonry wall; in the latter case a felt damp-proof-course strip should be placed between the wall plate and the masonry.

With the roof structure in place, the roof covering can be added. If translucent sheeting is being used, you will need to add purlins at intervals between the rafters, parallel to the wall plates, to give extra support to the sheets and to provide fixing points where the ends of the sheets overlap. If the roof is to be boarded and felted, or covered with tiles, sawn boards or chipboard sheets are nailed in place across the rafters before the final roof covering is added.

Before beginning to construct any addition of this sort to your house, you must check the requirements of the Town & Country Planning Act and the Building Regulations. The former, policed by your local authority's planning department, dictates whether your proposed structure is permissible; the latter, under the control of the authority's Building Control Officer or District Surveyor, in intended to ensure that it is structurally sound. The requirements of both are complicated, and it is generally best to check in advance whether your proposed alterations need formal approval under either or both sets of legislation. If they do, you must submit the required forms and plans several months in advance. Do *not* begin such work until your plans are officially approved (many an impulsive do-it-yourselfer has been obliged to dismantle work erected without approval). If approval is not needed, you can of course proceed with a clear conscience.

corrugated roofing panels, the manufacturer may make a special flashing strip that follows the contours of the roof panels, guaranteeing a weather-proof job. On felted roofs, you can use a strip of roofing felt to form the flashing, bedding it in bitumen mastic.

Access is frequently a problem with this job. If the roof is strong enough to bear your weight, use a half-sheet of chipboard, cut lengthwise, to form a working platform that will spread your weight over a number of rafters. If it is not strong enough, the best way round the problem is to remove panels or panes from the roof near the wall to install the flashing, and work from steps erected beneath the roof.

Where the sides of a lean-to structure meet other buildings, the junction can best be weatherproofed by sealing the gap with non-setting mastic. If the gap is irregular, pack it first with mortar before sealing the surface.

Outbuildings

The maintenance of timber outbuildings – sheds, greenhouses, summerhouses, and the like – is generally of lower priority than house maintenance. However, they are valuable structures, and expensive to replace these days, so they are worth their fair share of care and attention.

For a start, they are all too frequently erected on inadequate bases – sometimes on bare earth – and so the floor (if fitted) and the lower parts of the walls are particularly prone to rot. If possible, they should be built on concrete bases (see page 29), with damp-course strips laid beneath any timbers resting directly on the base. It may be possible to raise an existing building sufficiently to introduce preservative-treated timber bearers below the walls and floor, so that these are no longer in contact with the ground and have the chance to dry out sufficiently for rot to be treated and repairs carried out.

The roofs of timber outbuildings (other than greenhouses) are usually felted, and may need localised repairs. A porous roof can be weatherproofed with a coating of bitumen emulsion, although re-felting will be a better long-term proposition. Rotten glazing bars in greenhouses can be repaired tempor-

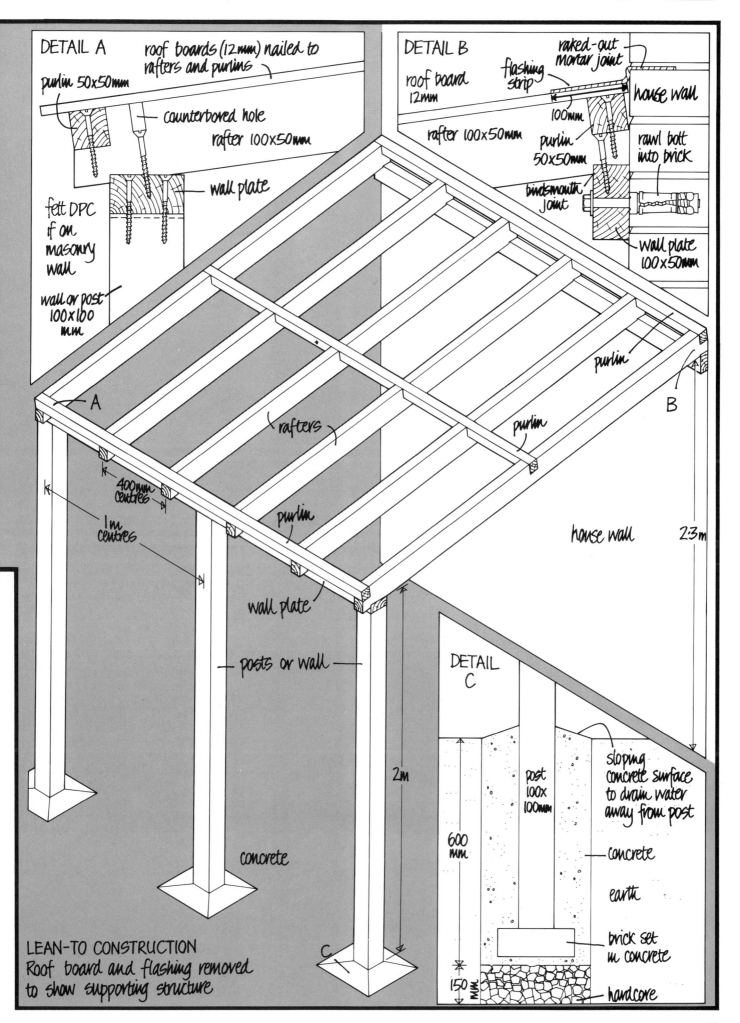

DETAIL A

roof boards (12mm) nailed to rafters and purlins

purlin 50×50mm

counterbored hole

rafter 100×50mm

wall plate

felt DPC if on masonry wall

wall or post 100×100 mm

DETAIL B

raked-out mortar joint

flashing strip

roof board 12mm

house wall

100mm

rawl bolt into brick

rafter 100×50mm

purlin 50×50mm

birdsmouth joint

wall plate 100×50mm

A

B

rafters

purlin

purlin

purlin

400mm centres

1m centres

wall plate

posts or wall

house wall

2·3m

2m

concrete

C

DETAIL C

post 100×100mm

600mm

sloping concrete surface to drain water away from post

concrete

earth

brick set in concrete

150 MM

hardcore

LEAN-TO CONSTRUCTION
Roof board and flashing removed to show supporting structure

arily with metal repair plates, and leaks can be patched with adhesive flashing tapes pressed over the glazing bars and on to the glass on either side.

Planked and panelled walls should be treated with two coats of a water-repellent wood preservative every two years or so to protect the wood and to enhance its appearance. Such regular and inexpensive maintenance will prevent the need for more drastic measures if rot really gets a grip on the structure.

Fences

Garden fences rarely receive the regular maintenance they deserve; it is more often than not a case of too little, too late when they blow down in a winter's gale. The following measures will help to lessen the risk of that happening.

Posts that have worked loose should be bedded in concrete on a hardcore or gravel base, which will allow water to drain from the foot of the post. If the fence is leaning, the post should be braced upright and enough soil excavated to allow you to check the condition of the post below ground level. If rot is advanced, either replace the post or fit a pre-cast concrete fence spur or a length of timber to which the sound portion of the existing post can be bolted for support. The spur should be set in the ground to a depth of around 750mm (30in) and bolted to at least 450mm (18in) of sound post. Angle iron may also be used for supporting fence posts, but it must be meticulously painted with bituminous paint before being set in the ground.

Project 2

Building a shed

Constructing a small garden shed is comparatively straightforward. The basic principle involves making a simple braced framework for each wall panel, cladding the framework with softwood planking or man-made board, and adding a simple roof. A timber floor is optional, but worth considering if the building is to be used as a workshop, since timber is more comfortable to stand on than concrete.

First decide whether you want a pitched or a lean-to roof, since this will affect the wall design. A shed with a pitched roof has two walls the same height and two gable ends; a shed with a lean-to roof has one wall higher than the one opposite it, and end walls with sloping upper edges. In either case, make sure you will have adequate headroom by making the minimum internal height at least 2m (6½ft).

Make the floor first, nailing your floorcovering (which can be preservative-treated softwood or exterior-quality plywood) to 50 × 38mm (2 × 1½in)

preservative-treated joists at about 450mm (18in) spacings. The wall panels will stand on the edges of the floor, their cladding overhanging slightly to protect the floor against the weather. Measure the width of opposite pairs of wall panels, remembering that one pair will overlap the other pair at the corners of the building. Then make up a lap-jointed frame of 50 × 25mm (2 × 1in) sawn timber for each wall, adding vertical and horizontal cross-braces. Notch in timbers to form window and door openings; rebates can be formed round these later by pinning on slim beadings. Clad the outside of each frame with tongued-and-grooved planks or exterior-quality plywood.

With the four walls erected, you can start to erect the roof. On a lean-to shed you can simply nail rafters across from front to back, adding softwood planks or chipboard panels with fascias all round ready to be covered with roofing felt. On a pitched roof, you can either make up two panels in the same way as the floor was constructed, and nail them to the tops of the walls so that they meet

at the roof apex, or you can erect a ridge between the tops of the end walls and notch rafters to it and to the eaves before covering them with planks or panels as already described. Unless the roofing felt is wide enough to cover the roof in one piece, cover the lower slopes first and overlap subsequent strips by about 150mm (6in). On a pitched roof, cover the lower slope of each face first, and then add a centrally-placed strip over the ridge. Finish off the building by glazing windows, hanging doors, and treating all the timber with two coats of water-repellent preservative.

Garden sheds and similar buildings do not usually require planning permission, although there are restrictions on their size, location, and the area of your garden you can cover with them. They are also exempt from Building Regulations approval so long as they are completely detached, have a floor area of less than 30m² (325sq ft) – which would be a very large shed – and are less than 3m (10ft) high. If you are in doubt about the building you want to erect, check with the appropriate authority before proceeding.

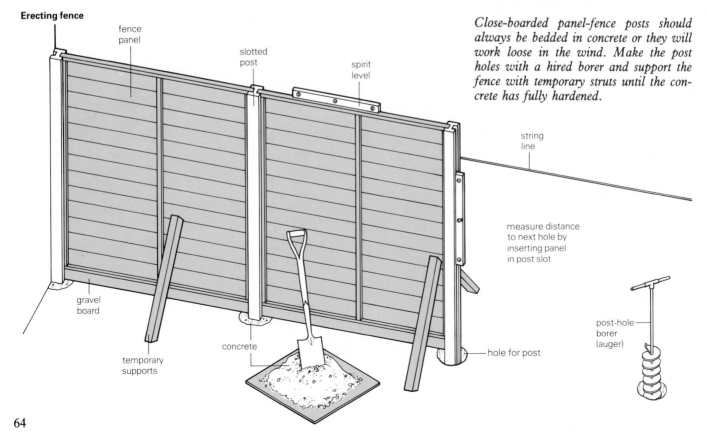

Erecting fence

fence panel

slotted post

spirit level

string line

Close-boarded panel-fence posts should always be bedded in concrete or they will work loose in the wind. Make the post holes with a hired borer and support the fence with temporary struts until the concrete has fully hardened.

measure distance to next hole by inserting panel in post slot

gravel board

temporary supports

concrete

hole for post

post-hole borer (auger)

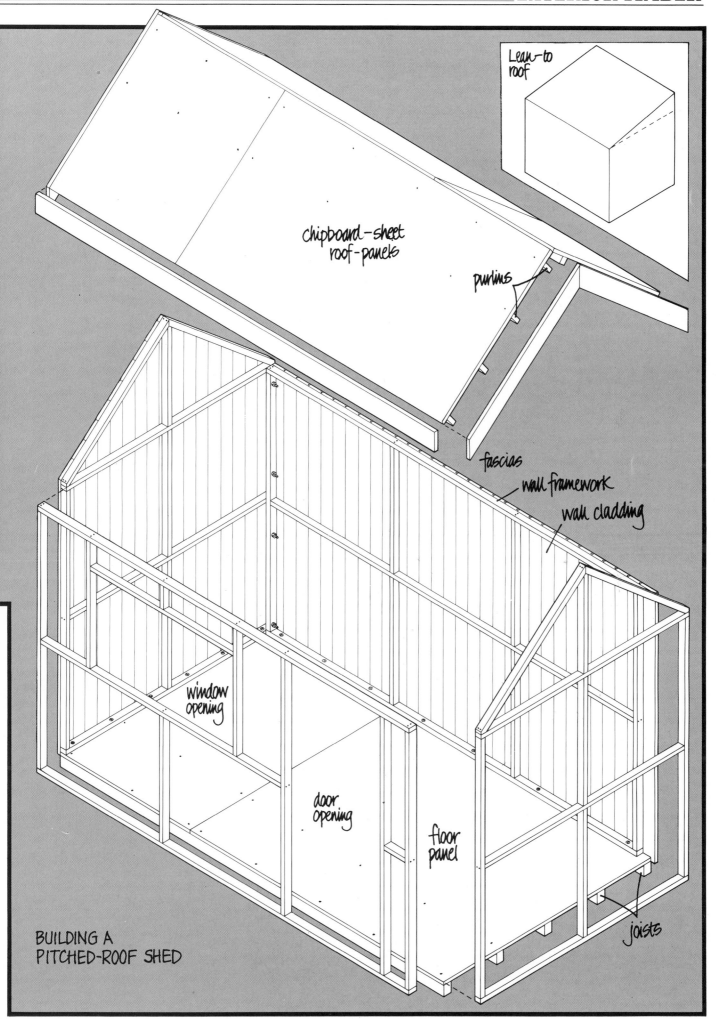

Lean-to roof

chipboard-sheet roof-panels

purlins

fascias

wall framework

wall cladding

window opening

door opening

floor panel

joists

BUILDING A
PITCHED-ROOF SHED

WALL LENGTHS

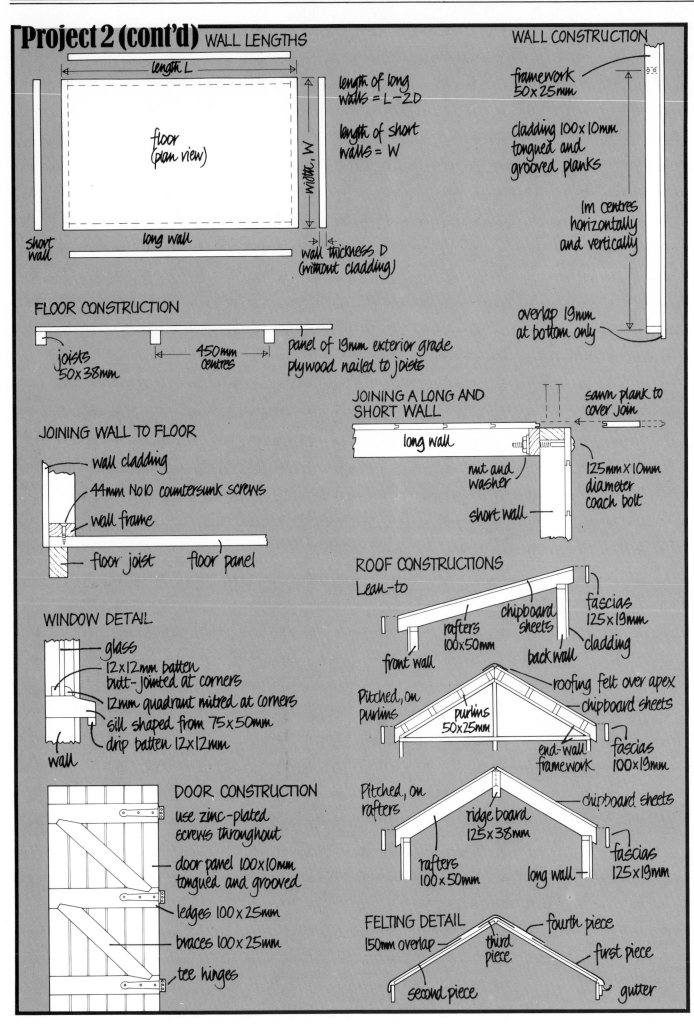

floor
(plan view)

length L

width, W

short wall

long wall

length of long
walls = L−2D

length of short
walls = W

wall thickness D
(without cladding)

WALL CONSTRUCTION

framework
50 x 25mm

cladding 100 x 10mm
tongued and
grooved planks

1m centres
horizontally
and vertically

overlap 19mm
at bottom only

FLOOR CONSTRUCTION

joists
50 x 38mm

450mm
centres

panel of 19mm exterior grade
plywood nailed to joists

JOINING WALL TO FLOOR

wall cladding
44mm No10 countersunk screws
wall frame
floor joist   floor panel

JOINING A LONG AND SHORT WALL

long wall

sawn plank to cover join

nut and washer

short wall

125mm x 10mm diameter coach bolt

WINDOW DETAIL

glass
12 x 12mm batten
butt-jointed at corners
12mm quadrant mitred at corners
sill shaped from 75 x 50mm
drip batten 12 x 12mm

wall

ROOF CONSTRUCTIONS

Lean-to

rafters
100 x 50mm

chipboard
sheets

fascias
125 x 19mm

front wall

back wall

cladding

Pitched, on
purlins

purlins
50 x 25mm

roofing felt over apex

chipboard sheets

end-wall
framework

fascias
100 x 19mm

Pitched, on
rafters

ridge board
125 x 38mm

chipboard sheets

rafters
100 x 50mm

long wall

fascias
125 x 19mm

DOOR CONSTRUCTION

use zinc-plated
screws throughout

door panel 100 x 10mm
tongued and grooved

ledges 100 x 25mm

braces 100 x 25mm

tee hinges

FELTING DETAIL

150mm overlap

fourth piece

third piece

first piece

second piece

gutter

The arris rails carrying the planking on boarded fences often shrink so much that they no longer engage in the slots in the fence posts. You can remedy this by screwing battens to the sides of the fence post to increase the post width and so hold the rails securely. If the ends of the rails have rotted, fit galvanised repair brackets to secure the rail.

Larch-lap and interwoven fence panels are nailed to wooden posts, or held in grooves between adjacent concrete posts. You should remove rusted nails and replace them with new galvanised nails, inspecting them every year to ensure that the panels are secure. With concrete posts, shrunken panels may keep popping out of their grooves; the simplest remedy here is to nail a preservative-treated batten down the edge(s) of the panel to increase its width slightly, and then slot the panel back into the grooves.

Gravel boards at the foot of fence panels are often the first part to rot. Remove rotten boards completely, and dig the soil away sufficiently to allow the new board to be fitted clear of the ground. Attach it to small blocks nailed to the inner faces of the fence posts.

If you are fitting new fence posts (which should already have been preservative-treated), give the ends that will be underground an extra dose of preservative by immersing them overnight in the fluid. When you have installed the posts, cap them to prevent water seeping in to the end grain.

Always use galvanised nails for fixing fence components and for general repairs. And ensure that all new wood used is liberally treated with preservative before being fixed.

Below Close-boarded fence boards may be 1 ship-lap, 2 feather edged or 3 square edged. Open-boarded fences are of many different types: 4 single- and 5 double-sized horizontal ranch, 6 double-sided vertical ranch and 7 post and rail.

Gates

Deal with loose or sagging gate posts in the same way as with fence posts. Posts fixed to walls may have defective fixings, and it is best to remove the post completely and re-fix it with rustproof screws driven into wall plugs. Before you replace the post, clean up the face that is fixed against the wall and give it a couple of coats of preservative (or prime, undercoat, and topcoat it, as may be appropriate).

If the hinges are sagging or rusty, fit new ones, making new fixing holes in the gate post or by plugging up the old ones first.

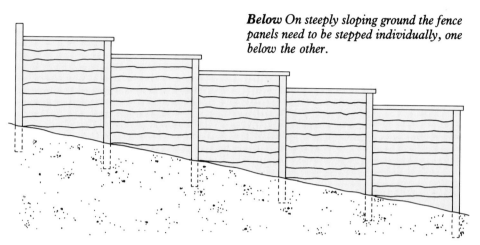

Below On steeply sloping ground the fence panels need to be stepped individually, one below the other.

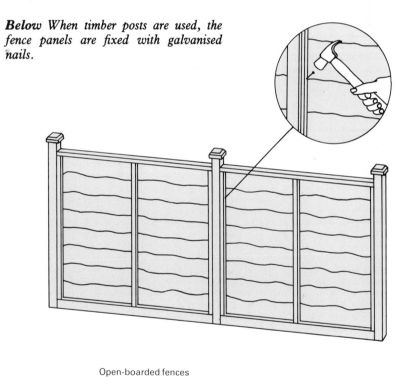

Below When timber posts are used, the fence panels are fixed with galvanised nails.

Close-boarded fences

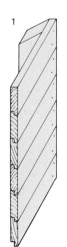
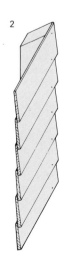
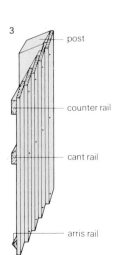

post

counter rail

cant rail

arris rail

Open-boarded fences

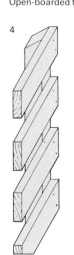
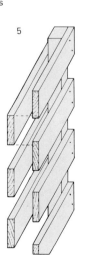
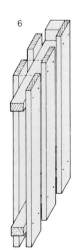

EXTERIOR DECORATING

Because exterior decoration plays such an important role in protecting your home, it is essential that you do it regularly. Putting the job off until the existing paint (or whatever) undergoes widespread failure not only gives damp and rot a foothold but lets you in for a great deal of work when you do eventually redecorate because of the amount of extra preparation involved.

How often is meant by 'regularly' depends on a number of factors, including the materials you use and even where you live. Some authorities say every three or four years; others, every five or six. In practice it is best to rely on your own eyes.

This does not mean you have to decorate the whole house in one go when the appointed year comes around. Instead, consider breaking the work up and doing it in stages.

However, unlike interior decorating, you cannot go out and paint the outside whenever you feel like it. You must take the weather into account. If wet paint is exposed to extreme cold, extreme heat, or to a lot of dampness in the air (let alone rain), you will end up with a sub-standard finish.

For these reasons, exterior decorating is traditionally always done around the end of summer. In England, September is ideal: it is usually neither too hot nor too cold, and it is the driest month. Do not begin painting too early in the morning: give the sun time to dry off any dew. Humid atmospheres should be avoided if you are painting bare metal surfaces: rust could be developing even while you are applying the paint.

Types of surface

Softwood Most of the timber capable of being decorated – windows, doors, weather-boarding, and the like – is softwood, and its most serious drawback is that it rots. So you must check for signs of rot before you decorate.

To prevent the wood rotting, you need to protect it against the weather with a good-quality exterior-grade gloss paint, an exterior-grade varnish, or a preservative stain. Paint is the usual choice, however, because most of the softwood commonly used in houses today is insufficiently attractive to be worth displaying. An exception to this rule is cedar, which you are most likely to find as a weatherboarding. Cedar is more than capable of looking after itself, suffering nothing worse than a loss of colour over the years. You can, if you wish, restore the colour by applying a water-based preservative stain, but many people find the silvery-grey colour of weathered cedar attractive.

Hardwood Normally found only in high-quality joinery, or as a sub-frame

Exterior decorating cycle

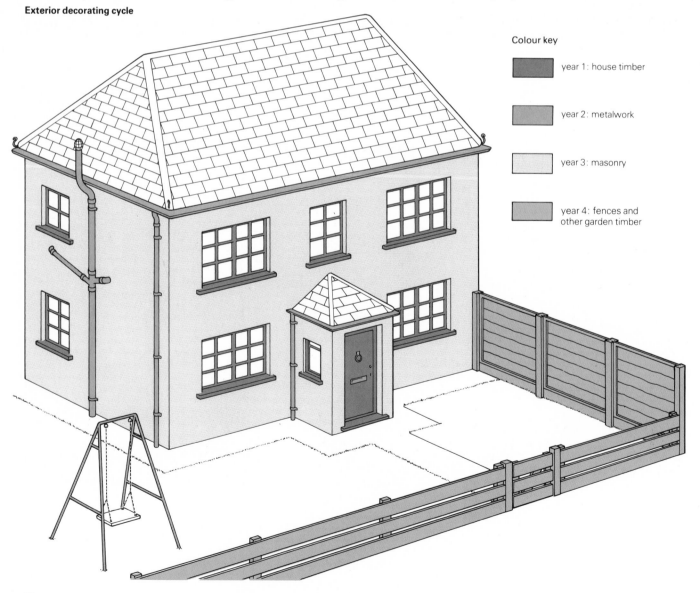

Colour key

year 1: house timber

year 2: metalwork

year 3: masonry

year 4: fences and other garden timber

to aluminium windows. It is stronger and more durable than softwood, but it still needs protection. Attractive in its own right, a varnish or a preservative stain is preferable to paint.

Metal Aluminium, zinc, and lead do not need painting. The galvanised steel used for windows and the cast-iron used for gutters and downpipes must be painted or they will be destroyed by rust. Gloss paint over a suitable primer and undercoat is the best choice.

Brickwork Another material that is attractive in its own right and well able to look after itself. Repointing is normally all that is needed to restore its appearance. If you want to weather-proof it, because the bricks are porous, or because they are exposed to the weather, use a clear silicon sealant or paint.

Stone Almost everything about surface treatments for brick applies also to stone, although cleaning stonework is a job best left to a professional.

Rendering Whether smooth or textured, rendering needs regular painting if it is to look its best. If it is particularly exposed to the weather, paint will also help to waterproof it.

Aggregate finishes Pebbledash and Tyrolean are perhaps the best known, but there are others using aggregates of various sizes and colours. Provided they are sound, there is no need to decorate. If they have begun to fail, you can patch and paint them – the paint is needed because otherwise the repair would not match the rest of the wall.

PAINTS, STAINS, VARNISHES AND SEALANTS

Paints for wood and metal A gloss finish is best for outdoors. It weathers better and is easier to keep clean than a matt or a semi-gloss finish.

Wood varnishes These are useful if you want to show off beautiful wood. Polyurethanes are not suitable for outdoor surfaces. Use oil-based varnishes.

Wood stains Exterior wood stains are basically mixtures of waxes, chemicals, and pigment suspended in a solvent so you can brush them on. There are two main types: those that lightly tint the wood, and those that colour it so densely it has the appearance of matt paint. As well as colouring, the wood stains keep out moisture and help to protect the timber from insects and fungi.

Paints for masonry There are four types of paint you can use on masonry. The cheapest is cement paint, so called because cement is its principal ingredient. It is available in white and a limited selection of pastel shades.

Exterior-grade emulsion paint is slightly more expensive and is a more durable version of the indoor type. There is a good range of colours.

Next comes stone paint, which is suitable for use on any kind of masonry. It is basically an exterior emulsion paint and has all of its advantages, although it is more expensive. The difference is that stone paint has mixed into it a quantity of mica, mineral, nylon fibre, or crushed stone to make it tougher and better able to cover tiny cracks.

Finally in this group is what is generally called 'masonry paint', a resin-based product giving a durable, semi-gloss finish. It is resistant to dirt, so it is a good choice if you live in an area that suffers from atmospheric pollution.

Masonry sealers A silicone-based sealer is the best material to use if you want to waterproof a wall without changing its appearance. Most of these sealers last for between five and 10 years, after which you simply apply another coat.

Choosing a primer

On timber an all-surface primer or an ordinary wood primer will be suitable in most situations. If the woodwork is subject to direct sunlight for most of the day, an aluminium wood primer will offer better protection and adhesion. Use this, too, on wood that has been badly scorched with a blowlamp, on very resinous timber, and on any hardwoods you wish to paint.

On iron and steel use a calcium plumbate primer. If you want to paint aluminium you should use either a zinc chromate or a zinc phosphate primer.

Masonry does not usually need priming before you paint it, but if the surface is noticeably dusty you can seal it with a stabilising primer. If you intend to use a resin-based masonry paint, however, you will need one of the all-surface primers.

Left A four-year redecorating cycle. **Right** *For most exterior woodwork the best finish is gloss paint: it is attractive, easy to maintain, and durable.*

Preparing wood

Preparing exterior woodwork and metal-work for painting is very important: if you skimp on it the elements will quickly expose any weakness in the paint and cause widespread failure.

If the existing paintwork appears to be sound – as it will be if you have redecorated regularly and efficiently – there is no need to strip if off, unless it has become so thick that it fills the drip channels on the undersides of window sills, or makes doors and windows difficult to open and close.

However, it is worth trying the 'sticky-tape' test just to make sure that the paintwork is as sound as it looks. Smooth a short piece of tape on to the paint, leave it for a few minutes, and then peel it off. If paint comes away with it, you will need to strip it back to bare wood and start again. Repeat the test in different places to get an overall picture of the paint's condition.

Assuming the paintwork is generally sound, scrape off any that has flaked or blistered, and fill the resulting depressions using either wood-stopping compound or an exterior-grade cellulose filler. Sand that down smooth and flush with the surrounding surface, then give the whole surface a thorough rub down using wet-and-dry abrasive paper used wet. Wash the surface clean, leave it to dry, and then lightly rub it over with a soft cloth before applying the new undercoat and gloss.

Coping with poor paintwork

If the paintwork is in very poor condition, strip it back to bare wood using a chemical or electric stripper near glass, and a blowlamp for the rest.

When you have finished stripping, fill any cracks that have appeared with an exterior-grade cellulose filler, and check for signs of rot as well as for other defects such as loose joints.

The next step is to sand the surface as smooth as possible, using medium-grade glasspaper or, for mouldings, wire wool. This will also get rid of any flecks of paint left behind after strip-

Repainting rusty steel window frames
1 Apply a chemical paint stripper thickly with an old paintbrush. 2 Leave the stripper to work for 10–15 minutes, then scrape off the softened paint. 3 Treat any rust with a rust remover, rubbing down the surface with wire wool. 4 After 10 minutes, paint on fresh rust remover, then wipe the surface completely dry with a clean cloth. 5 Apply a coat of metal primer immediately to prevent rust forming on the unprotected steel. 6 Finish off with a coat of undercoat, as here, followed by two of exterior-quality gloss paint.

ping. If you find that the wood grain is too open to give a smooth finish, apply a slurry of filler, then scrape this off using a steel ruler or something with a similarly straight, sharp edge, so that filler remains only in the timber's pores. Allow to harden before sanding it smooth with glasspaper.

Finally, paint any knots with a knotting compound, otherwise the heat of the sun may draw out any resin within the knots and lift off the paint above it. Then apply a thin coat of the appropriate primer. It is important to make sure this primer coat is *really* thin: you should be able to see the wood through it. If you find that a thicker coat would be needed to get a smooth finish, it means that you have not done the sanding properly.

Preparing metal

This is essentially the same as preparing woodwork, except that any stripping must always be done with a chemical stripper. If you use a blowlamp, the metal may become distorted, or even crack. You should also use wet-and-dry abrasive paper rather than glasspaper for any rubbing down.

One additional problem you will have to deal with is rust. If it is not too severe, scrape off any loose paint and rub down the metal underneath until it is bright. Wipe over with white spirit or methylated spirits to get rid of any grease; then, as soon as that is dry, brush on the appropriate primer. Any delay here can prove costly. In certain conditions, unprotected metal can acquire a surface layer of rust in a matter

coat of gloss to stray on to the glass in a band about 3mm (⅛in) wide. As long as the glass is clean enough for the paint to adhere – and a wipe over with white spirit should see to that – this will provide a complete seal and prevent rainwater running down the glass from getting under the paint film and causing it to lift.

When painting the leading edges of outward-opening doors and windows, as well as the top half of the runners on sash windows, avoid applying the paint too thickly or the door may 'stick' later on when you try to open it. (You can thin the paint slightly with white spirit to prevent too big a build-up on such surfaces. And check that the paint is absolutely dry before the door or window is closed.) Finally, make sure that you do not clog the drip channels on the undersides of window sills and steps with paint. They need to be clear to work.

We mentioned earlier that you should not begin painting until morning dew has evaporated. Starting late also allows you to use an old decorators' trick called 'following the sun'. Still-wet paint is harmed by direct sunlight; this method allows you to paint areas as soon as the sun's passage leaves them in shadow. The sun will not strike your new paint until the following day, so giving it plenty of time to dry out.

Finally, bear in mind that, however

clean you got the surface when you began to prepare it for painting, some airborne dirt is certain to have landed on it in the meantime. Always lightly dust each section of the work before you paint it. A professional decorator has a brush especially for the purpose, but you can use an ordinary paint brush provided it has clean, fairly soft bristles. It is a good idea to flirt the bristles of this brush through your fingers every now and then, to stop dust building up within them. If you do not do this, you will eventually be dusting dirt onto surfaces, instead of dusting it off.

Achieving the natural look

Preservative wood stains and varnishes are applied in much the same way as paint, but there are important differences at the preparation stage. Any defects or repairs to the wood that are visible when you have finished the preparation will still be visible when you have varnished or stained it. That is why this type of finish is suitable only for timber that is in more or less perfect condition.

If you need to strip off the existing finish, you cannot use a blowlamp. However carefully you work, you are

To protect woodwork without hiding its natural appearance, use an oil-based exterior varnish; this is more durable out of doors than polyurethane types.

of a few hours. Never paint over rust.

If you find that the rust is more extensive, use a wire brush (you can get one to fit on an electric drill) to remove any loose material, and finish with abrasive paper. It is important to remove all traces of the rust, as well as any metal weakened by it. Follow up by treating the affected area and surrounding metal with a rust-neutralising agent – available from any car-accessory shop – then, provided the instructions for using the neutralising agent permit it, apply a coat of primer. Any pockmarks and superficial damage to the metal can be taken care of by using a car-body filler before priming.

Painting wood and metal

An undercoat is an essential feature of the paint system on exterior surfaces. Many experts recommend two coats. This does *not* mean that the undercoat needs to be thick: on the contrary, use the least possible quantity of paint consistent with complete, even coverage. If you apply two coats, allow the first coat to dry thoroughly, then sand it down lightly and apply the second.

When painting the frames of windows and glass doors, allow the final

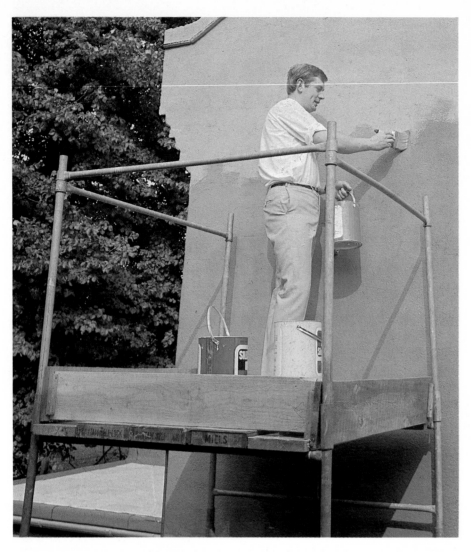

For the more arduous exterior-decorating jobs an easily assembled scaffold tower provides much safer, more convenient access than an extension ladder.

certain to scorch the wood here and there. A chemical paint stripper is the only alternative, but using it over large areas is expensive. In short, stripping paint from, say, a door in the hope of revealing the natural look is clearly an expensive gamble. To avoid wasting too much money, initially buy enough stripper to expose only a few sample areas of bare wood. From these, you should be able to get an idea of whether it is worth continuing or whether it would be better to have a painted finish after all. If it *is* worth doing, you may prefer to take your timberwork to one of the pine-furniture shops who are prepared to undertake stripping work in an acid bath.

You cannot use putty to seal glass into its frame in stained or varnished woodwork, because putty needs to be painted to last. You must cut out the old putty, and run a bead of flexible mastic around the join between glass and frame to form a waterproof seal. Into this, bed lengths of timber glazing

bead, cut accurately to size and mitred at the corners (like the joints in a picture frame). Fix these permanently in place with small panel pins.

PREPARING WALLS FOR PAINT
Brickwork

First, check the pointing. If it is crumbling, repoint (see page 32). Check also on the general condition of the bricks themselves. If any show signs of spalling (crumbling or flaking), chisel back to sound brickwork, and, as long as the damage is not too deep, make good with mortar, aiming to leave a brick-like profile. If most of the brick has eroded away, cut it out and replace it with a new one. If you find that there are so many bricks requiring this sort of attention that it is not a practical proposition, call in a professional and have the entire wall rendered.

Painting exterior walls

If you take a look at your home from the other side of the street, you will probably feel that, no matter how small it is inside, the outside walls look dauntingly large. Painting exterior walls is certainly one of the most tedious jobs for the do-it-yourselfer. But if you divide

walls into easily manageable sections, using the house's architectural features – corners, window bays, drain-pipes, and so on – to mark the boundaries, it helps to make the job seem smaller and less physically demanding. It has another, more tangible benefit, too. If you choose the section boundaries with care, they will help to disguise the 'dry-lines' that can appear between sections painted at different times.

Once you have decided on the various sections, aim to tackle each one in a logical order. If you are right-handed, start in the top right-hand corner (top left if you are left-handed) and work down and across until the section is finished. This reduces the amount of ladder and scaffold movement to a minimum.

Painting with a brush or roller

Exterior walls are generally a good deal less even and rougher in surface texture than interior ones. It is therefore important that you adopt a brush technique (or a roller technique: for this purpose they are the same) that ensures that you get even coverage, and do not leave unpainted patches through which moisture can find its way behind the surrounding paint film.

Load the brush fully and work the paint out, criss-crossing your strokes in all directions to produce a sort of ragged star. Once the brush begins to run dry, reload it and start another star next to it, allowing this to overlap the first sufficiently to cover all of the surface between the star centres. Do not expect to get a perfect finish at the first attempt. A second coat will almost certainly be needed, particularly if the wall is porous or has not been either primed or painted before. To overcome the porosity problem without wasting too much paint, it may be possible to dilute the first coat slightly – but check the manufacturer's instructions – or even to use cement paint as a sort of cheap undercoat. If the final coat is to be cement paint (but *not* if it is to be any other sort of paint) you can achieve the same result by simply soaking the wall with water before you paint it.

Finally, check that the wall has a damp-proof course and that this is doing its job (see page 29). If it does not, fit some form of DPC before you paint. Even though there may be no obvious signs of rising damp, it could still be there. The reason why you do not notice it is that the moisture evaporates as fast as it gets in. By painting the wall, you could reduce the rate of evaporation, or even stop it completely – and that will make the wall get steadily damper. At best, the dampness will lift off the paint; at worst it will leave the wall vulnerable to widespread damage by frost, which could lead to expensive repairs.

Painting blockwork and rendering
Smooth-faced, dense concrete blockwork and rendering over blockwork can be painted using a variety of proprietary paints. Ordinary oil-based paints are not suitable because they are incompatible with the alkalis contained in cement. The least expensive paint is exterior-quality emulsion paint, which, in sheltered locations, could have a life of up to five years before further treatment is necessary. More expensive but much longer lasting are chlorinated-rubber or acrylic- and resin-based paints, which are suitable for exposed sites and can have a life of about 15 years or more. Open-textured blockwork should be prepared for painting by bagging-in, as described for Tyrolean rendering.

Rendering
Whether it is rough or smooth, rendering on exterior walls is bound to have its share of cracks, and unless these are so narrow that the paint will cover them – certainly no more than 1 or 2mm – they must be filled. Cracks can be cleaned out with a cold chisel and brush, then filled with mortar before painting. For treating larger areas, see page 33.

Pebble-dash
Pebble-dash and other aggregate finishes are prepared for painting in the same way as rendering, except that you have to go over the surface with a stiff brush to remove any loose dirt and pebbles before applying the paint. Where the surface has become noticeably 'bald', there is a quick way to restore its appearance sufficiently for painting over. Chop out any remaining loose material with a bolster chisel and clean the hole with a brush. Apply a mixture of PVA adhesive, cement paint, sand, and water. Apply a second coat of the same mix, but this time load the brush more heavily and stipple it onto the surface to give the desired effect.

Painting with a spraygun
The finer details of technique depend on the type and model of spraygun you are using, and you should be careful to follow to the letter the instructions provided by the hire company. However, there are a few general points that are worth noting.

If the wall is to be covered evenly, using as little paint as possible, you must keep the gun moving at a constant rate, and as parallel to the surface as you can manage without over-reaching to the point where you risk falling off the ladder. It is best to work in a series of barely overlapping horizontal stripes, switching the gun off as you reach the end of each one and switching it on again only when it is in position and you are ready to start the next stripe. In this way, you work your way down to the bottom of the ladder, and finish off the foot of the wall from a pair of steps, or standing on the ground, before moving the ladder along and starting on the next stretch.

Even with the latest sprayguns, some paint is bound to stray, particularly if there is any wind about. A fine mist will drift away from the main jet. It is therefore advisable to mask carefully anything nearby that you do not want painted, using masking tape and either polythene sheeting or newspaper. This takes a little time but it does allow you to spray more quickly, and it guarantees good results even if you do get a little careless.

Repairing a large crack in rendering
1 Widen out the crack with a cold chisel and club hammer, undercutting the edges to provide a key for the repair. 2 Brush out any dust and loose debris, then soak the crack thoroughly by brushing in water. 3 Press mortar into the crack, using a filling knife or a small trowel. Take particular care not to trap pockets of air. 4 After smoothing off the repair flush with the surrounding area, work the wet mortar in order to match the texture on the surface of the rest of the wall. 5 To disguise the repair completely, the entire wall must be repainted after the mortar dries.

MAINTENANCE CHECKLIST

	SYMPTOM	FAULT AND REMEDY
CONCRETE	Cracks and potholes in paths or drives	Probably frost damage. Chip away loose pieces from hole, prime edges with PVA adhesive, and fill with concrete mix of 1 part cement, 2 parts damp sand, and 3 parts coarse aggregate. Fill cracks (after priming) with mortar mix of 1 part cement and 4 parts coarse sand.
	Cracked and broken edges of paths or drives	Subsidence or frost damage. Remove loose concrete, compact hardcore under damaged area, and fix timber shuttering along edge. Prime edges and fill with mortar mix of 1 part cement and 4 parts coarse sand.
BRICKS, BLOCKS & RENDERING	Faulty pointing on brick or concrete-block walls	Frost damage or erosion. Check for leaking guttering, or blocked drip groove if under windowsill. Rake out to depth of 12.5mm (½in) and repoint with mortar mix of 1 part cement, 1 part lime, and 6 parts sand.
	Efflorescence or mould growth on walls	Water dripping down or splashing up. Check for leaking gutter, downpipe, or overflow pipe. Treat with proprietary product and brush or scrape off.
	Damp patches inside rendered wall	Cracked rendering. Hack off loose rendering and undercut sound edges. Coat wall with PVA adhesive and render with stiff mortar mix of 1 part cement and 3 parts sand. Level off with straight-edge.
PAVING, PATIOS & STEPS	Wobbly paving slabs or treads of steps; puddles forming on patios	Settlement of foundations or broken bedding mortar. Lift loose slabs and chip off any mortar. Compact foundations, add hardcore as necessary, and cover with layer of sharp sand. Lay slabs as before, using long straight-edge to level them with surrounding slabs.
ROOFING REPAIRS	Damp patch on ceiling below roof	Leaking roof covering. Replace damaged or missing slates or tiles. Repair small leak in flat roof with bitumen; for larger leak, recover faulty section of roof.
	Water flowing over edge of gutter	Blocked or sagging gutter; or blocked downpipe. Fix any loose gutter brackets in new positions, using string line to achieve steady fall towards downpipe. Remove blockages from gutter. Clear blocked downpipe with wad of rag tied firmly to stiff wire. Prevent future downpipe blockage by fitting wire-netting dome over gutter outlet. Replace cracked or leaking guttering.
EXTERIOR TIMBER	Draughts around outside of window and door frames	Shrinkage of frames. Fill gap between frames and brickwork with non-hardening mastic. Fill inside gap with plaster or cellulose filler.
	Draughts around doors and windows	Shrinkage, warping, or missing putty. Seal around casement or door with draught excluder. Rake out cracked putty and replace.
	Sagging or binding gate	Loose joints or hinges, or loose post. Repair wooden gate by drilling through closed-up joint and dowelling. Remove loose hinge, plug screw holes and fix hinge with new screws. Set loose hinge pins in new mortar in brick pier. Replace rotten timber posts in concrete by boring out stump, enlarging hole to give extra 25mm (1 in) around new post, and filling in with mortar mix of 1 part cement and 4 parts coarse sand.
	Rotting timber	Check extent of rot with penknife blade: sound timber will hold point of blade when pushed in. Cut out small areas of rot, and shape and fit new piece of timber. Coat with preservative or paint. If rot is extensive, replace complete section or component.
EXTERIOR DECORATING	Flaking or blistered paintwork	Burn off or strip down paint to bare wood. Apply primer, undercoat, and at least two coats of gloss. Strip, scrape, and wire-brush down to shiny metal. Paint as for timber, but use metal primer.
PLUMBING	Water not draining from bath, basin, or sink	Blocked waste. Remove hair from bath or basin waste. Scoop water from sink and pour in boiling water and liquid detergent. Block overflow with damp cloth and operate sink plunger over plughole. Alternatively, unscrew waste trap and clean out.
	Dripping tap	Worn tap washer. Turn off mains stopcock (if kitchen cold tap) or gate valves on cold water storage tank. Replace washer. Operate stopcock and gate valves twice a year to prevent their seizing up.

	SYMPTOM	FAULT AND REMEDY
CENTRAL HEATING	Continual venting of radiators necessary; black liquid on venting	Corrosion. Drain and flush with proprietary product. Add corrosion inhibitor to feed and expansion tank.
	Radiators will not vent	Seized up ball-valve on feed and expansion tank. Push ball-float up and down to free valve.
ELECTRICITY	Spasmodic operation of appliance	Check plug and appliance for good flex connections, and tighten cord grips. Check flex for damage and renew if faulty.
	Plug fuse keeps blowing	As above or fuse of too low rating. Use 3 amp fuse for appliance up to 750 watts; 13 amp for over 750 watts.
	Circuit fuse keeps blowing	Damaged circuit cable (possibly due to rodents) or may be faulty appliance or plug wiring if on power circuit with unfused plugs. Replace faulty cables or check as above.
	Electrical fittings loose or askew on wall	Loose fixing screws. If askew, loosen screws two turns and straighten fitting—most types have adjustable lugs on box. Tighten, but do not overtighten, screws.
INTERNAL WALLS	Damp above skirting in ground-floor room	Probably bridged DPC. Check paths and soil adjoining house are 150mm (6in) below DPC.
	Bulging plaster on wall	Damp penetration. Check for faulty pointing or rendering (see BRICKS, BLOCKS & RENDERING).
	Cracks in plaster	Scrape out loose plaster and undercut edges of crack. Fill with plaster or cellulose filler flush with surface. Sand flat when surface has dried.
	Damaged corners	Nail temporary batten on one wall flush with surface of other wall and fill damaged area with plaster up to surface of batten. Allow plaster to harden, remove batten, and repeat on other wall surface.
CARPENTRY	Binding door	Plug screw-holes of loose hinges and fix. Plane down edge of door if it still binds.
	Squeaking floorboard	Loose nails. Lift board, drill and countersink nail holes, fix with 50mm (2in) × No. 10 woodscrews.
INSULATION	Condensation between panes of double-glazing unit	Moist air penetration. Check seals around edges of internal pane. Place sachet of silica gel crystals between panes to absorb moisture.
	Loose-fill roof insulation missing near eaves	Open cavity wall or draught under eaves. Cover cavity with boards laid flat between rafter ends and push insulation under eaves with brush. Do not completely block gaps under eaves as ventilation is important; boards laid on edge between rafters will reduce draughts.
INTERIOR DECORATING	Brown rings on painted timber	Unsealed knots. Strip to bare wood and apply shellac knotting to knots. Prime and repaint.
	Chipped paintwork	Rub down area of chip to bare wood with glasspaper and feather edges of surrounding paint. Prime, undercoat, and gloss paint.
	Lifting edges or bubbles under wallpaper	Apply adhesive with small brush to loose edge, allowing it to soak into paper, then press edge into place and roll it. Slit bubbles horizontally and vertically in form of a cross, and paste flaps.
	Damaged wallpaper	Cut piece of matching wallpaper larger than damaged area and tear edges to soften them. Peel back 3mm ($\frac{1}{8}$in) of backing paper all round area and tear off loose damaged paper. Paste new patch and apply to wall, matching pattern. Roll from centre outwards.
	Loose or damaged floor tiles	Lift loose tile and scrape or chip off adhesive from tile and floor. Apply adhesive to back of tile (or to tile and floor if contact adhesive) and re-lay. Chip or chisel up damaged tile and adhesive and replace with new one.
	Damaged sheet vinyl	Place patch large enough to overlap damaged area by 50mm (2in) all round and matching pattern. Use sharp knife to cut through both patch and sound edge of damaged area. Lift out damaged area. Patch will now exactly fit into its place; stick it down with adhesive.
	Frayed edge of carpet	Most commonly occurs in doorways. Cut off loose strands and fit binder bar to width of door. Alternatively, seal edge of carpet up to base of tufts with carpet adhesive. Stick carpet tape under edge, overlapping edge by 3-6mm ($\frac{1}{8}$-$\frac{1}{4}$in); then turn up overlap to base of tufts.
	Damaged wall tiles	Chip off old tiles (wearing protective goggles) and adhesive from wall, taking care not to damage plaster beneath. Apply adhesive to back of replacement tile using notched spreader, and push tile into position, inserting spacers between it and surrounding tiles. Allow 24 hours before grouting.

PART 2
INTERIOR

Interior maintenance and improvement projects connected with the services, structure, heating and insulation of a house are covered in this section under six major headings. Both routine and more complex tasks are dealt with: virtually everything from changing a washer on a tap and replacing an electrical fuse to laying thermal insulation in a loft and removing load-bearing walls. The enthusiastic handyman will even find details of how to extend electrical circuits and plumb in sink units.

Plumbing 78–89
Central Heating 90–5
Electricity 96–111
Internal Walls 112–21
Carpentry 122–37
Insulation 138–45

PLUMBING

Plumbing is no longer the mysterious art that it used to be. With the introduction of copper and plastic piping and easy-to-handle fittings, an inexperienced person can now do virtually any plumbing job around the home.

Plumbing can be divided into two parts: first, getting a supply of water to sinks, baths, basins, and WCs; and second, disposing of the used water.

The drawing shows a normal water supply system used in modern houses. Your local Water Authority pumps fresh water underground past your home. An offshoot pipe, complete with stopcock, usually situated on the pavement outside, diverts water to individual homes or to a collection of houses. This external stopcock is the Water Authority's responsibility and should not be touched.

The water enters your home via a rising main. This is often situated under the kitchen sink and is fitted with another stopcock. This one is your responsibility and controls all the water in your home. You should locate it, label it, and operate it at least twice a year to ensure that it remains usable.

From that rising main stopcock water is fed directly to a cold-water storage tank, often in the loft. On the way it feeds the kitchen sink to provide fresh water for cooking and drinking. It may also supply a basin upstairs, again to provide fresh drinking water, and any central-heating feed and expansion tank you may have.

The flow of water into the storage tank is controlled by a ball float and valve. All the other water outlets, including domestic water heaters, in the home are fed from the cold-water storage tank. Each tank outlet should ideally be fitted with a stopcock so that if any problems arise individual pipe sections can easily be isolated.

The only exceptions to this basic layout are in some old properties without a storage tank. In these rare cases, all outlets are fed directly from the rising main.

Waste systems

Modern homes are now built with what is called a single-stack waste system. In such a system, used water from the WC, bath, basin, and kitchen sink is fed via pipes with deep anti-siphon traps into one single soil pipe. This is sealed (though it has a vent at the top) and leads directly to the main drainage system. The single stack is generally built into the house, the only visible part being the vent.

Older homes have a two-pipe drainage system. Waste from the WC is fed directly via one pipe to the main underground drainage system, while other waste water goes via open hoppers and gullies to the drain. Hoppers are at first-floor level, gullies at ground level. The latter are basically traps permanently filled with water to prevent the escape of smells from the main drains.

Getting the water in

If you wish to make any addition or changes to your water supply system you will need to learn how to use the new copper piping, with its various bends, connectors, and other fittings.

Pipework

In older buildings that have not been modernised, lead piping may still be in use, and you should consider replacing it since it has a limited life.

Lead is not now used and is certainly not a material with which the do-it-yourself plumber can cope. The information provided here and on the following pages should enable you to remove and replace it yourself. Modern homes are now plumbed using copper

pipe for both hot and cold water supplies. Copper is an easily workable material.

The most common size of pipe is 15mm diameter – this is the external dimension – and is not quite the same as the old pre-metrication ½in diameter pipe. The latter was an internal measurement, but when used with compression fittings the two sizes are virtually interchangeable so that you can link old ½in copper pipes directly to new 15mm copper ones.

If you choose to use solder instead of compression fittings, you can obtain special ½in × 15mm adaptors, but ideally you should make the first connection with a compression fitting.

Copper piping of 15mm diameter is used to convey fresh water from the rising main stopcock up to your cold-water storage tank. This size also serves as the supply pipe for the WC, sink, and basin taps, often as an off-shoot from a larger 22mm diameter pipe used for circuits with several outlets. The hot and cold supply to the bath is always 22mm diameter pipe. Supplies to water heaters, however, are often made with 28mm pipe; so you could find that the outlets in your cold water storage tank are a mixture of 15, 22, and 28mm (approximately ⅗, ⅞, and 1⅛in).

Pipework must always be well supported, using correct-sized pipe clips at regular intervals, ideally no more than 1.2m (4ft) apart.

Fittings

The would-be plumber has the choice of two types of fitting for use with copper pipe; each has advantages and disadvantages.

Compression fittings are undoubtedly the easier for the beginner to use. They are made of brass with a copper 'olive' or 'cone' that is compressed firmly

against the copper pipe as a coupling nut is tightened. Two spanners are needed for fixing – one to hold the body of the fitting, the other for the nut. The joint can easily be tightened further or separated at any time. The disadvantage of compression joints is that they are bulky and comparatively expensive.

The alternative is a soldered joint, of

Plumbing pipes, fixtures, and fittings 1 Plastic waste pipe, available in 32mm (1¼in) and 38mm (1½in) sizes; 2 28, 22, and 15mm copper supply pipes; 3 22mm plastic cistern overflow pipe; 4 22mm plastic overflow pipe connector to cistern; 5 ½in and ¾in (12.5mm and 19mm) tap washers; 6 Bottle trap with universal compression-type outlet fitting (with washer and rubber 'O'-ring seal) available in 32mm (1¼in) or 38mm (1½in) sizes; 7 Bottle trap with push-fit outlet, also available in two sizes for bath, kitchen sink, or basin; 8 'U' trap with compression outlet; 9 Shallow 'U' traps for use where vertical space is limited, as under a bath; 10 Plastic pipe clips for water-supply pipes; 11 Copper pipe clips; 12 Yorkshire capillary tees, straight connectors, and elbows in 28, 22, and 15mm sizes; 13 Brass compression tees, straight connectors, and elbows in 28, 22, and 15mm sizes; 14 Reducing tee, 15 × 15 × 22mm (reducing tees are usually classified with the 'branch' diameter given last); 15 Reducing tee 22 × 22 × 15mm; 16 Bib-tap wall flange used to secure an outside tap to a wall (fitting has a compression joint for the water-supply pipe and a female threaded socket for the tap); 17 Straight swivelling tap connector (compression fitting at one end, female to iron at the other) used for linking copper supply pipe to tap; 18 Angled swivelling tap connector (this and 17 above need a fibre washer for

which the most suitable type is called a Yorkshire capillary fitting. This is made of copper and is supplied with a ring of solder already built into the fitting. Noticeably slimmer and neater than a compression type, the solder fitting is also cheaper; but it requires more careful preparation of the pipe, and also the use of a blowtorch.

use at the tap end); 19 Straight reducing connector for linking 15mm to 22mm copper pipe; 20 Cistern inlet valve with float and float arm (two nuts hold the unit to the cistern wall); 21 Flanged tank connector with nylon washers; 22 Straight connector, copper to female iron; 23 Straight connector, copper to male iron; 24 Drain cock with male to iron thread; 25 Common stopcock used to cut off water supply; 26 Gate valve, used as a stopcock and usually fitted to cistern outlets; 27 Waste pipe connectors, one end for solvent welding, the other for push fit; 28 Straight solvent-weld connectors; 29 Solvent-weld wastepipe sweep tees; 30 Solvent-weld elbows; 31 Waste pipe; 32 Waste-pipe clips for wall fixing.

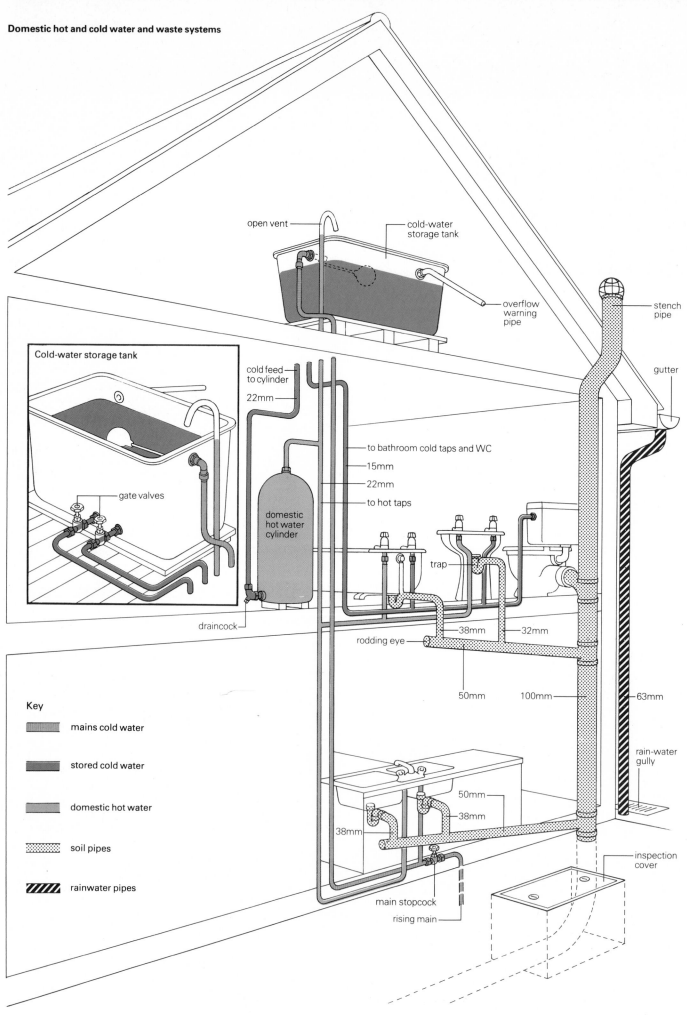

open vent

cold-water
storage tank

overflow
warning
pipe

stench
pipe

gutter

Cold-water storage tank

cold feed
to cylinder

22mm

to bathroom cold taps and WC

15mm

22mm

to hot taps

gate valves

domestic
hot water
cylinder

trap

draincock

rodding eye

38mm

32mm

50mm

100mm

63mm

rain-water
gully

Key

mains cold water

stored cold water

domestic hot water

soil pipes

rainwater pipes

50mm

38mm

38mm

inspection
cover

main stopcock

rising main

Tools & Techniques

Cutting copper pipe

Before proceeding with any cutting, measure the length of pipe required very accurately, and bear in mind that, with using either a compression or a solder fitting, the end of the pipe extends into the fitting by about 12.5mm (½in). If the pipe you intend to use has a damaged end, cut this off before marking out the required length.

Pipe can be cut in two ways. One is to use a junior or larger hacksaw with a fine blade. Clamp the pipe in a vice firmly enough to prevent it moving or turning, but take care not to compress the pipe. Your cutting line should be positioned about 25mm (1in) away from the vice, with the loose end of pipe supported. Cut gently, without forcing the hacksaw, and ensuring that the cut

is square. Clean off any burrs caused by the cutting with a fine file to leave a clean, smooth pipe end. Remove internal burrs with a round file.

The other method of cutting, which is considerably quicker if you have a lot of work to do, is to use the special plumber's tool known as a wheel pipe cutter. This tool is adjustable and it will cut pipes of different diameters.

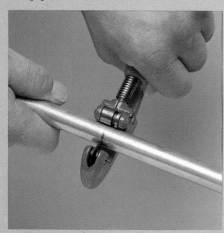

Below Plumber's tools 1 Hacksaw 2 Junior hacksaw; 3 Mole wrench (can be adjusted and locked onto nuts); 4 Adjustable spanner; 5 Stilson wrench (when fitted loosely over a nut, exerting pressure causes the jaws to grip the nut firmly); 6 Crowsfoot (or basin) wrench (essential for tightening or loosening tap-connector nuts in confined space); 7, 8 Pipe-bending springs (15 and 22mm sizes); 9 Pipe-bending machine with 15mm and 22mm formers (9a); 10 Adjustable-wheel cutter; 11 Round and half-round files.

Above and above right Two tools for cutting copper pipe: an adjustable-wheel cutter and a hacksaw. Left Pipe-joining equipment: blowtorch, jointing compound, solvent-welding cement, PTFE tape, steel wool, flux, and degreaser.

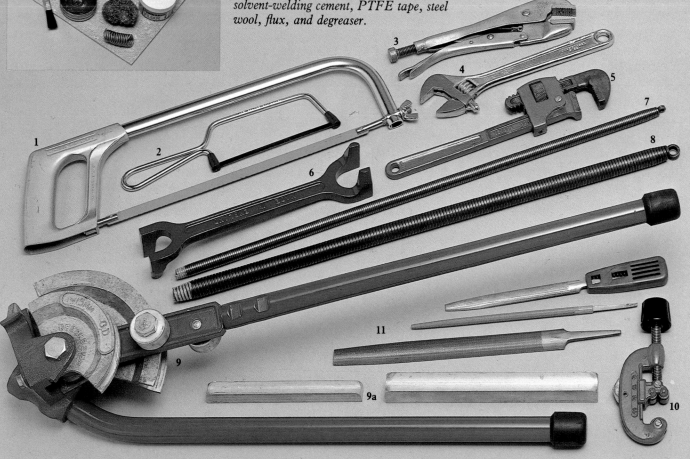

Making compression joints

Clean the end of the cut pipe using fine wire wool or fine emery cloth. Remove the relevant coupling nut from the compression fitting and slip this over the pipe end followed by the copper olive. Fit the pipe into the union, ensuring that it reaches the ridge or shoulder inside.

Keeping the pipe firmly pressed against the shoulder, slide the olive and coupling nut into position. Although it is not strictly necessary, a paste jointing compound can be smeared around the olive to improve the seal. Screw down the coupling nut as far as possible by hand, then use a spanner to make 1½ turns more. If the joint is still not tight and the pipe can be rotated by hand, use the spanner again until the pipe is locked firmly. Avoid over-tightening with the spanner, however, as this can lead to the olive breaking the copper pipe. Always use either a second spanner or a wrench to hold the body of the union while tightening the coupling.

Making a capillary solder joint

Cleanliness is essential when making soldered joints. The pipe ends must be spotlessly cleaned using wire wool or emery cloth; the inside of the fitting must also be cleaned.

After cleaning, slip the pipe end into the fitting, right up to the shoulder and mark on the pipe, in pencil, the depth

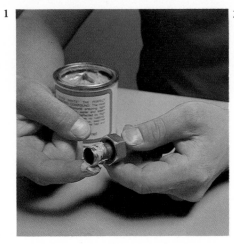

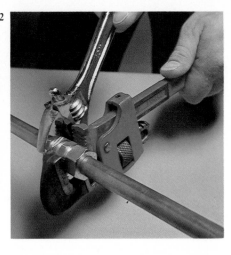

of insertion. This is to ensure that, when finally assembled, the pipe is fully inserted. Now remove the pipe and apply soldering flux to both the pipe end and the inside of the sleeve.

Unlike compression joints, which can be made one at a time, soldered joints made with a standard blowtorch on one fitting need to be made together. So if you are using a two-pipe connector or a T, all sections of pipe and the fitting should be prepared together. The reason for this is that metal is an excellent conductor of heat, and so the heat applied to one end of the fitting could travel along to the other end, causing its solder to melt.

Assemble the pipes and fitting. Apply heat from the blowtorch to the fitting,

Making a compression joint 1 Smear jointing compound around the olive before inserting the pipe into the coupling. 2 Hold the body of the fitting with the wrench, and tighten the nut with the spanner.

not to the pipes. Watch each joint carefully, and as soon as a ring of melted solder appears around the pipe, remove the heat and allow the joint to cool slowly.

If you are working close to a wall or to woodwork, use a sheet of soft asbestos behind the fitting to prevent the blowtorch doing damage.

Pipe bending

The easiest way to make a change of direction in pipework is to use an angled joint, but this means buying an extra fitting. Gentle curves and turns up to 90° can, however, be made by simply bending the pipe over your knee. Before doing so, you must insert into the pipe a bending spring to stop the pipe from being flattened. Slightly over-bend the pipe then return it to the correct angle; this will make it easier to remove the bending spring.

Linking to iron

Adding copper piping to existing threaded iron pipe requires the use of a special fitting, one end of which is normally a compression joint for the copper pipe, the other end being either a male or female threaded pipe section of imperial rather than metric size.

The female version most commonly used is threaded on the internal surface (to fit *over* the iron pipe), while the male

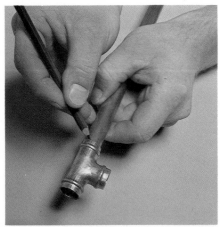

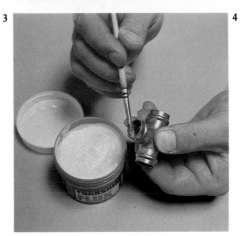

Making a capillary joint. 1 Use steel wool to clean the cut end of a length of copper pipe. 2 Push the pipe into the fitting right up to the shoulder and mark the depth of insertion on the pipe with a pencil. 3 Use a small paint-box brush to apply flux to the inside of the fitting. 4 Apply heat to the fitting. When a ring of solder appears at each joint, remove the heat.

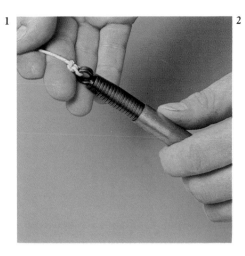

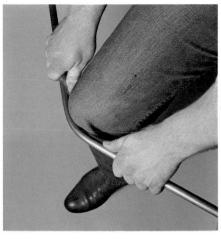

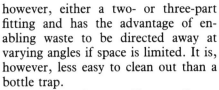

Bending copper pipe 1 If the bending spring has to be fully inserted, tie a piece of strong cord to the end or it may be difficult to remove afterwards. 2 With the spring inserted, bend the pipe around your knee.

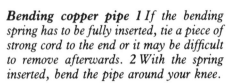

version is threaded externally. Fitting to iron is done with a special tape, PTFE, which is available from plumbers' merchants. You wind it *clockwise* around the thread. PTFE tape replaces traditional paste jointing compounds and acts as a watertight seal.

Getting waste water away

If you fit a new bath, basin or sink, apart from getting fresh water in, you will need to provide for the removal of waste water. Nowadays this is done almost entirely with push-fit plastic piping and fittings that require few tools, no adhesives, and little skill.

Piping is supplied in various colours, depending upon make, with white being the most common. Waste piping is classified by internal measurement, with 38mm (1½in) diameter pipe required for kitchen sinks and baths, and 32mm (1¼in) for basins.

Take care if you are planning to link new piping to old. External diameters differ between some makes and piping will not necessarily connect correctly with fittings. However, universal couplings are available that will accommodate varying diameters of pipe. These couplings are similar to compression fittings, having a threaded ring pressing a rubber 'O' ring against the pipe.

Every bath, basin, or sink requires a combined overflow and waste fitting

Solvent-welding plastic waste pipes 1 Cut the waste pipe to length using a hacksaw. Remove all burrs from the end of the pipe with a file. 2 Use glasspaper to roughen and clean the end on the outside. 3 Apply the solvent-weld cement to the pipe end and inside the fitting. 4 Push the pipe fully into the fitting with a slight twisting action, then leave to set.

that terminates in a threaded outlet projecting beneath the unit. A water trap is connected directly to this outlet pipe to prevent smells coming up from the drain. Two types of trap are in common use. The neater is a bottle trap. This is most suitable for kitchen use, since the entire base can be easily unscrewed by hand when it needs cleaning or unblocking. It is fitted to the sink outlet pipe with a threaded knurled ring, and a loose washer between outlet and trap provides a watertight seal. The outlet from the trap is generally a compression fitting, which needs no more than hand-tightening.

The other type of trap is the U-trap, which is connected up in much the same way as the bottle trap. It is,

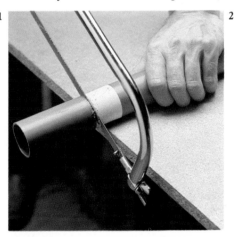

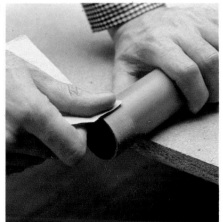

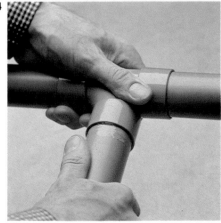

however, either a two- or three-part fitting and has the advantage of enabling waste to be directed away at varying angles if space is limited. It is, however, less easy to clean out than a bottle trap.

A bath or shower will normally require a much shallower trap since the bath outlet is close to floor level. Special bath traps are readily available.

Solvent-welded PVC pipes

Solvent-welded PVC waste pipes and fittings are still available and in regular use. These require the use of a special adhesive applied to both pipe and sleeve, and water must not be allowed to flow through the pipes for 24 hours after they have been fitted.

Cutting plastic piping

As with copper piping, measuring must be done with care. Plastic piping expands lengthwise when heated, so allowance must be made for expansion when making the joints.

Measure the depth of the internal shoulders of the push-fit fittings at one or both ends of the pipe run. Cut the pipe so that it fits with 10mm (⅜in) clearance at each end. Do *not*, however, make this allowance if compression couplings are used.

Cut squarely, using a hacksaw or other fine-toothed saw. Take care to remove all the burrs inside and outside

Project 1

Fitting a double bowl sink unit

The straightforward replacement of a kitchen sink with one of identical size should create no problems. The water supply and waste-trap connections (picture 1 at night) simply need undoing and refitting to the new sink (with the water turned off!).

However, many do-it-yourselfers will, if space allows, aim to fit a double sink with mixer taps and this will involve some additional plumbing work.

The first job is to shut off both the hot- and cold-water supplies. The cold will be cut off by closing the rising main stopcock, which is most likely to be under the sink. In a well-planned installation, the hot-water pipe will also have a stopcock under the sink; if it does not, trace the pipe back to the hot-water storage cylinder stop valve and close this.

When water has ceased to run from both taps, disconnect the pipes under the sink. If there is no easily accessible joint, use a crowsfoot wrench to reach behind the sink and undo the tap connectors (2).

Disconnect the waste also, by unscrewing the locknut directly under the sink outlet. Have a bowl handy to collect water from the trap, since this also will need to be removed. Now

release and remove the old sink complete with its taps.

Before placing the new sink in position, fit its taps, waste and overflow.

Most modern taps are supplied complete with nylon or rubber gaskets for use between the taps and sink, and no additional bedding compound is required. Lay the gasket in position over the ready-cut holes in the sink top and place the mixer-tap squarely in position.

With the sink resting on its front edge fit the washers and back nuts supplied, to the threaded tap tails (3). The nuts do not need much tightening; finger tightness followed by less than one turn should be sufficient to prevent the taps moving and any leakage of water.

Now for the water-supply connections. You will almost certainly have to alter the existing pipework to suit the new tap position, either cutting it back a little or extending it with new piping and elbows (4 and 5). You will need new tap connectors complete with their fibre washers.

Depending upon the position of your water supply pipe, you may be able to fit the tap connectors, together with short lengths of pipe, to the tap tails using PTFE tape, before placing the sink in position. The short lengths of pipe can then be

connected to the water supply using more pipe and joints. Corrugated pipe sections can prove most useful here. Available with tap connectors at one end, they can be bent by hand to link with existing pipework.

This, incidentally, is a good time to fit a stopcock in the hot-water supply pipe (6, bottom left) if it does not have one already. Ensure that the direction of flow indicated by an arrow on the side of the stopcock is right. Also fit a tee and extra stopcock into the cold water pipework to provide a water supply for a washing machine or dishwasher.

Next connect the overflow and waste fittings. Fit the waste outlet first, ensuring that the grid is seated squarely on its washer in the sink outlet hole. Some waste fittings require a bedding mastic (7); others do not. Place the threaded outlet on its washer under the sink and link the two halves with the centre bolt provided. Guide the flexible overflow pipe up to the overflow hole and fix in place.

Finally, fit either a bottle or U-trap to the sink waste outlet (8) and connect it to the existing waste pipe if this is plastic; alternatively, remove all the old waste pipework and fit new. The drawing (opposite page) shows how waste from each bowl enters a common waste pipe.

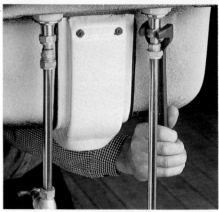

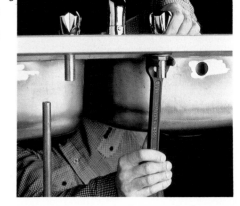

the cut end with a file. Chamfer the ends carefully at an angle to enable them to slip past the 'O' rings in each fitting without dislodging them.

Making a joint

Check that the rubber 'O' ring is correctly seated in the fitting. Apply a little silicone lubricant, petroleum jelly, or even washing-up liquid to the chamfered pipe end and push it into the fitting, right up the shoulder. Make a pencil mark on the pipe up against the fitting, then ease out the pipe by about 10mm (⅜in) using the pencil mark as a gauge. This is to allow for the expansion of the pipe.

As with water-supply fittings, numerous bends, tees, and connectors are available from your local builders' merchant. Careful planning of the waste

run is important to ensure a constant downhill flow. Remember, too, that plastic pipe cannot itself be bent safely, so that it is vital to avoid odd changes of direction. The piping must be well supported by brackets of suitable size at least every 900mm (3ft).

Tap maintenance

From time to time you will have to replace tap washers that have become worn. With the exception of the taps known as Supataps, which are fitted with an automatic, built-in cut-off mechanism (see drawing on page 88), you will always have to cut off the water supply to the tap before doing this job.

If your cold water storage tank is correctly fitted with stopcocks for each of its outlet pipe, and your hot water cylinder is also fitted with a stopcock,

cutting off your water supply should create no problems.

If there are no suitable stopcocks, then you will have to completely drain the cold water storage tank, at the same time preventing fresh water from refilling it. To do this, you will either have to turn off the rising-main stopcock or tie up the ball-float arm in the cistern, by placing a piece of wood across the cistern and tying the arm to this. Drain the tank completely by turning on all taps served by it. Remember to switch off the power to any electric water heaters that are fed from the tank.

Once water has ceased to flow you can tackle the offending tap. First, place the plug in position in the outlet pipe. This will prevent any small items falling down the drain if you drop them. Leave the tap open.

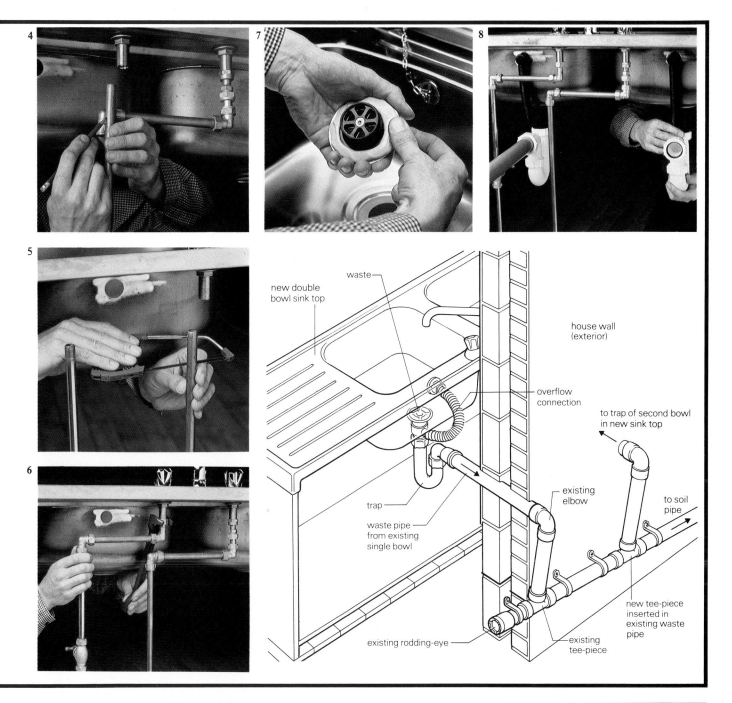

4

5

6

7

8

new double bowl sink top

waste

house wall (exterior)

overflow connection

to trap of second bowl in new sink top

existing elbow

to soil pipe

trap

waste pipe from existing single bowl

new tee-piece inserted in existing waste pipe

existing rodding-eye

existing tee-piece

Remove the tap top. With modern taps this often means carefully levering out the 'Hot' or 'Cold' disc on the top to reveal a screw underneath. Undo this screw and lift the top away from the spindle. Older taps are fitted with a cross-grip handle that is held in place by a grub screw that engages on the spindle. Below this is a shield, normally chromium-plated. This must be unscrewed and lifted off the spindle before you can gain access to the body of the tap. If you cannot unscrew it by hand, try pouring boiling water over it to break the seal that has been caused by the build up of dirt inside. If this is unsuccessful, wrap cloths round the shield to protect the chromium, then use a wrench to unscrew it.

The body of the tap will now be visible. The top nut is called the gland nut. Below this is a larger hexagonal nut, and this is the one that needs to be undone to remove the valve head. As you are unscrewing it, hold the tap spout to act as a counter lever.

Remove the complete valve unit. You will find the washer attached to a jumper at the base of the valve head. The old washer is held in place either by being slipped over a stud or by being retained by a brass nut (and brass washer). In the latter case, remove the small nut and discard the old worn washer, replacing it with a new one of precisely the same size, with its smooth side against the jumper.

Reassemble the valve, cleaning up all parts as you proceed, with the tap still open; then turn the water on again.

Stopcock washers are replaced in precisely the same way.

New taps for old
Old unsightly taps can be given a new lease of life with simple tap converters. As long as the old taps are made to British Standard 1010, and most taps are, all you need to do is cut off the water supply, remove the old tap head and body from the spout and screw in a new body with a modern handle. It is easier than changing a washer. New bodies are available for both bath and basin taps.

When replacing a stubborn tap shield you found difficult to remove, apply a little petroleum jelly to the thread so that it does not stick again.

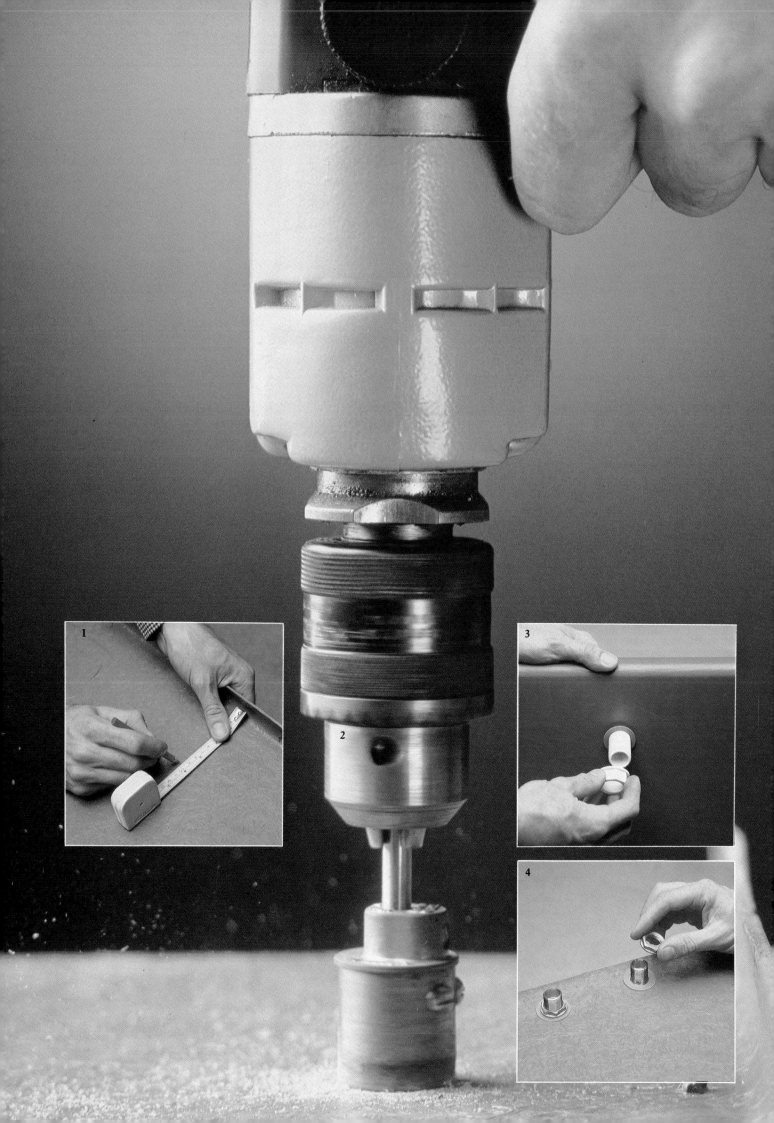

Installing a new cistern

Metal cold-water storage cisterns should be checked regularly to see that rust has not started to develop on the base or sides. If it has, consider replacing it completely with a new polythene or other non-metal type. Aim to do this on a day when water will not be required for a few hours. Turn off the rising-main stopcock and open all taps served by the tank to drain it.

Disconnect the inlet valve assembly and put it aside for re-use if it is still in good condition. Mop up any water still lying in the base of the old tank, then disconnect all outlets and remove the tank to make way for the new one.

If the old tank was merely resting on the joists, make a complete wooden platform for the new polythene tank. Put the new tank on its base and mark the positions for inlet and outlet holes, including the overflow-pipe outlet, which should be at a lower level than the inlet-valve hole and of larger diameter. Cut the holes to suit the size of the new flanged tank connectors you will be fitting. Use a hand or power drill with a special hole cutter or flat bit. Use a file to remove any burrs from the cut edges, then upturn the tank to get rid of bits and pieces of waste material. Make all tank connections using the nylon washers provided. These go *inside* the tank. Reconnect, fitting stopcocks to each outlet.

5

6

Cistern sizes

If you are thinking of replacing a cistern, you should contact your local Water Authority (its address is on your water-rate demand), since it will have drawn up specific size requirements for cold-water storage cisterns.

Knocking pipes

That irritating knocking in the pipes can be caused by several things. One is the lack of adequate support for the pipe runs: as water flows through the pipe, the latter vibrates and knocks against another pipe, the wall, or floorboards. Pipe clips should be fitted every 1.2m (4ft) or so.

Another cause is too high a mains-water pressure, causing valves and tap jumpers to vibrate in their sockets. Try reducing the water pressure by partly closing the rising main stopcock.

If the knocking occurs only when you turn off a particular tap, there is little you can do except turn it off more slowly so that the jumper in the tap does not rattle in its seating, thus causing the pipe to vibrate.

Air locks can also cause knocking or hammering in the pipes as water tries to flow past an air bubble. Generally this indicates a high point or oversharp bend in the pipework that has air trapped in it. This can lead in time to a complete stoppage.

Applying back pressure can often relieve the situation. If the offending tap is close enough to your kitchen cold tap fed directly by the rising main, fit a hosepipe to the kitchen tap. Attach the other end to the airlocked tap and open this one. Now turn on the kitchen tap. The rising water pressure is likely to be considerably greater and will force the air back out of the pipe.

Do not run the mains cold water for more than a short while since you will be feeding water into a hot or cold storage tank from the 'wrong' end and might cause an overflow.

Installing piping and float valve in a cold-water tank **1** *Mark the positions of all holes that need to be cut in the tank.* **2** *Cut the inlet and outlet holes in a non-metal tank with an electric drill and holesaw bit. Use a file to remove all burrs caused by the cutting.* **3** *Fitting the plastic overflow connector. The nylon washer goes on the* inside *of the tank.* **4** *Brass-flanged tank connectors are used for outlets. Position these about 50mm (2in) above the base of the tank.* **5** *Fit stopcocks (as here) or gate valves to all tank outlets.* **6** *Fit the inlet valve with its ball float.*

Installing a shower

One way of modernising a bathroom, and at the same time cutting down water-heating costs, is to install a shower. This can be done either by fitting a completely self-contained shower cubicle (if space permits), or by linking hose-type connectors to existing bath taps leading to a rose, or by changing your present taps to combined bath and shower mixer taps. With the last-named, water is directed either into the bath or up to a fixed or movable shower rose at the flick of a lever.

Removing the old taps is probably the hardest part of the job since they may have been in place for many years and access to the water connections may not be easy. You will need a 22mm size crowsfoot wrench to reach the tap connectors under the bath.

Turn off both the hot- and cold-water supplies. Using the wrench undo the tap connectors. Keep some rags handy to mop up water still in the pipe. When the tap connectors are separated from the tap tails, place more rags over their ends to prevent dirt getting into the pipe. Ensure that the rubber or fibre washers for the tap tails do not get lost.

Next, remove the hexagonal nuts and washers holding the taps in place. Do not allow the tap bodies to turn in their sockets as this could damage the holes cut in the bath. Hold the taps firmly, then lift them out when the nuts are removed. Clean away any bedding mastic left around the tap holes.

Fit the new shower-mixer taps using the nylon or plastic gasket supplied; bedding mastic is not usually required with modern taps. Holding the tap unit in place, fit the washers and backnuts to the tap tails. Tighten the nuts just sufficiently to prevent the taps moving. Bind PTFE tape clockwise around the tap tails and screw the tap connectors back into place, ensuring that the washers are seated correctly. (These washers may, incidentally, need replacing.)

Open the taps, turn on the water supply again, and check for leaks both when the water is flowing and when you have turned off the taps. If necessary, tighten any connections.

You will now need to make a wall fixing for the shower-rose holder. This generally means drilling and plugging the wall behind the bath to attach the holder. Make sure that you use rust-proof screws for the fixing.

Having fitted a shower, you must check that the gap between the wall and bath is completely sealed so that no water can run down the wall behind the bath, where it could cause wood rot or other structural damage. Seal the gap

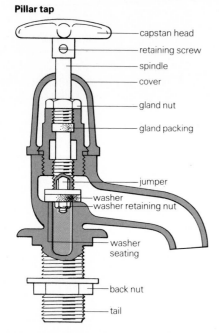

Pillar tap

- capstan head
- retaining screw
- spindle
- cover
- gland nut
- gland packing
- jumper
- washer
- washer retaining nut
- washer seating
- back nut
- tail

The pillar is the commonest type of tap. Most standard taps have internal workings similar to this one.

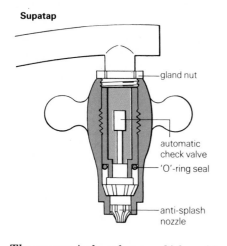

Supatap

- gland nut
- automatic check valve
- 'O'-ring seal
- anti-splash nozzle

The supatap is the only type which enables a washer to be changed without cutting off the water supply.

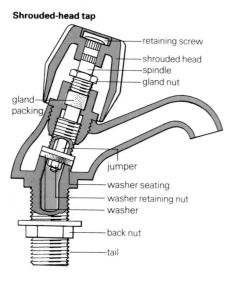

Shrouded-head tap

- retaining screw
- shrouded head
- spindle
- gland nut
- gland packing
- jumper
- washer seating
- washer retaining nut
- washer
- back nut
- tail

Basically the same as a standard pillar tap, this design has a more modern head covering the spindle.

with a silicone rubber bath sealant, following the manufacturers' instructions.

You will also have to fit either a rigid shower screen or a curtain at the side of the bath to prevent water from the shower splashing outside the bath itself. Rigid screens or curtains made of waterproof material are readily available complete with fitting instructions.

Gland nuts

If leakage occurs from around the tap shield and spindle rather than from the spout, the gland nut rather than the washer is the source of trouble. It may only require tightening slightly to prevent further leakage, but in time the hemp and petroleum-jelly packing or the rubber 'O'-ring washer inside may need to be replaced.

Supataps

You do not need to cut off the water supply to change a Supatap washer (see drawing at left) because an automatic cut-off is built into the tap. To change a washer, simply loosen the nut at the top of the nozzle. Hold the nut, then turn on the tap. At some point the automatic check valve will drop and stop the water flow. Keep turning until the nozzle comes free.

Push a pencil into the nozzle outlet to eject the combined jumper and antisplash device. Remove and replace the jumper, thoroughly clean the antisplash fins, and finally reassemble the tap in reverse order.

Waste blockages

Every once in a while waste water systems become blocked. The symptoms can be a general reduction in the flow of water away from a bath or basin or an almost instantaneous stoppage.

In nine cases out of ten the blockage occurs in the trap under the sink, bath or basin and affects only that outlet. If all outlets appear blocked and outside drains overflow, the cause is underground in the main drainage system.

Kitchen sinks

Blockages here are generally caused by the build up of food scraps and/or grease in the trap. The easiest way to unblock the pipe if food is the cause is to use a sink plunger – simply a rubber or plastic cup on the end of a handle.

With the overflow pipe opening firmly plugged with a damp cloth and water still in the sink push the plunger vigorously up and down on the waste outlet several times. The chances are that the pressure created by the plunger will force the blockage to break up and flow away normally.

If this is unsuccessful try poking a piece of flexible curtain wire down the outlet hole. With manipulation this will often break through a build-up of food scraps or grease, even twisting itself round the bend of the trap. Once a small hole has been cleared and is kept clear, hot water with washing-up liquid added will usually wash away the remainder of the blockage.

Failing everything else, you must tackle the trouble from under the sink. Put in the plug. With a bucket or bowl beneath the trap to collect water and debris, then undo the trap. A bottle trap simply unscrews to allow access to the waste pipe, and any solids can easily be scraped out. Lead waste piping generally has a small brass plug fitted at the bottom of the 'U'. With this unscrewed (do this carefully or you may distort the pipe), curtain wire can be inserted up both sides of the bend to release and pull out whatever is causing the blockage.

After clearing the blockage, run hot water through the waste pipe, adding washing-up liquid to dissolve grease.

Basins and baths

Blockages in bath and basin waste pipes are more often than not caused by hair becoming trapped in the waste pipe. After each successive hair washing more hair is added until the pipe is almost fully blocked.

Use curtain wire with an open hook attached to the end. Twist this hook round in the pipe to grip the hair blockage, and pull it to the outlet grid, where it can be removed.

Main drainage blockages

These will be indicated by gullies overflowing, or bath or WC waste running slowly away. You will need to open manhole covers to locate the site of the blockage. Start with the one farthest from the house. If this is clear the blockage must be closer to home, so open the next cover in line, and so on. Once you have discovered the blocked inspection chamber you will need drain rods to unblock it. These are basically flexible rods that are screwed together, and they can be hired. Various fittings can be attached to the end, such as a corkscrew head, scraper, brush, or rubber plunger. Feed the rods into the inspection chamber, aiming for the gulley and outlet at the bottom. Add more rods if needed. Remember to keep the rods turning in a clockwise direction at all times. If you turn them anticlockwise the rods may unscrew and become lost in the drain.

Once the rodding has cleared the blockage, use a hosepipe with a nozzle to spray and clean the inside of the inspection chamber. Always make a point of preventing the build up of leaves and dirt in gullies. They stop the free flow of waste water and can cause unnecessary blockages.

Dealing with bursts and frozen pipes

If you have insulated your home properly (see page 138) you should never suffer from frozen pipes, or, even worse, burst pipes. However, too many people choose to avoid the relatively small expenditure involved and as a result, bursts and freeze-ups occur. The cost of making-good the damage is often more than the cost of insulation.

If you do find you have a frozen pipe, resist the temptation to de-freeze it with a blowtorch: this would probably soften the pipe to the point at which it would fracture under the pressure of the unfrozen water. Open the tap or taps served by the frozen pipe. Using a hair dryer or other gentle form of heat, warm the pipe from the tap backwards along the run until the frozen section is reached and the water flows again. Leave the tap running for a while to ensure that all the ice is melted.

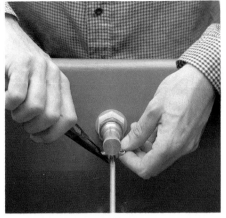

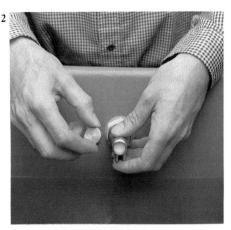

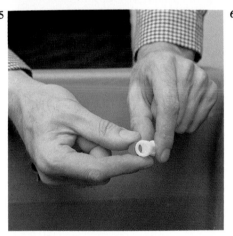

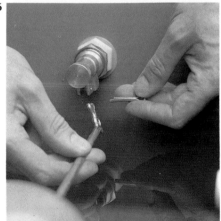

Burst-repair kits

A handy product to have available is a pipe- and hose-repair kit. This is just two types of tape in one pack for binding leaking or burst hot and cold pipes in the home, garden, or car. One tape covers the burst, even if it is still wet, the other is then stretched out and wound on top. It then shrinks to make a watertight repair. Two-part kits consisting of a rubber-lined clamp secured by a wing nut are also available.

Bursts

If a pipe does burst, relieve the water pressure in the pipe by turning on all taps served by it. Then stop more water entering the pipe by turning off the stopcock that controls the circuit. Mop up as much water as possible and put rags around the burst until the water flow has ceased.

If the pipe is of lead, call in a plumber: repairing lead piping is strictly a job for the professional. On the other hand, this may be the right time to consider replacing all lead piping.

Copper piping is less likely to burst, but if it does, take the steps described above, then cut out the damaged section and replace it with new copper, which you join up with compression or soldered connectors.

Changing a cistern washer

Taps and stopcocks are not the only plumbing fittings with washers liable to become worn. Storage tanks and WC cisterns also have washers and these too need to be replaced occasionally, as shown above, to prevent overflowing.

The water level of a cistern is normally controlled by a metal or plastic ball-float on a metal arm. As the water level rises the arm is lifted by the float and operates a piston, which incorporates a flat washer to shut off the flow.

Replacing the washer necessitates cutting off the water supply, as previously described. Remove with pliers the split pin holding the float arm in place (see picture 1), and allow the arm to drop down. If one is fitted, unscrew the end cap of the valve assembly (2). Using

a screw-driver in the hole vacated by the float arm, ease out the piston (3). Then, with the screwdriver in the piston's lever-arm slot, unscrew the cap holding the washer in place and remove washer (4). You can use pliers, but take care not to damage the fitting.

Insert the new washer into the slot at the end of the piston (5), and re-assemble the fitting, smoothing any roughness caused by the pliers with wire wool or fine emery cloth. Wipe petroleum jelly over the piston and refit it, with the lever-arm slot facing downwards. Before reconnecting the float assembly (6), check that it is in good condition and has not collected water inside the ball. If it has, unscrew its two halves and empty them. If a leak has developed, the ball must be replaced.

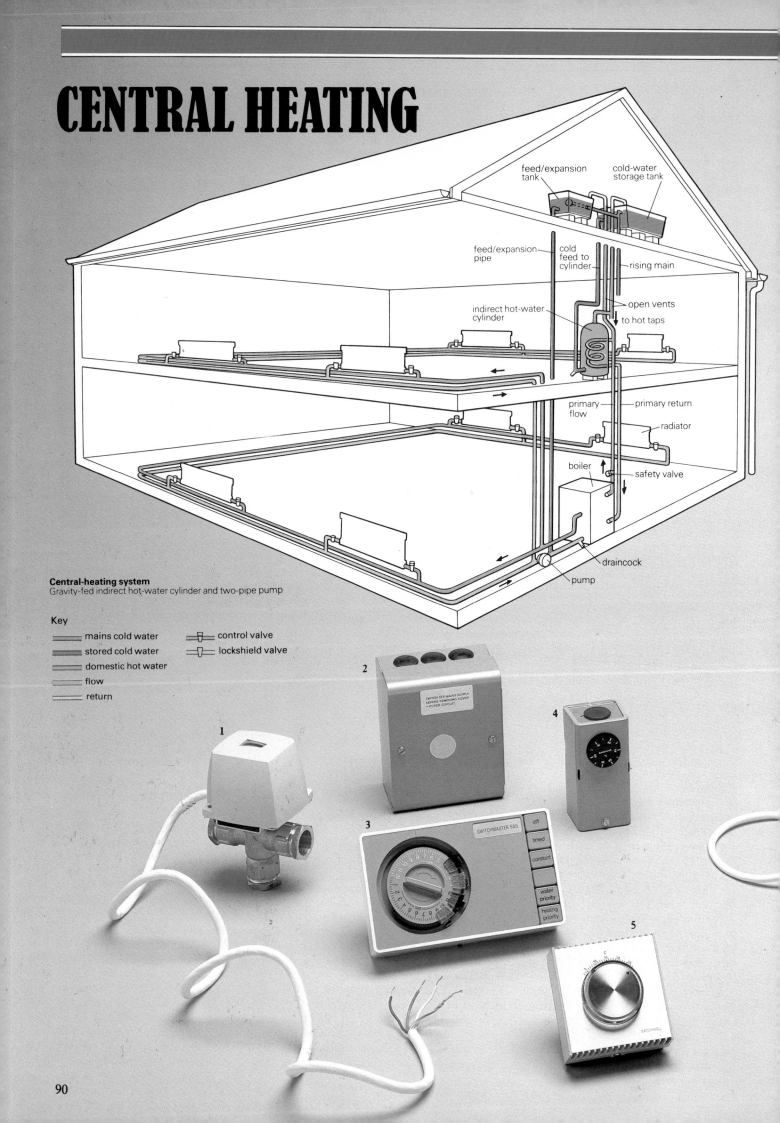

CENTRAL HEATING

feed/expansion tank

cold-water storage tank

feed/expansion pipe

cold feed to cylinder

rising main

indirect hot-water cylinder

open vents

to hot taps

primary flow

primary return

radiator

boiler

safety valve

draincock

pump

Central-heating system
Gravity-fed indirect hot-water cylinder and two-pipe pump

Key

mains cold water

stored cold water

domestic hot water

flow

return

control valve

lockshield valve

1

2

SWITCH OFF MAINS SUPPLY
BEFORE REMOVING COVER
— FUSED CIRCUIT.

3

SWITCHMASTER 500

off

timed

constant

water priority

heating priority

4

5

Of all the many methods of domestic heating, the most popular is central heating, providing overall rather than partial warmth.

A boiler is located in the house, running on gas, oil or solid fuel, heating water that is pumped to radiators fitted in each room.

That boiler may also either directly or indirectly heat water for household use.

The diagram on this page shows a typical central heating layout and is intended as a guide only, since there can be many variations, depending on the size of house and requirements.

The boiler is normally located at ground-floor level often either inconspicuously built into a line of kitchen units or, in the case of small-capacity boilers, attached to the wall.

For the boiler to operate efficiently and safely it must be provided with sufficient air for combustion and an adequate flue system to remove exhaust gases from the house.

Most modern gas- and oil-fired boilers are fitted with 'balanced flues', which lead directly to the outside of the house and require no chimneys. Air is drawn in through the lower section of

Safety First!

Do not be tempted to play around with parts of your central-heating system if you don't understand them. The rule is – if in doubt, leave it alone! Boiler servicing, for instance, should be left to professionals. Don't work on any electrical component without turning off the electricity supply first. Keep an eye on the various safety valves in the system for signs of leakage or corrosion, which may impair their operation.

the balanced flue for combustion with exhaust gases being expelled through the top vent.

Radiators may be of the panel type (single or double, with or without convection fins), or older style column radiators. The former are light enough to be attached directly to the wall, the latter stand on the floor and are bracketed to the wall.

Pipework in old installations will be iron, whereas modern installations use copper piping with the same connectors and fittings described in the chapter on plumbing. The size of pipework will depend on the circuit requirements, an average small-bore layout using 15, 22, and 28mm pipe.

With a less common microbore system 6mm, 8mm or 10mm copper piping will also be used.

The diagram shows also that the boiler is used to heat the water in the hot water cylinder. The water from the boiler circulates through a sealed section of pipes inside the cylinder, then it is returned to the main circuit on its way back to the boiler. The water you draw off from the taps (the domestic water, as it is generally called) is kept entirely separate from the water that heats the radiators.

The cylinder may also have an electric immersion heater fitted to provide alternative heating and may be pre-lagged with high-density foam.

The entire system is supplied with water from a feed and expansion tank normally sited in the loft alongside the main cold water storage tank. As its name implies, the tank not only keeps the system topped up, but also allows

Central-heating control equipment
1 Automatic motorised diverter control valve; 2 Relay junction box; 3 Heating system programmers; 4 Hot-water-cylinder thermostat; 5 Room thermostats; 6 Automatic motorised control valve; 7 Thermostatic cylinder valve with built-in sensor; 8 Thermostatic radiator valves (TRVs); 9 Radiator control valves.

for the expansion of hot water, providing a safety outlet.

In some homes where pipe runs are short and direct there may not be any form of pump fitted into the circuit, with water circulating simply by the natural process of hot water rising and cold water falling. Such a gravity feed system, as it is called, is often found in homes with iron piping and column radiators. It is not, however, unusual in such situations to find the last radiator seldom gets hot and the fitting of a pump would improve the situation considerably. The system would also operate more economically because the water would circulate more rapidly, becoming less cold and therefore requiring less costly fuel to re-heat it.

Modern systems, with their sophisticated valves and controls, are always fitted with a pump generally on the return pipe close to the boiler.

The efficient running of any system depends largely on maintaining all parts in good working order.

The maintenance of the boiler should

always be left to specialists, and an annual servicing contract is a worthwhile arrangement. However, you can take care of virtually all other jobs connected with the system.

The following pages describe the purpose of most fittings you will find on your system and how to operate and look after them.

CONTROLS AND FUNCTIONS
Thermostats
The most basic control for any heating system is a thermostat. The boiler will have a thermostat to control the temperature to which it heats the water, but in addition there could be what is known as a room thermostat. This turns on a boiler pump when the air temperature close by the thermostat cools beyond a pre-set level, thus sending hot water round the circuit. When the air temperature reaches a pre-set level the thermostat shuts off the pump, thus stopping the flow of water.

A single thermostat, normally sited in the sitting room or hall, controls the heat throughout the house.

This has drawbacks since if the air around the thermostat is warmed by another heat source, such as a living-room fire, the pump will not switch on, so radiators will not heat other rooms in colder parts of the house.

Any single thermostat must therefore be sited in such a position that it is unaffected by 'outside' sources.

Two control systems In the first system (top left) gravity pushes hot water from the boiler to heat the domestic tank: only the radiators are fed via a pump. In the second system (larger drawing) all heated water is pumped around the circuit.

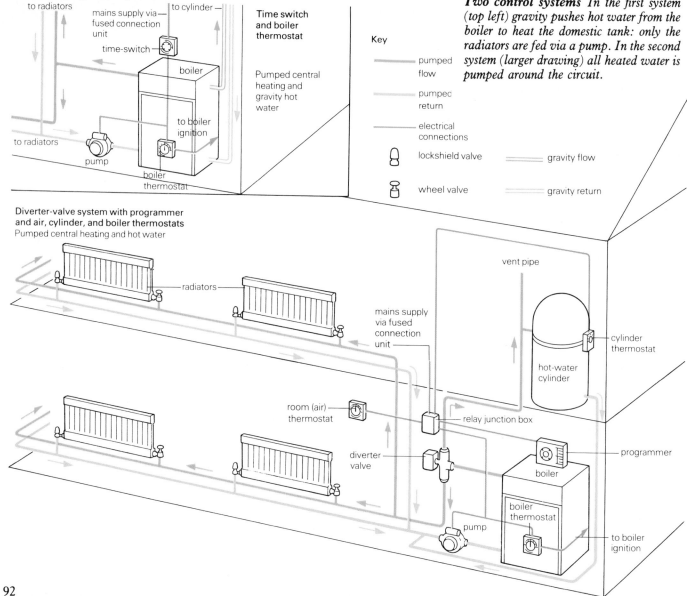

Central-heating control systems

to radiators — mains supply via fused connection unit — to cylinder —
time-switch —
boiler
to boiler ignition
to radiators
pump
boiler thermostat

Time switch and boiler thermostat

Pumped central heating and gravity hot water

Key
— pumped flow
— pumped return
— electrical connections
lockshield valve — gravity flow
wheel valve — gravity return

Diverter-valve system with programmer and air, cylinder, and boiler thermostats
Pumped central heating and hot water

radiators
vent pipe
mains supply via fused connection unit
cylinder thermostat
hot-water cylinder
room (air) thermostat
relay junction box
diverter valve
programmer
boiler
boiler thermostat
pump
to boiler ignition

A far more effective method of controlling the temperature in all rooms is to fit thermostatic radiator valves (TRVs) to every radiator in the home, dispensing with any other thermostats – except the one fitted to the boiler.

Radiator thermostats, then, control each room independently, allowing hot water into individual radiators as and when necessary. They are easily fitted to radiators in place of the standard on/off control valve.

It should be stressed that radiator thermostats need to be fitted to all radiators and that, apart from the boiler thermostat, there should be no other temperature controls built into the heating system.

Time clock controls

Few home-owners want their central heating operating non-stop. For this reason, time switches are incorporated into systems to control the number of hours and times the heating is on.

The simplest time switches can be set to run the heating for two periods in every 24 hours, and have an over-ride control should you wish to switch the heating on or off at any other times out of sequence.

It would be normal for this type of time control to be set to turn on the heating an hour or so before the family rises in the morning, to turn it off when the family sets out for work or school, then turn it on again before anyone comes home. It would finally shut down the boiler late at night.

Programmers

Time switches can, however, be far more elaborate than this, incorporating other controls as well, and in effect becoming complete programmers for the heating system.

They can be pre-set to allow the boiler to heat an indirect hot-water cylinder only or heat both radiators and cylinder or vice versa.

The diagram on this page shows a typical electrically controlled programmer. During the summer months it would be set to provide hot water only with no central heating on at all.

The programmer is an important part of any central heating system, ensuring that the most economical use is made of expensive fuel.

The pump

The pump, as described earlier, is responsible for circulating the heated water around the system. Electrically powered, the pump is generally situated close to the boiler on the return pipe.

It should be fitted with stop valves at each side because it may be necessary to

1

2

3

4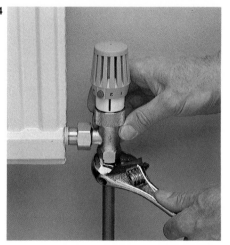

Replacing an on/off radiator valve with a thermostatic radiator valve
1 Bleed the entire central-heating system after turning all the controls to 'off'. Disconnect the old valve from the supply pipe and radiator. Remove the radiator tail pipe and coupling nut. (It should not normally be necessary to remove the radiator from its wall brackets.) 2 Fit the new tail pipe (it will have been supplied with the new valve) to the radiator, using PTFE tape to seal the joint. 3 Connect the thermostatic valve to the coupling nut on the radiator. 4 Re-connect the supply pipe to the new valve. You may have to shorten the supply pipe and/or remove the old olive and coupling nut.

open or remove it for maintenance or replacement. Stop valves ensure that this can be done without the need to drain the entire heating system.

The pump operates only when the boiler is running, being controlled by the thermostat in conjunction with any programmer.

Radiators

Modern radiators have three fittings. One, at the top, is the bleed valve used purely to allow air trapped in the radiator to escape. This valve is opened by a key just sufficiently to allow air out. As soon as water appears the valve is closed again.

The water inlet and outlet fittings are at each end at the bottom of the radiator. The inlet is fitted with either a standard on/off valve to control the water flow or a thermostatic radiator valve, as described earlier.

The outlet valve connected to the return pipe to the boiler is fitted with a balancing or 'lockshield' valve. This is a valve that, once adjusted correctly, is rarely turned or altered. Its purpose is to ensure that all radiators on a circuit get a fair share of hot water. Without it, the radiators first in line could use up most of the heat, leaving those at the end of the line unable to warm up.

When the radiators are installed these balancing valves are adjusted to ensure an even flow of hot water to all radiators, with no one radiator being capable of getting hotter than any other.

Drain valves

It may, on occasion, be necessary to drain water from all or part of the system. For this reason drain valves are fitted to the pipework at strategic points.

On a system with two circuits, one upstairs and one downstairs, there should be a drain valve fitted at the lowest point on each circuit.

Normally the valve will be connected

to a radiator outlet pipe below the lockshield valve. A hosepipe can be attached to the drain valve to carry water outside the house. The valve is opened with a spanner.

The boiler itself will also have a similar valve, so that the entire system can be drained.

Vents and safety valves

All systems, whether gravity fed or pumped, must have safety valves and vents built in to prevent the potentially dangerous build-up of pressure within the system.

For this reason, boilers are fitted with an automatic safety valve. Should the pressure within the boiler exceed a certain level the spring-loaded valve will open and release the pressure. Part of the servicing of any boiler should include a check that the safety valve is in working order.

The flow pipe from the boiler leading to radiators and any indirect hot water cylinder must extend up to and over the feed and expansion tank in the loft. This pipe is open-ended and serves as a vent in precisely the same way as the expansion pipe linked to the pipe carrying hot water to taps from the top of the hot water storage cylinder.

These vents or expansion pipes must never be blocked.

Feed and expansion tank

This is virtually identical to, but smaller than, a cold water storage tank. The water level in the feed and expansion tank is controlled by a normal ball valve.

The tank must be fitted with an overflow pipe with a larger diameter than that of the inlet pipe, to carry excess water outside the house.

Maintenance and fault finding

Apart from boiler servicing you should be able to maintain your own heating system, locating and correcting faults which develop.

Checking the feed and expansion tank At the start of every winter, before you turn on the heating, you should go up into the loft and check that the feed and expansion tank has water in it.

Lack of use in the summer months often causes the ball-valve assembly to stick in the closed position. With no water in the tank to keep the system topped up, several, if not all, radiators will remain cold.

If you find a dry tank, simply waggle the float arm up and down to release it and allow the water to flow again.

Turning the heating on Once the tank has filled up you can turn on the heating. Check that the clock or pro-

grammer is in an 'on' position, also that any centrally located thermostat is 'on' by turning up the temperature a few degrees. As you check the thermostat, listen for a slight click to indicate that it is in working order.

Bleeding the radiators As the radiators begin to warm up, go round each one in turn, starting with the lowest, and open the bleed valve. Hold a cup or cloth under the valve. A hissing noise will indicate air in the radiator. Allow this to escape fully, closing the valve when water appears.

If no hissing or water are apparent, turn off the thermostat and bleed the radiator while the pump is not running.

Bleed a radiator by turning the bleed-valve key anti-clockwise to allow air to escape. Close the valve when water appears.

Modern wall-mounted boilers fit unobtrusively into any kitchen, being made to lie flush with wall shelving units. Equally unobtrusive are the latest slimline panel radiators. The panelling increases their surface area and therefore their efficiency.

Pump maintenance Pumps are generally trouble free, but they do on rare occasions collect sludge or air that becomes trapped, reducing their effectiveness.

Pumps usually have an air vent fitted and can be bled in the same way as a radiator, using a screwdriver or key depending on the type of bleed valve.

To remove stubborn sludge, it is necessary to electrically disconnect and then dismantle the pump. If it is fitted with stop valves at each side, the pump can be removed without draining the whole system, and then cleaned out.

It is not, however, recommended that you attempt the complete dismantling

Project

Changing a pump

Central-heating pumps usually last for years. Eventually, however, they wear out and need replacing. It is quite an easy job that the average do-it-yourselfer should be able to manage. Provided the old pump has valves on either side to cut off the water supply, you do not need to drain the heating system: simply close the two valves, using a screwdriver (as shown at 1)

or a spanner. When the slot in the valve screw or nut is at right-angles to the direction of water flow, the valve is closed.

Now cut off the electricity supply, and remove the cover over the electrical terminals on the pump (2). Make a note of which wire goes where, then disconnect them and withdraw the cable from its grip. Using a wrench or suitable spanner, undo the coupling nuts on either side of the pump (3) and remove it. The pump will contain

some water, so have a bucket or mopping-up cloths handy. Fit a similar pump (4) in place of the old one. Feed in the power cable and remake all the connections (5), then replace the terminal cover.

Open the valves on either side of the new pump, set the speed of the new pump to match that of the old one (6), then turn on the power. Any time-control or thermostat in the system will have to be put in an 'on' position before the pump will begin operating.

unless you have some mechanical knowledge. This is a job for an expert.

Adjusting a lockshield valve If one radiator fails to warm up despite being full of water, one reason could be that the lockshield valve on this radiator is closed too far *or* that the same valve on another radiator is too far open. To balance the system more equally, fully open all on/off valves, unscrew and remove the cover on the lockshield valve on the hottest radiator. Using a spanner *close* the valve slightly in the direction indicated.

See if the colder radiator now benefits. If necessary unscrew and remove the shield from this one also and *open* the valve a fraction.

By carefully adjusting the lockshield valves, all radiators should reach the same temperature.

Blockages Heating system circuits can become partially or completely blocked by a build up of sludge in the pipes. This sludge is generally the result of corrosion in the pipes, and collects in bends preventing the free circulation of water. When this occurs, the entire system must be emptied and flushed out thoroughly.

Turn off the heating at the main control so that the boiler cannot operate. Attach a garden hosepipe to the drain plug by the boiler, leading the other end to an outside drain.

Close the inlet valve supplying water to the feed and expansion tank or tie up the float arm to a piece of wood stretched across the tank to stop fresh water entering the system.

Open the boiler drain plug and allow the system to empty. Without yet closing the drain plug, let water into the system again via the expansion tank to flush through the pipes.

When completely clean water eventually flows through to the outside drain, close the drain plug and allow the system to refill.

During the refilling process add a proprietary brand of corrosion inhibitor to the feed and expansion tank. Such liquids are available from builders' and plumbers' merchants and should be used precisely as directed. The system should remain clear for several years.

Air will need to be vented by means of the valve key from all the radiators as the system fills, and again after the heating has been turned on.

If after this a radiator fails to heat up, the problem may be due to an air-lock. Check that the on/off valve is fully open, then turn off all the other radiators and, with the pump running, bleed the faulty radiator. When it has warmed up, turn on and bleed again all the radiators above it.

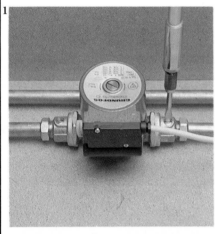

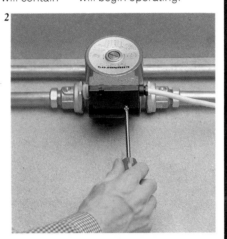

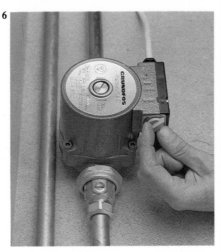

ELECTRICITY

Electricity reaches our homes through underground or overhead cables. Where these enter the house, they pass first to the Electricity Board's service terminal box, a small sealed unit containing the main service fuse. This fuse, which should never be tampered with, allows the board to cut off the house supply to allow repairs or replacement of the electricity meter or the mains distribution equipment. From this terminal box, two leads pass to the electricity meter (or meters: some houses have more than one). Up to this point the cabling and equipment are the board's property and must not be interfered with in any way; beyond this point, the entire house wiring system is the responsibility of the householder.

From the meter, two leads pass to the fusebox. In an old house there will be a main switch unit, to which are connected a number of separate switchfuse units, each controlling an individual circuit in the house. In a modern installation, there will be a one-piece consumer unit – a control box containing a main on/off switch that cuts off the house supply and a number of separate fuseways; again, each controls an individual circuit.

Old-fashioned switchfuse units should be labelled to show which unit controls which circuit in the house; a modern consumer unit should have a panel inside the cover that lists the various fuseways, stating which each one controls. In the latter case, you will find that the fuseways are colour-coded to help you identify them – a white dot for lighting circuits, a red dot for power circuits, and other colours for circuits feeding fixed equipment such as cookers and immersion heaters.

Where the labelling is unclear or non-existent, the first thing to do is to identify the circuits and label each one for future reference. If you have switchfuse units, turn off each one in turn and tour the house switching on lights or plugging in appliances to pinpoint the dead circuit. With a consumer unit, turn off the main switch, remove the first fuse and restore the power to the other circuits before touring the house as before checking what does not work. There are normally two lighting circuits, two or perhaps three power circuits, and one or more circuits to fixed appliances. Note your findings on a card and keep it by the fuseboard.

Understanding electricity

Electricity flows from point to point because of a difference in 'electrical pressure' between the points, rather as water pressure feeds our plumbing systems. This pressure difference is properly called potential difference or, more commonly, voltage – about 240 volts in this country, less in most other European countries.

Electric current flows through electric cables under this pressure difference, forward along one wire – the 'live' wire – to wherever it is needed, and back along another wire – the 'neutral'

Typical Domestic Mains Installation

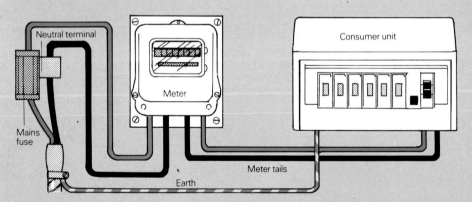

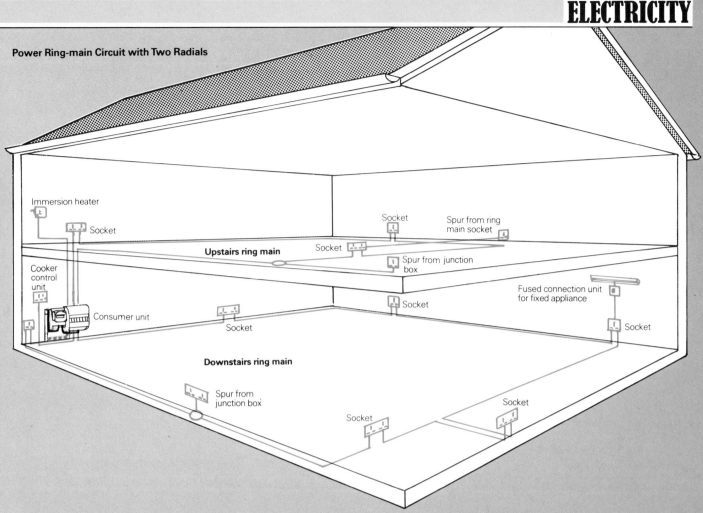

Power Ring-main Circuit with Two Radials

Immersion heater

Socket

Cooker control unit

Consumer unit

Socket

Downstairs ring main

Spur from junction box

Socket

Socket

Socket

Upstairs ring main

Socket

Spur from ring main socket

Spur from junction box

Fused connection unit for fixed appliance

Socket

Socket

Socket

Above *A typical ring-circuit installation. Note the separate radial circuits to cookers and fixed appliances.* *Opposite page, above* *The house electrical supply passes through a main fuse and meter, then to the consumer unit.* *Opposite page, below* *1 to 4 4mm², 2.5mm², 1.5mm², and 1mm² PVC-sheathed two-core-and-earth circuit-wiring cable; 5 1mm² three-core-and earth cable (for two-way switching); 6, 7, 8 Braided (non-kink), rubber-sheathed (heat-resisting), and PVC-sheathed three-core appliance flex; 9, 10, 11, 12 Circular, flat, parallel-twin, and clear-PVC-sheathed two-core flex; 13 Bell wire; 14 Co-axial television-aerial cable.*

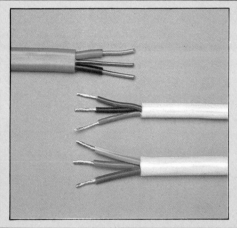

Colour codes

Mains wiring cable (top) has the live core colour-coded red and the neutral core colour-coded black. The earth is unsleeved, but when exposed to make connections must have green-and-yellow PVC sleeving. The cores of flexible cords are colour-coded brown for live, blue for neutral, and green-and-yellow for earth (bottom). Flex on appliances manufactured before 1970 (centre) have red (live) and black (neutral) cores instead of brown and blue.

wire. The third vital ingredient in an electricity supply is earthing. If for any reason the electricity flow along the live and neutral wires is disrupted, it 'flows to earth'. This is because the neutral side of the electricity supply from our power stations is (literally) connected to earth. An electrical circuit is completed in one of two ways: the electricity can either flow to earth down the electricity supply cable's neutral conductor, or it can flow directly to earth. In practice, it will take the line of least resistance and flow directly to earth.

This question of resistance is important. Good conductors of electricity, such as the copper wires that carry electricity round the circuits of a house, have low resistance and allow electricity

to pass along them easily. Bad conductors have high resistance: that is, they resist the passage of electricity. If current passes along a conductor of high resistance, it generates heat. The element of an electric fire, for example, has a higher resistance than that of the cables carrying electricity to it. Materials with extremely high resistance are, in fact, not conductors but insulators, actually preventing the passage of current. The insulation around copper cables in our homes performs this function. Air is also an excellent insulator, and overhead power lines use this property of the atmosphere to keep the current within their cables. (The insulation can, however, break down if the voltage is high enough.)

The principle of earthing the electrical circuits of a house is in the cause of safety: it protects both the circuits themselves and, more importantly, their users. It means that, when a fault occurs, electricity can flow harmlessly to earth through the low-resistance earthing conductor – the third wire in an electrical cable or flex. This earth-continuity conductor runs alongside the live and neutral conductors and is connected to electrical appliances and to fixed electrical accessories such as power points. All the earths in the house are connected to one central point, usually the outer metal sheath of the main underground supply cable or to an earthing rod driven into the ground beneath the house.

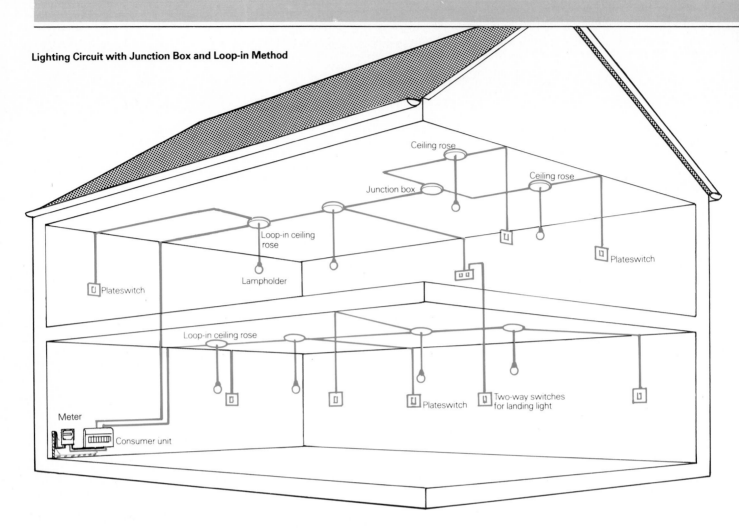

Ceiling rose

Ceiling rose

Junction box

Loop-in ceiling
rose

Plateswitch

Lampholder

Plateswitch

Loop-in ceiling rose

Meter

Consumer unit

Plateswitch

Two-way switches
for landing light

Modern lighting circuits are connected up using loop-in ceiling roses: the circuit cable loops from rose to rose, and switch cables run from the rose to the switch position; junction boxes connect branch circuits.

Each circuit in the house, then, consists of a live conductor, a neutral conductor, and an earth conductor. The live conductors are connected to one side of the bank of fuseways in a consumer unit, the neutrals to a neutral terminal block, and the earths to an earth terminal block. The incoming main supply is split, the live cable going to the other side of the bank of fuseways and the neutral cable to the neutral terminal block. The main switch 'breaks' both the live and neutral cables when it is switched off.

Understanding fusing
Fuses are another protective device, the purpose of which is to isolate circuits or appliances from the electrical supply in the event of a fault. Such a fault may cause the flow of current in the live conductor to rise. A larger current makes the conductor heat up, and over-heated conductors can start fires. A fuse is a short piece of special metal designed to melt if it gets hotter than it should; by melting, it breaks the flow of electricity and so the supply to that circuit or appliance is cut off.

The fuse is placed on the live side of the circuit in a modern electrical system and will melt (or 'blow') for any of three main reasons: first, if too much current is being drawn from the circuit; second, if a fault develops on an appliance and it draws too much current to itself as a result; third, if electricity is leaking to earth and the total current flow is thereby increased.

A modern alternative to a fuse is a device called a miniature circuit breaker (MCB). This is an electromechanical switch that detects a higher-than-normal electric current and switches itself off, so isolating the circuit concerned. Such circuit breakers are a more reliable substitute for fuses.

There is also a different type, called a residual current circuit breaker (RCCB), which detects the slightest flow of current to earth. Such leakages of current are often not big enough to blow a fuse or switch off an MCB, but they can give fatal shocks if the current happens to be flowing to earth through a human body. However, RCCBs cannot do some of the things that a fuse or MCB can do, such as detecting a large current in the live and neutral conductors when there is no leakage to earth, so they must be used in conjunction with fuses or MCBs. They also act as a mains on/off switch and may replace this switch in the consumer unit.

Your electrical system
Whether your switchboard has separate switchfuse units or a one-piece consumer unit, you will probably find that each circuit is protected by a rewireable fuse – a length of fuse wire held in a ceramic holder between two screw-down terminals. Fuse wire of different ratings is used to protect different circuits, according to their normal current demands – thin 5-amp wire for fuses protecting lighting circuits, 15-amp wire for fuses protecting fixed appliances such as immersion heaters, and thick 30-amp wire for protecting power circuits. It is imperative that fuse wire of the *correct rating* is used for each circuit, otherwise the fuse will not provide the overload protection it should. It is extremely dangerous to replace the fuse wire with any other metallic object such as a nail, a paper clip, or a strip of silver paper.

Some circuit fuses are of the cartridge type, in which a manufactured fuse containing fuse wire of the correct rating simply clips into the fuseholder. Different-sized cartridges are used for each rating, so it is almost impossible to fit one of the wrong rating into a particular fuseholder. These circuit cartridge fuses are larger than those used in modern plugs and are not interchangeable with them. Their one drawback is that, when a fuse blows, it is often difficult to see which one is affected (although if the fuseways are labelled correctly you will at least know which circuit is involved).

Fuseholders of both rewireable and cartridge fuses are colour-coded according to their rating:

Circuit	Rating	Colour
Lighting	5 amp	White
Immersion heater	15 amp	Blue
Storage heater	20 amp	Yellow
Power circuit	30 amp	Red
Cooker	45 amp	Green

As previously mentioned, some modern electrical installations have MCBs instead of fuses, while some other systems are also protected by an RCCB, which can trip off and isolate the whole house.

From the consumer unit or switch-fuse units, cables carry the electricity to where it is needed in the house – at lighting or power points and to fixed appliances. Most of these circuits are what electricians call radial circuits; one cable runs to its furthest point, feeding one or more draw-off points on the way. In older houses, all circuits were of this type, but in the case of power points it was found that each radial circuit could feed only a relatively small number of

points, and as the number of power points needed for the appliances used in the average house grew, so did the number of radial circuits required. So the ring circuit was devised.

This differs from the radial circuit in that a continuous loop of cable runs from the consumer unit, supplying electricity to a larger number of power points on the way, and then returns to the same live terminal of the consumer unit. The effect is that electricity can flow in either direction along the live cable to where is is needed. In a typical modern installation, there will be one ring circuit for the ground floor, one for the first floor and possibly a separate one for the kitchen, which these days is the room where the most appliances are used. The only restriction as far as a ring circuit is concerned is that each can serve a floor area of up to $100m^2$ (1,076sq ft); there is, however, no limit to the number of sockets that can be fitted within this area.

Sockets on a ring circuit can be either single or double, and there are fused connection units for appliances such as freezers and heaters, which are normally kept permanently plugged in. In addition to the main circuit, sockets can also be supplied by branch lines called

How old is your wiring?
If your house has separate switch-fuse units at the fuseboard and your power points take plugs with round pins, then it is probably at least 25 years old. While the equipment itself may be in reasonable working order, the cable will most probably be insulated with rubber rather than with the modern equivalent, PVC. Rubber insulation perishes in time, and so the wiring becomes unsafe. Old systems were not designed to cope with the much higher electrical demands likely to be put on them nowadays. Overloading could cause a fire, while perished insulation may make parts of the installation 'live'. If you have reason to believe your wiring is in any way suspect, have it inspected by a qualified electrician, and be prepared to have your house completely rewired, with modern accessories and a consumer unit containing miniature and earth-leakage circuit breakers for the best electrical protection.

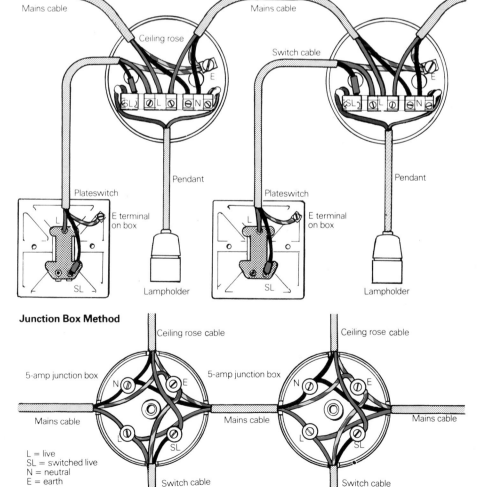

Loop-in Method

Junction Box Method

L = live
SL = switched live
N = neutral
E = earth

Left, above With the loop-in system, the 'mains-in', 'mains-out', and switch cables are connected up as shown. *Below* With the junction-box method, two mains cables, one switch cable, and cable to a ceiling rose are connected like this.

'spurs'. These are sometimes fitted during installation to save cable, but more importantly they are an easy way of adding extra sockets later (see page 106). There can be as many spurs as there are sockets on the ring circuit, but each spur can serve only one more outlet – one double or one single.

Appliances with a rating of up to 3kW can be plugged into a ring circuit; those with a higher rating, such as cookers, instantaneous showers, and immersion heaters, must have an individual circuit run directly from a separate fuseway in the consumer unit.

Lighting circuits are radial circuits, with a single cable leaving the consumer unit and running to a number of lighting points in series. Most houses have two lighting circuits, one upstairs and one downstairs. They are wired in one of two ways: the loop-in method or the junction box method.

With the loop-in method, the mains cable runs to each ceiling rose in turn. A second cable runs from the rose to the light switch, and sometimes a third cable runs from the rose to supply another lighting point controlled from the same switch. All the connections are made within the ceiling rose, which has a bank of terminals to take them.

In the junction box system, the mains cable runs to a number of four-terminal junction boxes fixed above the ceiling. One cable from this box feeds the first ceiling rose, another the switch controlling it, while the fourth cable passes on to the next junction box.

Most modern lighting systems are wired with the loop-in method, because it is cheaper and easier to install. It is also easier to add to if extra lighting points are needed in the future. However, it is not unusual to find hybrid systems, with the occasional junction box used on what is otherwise a conventional loop-in system.

Each lighting circuit can serve up to 12 lampholders fitted with bulbs not larger than 100 Watts, although in practice the number of points is usually limited to eight so that larger bulbs or multi-bulb fittings can be used.

The electric cable that carries current round these various circuits has a stout outer PVC sheath, usually coloured white for surface-run wiring, and grey for cable runs buried in walls and under floorboards. The cable has a cross section like a flattened circle, and with the special exception of cable for two-way switching of lighting circuits (see page 110) contains three wires or 'cores'. Two are colour-coded with inner PVC insulation – red for live, black for neutral. The third core is a bare copper earth continuity conductor. Any part of

this which is exposed by the removal of the cable's outer insulation to make a connection to an electrical accessory must be covered with a piece of green-and-yellow striped PVC sleeving, so that there is no risk of accidental contact within the accessory between the earth core and either the live or the neutral one. The name in the trade for this sort of cable is 'two-core-and-earth PVC-sheathed cable'.

Different circuits require cable of different current-carrying capacity and each is rated according to the diameter (or, strictly, the cross-section area) of the copper conductors. For wiring lighting circuits, adding single lights, and wiring up such accessories as clock connectors and shaver sockets to existing lighting circuits, 1.0mm^2 cable is used. There is also a 1.5mm^2 size, sometimes used for wiring complete lighting circuits. Ring or radial power circuits and spurs from ring circuits are always wired in 2.5mm^2 cable, as are circuits to fixed appliances such as immersion heaters, instantaneous water heaters with ratings below 4.8kW and storage heaters, For cookers up to 12kW and water heaters over 4.8kW, 4mm^2 cable is used, and there is also 6mm^2 cable for large (over 12kW) or split-level cookers. You are unlikely to need anything larger than this in a domestic installation.

We have now piped our electricity to various circuits around the house and

need to be able to extract it from the circuits to power lights and electrical appliances. This is where electrical accessories come in. Power for electrical appliances is supplied via socket outlets into which the appliance plugs are inserted. These socket outlets nowadays have three rectangular holes, but older systems had socket outlets with round holes of different sizes according to the current the outlet was wired to deliver; 2-, 5-, and 15-amp sockets were used.

Single or double socket outlets are available, some with their own switches. For appliances that need to be permanently connected to the ring main, a fused connection unit replaces the socket outlet; the appliance is connected to the unit through a hole in its faceplate. Fused connection units can also be switched or unswitched, and may incorporate a neon light to show that the appliance is on.

Cookers are permanently wired to cooker control units fitted with a main switch and, usually, an indicator light. Cooker units are also available incorporating a switched socket outlet – a useful way of getting an extra socket outlet near a worktop.

There is less hardware involved in the average lighting circuit. Ceiling roses provide the connection between the lighting-circuit cables and the actual light fittings, while wall-mounted light switches (or cord-operated, ceiling-mounted ones) allow the lights to be switched on and off. Wall lights are usually fixed to the wall over small

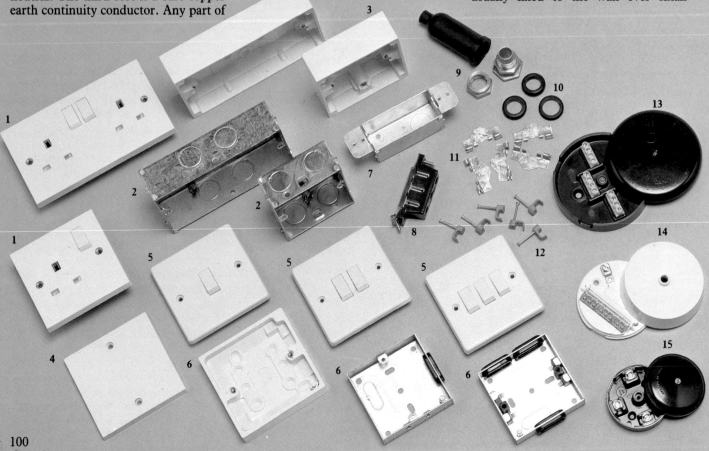

recessed boxes, which contain the connecting block between the circuit cable and the light fitting.

The last components of an electrical system are the plugs that connect appliances to socket outlets and the light bulbs in the various light fittings. The three-pin plug with its rectangular pins is a familiar sight, but there are also switched plugs and adaptors that allow more than one appliance to be plugged into a single socket.

Light bulbs come with a choice of three types of glass – clear, pearl, and silica-coated. There is a wide variety of shapes available, although pear and mushroom are the most popular. Most have a two-pin bayonet fitting, but some bulbs, for use in spotlight fittings for example, have a screw-in fitting. The latest development is the SL lamp, which has a small fluorescent tube within a tough cylindrical glass envelope and uses far less power than an equivalent ordinary bulb. Fluorescent tubes give between three and five times as much light as a filament bulb of the same wattage.

The final link: flex and plugs

Light fittings and electrical appliances are connected to the 'fixed' wiring of lighting and power circuits by 'flex' (an abbreviation for 'flexible cord'). Flex comes in many more types than cable, and a distinguishing feature is that nowadays the cores are colour-coded differently from those in cable (the same code was once used for both). The live core is now coded brown, the neutral blue, and the earth green-and-yellow striped. Not all flex has three cores; that for use with double-insulated appliances and for fitting pendant lights to ceiling roses has only two cores: live and neutral.

For connecting most domestic appliances, circular three-core PVC-insulated-and-sheathed flex is used. This comes in ratings from 0.5mm² (for appliances taking up to 700 Watts) to 4mm² (for ratings up to 6kW), so it is important to choose flex of the correct rating for the appliance involved. For kettles, irons, and other portable appliances, use circular three-core unkinkable flex, which has a flexible outer sheath sometimes covered with coloured braiding. Where high local temperatures exist (the flex to an immersion heater for example), heat-resisting flex should be used.

Two-core flex is used only for double-insulated appliances such as power tools, for table lamps with non-metallic fittings, and for pendant lights. Circular two-core flex is the most widely used, but you can also buy flat two-core flex (with the same cross-section as cable) and twin two-core flex, which has a figure-of-eight cross-section.

Special bell wire with solid conductors is used to connect battery bells and to connect transformer terminals to mains-operated bells. And special coaxial television feeder cable is used to connect a TV set to its aerial.

On a modern electrical system with rectangular-pin plugs, a small fuse is fitted within the body of the plug to protect the appliance from an overload on the circuit and to protect the circuit itself if there is a fault in the appliance. There are two fuse sizes, 3 amp and 13 amp, colour-coded red and brown respectively. The 3-amp fuse is used on appliances taking less than 720 Watts, the 13-amp fuse on all others. The one exception to this is that a 13-amp fuse *must* be used with a colour television, even though its stated rating is less than 720 Watts, because the starting current of the set may exceed 3 amps. These small cartridge fuses are also used in fused connection units. In both cases they clip into a sprung holder over the live terminal.

Some electrical sockets and switches
1 One-gang and two-gang switched sockets; 2 One-gang and two-gang flush-socket boxes; 3 One-gang and two-gang surface-socket boxes; 4 Blanking-off plate for one-gang box; 5 One-gang, two-gang, and three-gang plate switches; 6 Surface and flush (plaster-depth) plate-switch boxes; 7 Flush box for architrave switch; 8 Terminal block for box mounting; 9 Armoured-cable gland, locknut, and sheath; 10 PVC grommets; 11 Plasterboard fixings lugs for metal boxes; 12 Cable clips; 13 Three-terminal 30-amp junction box; 14 Loop-in ceiling rose with earth terminal; 15 Four-terminal 5-amp junction box; 16 Flush cooker-switch box; 17 Cooker switch; 18 Cooker-control unit; 19 Cooker cable outlet; 20 Bathroom shaver unit; 21 Bedroom shaver socket; 22 Twin-element immersion-heater switch; 23 Water-heater switch; 24 Unswitched fused connection unit; 25 Switched fused connection unit with neon and flex outlet; 26 20-amp double-pole switch with neon; 27 Lampholders; 28 20-amp double-pole cord-operated switch with neon; 29 5-amp cord-operated switch; 30 Cord for 28 and 29; 31 BESA box with back outlet; 32 Batten-holder.

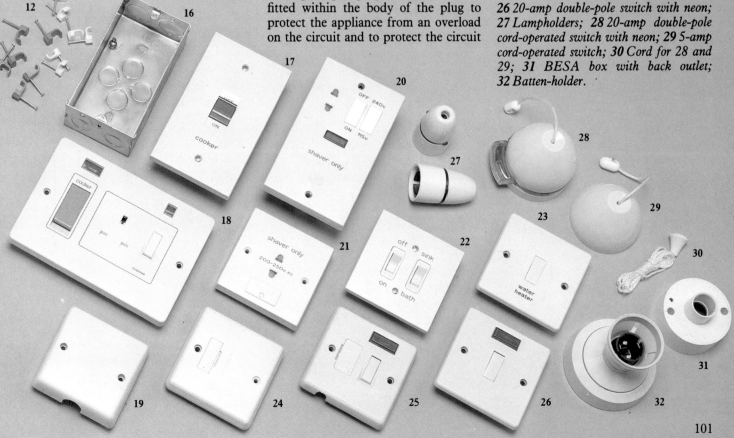

Tools & Techniques 1

A small electrical tool kit is useful even if you intend to do little more than wire up the occasional plug. Essential items are a small electrical screwdriver to make connections to plug terminals, a pair of wire strippers, a sharp knife, a roll of electrical insulating tape, spare plug fuses in 3-amp and 13-amp ratings, a card of fuse wire (or the appropriate cartridge fuses) for repairing circuit fuses, and a torch so you can see what you are doing when the lights go out.

If you are intending to do some work on your house's fixed wiring system, add a pair of pliers with insulated handles and cutting jaws for cutting cable and twisting cores together, a mains tester for checking the continuity of your connections, and some green-and-yellow PVC sleeving for covering bare earth wires.

In addition, an extension cable is useful, to provide light or power in a room where the power is off. Buy a cable ready-made on a reel, or make one up from a length of 1.25mm^2 three-core flex, a moulded-rubber plug, and a moulded-rubber trailing socket.

A selection of other tools is also necessary – woodworking tools for lifting floorboards, drilling holes for cables to pass through joists and so on, and masonry tools for chopping out cable runs in walls and fitting flush-mounted electrical accessories.

Mending a fuse

A fault on the fixed wiring of your house will blow a circuit fuse, usually with a loud bang! If you have labelled all the circuits, you will know which one is affected by the loss of power; otherwise turn off the main switch, and remove each fuseholder in turn until you find the one that has blown. If it is a rewireable fuse, the wire will probably have been destroyed, blackening the fuseholder. Remove the remains of the old fuse wire and fit a new piece of the

correct rating between the fuseholder terminals. A glance at the other fuseholders will show how it is done.

With cartridge fuses, it is not easy to tell at a glance which fuse has blown. Test these fuses with a mains tester, or make up a simple test circuit using a torch bulb and battery and a short length of wire. If the fuse is sound, the bulb will light. Alternatively, test the fuse by holding it across the open end of a metal-cased torch, with one end of the fuse on the end of the battery and the other on the metal casing of the torch. A sound fuse will light the torch when it is switched on.

Of course, if the consumer unit is fitted with MCBs, a circuit fault will merely trip the MCB off. Simply switch it on again to restore the power. You will not be able to do this if the fault is still present; a persistent fault will also keep blowing a rewireable or cartridge fuse. In this case, go round the affected circuit checking all connections and disconnecting suspect appliances until the fault is isolated and the new fuse does not blow. If fuses blow repeatedly, call in a qualified electrician.

Fitting a plug

Correct and safe connection of plugs to appliance flex is imperative. Begin by stripping off about 38mm (1½in) of the outer sheath from the flex by drawing a sharp knife along it, between the cores, taking care not to damage the insulation on the cores themselves. Lay the flex over the open plug and cut each core 12.5mm (½in) longer than necessary to

Electrical tool kit 1 Extension cable and reel; 2 Torch; 3 Long-bladed screwdriver with insulated handle; 4 Combined mains-tester and small screwdriver; 5 PVC insulating tape; 6 Ring-main tester; 7 Card of fuse wire (5-, 15- and 30-amp ratings); 8 Earth sleeving; 9 Handyman's knife; 10 Cartridge fuses for flat-pin 13-amp plugs; 11 Pliers with insulated handles; 12 Wire stripper/cutter.

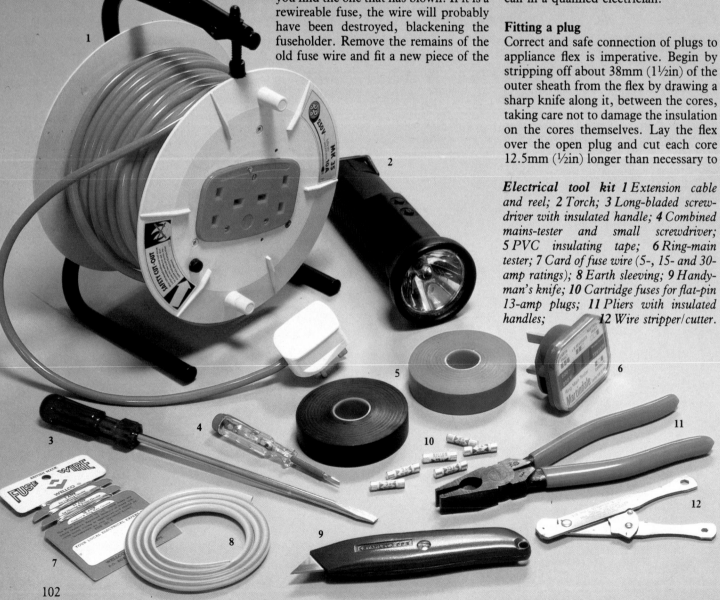

reach its correct terminal. Strip 12.5mm of insulation from each core and twist the strands of each tightly together. Next, position the flex in the cord grip, by pressing it down into the nylon jaws or by screwing down the fibre strip securely. The cord grip should grip the outer sheath of the flex, not the cores, if you have cut the insulation correctly, and the insulation on each core should stop just short of its terminal. Check that the flex is firmly held; if it comes adrift when pulled, a core could pull away from its terminal and touch another with dangerous results.

Attach each core to its correct terminal. The brown core goes to the bottom right terminal (L), the blue core to the bottom left terminal (N) and the earth core to the remaining terminal at the top of the plug (E). For stud terminals, wind the exposed wire clockwise round the post and screw on the stud. For pillar terminals, double back the wire on itself, insert it and tighten down the top screw fully.

In a fused plug, replace the fuse. Finally, replace the plug top and tighten the fixing screw, making sure that the top fits properly. If the plug case is damaged, replace it with a new plug; such plugs are dangerous and should never remain in use.

Rewiring a pendant light

Lighting flex supporting a pendant bulb and light fitting not only carries electricity to the light but also supports it. Such flex may become frayed and worn and the connections at the ceiling rose and lampholder can pull away, causing a short circuit. To replace worn flex, isolate the lighting circuit by removing the circuit fuse or switching off the appropriate MCB. Supporting the light fitting, unscrew the ceiling rose and disconnect the old flex, noting which terminals were used. Prepare a new piece of two-core circular PVC-sheathed flex of the required length, trimming off the outer and inner insulation as necessary. Thread one end through the lampholder cover and attach it to the two lampholder terminals, looping the cores over the small anchorages on the body of the lampholder. Thread the other end of the flex through the ceiling rose cover and connect the cores to the terminals from which the old flex was disconnected. Again, loop the cores over the celing rose anchorages; these prevent the weight of the light fitting from straining the connections. Finally, replace the rose cover, after checking that the outer insulation of the flex passes into the rose; the cores should not be exposed.

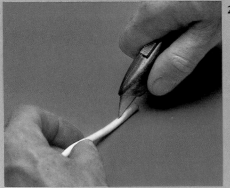

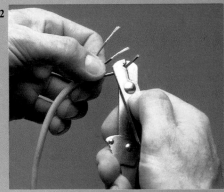

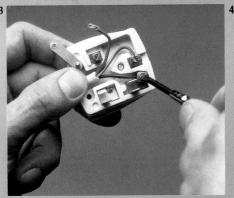

Above: Wiring a plug 1 Split the PVC sheathing without cutting the core insulation. 2 Strip the core insulation with wire strippers. 3 Connect the cores to the correct terminals. 4 The plug properly wired up.
Right: Replacing a pendant flex 1 Unscrew the rose cover after isolating the lighting circuit. 2 Prepare the cores of new flex, connect to the lampholder terminals, and slip on the lampholder cover. 3 Thread the flex through the rose cover and connect it to the rose terminals.

Rewiring an electrical appliance

New flex can be fitted to an electrical appliance following a similar sequence. First, open up the appliance after unplugging it from the mains and identify the flex terminals. Buy new flex of the correct type and rating, cut to the length required and bare the cores by cutting away the outer sheathing carefully. Strip each core, pass the flex through the opening in the body of the appliance and anchor it in the cord grip, if one is fitted, by tightening the small screws. Connect the cores to the correct terminals, which will be labelled L, N and E. Close up the appliance and attach the plug to the end of the flex.

Replacing old wiring accessories

Existing socket outlets and plate-switches can be damaged accidentally, and should be replaced. You might also want to fit accessories of more up-to-date colour or design. Provided the existing accessories are of reasonably modern design, the old faceplates can simply be unscrewed and replaced with

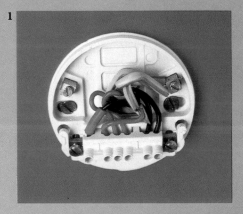

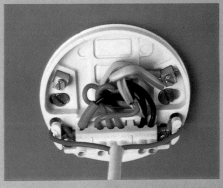

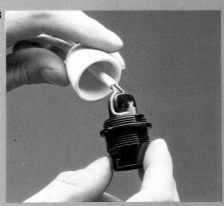

new ones. Outlets and plate switches are fitted to a mounting box, screwed to the wall. This box can be either hidden below the surface of the wall, in which case it is said to be flush-mounted, or on view, when it is described as being surface-mounted. The box has threaded lugs to receive the fixing screws of the socket or switch.

First isolate the circuit concerned by removing the appropriate circuit fuse or switching off the MCB. Unscrew the fixing screws in the accessory face-plate and ease it away from its mounting box. Note which cable core is fixed to which terminal and disconnect them by loosening the terminal screws. Connect the cable cores to the terminals in the new accessory, ensuring that the red core goes to the terminal marked L and the black to that marked N. The earth continuity conductor, which should be sleeved if it is bare, may be connected to the accessory itself; if this does not have an earth terminal (a light switch, for example), connect the earth instead to the earth terminal of the box in which the accessory is fitted. Finally replace the fixing screws in the accessory face-plate to attach it to the mounting box.

If the accessory you wish to replace is of an old style not compatible with current accessory dimensions, you will have to replace the mounting box also – easy if the accessory is surface-mounted, but trickier if it is of the flush-fixed type, since a new wall recess to take the box will have to be cut – see page 105. If you find when investigating the possibility that your mains cable is of the rubber-covered type, you should consider replacing it with PVC-sheathed cable instead.

Running cable
When replacing old cable with new, it may be possible to connect the new to the old then to draw out the old cable, pulling the new cable along the same run. This is possible, however, only where the cable runs loose under floorboards, or in conduit buried in the walls. Otherwise you will have to run the new cable to where it is required using one of the following methods.

Cable to lighting fittings and ring mains on one floor can be run under the floorboards. To do this, you will have to lift one or more boards, depending on the direction of the cable run. Cable crossing the line of joists should be passed through holes drilled in the joists at least 50mm (2in) below their tops to lessen the risk of nails damaging them. Cables running parallel to the joists should be fixed to their sides, but can be left lying flat on ceilings or on the earth beneath ground floors.

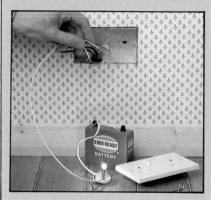

To pass a cable under a floor, take up a board at each end of the run, tie a loop in the end of the cable and push it down the gap at one end of the run. From the other end push in a length of stiff wire with a hook at the end and grab the looped end of the cable. Draw through the cable to the other end of the run.

Cable can also be concealed behind skirting boards and architraves. Prise the architrave away from the door frame to expose the gap between wall and frame and clip the cable to the frame

before replacing the architrave. As for skirtings, either chisel away the plaster just above the skirting and feed the cable down behind it, or else remove the skirting board altogether and run the cable along the wall with cable clips. Either method is useful in a room with solid floors.

When the cable run has to run down or across a wall, it is buried in the plaster. To minimise the risk of damage should anyone chance to drive screws or nails into the wall later, cable runs are always made vertically or horizontally, never diagonally. A groove is chiselled out of the plaster and the brickwork behind if necessary. The cable is then placed in it, held in place with small plastic cable clips. For additional protection, it can also be covered by slim protective trunking before the groove is replastered.

Cable can also be inserted into the cavity of exterior cavity walls (so long as they have not been insulated) or within internal stud partitions. Start by making a hole in the wall where you want the cable to emerge from the the top of the wall. Drop a weighted string down inside the cavity and fish its end out through the hole. You can then tie the cable to the string and pull it up through the cavity. With stud partition walls, horizontal timber studs will block the way. Scrape the plaster from the top of the studs and cut a groove in them to allow the cable to pass.

Cable can also be run on the surface, but in this case it should be protected by being run in surface-mounted plastic trunking. Several proprietary systems are available.

Fitting mounting boxes
Surface-mounted boxes are simply screwed to wall plugs in holes drilled in the wall. Cable can be concealed, emerging through the back of the surface-mounted box, or can be run to it surface-mounted in trunking. However, for the neatest finish the mounting boxes are recessed into the wall so that the accessory face plate fits almost flush with the wall surface.

To fit a flush-mounted box, mark its outline on the wall where it is to be fixed. Chip away the plaster and use a brick bolster and club hammer to chop out a recess slightly deeper than the box itself. If you chop too deep in a solid wall, put a dab of mortar in the back of the recess before fitting the box. Drill holes for two wall plugs and screw the box into position in the recess. Check that it is horizontal; the screw slots in the box allow you to make slight adjustments. Make good round the box with plaster or filler. In a cavity wall, the

Installing a socket 1 Pencil around the box position on the wall. 2 Mark the cable run to the box. 3 Cut away the plaster with a club hammer and bolster chisel. 4 Drill holes in the underlying brickwork or blockwork. 5 Complete chopping out the recess with hammer and bolster. 6 Fix the box in place and thread the cable down the run and into the void beneath the floorboards prior to connecting it up to the circuit. 7 Fill the cable channel neatly with plaster before repapering. 8 Connect up the socket and screw it to its box.

single brick thickness will not allow you to cut a deep recess without breaking through into the cavity. In this case choose a box that is only 25mm (1in) deep and team it with an accessory with a deeper-than-usual faceplate.

Before finally fixing the box in place, check the direction of the cable run to it and push out one of the circular knockouts in the sides or back of the box. Fit a rubber grommet into the knockout in order to protect the cable, and feed it into the box so that it is ready to be connected to the accessory.

In stud partition walls, a flush box can still be fitted, either using small metal lugs clipped to the side of the mounting box, or by using a proprietary mounting box with spring-loaded lugs that grip the sides of the plasterboard.

Ceiling roses must be screwed to the underside of a joist, or to a batten fixed between the joists above the ceiling.

Installing extra socket outlets
It is possible to extend a ring circuit to provide more socket outlets in a number of ways. The first is to add a spur from an existing socket on the ring circuit – see drawing, page 106 overleaf. Begin by planning the cable run from the new socket position (A) to a conveniently-sited existing one (B). Then fit the mounting box at A, feed the cable through one of its knockouts and run it back to B by one of the methods outlined previously. Connect up the faceplate at A (remember to sleeve the bare earth wire) and fit it to its box. At B remove the face-plate after isolating the circuit, push out one of the knockouts and feed in the spur cable, fitting a rubber grommet if the box is metal. Then connect up the cores of the new cable to the L, N, and E terminals of the existing socket, replace the faceplate and restore the power.

The second method is used when there is no conveniently-sited socket outlet from which to run the spur. Instead, the spur is connected directly to the ring, using a 30-amp joint box. Locate the ring circuit by tracing the cable back from a socket known to be on the ring. At a convenient place under the floor, screw the joint box to the side of the joist at least 50mm (2in) below its top edge. Run the cable from the new socket to this joint box. Switch off at the mains, cut the ring cable and connect the three cable ends at the joint box. It does not matter which terminals are used as long as all the live cores go to one terminal, all the neutrals to a second and all the earths to a third. Fit the joint-box cover and restore the power.

The third method is used when there is an existing socket that is no longer needed, perhaps because it is hidden behind a piece of furniture. It is simply used as a junction box instead (and can therefore be brought back into commission in the future). The existing socket faceplate is removed and the cable from the new socket run to this point. A three-way insulated terminal block is then placed inside the existing mounting box and the cable cores connected to it – live wires to one terminal, neutrals to the second and earths to the third. Then a blanking-off plate is fitted to the existing mounting box.

Note that all these instructions refer only to extending ring circuits. You should not attempt to extend radial circuits without first seeking the advice of a qualified electrical engineer.

Cooker control units

A cooker must be powered by a separate circuit from a 30-amp or 45-amp fuseway at the consumer unit, using 4mm^2 or 6mm^2 cable respectively, according to the wattage of the cooker. The cooker itself is connected via a control unit, which should be no more than 2m (6½ft) away from it. Both parts of a split-level cooker must be within 2m of the control switch, although they can be on either side of it.

The cooker control unit may be flush- or surface-mounted, and is fitted to a mounting box. Cable of the same rating as the circuit runs from it to the cooker. The terminals must be clearly identified by suitable labels; they may be marked 'mains' and 'cooker' or 'load' and 'feed'. Both cables from split-level cookers can go to the same terminals, or you can, if you prefer, connect extra cable from the feed terminals of one control to a second control.

The connections for a freestanding cooker can most conveniently be made via a terminal box that should be installed fitted low down on the wall behind the cooker. The cable between the cooker control unit and the terminal box can be flush- or surface-mounted. Flex is not used to connect the cooker itself to its terminal box; cable is used instead. Leave enough slack in the cable to allow the cooker to be pulled out from the wall for cleaning.

*Left You can connect a spur by running a cable from an existing socket on the ring main to a new socket position. **Below, left** If there is no socket nearby, you can connect a spur into the ring main using a three-terminal junction box. 1 Cut off the tongue between adjacent floorboards (the batten shown here acts as a saw guide). 2 Drill a saw-access hole alongside a joist and cut across the board with a padsaw. You can locate the position of the joist by tapping the floorboards. 3 Cut the ring cable (make sure that you have switched off the power first). 4 Screw the junction box to a joist. 5 Connect up the mains and spur cables. 6 Screw a support block for the floorboard to the side of the joist.*

Installing a Spur

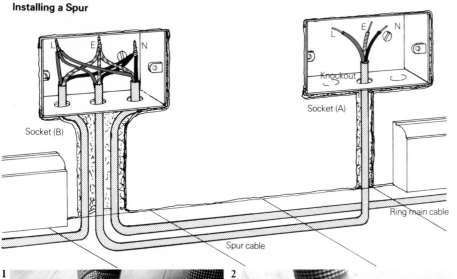

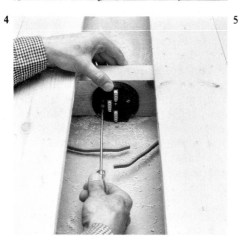

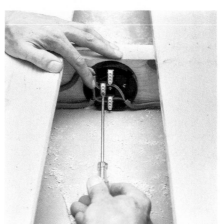

Shaver units

In a bathroom a shaver supply unit must conform to British Standard BS 3052. It contains a transformer that provides an earth-free 240-volt supply so that there is no risk of an electric shock if the shaver develops a fault. No other appliance can be used from a shaver socket, which contains a thermal cut-out device to prevent overloading. This type of unit can be flush- or surface-mounted; in the former case a deep box is needed to contain the unit.

In any other room, you can install what is known as a shaver socket outlet, which is the same size as a socket outlet and goes in an ordinary flush- or surface-mounted box. This has the same two-pin outlet and thermal cut-out as a shaver supply unit, but no transformer, and is therefore somewhat cheaper. It also contains a special 1-amp fuse to protect the cut-out.

Both types of shaver unit can be connected as spurs from a ring circuit (see sketch, page 106), or as extensions of lighting circuits, whichever is the more convenient in terms of the cable run.

Immersion heaters

As with a cooker, an immersion heater must be connected to a separate circuit run from the consumer unit and protected by a 15-amp circuit fuse or MCB. The circuit is wired in 2.5mm^2 cable to a point near the heater, where a switch is installed. For single-element heaters and dual-element models with an integral changeover switch, this must be a 20-amp double-pole isolating switch, preferably with a neon indicator. Dual-element types without their own switch need a combined changeover and double-pole switch. The connection between the switch and the immersion heater itself is made with three-core heat-resisting flex; the latter must have a rating to match that of the heater.

Extractor fans

An extractor fan in any room except a bathroom can be connected either as a spur from the ring circuit or an extension of the lighting circuit – see page 110. Most fans have integral on/off switches, but where a separate switch is needed – for a wall or ceiling fan – the wiring should be in 1mm^2 cable.

In a bathroom, the cable to the fan must be run via a fused connection unit within the bathroom if you are taking power from the ring circuit, or via a cord-operated isolating switch mounted on the ceiling if it is connected to the lighting circuit. Again, 1mm^2 cable should be used and the connection unit should be fitted with a 2-amp fuse.

Project 1

Turning single sockets into doubles

The simplest way of getting more socket outlets with the minimum of upheaval is to fit double sockets in place of existing singles, as shown in the three examples below. First, however, make sure the socket you want to replace is not on a spur.

Unscrew and disconnect the existing faceplate. If it is flush-mounted (1), take out the single box, enlarge the hole (2, 3) and fit a double box (4); or buy a surface-mounting box and fit it over the old single box (5, 6). If the socket is surface-mounted, remove the existing single box and fit a surface-mounted double box in its place (7, 8); or better still make the socket a flush one by chopping out a recess in the wall to take the new box.

When the new box is in place, simply connect up the cable or cables to the terminals on the new double socket faceplate. Make sure that all the red cores are firmly held in the live terminal, all the blacks in the neutral, and all the earths in the earth terminal. Finally, screw the new faceplate to its mounting box.

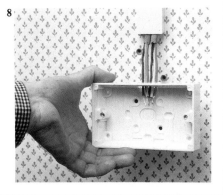

Fused connection units

Connection units are used instead of socket outlets to connect appliances that should not be accidentally disconnected – fridges, freezers, central heating pumps and so on. They are also useful for appliances in constant use, such as washing machines and waste disposal units, since they save the chore of plugging-in and unplugging.

A connection unit fits a standard mounting box and so can take the place of a socket outlet. Alternatively, it can be wired as a spur from the ring circuit. The sketch shows the connections at the unit; there may be two mains cables, rather than the one shown. The flex from the appliance passes through the unit's faceplate and is secured in a cord grip to prevent it being pulled out. Its cores are connected to the terminals marked 'load'. A fuse of the correct rating for the appliance concerned is housed in the small fuse carrier, which is accessible from the front of the unit.

Fused connection units are available switched or unswitched, with or without neon pilot lights.

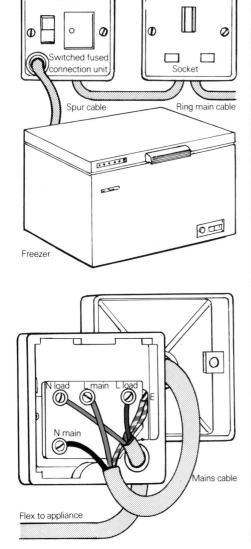

Switched fused connection unit

Socket

Spur cable

Ring main cable

Freezer

N load   L main   L load

E

N main

Mains cable

Flex to appliance

Project 2

Extending power to outbuildings

Temporary extensions to provide power and light to outbuildings such as sheds and garages are dangerous, and have a nasty habit of becoming permanent (when they are in breach of the wiring regulations). Installing a proper permanent link-up is the answer – a quite easy operation for the handyman, as illustrated in the photographs below.

The heart of such a circuit is an underground link of 4mm^2 twin-core armoured and sheathed cable (1) buried in a trench at least 600mm (2ft) deep between house and outbuilding. It is fed through the wall of each building, and terminates at each end in a 3-way terminal block. From there the rest of the circuit is made up with ordinary PVC-sheathed cable (see photographs on page 96). At each end of the underground cable, a standard metal mounting box (2) is installed. The armour and sheathing are cut back and a screwed gland fitted (3). This is then secured in one of the box's knockouts with a locknut and bush. The armour acts as the earth conductor, so that some of the cable's outer sheath must be removed before the gland can be fitted.

The other two cores of the armoured cable are connected to the red and black cores of the ordinary circuit cable via the terminal block, which is fitted in the metal box (4). The earth core of the ordinary cable should now be connected to the earth terminal on the metal box at each end of the underground cable run.

At the house end of the circuit, the 4mm^2 PVC-sheathed cable is run either to a spare 30-amp fuseway in the consumer unit, or to a separate switchfuse unit. At the garage or outbuilding end of the circuit, the PVC-sheathed cable is run to another switchfuse unit (5 and 6), and it is from there that the new sub-circuit is wired up.

For example, cable can be run on to a double socket outlet to provide power for plug-in appliances, and then it can be continued on to a fused connection unit with a 3-amp fuse which controls the building's lighting.

From this connection unit 1mm^2 cable is run up to a loop-in ceiling rose, and from there down to the light switch controlling it.

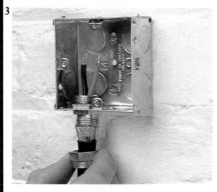

Project 3

Instantaneous showers
An instantaneous shower is yet another appliance that needs a separate circuit run from a 30-amp fuseway or MCB.

The circuit is run in 4mm² cable to a double-pole, cord-operated isolating switch (right) mounted on the bathroom or shower-room ceiling. The switch should be screwed to a joist, or to a batten nailed between the joists above the ceiling, to provide a firm fixing. The sketch shows how the connections to the switch are made. The same size cable is then run from the switch to the shower heater unit (below), following the shower manufacturer's instructions carefully.

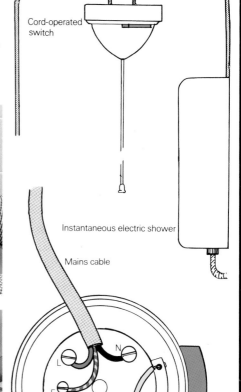

Mains cable
Switched cable
Cord-operated switch

Instantaneous electric shower

Mains cable

Neon light

Switched cable

Switchfuse units
If extra circuits are required but there are no spare fuseways in the consumer unit, either have a larger consumer unit fitted by an electrician, or install a separate main switch and fuse unit, known as a switchfuse. This is screwed to the fuseboard near the consumer unit, on the meter side. The circuit is fed in through the entry hole and connected to the terminals marked 'load'. Next, two lengths of 16mm² single-core PVC-insulated cable, one red and one black, are run from switchfuse to meter; the connections to the meter *must* be made by the electricity board.

Most electricity boards are reluctant to connect more than one pair of leads to their meters and instead require a multi-way service connector box into which the various meter leads are connected and out of which the final cables to the meter are run.

The switchfuse unit must be properly earthed, via a length of 6mm² PVC-insulated earth cable run from its earth terminal to the earthing terminal of the whole installation.

Extending lighting circuits
As already explained, lighting circuits are wired as radial circuits, on either the loop-in or the junction-box principle. Extending them is relatively straightforward, with one limitation to prevent overloading. Since the total loading of a circuit with a 5-amp circuit fuse must not exceed 5 × 240 = 1200 Watts, you are allowed a maximum of 12 lighting points on each circuit (it does not matter if you always used 40-Watt bulbs; the regulations count all lighting points as a nominal 100 Watts). So you must first count up the number of lights (and other connections to the circuit, such as extractor fans and shaver units) on the circuit you want to extend to see if your quota has been used up.

A lighting circuit can be extended in two ways. In the first, the existing circuit is cut into at a convenient point and a junction box installed. Use a four-terminal box (below, left) and run two cables from it – one to the new fitting and the other to the new switch. Or use a three-terminal box (below, centre) and run one new cable to a loop-in ceiling rose at the new lighting position, connecting the switch cable to the rose instead. Which you choose will depend on the relative positions of the fitting and switch; one will use a lot less cable than the other.

With the three-terminal junction box, install a loop-in rose at the new lighting position and connect up its switch cable. Run the mains cable back to the junction box position, switch off at the mains to isolate the circuit and cut the existing cable. Connect up the three cable ends as shown in the photographs – all the live cores to one terminal, all the neutrals to the next and all the earths, properly sleeved, to the third. Fit the cover. Then add the pendant flex at the ceiling rose and connect the switch cable up to the new switch position to complete the job.

With the four-terminal junction box, the connections are a little more complicated. To terminal 1 go the red cores of the two mains cables, and the red core of the switch cable. To terminal 2 go the black cores of the two mains cables and the fitting cable. To terminal 3 connect the red core of the fitting cable and the black core of the switch cable; since this latter core is technically live, it should be so identified with a 'flag' of red tape or a blob of red paint. Note that only two cores go to this terminal. The four earth cores are connected up to terminal 4. The switch cable is run to the new switch position, the fitting cable to the new rose, where it is connected as shown in the bottom photograph.

The second method of extending a lighting circuit is simpler to describe, but can be used only where the existing system uses loop-in ceiling roses. Here a cable is simply connected up to the rose. Bear in mind that if there are only two cables present, the rose is the last one on the system. It is then run on to the new lighting position and connected to a new loop-in rose complete with its own switch cable.

Light switches
A light switch is perhaps the simplest electrical accessory to wire up if it controls one or more lights on a one-way system – in other words, if it is the only switch controlling those lights.

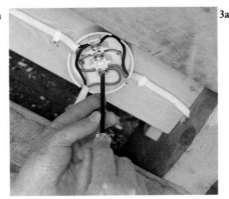

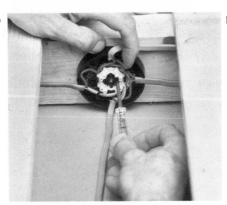

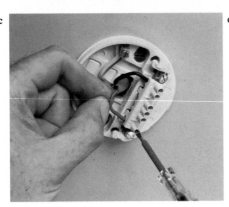

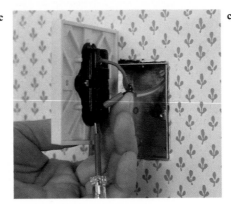

Above: Extending a circuit with a four-terminal junction box 1a Cut the existing cable and connect to the box. 1b Connect up cables to the new fitting and switch. 1c Connect the fitting cable to a new loop-in rose.

Above: Using a three-terminal box instead 2a Cut the existing cable and connect the cut ends and the spur cable to the box. 2b Connect the spur and switch cables to the new loop-in rose. 2c Connect up the cable at the switch.

Above: Converting a one-way switch for two-way switching 3a Disconnect the old switch. 3b Run three-core-and-earth cable to the new switch position, and fit a two-way switch there. 3c At the old position, connect up both cables.

From each light a single cable will run to the switch, which simply breaks the live connection. So, although the cable contains red and black cores, both are technically live and the black core should be marked with red tape. The earth core of the switch cable should be connected to the earth terminal of the mounting box. If there is more than one cable, red cores are connected to one switch terminal, black to the other.

Where two (or more) switches control the same light, as on a staircase with switches at the top and bottom for the landing light, the connections are more complex. Special switches with three terminals are needed, and also special cable with four cores – three-core-and-earth cable, with the three cores being insulated in red, yellow and blue sleeving (the earth is bare, as always). Each two-way switched circuit has one switch connected to the light via the standard two-core-and-earth cable; the second switch is connected to the first switch with the three-core-and-earth cable.

Converting an existing one-way switch to two-way operation is relatively straightforward. The existing switch is replaced by a two-way switch and the three-core-and-earth cable is simply run to the new switch position and connected (page 110, right).

Installing other light fittings

If you want to fit a light close to the ceiling in place of an existing pendant light, dismantle and remove the ceiling rose. The new fitting will probably have a base plate to which everything is fixed. Pull the circuit cables through the base plate and screw it firmly to the ceiling – either to a joist or to a batten nailed between two joists. Connect up the terminals of the fitting, following the manufacturer's instructions. If the fitting does not have terminals, but just a length of flex emerging from it, recess a round conduit box (see right) into the ceiling, screwing it to a batten nailed between the joists, and link the flex and circuit cable using small connector blocks. Mount the fitting over the box.

Dimmer switches

Installing a dimmer switch is quite straightforward, since it usually replaces an existing conventional light switch. But first you must be sure to select the correct type, by rating and by the number of gangs or individual controls it has. You can buy dimmers in 1-, 2-, 3-, and 4-gang versions independently. The 1- and 2-gang versions usually fit the box of a 1- or 2-gang light-switch; the larger versions require a double box. Ratings range from 258 Watts up to 500 Watts, but more im-

Project 4

Installing wall lights

Wall lights are installed over a mounting box – either a long narrow type known as an architrave box (lower pictures below), or a conduit box supplied with the fitting (as shown in the upper pictures). The cable to the fixing point is connected to the light flex by means of an insulated cable connector, as shown upper right. The actual cable connections vary according to the sort of switching you want.

If the wall lights replace an existing ceiling light that will no longer be wanted, a junction box is installed above the ceiling instead, linking the existing mains and switch cables and the new cable to the wall light position. But if you want wall lights as well as a ceiling light, you have two choices: to have them switched on at the same time as the ceiling light, or to have them switched independently. In the first case, simply run cable from the ceiling rose to the wall light position. In the second, the most convenient method is to replace the existing light switch with a two-gang switch that fits into the same box. One switch will control the ceiling light, the other the wall lights. To wire this up, trace the main lighting circuit above the ceiling, and fit a four-terminal junction box at a convenient position. Two cables will be the main cable at that point; the third goes to the wall light, the fourth to the new wall-light switch. The existing switch cable controlling the ceiling light is then connected to the other gang of the two-gang switch.

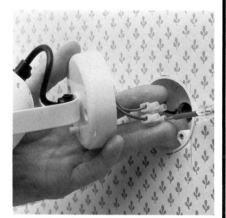

portantly there is usually a minimum rating, too: many dimmers will not work satisfactorily if the wattage of the light is below 50 Watts. So ask for advice from your dealer.

Repairing cord-operated switches

If the cord on a cord-operated switch breaks or needs replacing, the job is quite straightforward as long as the break is below the threaded connector at the top of the cord. All you have to do is unscrew it, remove the old cord and thread a new piece through the connector and the pull knob, knotting each end of the cord in order to retain it in the top and bottom fittings.

If it breaks at the top, between the connector and the switch, you will have to remove the switch cover. Do not disconnect the mains connections (but take care to make sure that the circuit is isolated); just undo the screws holding the switch block to the cover. Hold the block down as you do this, or the spring inside will shoot bits everywhere when you undo the screws. Now lift the switch block off carefully, and pull the knotted end of the cord away carefully from the nylon holder below it. Fit a new piece of cord and press the switch block back into place, checking the on/off action by pulling the cord. Replace the screws and re-fit the switch cover.

INTERNAL WALLS

Builders and architects classify your home as having two types of wall – external and internal. External walls are those that form the exterior shell of your home. Internal walls divide up the space inside the shell into a series of upstairs and downstairs, rooms.

The way the rooms are set out at present – either by the original builder or as a result of conversions carried out later by previous householders – may not suit you, and it is possible to rearrange them, although not always as a do-it-yourself project. This arrangement can consist of removing an existing internal wall, so that two rooms are turned into a single, larger one. Or you can erect a new internal wall, creating two smaller rooms from one large one. Internal walls are basically of two kinds:

load-bearing and non-load-bearing. The former are part of the house structure, actually helping to hold the building up. Non-load-bearing walls merely divide up space; they are also known as partition walls.

Removing a load-bearing wall is much more complicated than merely removing a partition, so if you are thinking of re-planning the interior of your home, you must first of all identify which of the internal walls are load-bearing. How can you do so? It is difficult for anybody other than an expert to be 100 per cent sure in every case, but there are several pointers.

An internal wall can be either solid (built of masonry – brick or insulating block) or it can be hollow, in which case it will consist of a timber framework with a cladding of some sort on both side. A hollow wall is most likely to be a partition, whereas a solid wall will usually be load-bearing, although this is not always the case. A good test is to see if a load-bearing wall is parallel, or at right angles, to the joists of the floor above. If it is at right angles it may well be helping to hold them up. If it is parallel it is probably offering no support. (Incidentally, you can easily tell the direction of the joists by looking at the floorboards. These are fixed at right angles to the joists below.)

Thus the wall between living and dining rooms in a typically small semi-detached house is probably supporting the joists of the floor above, for these usually run from the front to the back of the house. Similarly the wall beween front and back bedrooms is probably supporting the ceiling joists. However, a wall between front bedroom and box-room, which would be parallel to the joists in such a house, is likely to be non-load-bearing.

Similarly, the walls of a small, brick-built pantry off a kitchen may well be just partitions. However, in the last resort only an expert can decide.

How do you distinguish between a solid and a hollow wall? Tap the surface of the plaster with the knuckles: a solid wall will have a totally different 'feel' from a hollow one. Another way is to take a test boring with a drill and bit in an inconspicuous spot. In a solid wall the bit will meet resistance beyond the plaster, but will not do so in a hollow wall, unless by coincidence you strike part of the timber frame. Even then you will easily recognise the difference be-

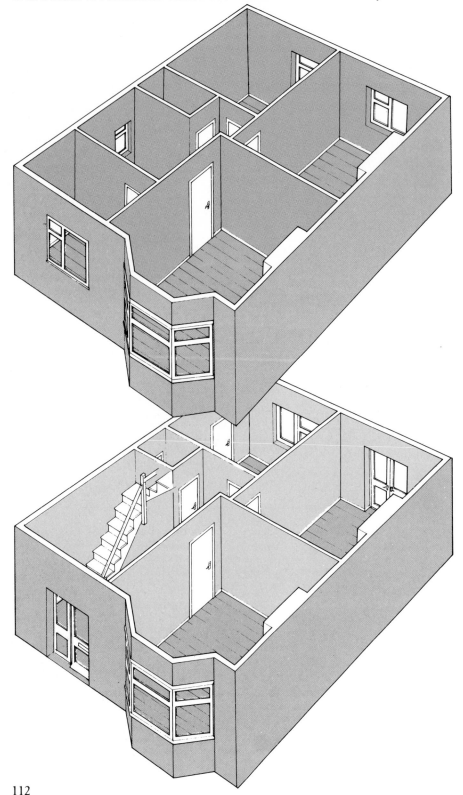

Left Internal walls split up the typical small house into a sometimes fussy arrangement of little rooms. You may be able to create a new spaciousness by removing one or more of these walls.

tween this and masonry. Examine the dust thrown out by the bit. Bright red dust will be from brick, black dust will be from some form of building block, sawdust will indicate timber.

Solid internal walls are built in exactly the same way as the external walls: brick is laid on brick (or building block on building block) and held in place with mortar. However, an internal wall will normally be much thinner than an exterior one. Moreover, whereas the external walls of a modern house are of cavity construction, consisting of two separate 'leaves' with a gap of 50mm (2in) or so between them to stop damp from passing into the house, this will hardly ever be true of internal walls.

At the heart of a hollow wall is a timber framework, the members of which are usually either 75 × 50mm (3 × 2in) or 50mm square. There will be horizontal members, called 'plates,' going the full length of the room at floor and ceiling level, and vertical ones, known as studs, at each end and spaced between the plates at intervals of anything from 400mm (16in) to 600mm (24in); between the studs are intermediate horizontal members (called noggings) about halfway up.

In older houses this framework is covered by lath and plaster. A series of thin, horizontal timbers (the laths) are nailed to the timber uprights act as a key for the plaster, which is skimmed on to them. A lath-and-plaster wall often has a springy feel when pressed. Modern hollow walls are most commonly clad with sheets of plasterboard, although in some cases such walls will have been built up from factory-made partitions.

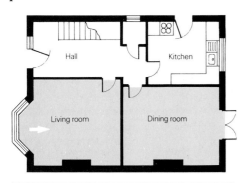

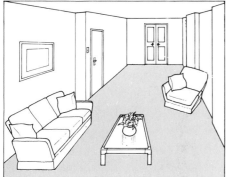

Re-arranging your home
One of the best ways of making a small home seen less cramped is to take down a dividing wall between two poky rooms and turn them into one large one. Anyone who has ever carried out such a conversion is amazed at the sense of spaciousness achieved. You appear to gain much more than the space previously occupied by the wall.

Most people planning to carry out such an alteration usually think in terms of removing the wall between the living and dining rooms in order to create a through lounge, but there are other possibilities; the walls between the hall and living room, for instance, and between the kitchen and dining room. Let us look at each in turn.

The wall between living room and dining room
This is a favourite dodge. Because you get the benefit of a window at each end, you can see both front and back gardens from one room, and you get an immediate sense of additional light and air. But not only that. Because you can dispense with the door into one or other of the rooms, you actually do gain considerable extra space.

You have to take care in the furnishing and decoration of your new through lounge, otherwise it will still look like two rooms turned into one. One way to avoid this pitfall is to take out and block off the old dining-room fireplace, and to fill the alcoves each side with bookshelves or similar built-in furniture to disguise the chimney breast. Or you can remove the chimney breast to create extra space. Another point is that, now that you are warming a much bigger area up to the comfort standards you expect in the living-room, your heating

Left The internal wall that is most often removed is that dividing the living room from the dining room, in this example to create a through lounge which has the advantage of receiving light from windows at both ends. *Right* An alternative scheme could combine the kitchen and dining room, which would not only increase the effective space available in the kitchen but would allow a much greater flexibility in planning the combined cooking and dining areas.

bills will undoubtedly rise, especially if, as is often the case, you have large, single-glazed french windows in what was once the dining-room. So double-glazed patio doors will become an important priority.

The wall between hall and living room
Your lounge will increase dramatically in actual size as well as looking more spacious if you adopt this scheme. And if you replace your present staircase with a modern open-tread one, the visual effect will be stunning. Since it is against the regulations for the door of a WC to open directly off a living-room, you cannot remove this wall if you have a downstairs cloakroom in the hall. Indeed, some local authorities would say that this type of conversion brings the lavatory door on the first floor landing into the living room. However, you can generally persuade them not to press that point too far.

There is a heating problem again, for your bills are certain to rise as you have to warm the hall, stairway, and landing up to living-room temperature. Moreover the fact that the front door opens directly into your living room will send a few draughts in. Good draughtproofing and a porch can go a long way to curing this problem, however. Another problem is the fact that if you have young children the noise from the TV set and audio equipment might be audible in their bedrooms.

The wall between kitchen and dining room
You may have seen in the glossy brochures kitchens large enough to have their own dining annexe. Well, you can

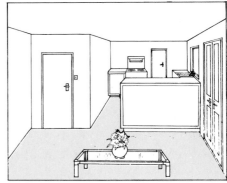

create such an annexe in your kitchen by removing the wall that divides it from the dining room. Such a reconstruction makes excellent use of a tiny kitchen and dining room (especially if the latter is a room you seldom use). For you can rearrange things as you wish, extending the kitchen into the former dining-room, or the dining section into the kitchen, according to the relative size of each. Moreover, if the diner has french windows or patio doors, that give on to the garden, these can take over as the 'back door' from the kitchen to the outside. The former door can be bricked up, giving you more usable kitchen space.

It is a fact that some of us, while more than happy to breakfast in the kitchen, do not like to take more formal meals there, especially when we are entertaining guests to lunch or dinner. But a servery between the two sections will make the dining area less utilitarian, and you could always fit a blind to the ceiling above the servery and lower this when you have guests.

The wall between front bedroom and boxroom
Boxrooms often give the impression of being mere space-fillers rather than deliberately planned areas of the house. In this scheme, removing the intervening wall adds interest to the shape of the resultant room, and it creates space for additional wardrobes and other storage units or allows division of the room into sleeping and dressing areas.

The wall between bathroom and WC
Although a separate WC has advantages, removing this wall may be the only way of making enough extra space to permit the installation of, say, a shower unit independent of the bath.

The building regulations
You cannot remove an internal wall in your home without first getting approval under the Building Regulations. You must submit 'before' and 'after' plans to your local authority – your builder or a local drawing office should be able to help you with this – and the council's Building Control Officer will visit your home to make sure, stage by stage, that the work is being carried out properly.

His main concern will be to satisfy himself that what you are doing will not interfere with the structure of your building. But there are other points. For instance, the Building Regulations lay down stringent rules about, among other things, the size of windows, ventilation, and ceiling height a room must have. The local authority will want to satisfy itself that the room still complies with these rules after your plans have been carried out. Provided that both sides of the wall were used for living in previously, there should be no trouble. You might encounter problems if you would be bringing what was, say, a windowless store area with a low ceiling into the living room.

Below left Bring the WC into the bathroom, and you may make enough extra space to fit additional facilities, such as a shower cubicle or a bidet. Below right If you remove the wall between a somewhat cramped bedroom and a boxroom you will have space for more furniture or, say, a fitted wardrobe.

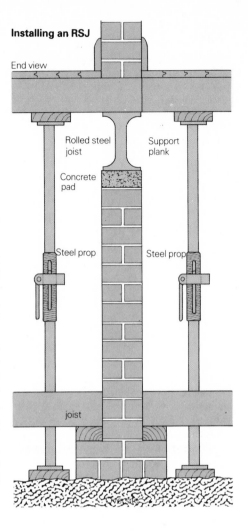

Installing an RSJ

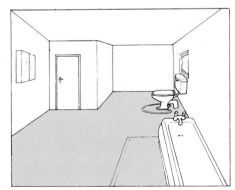

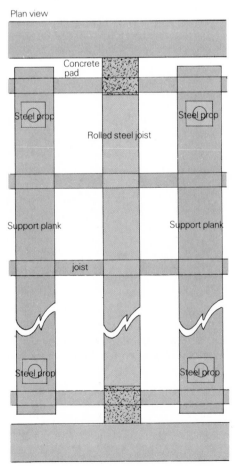

114

Knocking down a load-bearing wall

This is definitely not a task for any but the very experienced do-it-yourselfer, both because the work is so heavy and, unless you know what you are doing, you can cause serious damage to your home. It is also a job that will create a lot of dust and dirt in the house. However, let us detail what is involved to help you to take an interest in the work and, perhaps more important, so that, if you find a co-operative builder, you can tackle the less-skilled parts of the job yourself and lower the bill accordingly.

Taking down a structural wall involves removing one of the vital props of your home, so something else must be put in its place to do the job instead, usually a rolled-steel joist (RSJ). This is a length of I-section steel that spans the whole width of the room and usually rests at each end on a short length of wall left in place during the demolition or on a specially built pier. Only an expert can decide if such an arrangement is strong enough, and only an expert can work out the size of the RSJ required (see drawings at left).

The house will need support while the work is being carried out and this is normally provided by adjustable steel props. A plank of 150 × 50mm (6 × 2in) timber is laid across the room on the floor and at ceiling level on each side of and parallel with the wall and about 600mm (2ft) away from it. A series of the props is braced between the planks.

Mark on both sides of the wall in chalk the size of the RSJ and the shape of the opening to be cut out. With a bolster chisel and a club hammer, make a neat cut along the lines on both sides of the wall. Next, using the chisel and hammer, hack off the plaster over the entire area on both sides, until the brickwork is exposed.

Start to remove the brickwork. Choose a brick near the middle, chop out the mortar around it, and remove it. Once you have taken the first brick away, the others should come quite easily. On top of the brickwork that has been cut out to form a housing for the RSJ a concrete pad has to be formed to make a bearing for the joist. Levering the RSJ into position on the pads is one of the trickiest and most laborious parts of the job.

The support props are left in position for a few days to let the concrete pads harden. When they have been removed, the task of making good can start. The RSJ is hidden by plasterboard fixed to a timber framework nailed to wedges hammered between the flanges of the RSJ. The exposed edges of the piers of the wall must be covered, too.

Removing a load-bearing wall 1 Take out the first bricks, from top centre of the wall. 2 Instal temporary supports for the ceiling. 3 Always wear a safety helmet for work in such a confined space. 4 The RSJ is supported until the concrete pads are installed on top of the brick piers at each side of the room. 5 A piece of timber frame is nailed to a wedge hammered into the flange of the RSJ, which will then be enclosed within a box made of plasterboard nailed to the frame.

Taking down a partition

Taking down a partition wall is a much easier business, although here, too, you will create a certain amount of dust and mess. But since the wall is not supporting a floor above, there is no need to insert any compensating structure, such as an RSJ.

Begin by taking off the outer covering. If you are working on lath and plaster, the best tool to use for this is a hefty claw hammer. Force the claw through the plaster covering, and use it to wrench away the laths, which are nailed to the timber studs. As the laths come away, they will bring the plaster with them. When all the plaster and laths have been removed only the timber framework will remain. If the framework has been screwed in place, merely withdraw the screws and remove the pieces. It is more likely, however, that the members will have been fixed with nails, and you must prise them away, using an old chisel or a stout screwdriver, perhaps in conjunction with a claw hammer.

Removing plasterboard is an easier, less messy job. The sheets of board are nailed to the timber framework, and can merely be prised away. Remove the studs and other framework as for those of a lath and plaster wall.

Building a Partition

If you want to divide a large room into two smaller ones, it is a relatively easy job to do by means of a simple wall of plasterboard fixed to a timber framework. Remember, though, that such a wall is merely a partition; it is not designed to be load-bearing.

Working with plasterboard Plasterboard comes in sheets 12.5mm (½in) or 9.5mm (⅜in) thick. The former are more expensive but need fewer supports in the framework, and so may well be cheaper in the long run. It is worth while doing a few sums to make sure. The sheets of board are 1200mm (about 4ft) wide, and 1800mm (6ft) or 2400mm (8ft) long. Larger ones are available to special order. The length of board you choose will be determined by the height of your room. The best type of board to use has an ivory-coloured surface and tapered edges to help in disguising the joins once the boards have been fixed.

Few tools are needed to work with plasterboard. The board is cut ivory side up, with a fine-toothed saw. Short lengths can be cut off if you score the ivory side deeply with a sharp knife, then snap off the waste over a straight-edge, cutting through the lining on the backing with the knife.

If it is necessary to cut a hole in the middle of a sheet – to take light switches or electric socket outlets, for example – do so by first marking the outline on the board then drill a row of starter holes and cut out the shape with a keyhole saw. Cut edges should be sanded lightly to remove paper burrs before the material is fixed in place.

The board is fixed to the timber with special galvanised nails, for which you will need a hammer. You will also need a ruler and a pencil for marking. A few additional items are required for constructing the framework: screwdriver, drill for drilling pilot holes for the screws, plus a spirit level and plumb line and bob to make sure the frame is truly vertical. A footlifter, a piece of triangular-section timber which you can make yourself from a piece of 250 × 50mm sawn softwood, is useful while you fix the sheets. There are also special jointing tools required for hiding the gaps between the sheets.

Technique

Removing a fireplace

Taking out an old fireplace presents no problems, although it is rather a muscular job. The fire surround itself is held to the wall by means of screws driven through small lugs fixed to the side of the surround. The lugs are hidden under the plaster and must be exposed. Using an old chisel or screwdriver and a hammer, chip away a band of plaster, about 25mm (1in) wide around the surround to reveal the lugs - there will be one or two on each side. Withdraw the screws and lift clear the surround. Be careful! The surround will be very heavy and you will almost certainly need a helper for this.

The fireplace hearth, known to the builder as a superimposed hearth, sits on a constructional hearth, which is a slab of concrete set into the floor and projecting from the chimney breast. The superimposed hearth is cemented to the constructional hearth; in order to lift it clear, the bond must be broken. Chip all round the hearth with a hammer and cold chisel, then wedge a garden spade

between the two hearths at the front. Press on the handle and lever the superimposed hearth clear of the constructional hearth.

If you propose to remove just the fireplace and leave the chimney breast in position, you have to disguise the fire opening. The usual way is to brick it up and make good with plaster. An easier way for the do-it-yourselfer is by means of a sheet of plasterboard, using an adaptation of the methods explained in the Building a Partition section that follows.

Remember, though, that although you have got rid of the fireplace, there is still a flue behind it, put there to carry smoke and other combustion gases safely up the chimney. This will need ventilation if you are to keep it clear of damp, which would appear on the walls higher up the house. The usual method is to fit a small metal grille into whatever you use to cover the old fireplace opening.

Taking out a fireplace will reveal the concrete of the constructional hearth, but this can be hidden below the new floorcovering.

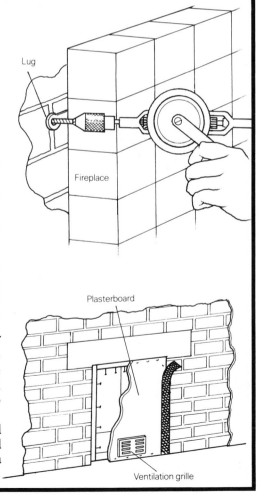

Lug

Fireplace

Plasterboard

Ventilation grille

Planning the wall A plasterboard partition should be built on a framework of 75 × 50mm (3 × 2in) timber. If there is to be a proper habitable room on each side of the wall, both sides of the framework should be clad with plasterboard. But where the wall is being built merely to form, say, a store room, you need to fix board only to the living-room side of the partition. Should a high degree of sound insulation be required, fix two sheets of 12.5mm (½in) thick board, their joints staggered, to each side of the timber framework.

Will there be a door in your wall? If so, it is better to buy a standard-sized, ready-made one, rather than try to make one yourself. Flush doors suit a modern house and are readily available; panelled doors, in the style of those common in older houses, can also be bought. Make sure that the door frame, especially the architrave, matches those elsewhere in the house.

Work out in advance the position on the partition of any heavy objects, such as washbasins in a bathroom or cupboards in a kitchen. Extra noggings (horizontal timbers) may be needed to receive the fixing screws.

The framework of the partition must be fixed at the top to the joists of the ceiling above, so when deciding on its precise location make sure that there are joists in the correct position to receive the fixing screws. Where the partition is at right angles to the joists, there will be no problem; but if the partition is parallel to the joists, your chosen position for it might well be between two joists. In such instances it is best, where possible, to alter the position of the partition so that it is directly under a joist, otherwise you will have to fit noggings between the joists to receive the fixing screws. Fitting noggings might not be very difficult for a top-storey room, where you can get at the attic above; but it will cause a great deal of disruption if there is a floor above, and the floorboards have to be removed.

How can you pinpoint the positions of the joists? In a top-floor room, simply poke your head through the loft opening and you will see them. If there is a room above, look at the fixing nails of the floorboards, for these are driven into the joists. Should the boards be covered, tap the ceiling in the room below with your knuckles – there will be a solid 'feel' when you touch a joist; a hollow sound when you tap the plaster in between. Alternatively, make test borings with a drill; the holes can be filled and covered during the redecoration of the room that will be necessary once the partition has been built.

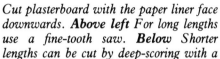

*Cut plasterboard with the paper liner face downwards. **Above left** For long lengths use a fine-tooth saw. **Below** Shorter lengths can be cut by deep-scoring with a sharp knife, then snapping the waste off. **Above right** Holes can be cut out with a padsaw (or keyhole saw) after a starting-hole has been drilled.*

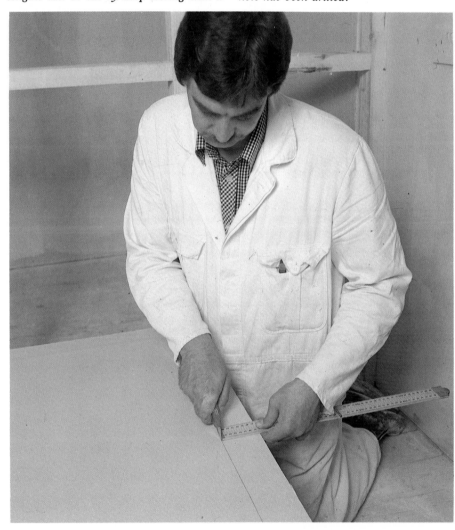

Constructing the framework Begin by marking on the floor the exact position of the wall, indicating where the door, if there is to be one, will go. Along the centre line of the partition fix to the floor the first piece of the framework – a continuous length of timber, broken only for a door opening. This timber, known as the sole plate, should be screwed or nailed at 600mm (24in) centres. The plate can be fixed directly into the floorboards or, for a stronger structure, into the joists below.

Immediately above the sole plate – use a plumb line, or a spirit level and a straight piece of timber, to ensure the accuracy of your positioning – fix a length of timber to the ceiling by means of screws driven through it and the plaster, and into the joists above. This ceiling plate should be a continuous length. Only in the rare cases of a very

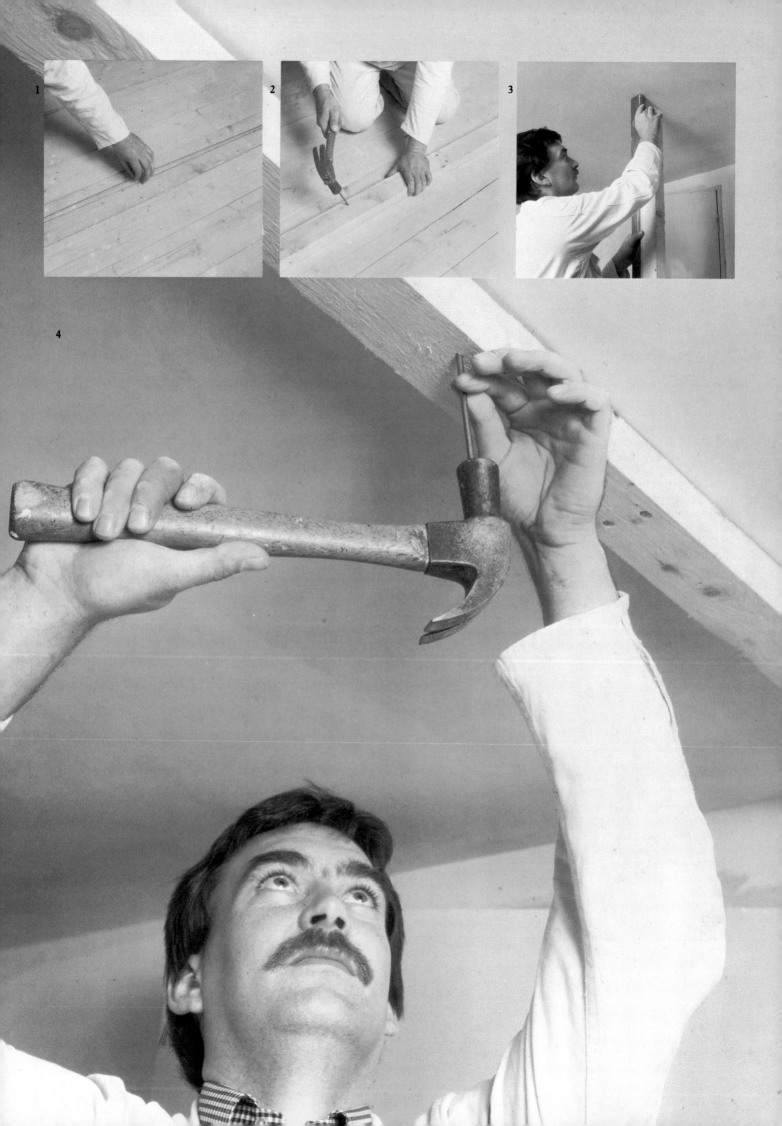

Left: Building a non-load-bearing partition with plasterboard panels Begin by erecting the timber framework, to which the panels will be nailed. *1 Mark the position of the sole plate on the floor by snapping a taut chalked string. 2 Nail or screw the sole plate to the floor. 3 Locate the head plate exactly above the sole plate by using a plumb line or (as here) a straight-edged piece of timber and spirit level. 4 Nail or screw the head plate into place with fixings long enough to pass through the ceiling plaster into the joists.*

low ceiling or exceptionally tall door, where the door is as high as the wall, should it need to be broken.

Vertical studs can now be fixed between the two plates. They are required at 400mm (16in) centres for 9.5mm (³⁄₈in) thick board, or 600mm (24in) centres for 12.5mm (½in) thick board. In addition, they will be needed each side of any opening.

The studs must be truly vertical – use a spirit level or plumb line to ensure this. They are fixed by skew-nailing: a nail is driven through the side of the stud at an angle so that it emerges through the end of the timber and passes into the plate above or below. Halfway up the studs, horizontal noggings should be fixed, as should any noggings required to provide support for fixtures. Once again, use skew-nailing.

Fixing the boards The boards are fixed with galvanised plasterboard nails at 150mm (6in) centres, and 12.5mm (½in) from the edge of the board. They are driven in until the head dimples the surface of the board, but not so far that the paper liner is fractured.

Cut the board 25mm (1in) less than the height of the partition and hold it firmly against the ceiling whilst nailing. An efficient way of holding it in place is with a footlifter (picture 7), which you can make from a triangular piece of wood.

Hiding the joins The joins between the boards are hidden by a method that involves the use of a joint filler, joint finish, and joint tape. Three special tools are needed – a 200mm (8in) wide jointing applicator; a 50mm (2in) wide taping knife, and a jointing sponge. All the tools and materials can be bought from the merchant who supplies you with the plasterboard.

Because the boards are taper-edged, a shallow depression is formed where two boards meet, and this is filled by a band of joint filler. A length of the tape is bedded into this band, using the taping knife, and immediately another band of filler is applied to fill the taper, so it is level with the surrounding boards.

Completing the partition *1 Measure the height of the ceiling with two overlapping battens at every point where you will need to erect vertical studs. 2 Instal the studs by skew-nailing. 3 Skew-nail the horizontal noggings. 4 Or position them at different heights and end-nail them. 5 Instal an extra stud over door-opening. 6 Add noggings to support screws of built-in wall fittings. 7 Position panels with the footlifter. The nails should be at least 12.5mm (½in) from the edge of the panels. 8 Trim the waste from the panel after you have nailed it to the frame.*

When the filler has set, a thin layer of joint finish is applied and the edges are feathered with the damp sponge – working in light, circular strokes.

After the first coat of joint finish has dried, another is applied in a broad band and feathered.

Finally, even up the difference in surface between the board and the join by distributing a thin slurry of joint finish over the whole wall. Full instructions on how to use the tools and materials are given with the pack.

When a professional treats plasterboard in this way, it is impossible to detect where the joins are; with a little practice the do-it-yourselfer can produce an attractive finish.

The join between wall and ceiling can be concealed with plasterboard coving, cut to length and glued in place.

A skirting board will need to be fitted, to cover the gap between the wall and the floor; this can be bought from a timber merchant, and is nailed to the studs. Finally, the door frame is nailed, or screwed, to the studs.

Wall & Ceiling Fixings

Disguising the panel joints 1 Fill the tapering edges of each plasterboard panel with joint filler. 2 Bed in joint tape. 3 Cover the tape with more filler. 4 When the filler sets, apply joint finish. 5 Feather the edges of the finish with a jointing sponge. 6 Add a final coat of joint finish. To complete the work, fill in nail holes, coat the wall with a slurry of thinned joint finish, seal the surface with a special primer, then paint or paper as required after fitting a skirting board.

All walls appear to be 'solid' to the person faced with the problem of fixing shelf brackets or other items to them with nails or screws, but it is essential to establish just how 'solid' the inside leaf is. If it is brick or stone it will not be possible simply to hammer ordinary nails into it, as you can with early forms of insulating block – known as breezeblock, which has the texture of ground coke particles held together. You can tell if you have these walls if the dust that comes out when you drill it is dense black or dark grey.

When you want to use screws, or when you have to because your wall is not soft enough to take nails, you have to drill holes first, so that you can put little plugs in them of material that will hold screws – wood, fibre or plastic. Plastic is generally the most satisfactory in brick, stone and concrete, provided you can get clean, accurate holes to fit the specially moulded plugs. Drills for masonry have very hard tungsten carbide tips brazed on to steel shanks. They become very hot if used blunt, or in deep holes choked with drilling dust, or if used with too high a drill speed, so if your drill has a lower speed, use it and withdraw it from the hole about every 12.5mm (½in) with the drill still running, to clear out the debris. Use hammer action if your drill has it for hard walls. It isn't necessary on breezeblock or other insulating blocks.

Several manufacturers now market plastic wall plugs that will accept any screw size from No.6 to No.12. This means that you can stock a single plug size, one masonry drill – usually a No.12 or No. 14 – and know that you can cope with most fixings in solid walls. The two materials that might cause problems when fixing screws are breezeblock and concrete. The former contains large, irregular particles which cause the drill to wander making unstraight, oversize and off-centre holes. To solve the problem, drill a very much larger hole than you need – say 12.5mm (½in) or even 16mm (⅝in) – push in a length of dowel, and screw into this. If even that should prove a less than tight fit, cement the dowel into the hole with, a plaster filler; when this has set, insert the screw.

Concrete is much tougher than insulating blocks and requires hammer action when drilling, but you might encounter a steel reinforcement rod near the surface of the wall. If this happens, the only solution is to find another place to bore the hole. Sometimes it is necessary to stick wide battens on to concrete walls with contact adhesive before screws can be used.

Most walls have a surface layer of mortar and plaster, which is too weak to hold much more more than a picture hook. Holes for plugs, therefore, must be at least 38mm (1½in) deep, to penetrate a good 25mm (1in) into the solid part of the wall and give a good grip; screws should be long enough to penetrate equally deeply. For a heavy-duty fitting, such as a shelf bracket to support a bookshelf, aim to have 50mm (2in) of screw thread plugged into the brick or stone. If the plug is a short one, engage one or two screw threads in it and use the screw as a punch, lightly tapping the plug down into the solid part of the wall before you begin to use the screwdriver.

Alternative fixings to ordinary nails and screws are hardened-steel masonry pins, which can be tapped into quite hard walls. The fixings made with these should be permanent, since you would have to lever them away if removal was necessary instead of just unscrewing. Multiple, light, firm taps give better results with masonry pins than heavy hammer blows. For heavy-load items such as pivoting support brackets, it is better to use expanding bolts than screws. These have a soft iron plug around the bolt stem. When the bolt is tightened in the hole, the plug is forced against the sides, forming a tight fit.

Hollow wall panels and ceilings need special fixings, of which there are two main types. One is a toggle fastener, which is a bolt with a type of nut consisting of two broad, hinged wings, which fold down on its shank. Unscrew the hinged nut and thread the bolt through the item to be fixed; screw the nut back on again a few turns and push it with wings folded through the hole until the wings open in the cavity. As the bolt is tightened, the wings spread themselves on each side of the hole. Once a toggle fastener is tightened, it cannot be retrieved. These fasteners are very strong, as they spread the load over a wide area. Bigger ones will even support quite large central heating radiators on wall panels.

For lighter jobs, several kinds of simple plastic screw-anchor are available. Some work like small umbrellas, springing out at the base as you push them through a hole on the end of an ordinary woodscrew. Others resemble masonry plugs, but have scientifically arranged splits that collapse as you tighten the woodscrew, forming a mushroom-shaped nut on the blind side of the panel. There are also metal versions of these fasteners, with bolts instead of screws. When these are compressed by tightening the bolt, they form a permanent screw-socket. The bolts can be removed and replaced as often as you like.

An alternative way to fix to hollow

Typical Wall Fixings

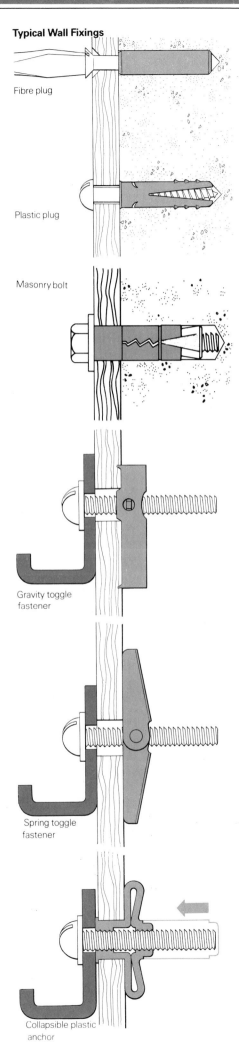

Fibre plug

Plastic plug

Masonry bolt

Gravity toggle fastener

Spring toggle fastener

Collapsible plastic anchor

walls is to screw into the timber supporting framework behind the cladding, although the location of these studs may differ from the position you had intended to hang the item.

Adhesives

Whilst modern adhesives can perform miracles in some situations, you should be cautious about using them instead of nails or screws, because the strength of the bond depends more often than not on the adhesion of a layer of paint to the plaster. If you can use adhesive over a broad expanse of wall, however, it is unlikely to let you down. Always degrease the surface to which you are applying adhesive, with white spirit or meths or a strong detergent solution. Don't forget to rinse and dry the surface if you use detergent. Neoprene-based adhesives are available which can be squeezed from a tube or gun to fix thin wall panels. They will take up minor irregularities in the wall surface, up to about 6mm (¼in), but if it is badly out of true you may have to make a batten frame to mount the panels on.

Tap-in screws
If you have a large number of screws to plug into masonry, it may save a lot of time and trouble to use tap-in screw/plug systems. Having made the necessary hole in the wall, simply put screw and plug into it and hammer home.

Lubricate wall plugs
Especially on tight-fit wall plugs, it makes for much easier screwing in if you put a little soap, light grease, or silicone lubricant (such as that used for plastic waste fittings) on the screw end.

Caulking loose plugs
You often get oversize holes in masonry, despite the utmost care. If the degree of looseness is slight, you can cure the problem by inserting spills or used matchsticks to take up the slack.

Look for the joists
When fixing things to ceilings, always discover where the joists are, so that you know where you can put woodscrews straight in without toggles or other hollow-panel devices. If it is not obvious where they are (paler strips on the paintwork or different notes in response to knocking are tell-tale signs), drill a series of tiny holes until you meet resistance.

CARPENTRY

'Green' timber, straight from a newly-felled tree, would be wet, sticky, and difficult to work with, so before it is of any use around the house it must be dried out. There are two reasons for this. The first is that cut timber may stain or rot if its moisture content remains above 20 per cent over a long period; the second reason is that wet timber tends to shrink and warp in the dry conditions of a modern home.

Wood used to be 'seasoned' by stacking if for long periods – sometimes years – in open-sided sheds. Houses were moister in the days before central heating became common, so wood was considered dry when its moisture content was down to 16%. By the time it

was made into furniture, window and door frames, and so on, it would contain about 12% of moisture, as did the air in the house. Central heating may reduce the moisture in the air to about 9 per cent, so wood now needs to be drier before it can be used. Partly for this reason, and partly because no merchant can now afford to keep wood for years before selling it, drying is nowadays carried out in kilns using carefully controlled proportions of hot air and steam.

Hard and soft woods

Hardwood comes from broad-leaved trees such as oak, softwood from cone-bearing trees, such as pine, larch, and spruce. The definitions 'hard' or 'soft' do not always give a reliable indication of the wood's physical and working characteristics; some hardwoods are quite soft and easy to work, and some softwoods are extremely tough and difficult. Balsa, for example, is technically a hardwood and pitch pine a softwood, although their properties suggest the opposite. In general, however, hardwoods are denser, closer textured, tougher surfaced and – size for size – stronger than softwoods. Most take longer to grow to maturity, so tend to be more expensive. But softwoods are by no means to be despised. They are used extensively in house construction, not only because they are economical in

cost, but also because they have a high strength-to-weight ratio and are easier to cut, drill and shape than hardwoods.

Nominal and actual sizes

The nominal size of a timber section is how it is straight from the saw. If, as is more likely, you are buying your wood PAR (planed all round), its actual measurements will be about 3 to 4mm less. A batten nominally 50 × 25mm (2 × 1in), therefore, will be planed to approximately 46 × 21mm (1⅞ × ⅞in). Unless you are buying very rare hardwoods, which are sometimes sold by weight, natural timber is nowadays sold in Britain by the metric unit, sometimes confusingly called the 'metric foot',

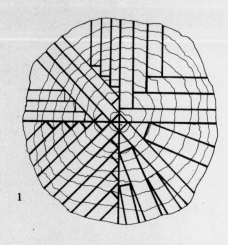

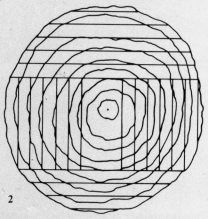

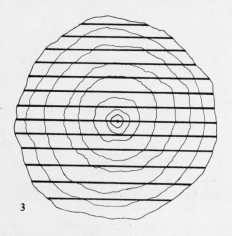

Maximum distances recommended between shelf supports

Material	Boards supported each end	Ends unsupported
13mm chipboard	400mm	450mm
16mm chipboard	500mm	600mm
19mm chipboard	800mm	900mm
17mm veneered chipboard	700mm	800mm
19mm veneered chipboard	950mm	1 m
13mm plywood	500mm	900mm
16mm plywood or blockboard	950mm	1 m
19mm plywood or blockboard	1300mm	1800mm

Intervals between supports may be increased by as much as 50% if a shelf is supported continuously under the back edge – by a batten screwed firmly to an alcove wall, for example.

which is a length of 300mm (just over 11¾ inches).

Price varies according to the basic quality of the timber, the area of the section, the finish – sawn or PAR – and the amount of moulding, rebating, or grooving there may be. If you buy a little more than you will need, you can use the spare wood for making trial cuts, matching reinforcement blocks, and many other purposes.

Commonly available types of wood
Pine/deal/redwood is by far the commonest timber on sale in Britain. The better grades have few knots, straight grain and fairly close annual rings. This is the only wood stocked by many DIY shops. Builders' merchants may have meranti, a coarse mahogany, and cedar; but for oak, teak, African or Brazilian mahoganies, and other hardwoods, you may have to go to a specialist.

Above: Typical manufactured boards 1 Perforated hardboard; 2 Pegboard; 3 Melamine-faced hardboard; 4 Hardboard; 5 Melamine-faced chipboard; 6 Veneered chipboard; 7 Chipboard; 8 Veneered plywood; 9 West African blockboard, hardwood-cored and faced; 10 Birch-faced Finnish blockboard, softwood cored; 11 Veneered blockboard; 12 Slab-sawn softwood board. Opposite page, below: Sawing patterns 1 Quarter-sawn to show ray markings in hardwood; planks will not warp; 2 Boxed-heart method, gives attractive ring-marks on pine; 3 Slab, or through-and-through, sawing – only centre planks resist cupping.

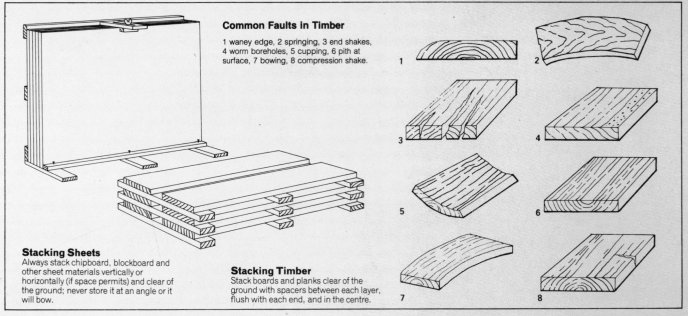

Common Faults in Timber

1 waney edge, 2 springing, 3 end shakes, 4 worm boreholes, 5 cupping, 6 pith at surface, 7 bowing, 8 compression shake.

Stacking Sheets
Always stack chipboard, blockboard and other sheet materials vertically or horizontally (if space permits) and clear of the ground; never store it at an angle or it will bow.

Stacking Timber
Stack boards and planks clear of the ground with spacers between each layer, flush with each end, and in the centre.

Tools & Techniques 1

The closer a joint fits together, the stronger it is and the better it looks. Most joint-marking and cutting operations use the faces, edges and ends of their components as a starting base, so the squarer and straighter these are, the more likely you are to get an accurate fit. This is where the bench plane can help. It is used two-handed (the wood is supported on a bench) and it has a big cutter, anything from 38 to 75mm (1½ to 3in) wide, ideal for flattening broad surfaces.

Standard bench planes have double cutters (blades or irons), the lower one in tool steel, which has to be sharpened frequently, and the top one in mild (unhardenable) steel, which rarely needs attention as its main job is to curl and break the shaving at an acute angle.

Block plane

This is a small, one-handed plane for lighter jobs. The cutter is single, sharpened in the same way as a chisel or bench-plane lower blade (see page 125), but must be fixed in the plane bevel uppermost to produce a cap-iron action.

Shooting board

All bench and block planes can be used in shooting boards, which are thick baseboards rebated to make a shallow guide for the plane to slide along on its side. At the front end, the vertical cutter passes very close to a cross-bar at right angles to the rebate side and plane sole, so that wood placed against the bar is planed square. The board is used mainly when planing end-grain. To make your board, see page 145.

Duplex rebate plane

Particularly simple to use is the duplex rebate plane, so called because the cutter has an alternative mounting position at the front for working into rebates closed at one end. A little of the closed end is chopped out with a chisel to give the short nose of the plane room to work. The duplex has depth and side stops, both adjustable, for pre-setting the required rebate size, and also features spur cutters that can be lowered at either side of the body for cutting across grain to make lap joints.

Plough plane

The plough plane has a very thin sole – like a skid – which takes a narrow cutter able to produce long, straight grooves in the centre of the wood. Some models can also be used to make rebates and mouldings. It has depth and width stops and cross-grain spurs, like the duplex. The cutter is usually honed at 35°, to give a strong edge.

Router plane
What this clever plane does is to surface the bottoms of housings and slots absolutely evenly and parallel with the top surface. The base is a flat plate with one or two holes or gaps in it for the cutter to poke through. These are shaped rather like a riding boot. The leg clamps to a short pillar on the base, and the foot – which may be square or pointed – cuts only at its toe, so that it works rather like a sharp shovel.

Hammers
There is probably no other tool made in such a wide range of types as the hammer, so there is no excuse for not using the right one for the job: for 150mm (6in) nails, a 680g (24oz) claw hammer; for 100mm (4in) nails, a 454g (16oz) claw hammer. Use a Warrington hammer of a weight you feel comfortable with for nails up to 75mm (3in), and a Warrington pin hammer of about 100g (3½oz) for pins and tacks.

Below: Woodworking tools and equipment 1 Woodworking and impact adhesives; 2 Combination/plough plane; 3 Duplex rabbet plane; 4 Jointer plane; 5 Block plane; 6 Bar cramp; 7 G-cramps, edging cramp; 8 Cramp heads for DIY wooden bar; 9 Beech mallet; 10 Warrington (cross-pein) hammer; 11 Steel-shafted claw hammer; 12 Nail punches; 13 Twist bits ('jobber' drills); 14 Spade bits for power wood-boring; 15 Auger bits for

Screwdrivers
You may have to file a tip occasionally to get a good fit. Ideally, a tip should not quite reach the bottom of a screwhead slot, but should grip on the top edges, and it should never be wider than the screw head. A good all-round cross-point driver to have would be a No. 2 Supadriv, but remember you need a No. 1 for screws smaller than No. 6 and a No. 3 for Nos. 12 and 14. There are both slotted and cross-point bits to fit braces, which take much hard work out of screwdriving. Another type of driver is the spiral ratchet, which is easy to work because you push instead of twist; it can be locked to allow normal driving, with or without left- or right-hand ratchet action. It will also bore small holes with a special drill kit.

Braces
A bit outdated for short-hole work, braces are still useful for boring deep ones. Dowel-hole boring should be

hand brace; 16 Firmer bevel-edge chisels (can be struck with hammer or mallet); 17 Mortise chisels (thick, strong blades, leather washer, and long handle; 18 Ratchet brace; 19 Enclosed-gear hand drill; 20 Spiral-ratchet screwdriver with detachable bits; Supadriv cross-point bit in chuck; 21 Engineer's hexagon-handle screwdriver; 22 Hand-ratchet screwdriver; 23 Cabinet-handled screwdriver.

Technique
Sharpening chisels
Firmer, bevel-edge, and mortise chisels depend on sharp cutting edges. They are honed on an abrasive block lubricated with mineral oil. With its angled end facing downwards, hold the chisel at an angle of 30° to the stone and move it to and fro to produce a clean bevel. You can buy a honing guide (top picture) to keep the chisel at the correct angle. When a fine burr has formed along the entire blade, turn the chisel over, lay it flat on the block (centre picture), and draw it back towards you several times until the burr has disappeared. When regrinding to get rid of nicks, the blade is held at the correct angle by a tool rest (bottom picture); the grindstone revolves *towards* the cutting edge.

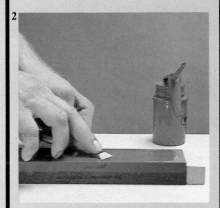

done with special dowel bits, which are much nearer their stated diameter than normal auger bits. Countersink bits are available for braces, as are dowel sharpeners. Apart from the usual U-shaped braces, you can get joist braces, which are T-shaped for getting into tight spaces and corners.

Adhesives

'Miracle' quick-setting, stick-anything adhesives are not the most suitable for general woodwork, whatever their merits in other areas. Neither are contact adhesives, except for sticking laminates to boards, as they retain a lot of flexibility when set. Modern resin-based adhesives come in three main types for wood. Two-part adhesives allow the longest working or 'open' time between application and cramping because the resin is put on one part of the joint and the hardener on the other, and neither sticks nor sets until they are put together. Two-part products are normally waterproof, but there are waterproof ones in single-mix form – usually a powder to mix with water. Open-time with these at room temperatures is about 20 minutes; the surplus leaves no stains when it is chiselled off. Perhaps the most useful for DIY work is the cold PVA (polyvinyl acetate) type, sold as a ready-mixed, thick white cream. You have only about 10 minutes to get everything cramped up after putting the first dab on, but you need to apply it to only one half of the joint and it sets quite firm in about two hours. Surplus squeezed out can stain some woods a little, so wipe it off with a damp rag before it sets.

Cramps

A G-cramp has a G-shaped frame and screw-threaded 'tail' and is used as an extra hand for holding a work-piece steady. Normal capacities are 75, 100, and 135mm (3, 4, and 6in). Edging cramps have a second screw in the centre to press edgeways on to a board. Bar cramps, for longer work, have one fixed, screw-adjusting jaw and one that will slide along the bar to locate in one of a number of holes along it, according to the length of the article being cramped. These are usually used in pairs for even pressure on frame assemblies. Picture frames have their own special type – mitre-corner cramps. Some are of steel and some of plastic; but they all employ the same mechanical principle – four L-shaped corner pieces drawn together by a connecting draw-cord or wire.

Irregular shapes can be cramped with web-clamps – long nylon or other straps looped into a ratchet mechanism.

Tools & Techniques 2

Rule

Even if you are only putting up a loose shelf, or fitting a wooden door-stop, you have to determine how much room there is for your finished product and then cut down larger pieces of wood to the required dimensions. Traditionally, carpenters have done all this with a stiff, folding rule, but there are many advantages in using a retractable tape rule, with an end-hook that slides to compensate for its own thickness and a locking mechanism.

Straightedge, square, and bevel

A straightedge is a flat strip of steel, bevelled on one edge, which is ground accurately straight. Good ones are constructed of hardened steel so that knives do not wear them out of true. The 600mm (2ft) size is an adequate length for most jobs, as you cannot make a cut much longer than that without stopping to shift your grip on the tool. Cuts longer than 600mm (2ft) can be made after you have joined up marks that are under the length of the rule apart.

A carpenter's square is an L-shaped straightedge available in various sizes, usually square-edged and graduated.

The trysquare or mitre square consists of an oblong stock with a thin, hardened-steel blade let into one end. With the blade lying on your wood, the stock is held firmly against its edge, allowing a line to be scored at an accurate 90° or 45° to that edge.

A sliding bevel is an adjustable trysquare, with a long, thin blade that pivots from a bolt at the top, locking at a chosen position by means of a wing nut. The range of angles possible is from almost 0 to almost 180°, but you must put enough blade on the wood to allow you to hold them firmly.

Sawing square

If you have difficulty sawing square to a horizontal surface, stand a trysquare, blade vertical, on the bench in front of you to give yourself a visual fix.

Don't lose any marks

It is easy to lose sight of knife nicks when marking out long lines on coarse surfaces such as chipboard. Ring them with a pencil as you make them so they are easy to spot later.

Marking and mortise gauges

These are devices for scoring lines parallel to a true edge. A marking gauge has a sharp pin or spur set in a wooden arm about 170mm (6¾in) long. This arm is fitted through a sliding stock, which can be locked at any position along it, the working maximum being about 150mm (6in). The stock is held against the edge of the wood to be marked and the point lightly pressed in as the tool is drawn along. A mortise gauge has two pins, the distance between them being adjustable separately.

Profile gauges

When fitting a board edge-on to a wall featuring a picture rail, skirting, or other projections, the best tool for transferring their shapes to the board for marking the cut-outs is a profile gauge. This consists of fine steel rods set in a flat clamp, in which they can slide but are held firmly enough to retain their positions when their ends are pushed against the projection. As all rods are the same length, you can then use the opposite side of the gauge to draw round for the cutout.

Saws for basic cutting

Handsaws have long, springy blades for heavy jobs. There are sizes from 500 to nearly 700mm (20 to 28in) to suit all normal arm (or stroke) lengths. Their teeth have to make a cut-width or 'kerf' wider than the blade, or it would jam, so they are bent or 'set' alternately right and left. Better-grade saws have blades ground thinner towards the top, so need less set and take out narrower kerfs. Crosscut saw teeth are like knife points, being designed chiefly for cutting across the grain. They *will* saw along it, but tend to follow grain lines rather than the one you have drawn. Coarseness and speed of cut are indicated (despite metrication) by the number of teeth per inch (tpi) or points per inch (ppi), usually 10 for shorter saws and 8 for longer ones. Ripsaws have teeth like chisels, work rapidly and accurately along grain with their 5 to 6 tpi 'pitch', but produce ragged cuts across grain. Padsaws have thin flexible blades for sawing round curves and are used for such purposes as cutting keyholes.

Saws for precise, straight cuts

The backsaw has an untapered, inflexible blade, reinforced along the top to keep it straight, and fine, cross-cut

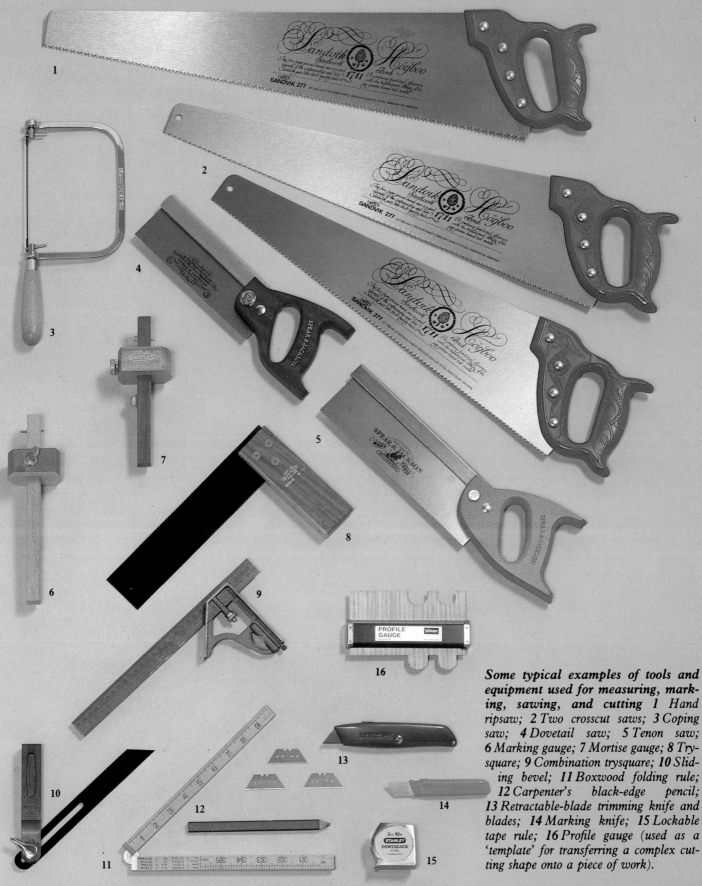

Some typical examples of tools and equipment used for measuring, marking, sawing, and cutting 1 Hand ripsaw; 2 Two crosscut saws; 3 Coping saw; 4 Dovetail saw; 5 Tenon saw; 6 Marking gauge; 7 Mortise gauge; 8 Trysquare; 9 Combination trysquare; 10 Sliding bevel; 11 Boxwood folding rule; 12 Carpenter's black-edge pencil; 13 Retractable-blade trimming knife and blades; 14 Marking knife; 15 Lockable tape rule; 16 Profile gauge (used as a 'template' for transferring a complex cutting shape onto a piece of work).

teeth, usually 24 per inch. Blade lengths range from 200 to 300mm (8 to 12 in). It is also commonly called the tenon saw, except for a small version with 32 tpi, sold as a 'dovetail saw', for very fine work. Tenons are cut entirely with backsaws, unless they are large, when the down-grain cuts can be ripsawn.

Profile-cutting saws

Curves and irregular shapes can be cut with a coping saw, which has a U-shaped steel frame, sprung to keep its fine, narrow blade taut. Pegs at each end are lined up to prevent the blade twisting and the setting is locked by the screw-in handle. The teeth can be set at any angle in relation to the frame. Cutouts that cannot start at the edge of a board have to begin with a small hole, through which the blade is threaded before re-fitting it to the saw. The distance from the edge at which you work is limited by the depth of the saw frame; extra-deep ones are available.

Tools & Techniques 3

A power drill is a valuable part of the household toolkit, even if it is used only to make holes in walls for screw fixings. If that is virtually all you ever going to ask of it, one of the modestly priced, light, two-speed hammer drills will be the most suitable. For masonry drilling, a second, lower speed to give you extra twisting-power (torque) is required. Low speed, coupled to rapid, wood-pecker-style hammer action pulverises stone, brick, and concrete, instead of polishing it and overheating the drill tip as rotary action alone tends to. These small drills are also conveniently short for close-corner work; there are versions with reverse-action for extracting a jammed drill-bit.

Lighter drills are inevitably limited as to power and the more advanced speed-control systems. There are available medium-price, medium-powered drills with two simple, mechanical gears and a 12.5mm (½in) chuck that will take heavy-duty bits; the operator supplies the necessary fine control. Electronic speed-control drills are also available.

In its simplest form, electronic control provides you with a facility for varying speed from 0 to the maximum in a chosen gear, usually by means of an acceleration trigger, which makes the

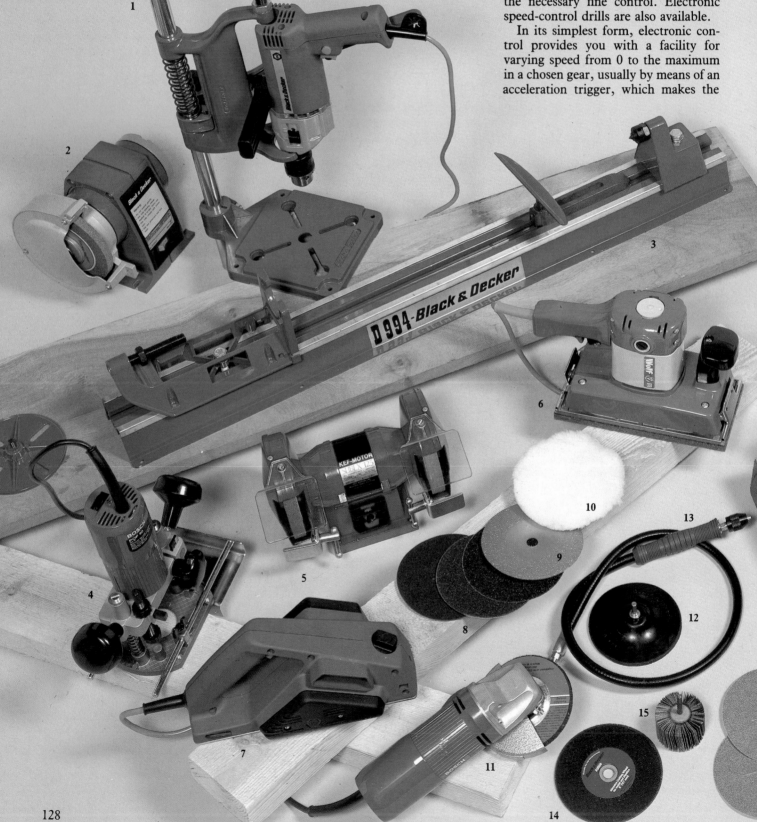

motor turn faster the harder you squeeze it. Full micro-chip electronic control is a good deal more versatile than this, however. It gives you the acceleration-trigger feature greatly enhanced, keeping constant track of motor speed and continuously altering the power fed to the windings to maintain the chosen chuck speed whatever resistance the drill meets. If you hit a soft patch of brick or a hole, there will be no sudden surge of unwanted revolutions. The micro-chip incorporates complex circuitry to prevent motor overloading; and it provides a soft start, so the drill does not jerk into action as you switch on. Soft-starting not only protects the motor, but also makes the drill very docile in the hand. There may be up to seven speed selections in each

mechanical gear, and with the appropriate one (defined in the manufacturer's literature, or printed on the drill itself) it is possible, for example to drill into ceramic tiles without indenting a mark first, or to drive and withdraw screws without any special attachment.

Attachments for drills

Few manufacturers now make the wide ranges of drill attachments that were the norm only a few years ago, preferring to cater for the modern demand for self-powered tools designed for a specific job. There are still attachments on the market for circular- and jig-sawing, for sanding, and for lathe-turning and flexible drives that allow operation at odd angles or in restricted spaces. Your choice of drill depends upon the attach-

ments required because not all drills – even of the same make – have facilities for every attachment.

One useful accessory is the pillar drill stand, or vertical drill stand, in which the drill is mounted so that it can be switched on and left running while you lever it gently down onto an article held on a horizontal baseboard. It is a great help for drilling square to a surface in precise positions and steadies the hand enormously when screw-drilling or plug-cutting is being done.

Grinders

Bench grinders take the form of abrasive wheels 125 to 150mm (5 to 6in) in diameter mounted on a horizontal spindle driven by a central motor. Chisels, cutters and so on are held against them

Typical power tools and accessories 1 Power drill in bench-drill stand; 2 Power centre (power take-off point at one end; grinding wheel at other end); 3 lathe attachment for power drill or, without cradle, for (2) above; 4 Plunge-action router (for grooving, rebating); 5 Bench grinder (for sharpening tool blades); 6 Orbital sander; 7 Power plane; 8 Sanding or cutting discs; 9 Carbide-grit-coated steel sanding disc; 10 Lambswool polishing buff; 11 Angle grinder (for

power filing, cutting, grinding, or coarse-disc sanding); 12 Flexible backing pad (for sanding discs); 13 Flexible drive shaft (attaches to power drill for drilling or, with burrs, for grinding in awkward corners or on complex shapes); 14 Cut-off wheel (for angle grinder); 15 Flap-sander (for general sanding); 16 Fabric-backed sanding discs; 17 Circular saws; 18 Power jigsaw; 19 Jigsaw blades (bright for cutting wood or plastics, red for cutting metal); 20 Portable power drills; 21 Woodboring spade bits; 22 Twist bits (jobber drills).

Power drill chucks
For long life and easy working tighten the key in each of the three holes in turn. To remove the chuck for fitting accessories, insert the key normally and tap it smartly but gently with a light hammer or a piece of wood. If the chuck sticks, put the short end of a hexagonal Allen key in as if it was a drill, tighten up, and tap the key.

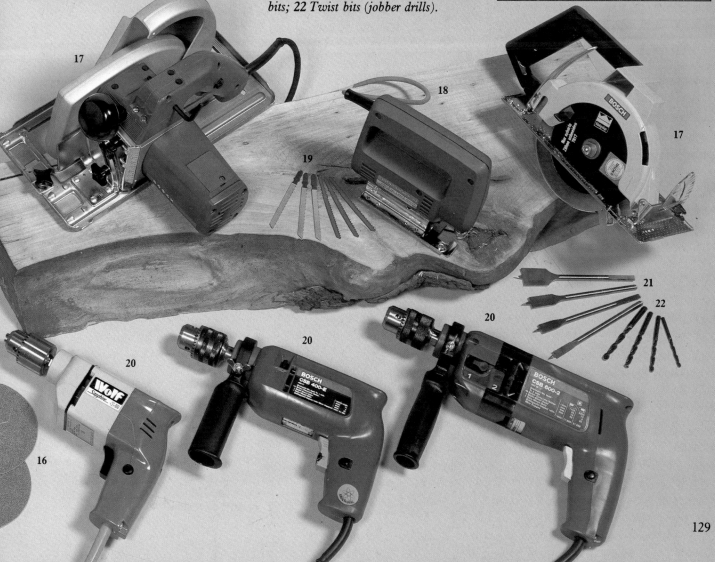

somewhat above centre, supporting them on a special tool rest bolted to the casing. This should be set very close to the wheel. Even if there is an eye shield fixed to the machine, you should wear safety goggles, just in case, and heavy gloves, too, for jobs demanding an extra-firm grip. Most grinders have two wheels – one coarse and one fine – but power-centre machines substitute a power take-off point for one wheel to drive lathes, flexible drives, sanding discs, drills, or wire brushes.

Angle grinders are portable, body-grip tools carrying a high-speed abrasive wheel at right angles to the motor. They will quickly grind away metal, fillers, plastics and masonry, throwing out debris at a high rate, so goggles are a must and breathing masks and heavy gloves useful on many jobs. DIY grinders are mainly small, 100mm (4in) diameter wheel tools, which convert easily to sanders, using coarse or medium discs with flexible rubber backing pads in place of the wheel. They are useful for roughing-down work.

Sanders
Sanders range from simple disc accessories for drills through flat-pad orbital machines with a gentle scrubbing action to rotary flap-sanders capable of smoothing or even stripping profiled and moulded woodwork. At least one of these can also drive a 175mm (7in) resilient, flat disc fitted with self-adhesive abrasive discs for fast work on large surfaces including gentle contours. Most sanders will work on wood, plastics, metals, or fillers so long as the abrasive is suited to the job. At the top end of the orbital-sander range is a machine which can be set to oscillate backwards-and-forwards instead of in tiny circles. This feature gives a finer finish than orbital motion on wood if used parallel to the grain.

Jig saw
The jig saw is more versatile than a circular saw, but not so fast. It drives a short, thin blade up and down, so there is no adjustment of cutting depth. When fitted with a strong, stiff blade, the saw can be tilted to cut into a board from the top, without drilling an access hole. In this way it is possible to cut out a circle or other curved profile from the middle of a sheet. Narrow, fine scroll blades can cut intricate shapes and there are also special blades for cutting. Speed controls vary from none at all through two-speed switches to electronic systems. Top-price models usually feature both electronic control and orbital blade action, permitting faster cutting on thick materials.

Circular saws
Circular saws drive a disc-shaped saw blade at high speed. The blade is mounted vertically and can be raised or lowered to suit the thickness of wood being cut. It can also be tilted sideways to make bevel cuts up to 45°. The blades rarely exceed 125mm (5in) in diameter, cutting maybe 30mm (1³/₁₆in) at right angles. A 150mm (6in) diameter saw may cut 45mm (1¾in) deep and a 182mm (7¼in) model up to 63mm (2½in). In all cases, cutting capacity is reduced when the saw is cutting at an angle. Circular saws are for fast cutting in straight lines and are at their best when used with man-made boards.

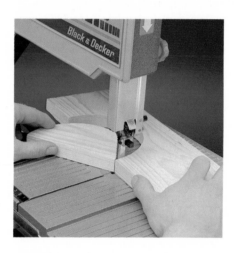

Bandsaw
The bandsaw has a blade made from a continuous band of steel which rotates through the article being cut. It differs from a jigsaw in cutting in one direction only, downwards in front of the operator on the machine shown here. It works at a slower speed than a jigsaw and has teeth set more closely together. It is therefore quieter in operation and produces a more accurate cut with a perfect finish on the side from which the blade enters the material. It is ideal for producing high quality articles.

Keeping to the point

When drilling into ceramic tiles, stick masking tape over the surface and mark on that the position of the hole. This will stop the drill point wandering off before it has penetrated the tile.

New blades from old

Worn jig-saw blades – if they are thick enough – can be given an extra lease of life on thin materials by deliberately breaking them, to bring a fresh set of teeth to bear. This works for machines with straight push-in blade slots.

Power router
Basically, this is a vertical motor directly driving a simple chuck, which takes a wide variety of shaped cutters – square, profiled, concave, convex, and tapered. The motor is fixed in a flat base in which it is raised or lowered to alter cutting depth. The machine can be guided either by the wood's edge or against battens cramped to it. A router works fast, is easy to control, and puts many skilled woodwork operations within reach of the do-it-yourselfer.

Power plane
This looks a little like a hand plane, but the cutter is a high-speed cylinder with two hardened steel blades set in it. Turning at about 12 to 14,000 rpm, a power plane removes a lot of wood very quickly and leaves a fine finish. Depth-of-cut adjustment usually consists of a rising front sole plate controlled by the front knob. The blade comes to the sides of the base, making rebating possible, with a supplementary fence.

Glue gun
This handy device produces a continuous stream of glue from a solid stick, liquefied by an internal heating element which operates as soon as the gun is switched on. It has the advantage of instant availability without mess.

Joints & Joining

Nails The simplest and most obvious way to join two pieces of wood together is to drive nails through one and into the other. It is also one of the strongest joints, if the nailing is done properly. A nail gets its grip by forcing apart the wood fibres, which hold it in place by trying to spring back to their original positions.

You can drive nails flush with the surface if you have a hammer with a slightly domed face. When nailing two thin pieces together, you can bend the nails over and bury the points in the under surface. This is called 'clenching', 'clenching over', or 'clench nailing'.

Straight-nailed joints can be made stronger by angling alternate nails left and right to produce a dovetail effect, making it more difficult to pull one piece of wood from the other than if all nails were driven straight. The only nails that must always be put in straight are the corrugated type used to reinforce corner joints in softwood.

Screws Size for size, screws offer a better grip on wood than do nails. This is because, in addition to a central core, which acts in much the same way as a nail, they have a thread, which digs into the wood to resist both sideways leverage and upward pull.

Like nails, screws are made from wire. They are available in a number of thickness, defined by the measuring-gauge number of the wire used, the commonest being Nos. 4, 6, 8, 10, 12, and 14. Irrespective of its length, each screw of a given gauge size will have the same diameter head, shank (the unthreaded part immediately under the head) and core of its threaded point. Heads are of three basic types: countersunk (flat on top, tapering down to the

shank); round-head (domed on top and flat underneath); and raised countersunk (a countersunk head slightly domed on top).

Countersunk-head screws are generally the most useful for wood because they can be set flush with the surface. Round-head screws are designed for jobs where the main need is for strength, their flat-underside heads giving an excellent grip on flat metal. For this reason, they are often used with washers under the heads to spread their pressure over a wider area.

There are two methods of screwdriving: the traditional slotted one and the more modern cross-head. Slotted screws are driven by normal, flat-bladed screwdrivers and cross-heads by special pointed-end drivers. All types of screw can be bought with either kind of head. Cross-point screws made in Britain are mostly of the modern Pozidriv or

Right: Nail types 1 Round-head; 2 Oval wire; 3 Round lost-head; 4 Oval brad; 5 Ring-shanked; 6 Veneer pin; 7 Panel pin; 8 Hardboard lost-head; 9 Masonry; 10 Cut-steel floor brad; 11 Carpet tack; 12 Galvanised clout; 13 Screw-nail; 14 Alloy dowel (for reinforcing joints).

Below: Screw types 1 Coach; 2 Clutch-head (security); 3 Slotted self-tapping; 4 Supadriv countersunk-head chipboard; 5 Supadriv countersunk-head wood; 6 Dome-head (for mirrors); 7 Round-head wood (japanned steel); 8 Round-head wood (bright zinc-plated), slotted; 9 Round-head wood (solid brass), slotted; 10 Countersunk, raised head (alloy), slotted; 11 Countersunk, raised head (bright zinc-plated), slotted; 12 Countersunk-head wood (solid brass), slotted; 13 Countersunk-head wood (bright steel), slotted.

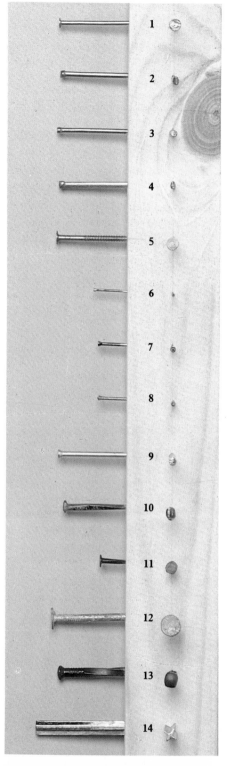

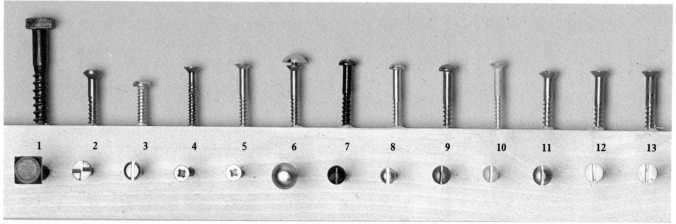

Technique

Making a halving joint

1 Mark the half-way line on both components, using a marking gauge. **2** Saw across grain of cross rail after sawing down gauge line. **3** Mark width of cross rail on side rail. **4** Chisel waste after sawing at knife marks and in middle to gauge line.

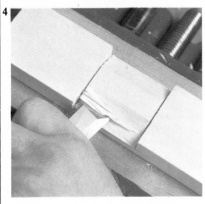

Technique

Making a mortise-and-tenon joint

1 Set the mortise gauge points to the exact width of the chisel blade. **2** Set the gauge stock to position the cutting marks in the centre exact of the wood. **3** Mark the tenon shoulders and mortise length with a try-square and knife, then mark the width lines within these limits using the gauge. **4** Saw down the tenon lines to the shoulder. **5** Saw the shoulder square and within the waste area, then chisel to the line. **6** Bore out the bulk of the mortise waste with a bit slightly narrower than the marked width. **7** Chisel the sides true to the marks. **8** Glue the mating surfaces, and clamp them together.

Supadriv type, imported screws more likely being the older Phillips kind. Phillips and Supadriv screw heads look similar: those with plain cross-sockets are Supadriv; those which are V-shaped in cross section are Phillips.

Bolts and coach screws Bolts may well offer a stronger fixing than screws for really heavy woodwork. Some woodwork bolts have a square shank under the head to stop it turning in the hole while the nut is tightened on to the washer. Others have a countersunk head for flush fitting. Screw-bolts have no heads – just a screw-point at one end and a straight, threaded shank at the other. These are screwed in by tightening two nuts against each other on the bolt part to give a turning hold. Once the screw is tight, the nuts are taken off.

Coach screws are thick woodscrews with coarse threads and heads shaped like nuts, so that they can be tightened with a spanner. They make very strong fixings, but the bigger ones can be quite hard to turn in tough timber.

Glued joints

Pieces of wood can be strongly fastened to each other without nails, screws or bolts, using only adhesive. This works extremely well where the pieces are joined together by close-fitting tongues and grooves, by hardwood dowel pegs, or by wedge-shaped, interlocking dovetails. It also works where the strain on the joint is spread over a sizeable area of glued surface, such as when sticking long boards edge-to-edge—although in these cases the fit between the glued parts has to be very true and snug. If an accurate, intimate fit is not possible, these 'butt' joints should be reinforced by nails or screws, which hold the joint firm whilst the glue sets and remain as insurance in case it fails later under stress. This 'belt-and-braces' treatment is advisable in all joints in which there is no enclosure of one component by the other sufficient to produce a dry grip; examples include butt, lap, bridle, and mitre joints.

The most commonly used glued joints are the mortise (oblong slot) and tenon (oblong tongue), the dowel (round pegs), and the dovetail (wedge-shaped interlocking tongues). Tongued-and-grooved joints as used in floorboards, and the 'spline' joints using separate tongues in grooves either side are in the same category, but they are usually factory-made. All the self-sufficient joints have to be cramped tight until the glue is firmly set and in general demand a bit more dedication and equipment than pinned or screwed joints do.

Technique

Making a dovetail joint

The key to successful dovetail joints is to cut the edges of the tails to exactly the correct angle. The simple template (see drawing below, right) enables you to do this and also saves you a good deal of time. Make the template from a piece of aluminium sheet. Turn the two ends up and down at right angles to the rest. Make the length of the template 1½ times that of the wider end and three times that of the narrower end.

Both pieces of wood must be of same width and thickness, with ends perfectly square. First, set your marking gauge to the thickness of the wood and lightly inscribe a gauge line parallel to the ends on both pieces. **1** Mark the tails using the template shown in the drawing (right) to make the correct taper angles. **2** Cut down the waste side of tail lines with a dovetail saw. **3** Remove the bulk of the waste with a coping saw working inside waste area. **4** Shave the waste lines exactly with a sharp bevel chisel. **5** Use the tails as a template to mark the pins on mating piece of wood. **6** Saw and chisel to make pins, then make a true fit. Glue, assemble, and cramp.

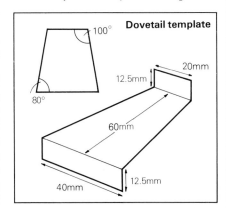

Dovetail template — 100°, 80°, 20mm, 12.5mm, 60mm, 40mm, 12.5mm

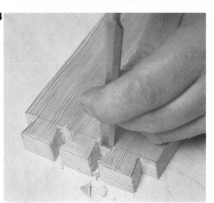

Timber Finishes

Both natural timber and wood-veneered boards look fresh, clean and attractive when newly planed or sanded, so why go to the extra trouble and expense of applying a finish? Being a natural material, wood is porous, absorbing and giving up moisture readily, so it will probably swell or shrink more rapidly if unfinished than if you seal it. Some woods react more quickly to atmospheric change than others, Parana pine being particularly sensitive, for example. Unsealed wood is liable to all kinds of attack on its good looks – from heat, staining liquids, spirits such as alcohol, perhaps abrasion, and in some situations sunlight.

Petroleum jelly
Good, old-fashioned petroleum jelly may strike you as an unlikely finish for wood, yet it is one of the simplest to apply and one of the easiest to maintain. All you do is coat the surface with it fairly generously and leave it to soak in. This will happen more quickly if you mix the petroleum jelly with a little turpentine (the proportion is not critical, so start at 10% and see how it goes). When the wood has drunk its fill, wipe off any surplus and polish it with a soft rag. The surface will not be sticky, but will have a soft, lustrous sheen, which you can restore at any time by giving it a further treatment.

Oil
Like vaseline, oil finishes soak into wood, enhancing colour and grain, giving a soft sheen and good protection against water or moisture penetration, though they do not offer much resistance to spillages of alcoholic drinks or to hot cups or plates. But for appearance they are very attractive, especially on darker woods. Olive oil is used only for food utensils – bread boards, spoons, salad bowls – and is the only oil treatment applied neat. One of the proprietary teak oil finishes is perhaps the best choice for smaller jobs. It consists of oil and spirit in a balanced formula to give good penetration and drying characteristics, but it can take quite a lot to do a big job and you may consider making up your own oil finish, putting up with a less elegant product and longer drying time to save money.

Raw linseed oil and turpentine in about equal proportions is a good mixture. You can use boiled linseed oil, but it is a bit more treacly. Both teak oil and linseed oil are difficult to get out once they are in the wood. This means that you are stuck with an oiled finish for the life of the object. If you think you might change your mind later about the finish, it is better to use Danish oil, as you do not have to remove it before applying a lacquer finish.

All oil finishes should be applied sparingly – a light application, followed by thorough drying (at least six hours; more if it is linseed) and another light oiling-and-drying, then another, until the wood will not take any more. Wipe off any surplus, then apply wax if required. If you have a fairly powerful drill fitted with a backing pad and lambswool bonnet, you can get a superb shine on oiled wood without wax. Once you have waxed, you have to de-wax before re-oiling, but you can put more wax on, of course.

French polish
Traditional french polish is by far the best finish for revealing the full beauty of fine wood, but it consists of shellac dissolved in meths and has no resistance whatsoever to spirits or heat. Its glass-like perfection is due to the fact that it dries before dust and insects can become embedded in it. This feature makes its application in traditional formulations a very skilled operation, one of the difficulties being the removal with the last few wiper-strokes of the film of white oil used as a lubricant. This can be removed chemically in certain home french-polish products, so provided you can achieve an extra-fine sanded surface, with no scoring across the grain or other blemishes, you can do your own french polishing.

Synthetic lacquers
There are three basic alternatives if you decide on a modern, hard, synthetic-resin lacquer finish. First is clear polyurethane, which is in fact slightly brown, and will darken lighter timbers such as pine and sycamore. Second is water-clear two-part lacquers which may be preferred for these woods. Once the two parts are mixed, 'pot-life' is about six hours, but apart from this they behave and wear very similarly to polyurethane lacquers – some of which are themselves two-solution products, called 'catalytic' because one part induces the other to set. These lacquers do not resist sunlight as effectively as pigmented paints, so for outdoor wood get the kind with a UV (ultraviolet) inhibitor.

2

1

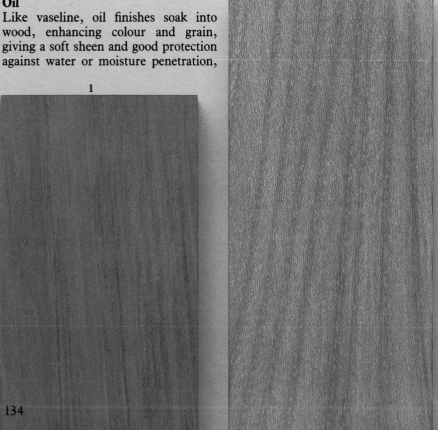

3

The third alternative is a coloured, translucent polyurethane, which can give a new and lively appearance to quite humdrum white or light wood. Application and performance is the same as for the other polyurethanes. The effect is totally different from that of opaque paint, since the grain shows through and is highlighted by the colours, of which there is a fair choice, including blue, yellow and red.

Synthetic lacquers do not like anything else between themselves and the wood – especially oil or wax – so clean up with white spirit before you start. Letting the first coat down with 50% white spirit is advisable for absorbent wood. A second coat can have 30% spirit, a third 10% and subsequent coats can be neat. Always rub down with steel wool (fine – grade 00 or 000 if possible) between coats and allow thorough drying of each application before rubbing and recoating. Clear and coloured polyurethanes produce darker shades as more layers are applied, whereas clear lacquers do not. If you want a matt finish, make the undercoats gloss and the top one matt; but by and large it is not a good idea to use matt lacquer under gloss unless it says you can on the tin. Waxing over polyurethane gives a soft-sheen finish if you rub the wax in with very fine steel wool.

Special effects

Softwood with pronounced grain – like pine – can be scorched with a blowlamp and wire-brushed with the grain to produce a rich, scrubbed-board effect before sealing. Oak may be 'lined' by brushing it with a paste made of garden (slaked) lime and water. Let it dry, then fine-sand, leaving the wood a grey/brown colour with white flecks in the pores of the grain. Clean with a dry rag.

To get a weathered look on oak, again mix lime with water, but don't brush it on straightaway. After the undissolved lime has settled, decant the lime-water off and use it to soak the timber. Just put it on evenly and allow it to dry. This treatment gives a pleasantly subdued colour, with no white flecks, but you have to be careful to seal it with something that will not alter its appearance. One of the wallpaper-protection products is the best for this purpose.

Pine and other well-striped softwoods can be made to look striking by 'pickling' with chemicals to increase the contrast between dark and light parts of the grain. This is a fairly hard-earned effect, as you have to apply nitric acid to the wood in a strength of one part added to eight of water. As the acid is highly corrosive you must protect yourself, the bench, and other items nearby from accidental splashes. Cover the surrounding area with polythene sheet. Rubber gloves are essential for hands and suitable goggles for eyes; all plastic goggles are proof against acids. Above all – *never add water to strong acid*. The reaction produces instant heat enough to boil it and make it spit. Add the acid to the water, slowly, while stirring gently, and put the stirrer somewhere safe until you can dispose of it. If you make a splash on your skin, wash it immediately with lots of water.

Apply the dilute acid evenly to the wood and leave to dry. When dry, sand it lightly with very fine abrasive paper, along the grain. Then stain the wood a bit darker using a weak solution of potassium bichromate. Fine-sand again when dry and protect with very dilute synthetic lacquer.

Grain fillers

For a glass-smooth finish when using synthetic lacquers or french polish, use a proprietary grain filler to bridge the indentations of the natural grain pores before sealing. It is wiped on, left to dry, then rubbed in with a rag.

Pre-coloured stoppings

Some wood stoppings cannot absorb stains as readily as wood does, so they have to be stained before they are used to fill the holes. Plastic wood has absorption characteristics similar to those of wood. Although it tends to shrink and fall out of the hole, it can easily be replaced and held with an epoxy adhesive.

Finishing chipboard edges

Polyurethane lacquers applied fairly thickly to unfilled chipboard edges take away the roughness of the wood and give an interesting textured appearance.

Progressive sanding

For heavy stock removal with orbital sanders, start with a coarse grit. For really rough surfaces, look for an industrial tool stockist and try to get some of the extra-coarse 46 grit professional sheets. Work down progressively from coarse through medium to fine grades and, towards the end, lift the machine very slightly in order to get a finer finish.

5

Timber finishes: 1 Teak oil, a soft, lustrous finish, with little solvent or knock resistance; 2 Wax – resists moisture but not solvents; 3 French or button polish makes a high-grade finish; 4 Copal varnish, resists sunlight; 5, 6 Polyurethane, resists everything except sunlight.

4

6

Door Furniture

'Lay-on hardware' does not mean a bed of nails, but items such as hinges, catches, pulls, and cover plates for keyholes (escutcheon plates) that are simply screwed to the wood surface, needing no recess to locate them. This means that you have to locate the fitting freehand, there being nothing to hold it in position while you drive in the screws. Positioning is easier if you pencil-in the screw-hole locations while holding the fitting in place, then remove it, lightly centre-punch the marks and drill pilot holes of a diameter to suit the size of screw. A push-drill is a valuable aid in these situations; it is a one-hand tool with a spring-loaded spindle that turns one way as you push and the other way as you release pressure, so that the drill point is working on both strokes. A magazine handle holds several points with suitable diameters for holes.

Bell pushes

Theoretically, bell pushes are simple to fit, needing only a hole through the door jamb for the wire. Some of the antique ones may have a hump in the middle at the back of the plate, and this must have its own recess. Make that before the main hole, either with a large auger or with a mallet and chisel. The other difficulty with bell pushes is hiding the wire, which can look unsightly when trailed across the frame, fastened by insulated staples. The mortising techniques already described can be employed to make long, shallow grooves to bury the wire, provided it is carrying only 6 to 12 volts.

Technique

Let-in hinges

Precise marking out is the key to success in let-in hinges. Butt hinges – the ordinary door and window kind – are designed to be recessed in open-sided mortises cut in the opening frame or door and the fixed frame; the mortises should be cut to a depth slightly less than half the width of the hinge's spine, because the two frames should not press together too tightly when the hinge is closed Measure down from the top of the frame for all hinge positions, rather than from top and then bottom. To give the opening frame or door adequate clearance at the top, measure and mark for the hinges on that first (see 1, below), then add on 1 to 2mm to each measurement when marking out the frame.

The outline for each hinge mortise can be marked with a knife and try-square (2) for the horizontals. Waste wood can be removed entirely with mallet and chisel. Use a sharp firmer chisel, slightly wider than the required mortise and make a series of shallow incisions across the grain (3). Make the final chop (4) with the flat of the chisel facing away from the mortise. So long as the incisions are close enough together, their effect will be to crumble the wood neatly inside the mortise, which can then be removed using the chisel sideways or, preferably, along the grain (5).

Mark the screw positions, drill pilot holes, and fix the hinges (6) to the opening frame or door. Chop out the fixed-frame mortices in the same way and drill pilot holes; you are now ready to hinge the two frames together. If it is a large door, use timber wedges or packing pieces to lift it off the floor bringing the hinges exactly into line with the mortises. Insert the centre screw in each hinge and close the door to check the alignment and fit. Adjust the mortises if necessary.

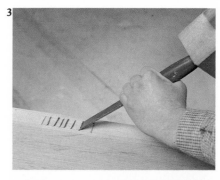

Technique

Lock mortises

Cylinder locks consist of two parts – a key block on the outside and a latch unit on the inside. The two are connected by a large hole, normally 32mm (1¼in) diameter, which takes the bulk of the cylinder mechanism and allows a connecting rod to pass to the latch. Most latches have a flange, which must be let into the door edge, and the metal housing for the jamb may need similar accommodation. These cut-outs are small mortises, just like those for the hinges, and are cut in the same way.

Mortise locks, however, are set into the centre of the door edge, often quite deeply. You can save a lot of chopping work by using a dowel jig – a device for keeping twist drills square to the surface and precisely positioned – to bore a series of holes the same width as the lock, removing most of the waste quickly. The remaining waste is removed from the slot with a broad chisel 32 or 38mm (1¼ or 1½in) to get the long sides accurate. It is a good idea to bore the small hole for the doorknob-spindle first. A little more work is necessary to let-in the lock plate on the door edge. Insert the lock as far as it will go, until the plate is flat on the door edge and draw round it with a sharp pencil. Remove the lock and chisel bevel inwards. Using a chisel narrower than the plate, make mortise chops across grain and chisel out until the plate fits flush (if there is a second cover-plate, allow for that, too).

Below Fitting a mortise lock. 1 Marking position on door edge. 2 Marking slot width. 3 Boring doorknob spindle hole. 4 Drilling slot. 5 Chopping out waste. 6 Marking outline for flush fit.

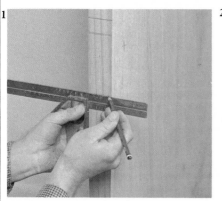

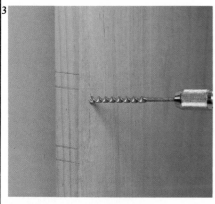

Mortise lock trial fits

Mortise locks sometimes feel as if they are going to fit easily when you push them in for a trial fit, then jam firmly half-way. Old established ones can also present removal problems. It is often possible to use a large screwdriver – either through the spindle-hole or as a gentle lever at the front – to coax them free.

Cutting lock mortises in situ

To hold a door firmly open to allow the cutting or drilling-out of a mortise without taking it off its hinges, use a wooden wedge, tapped firmly in with a hammer, between the bottom of the door and the floor. If the gap is too great for a one-piece wedge, you can improvise with a short plank and a block or brick to produce the same effect.

Hanging a door

Plane the new door to allow clearances of 3mm (⅛in) at top and sides and 6mm (¼in) or more at bottom. Then, supporting the door at correct height with wedges and timber stand, bring the butt stile into the door frame, re-check clearances, and mark position of hinges on stile, using the hinge recesses in the frame as a guide. The hinges should be about 150mm (6in) from the door top and 200mm (8in) from the bottom respectively. After fixing the hinges, bring the door on its wedges to the frame again, drill holes for each hinge in its recess, and drive in the screws. If the closing stile binds against the frame, one hinge recess is too deep; pack it with card.

There are several different types of hinges available: ordinary butt hinges, of which the most useful are the rising type which keep the door clear of the carpet when opened; parliament hinges which allow the door to be opened through 180° and swing hinges which close the door automatically.

Letter plates

Fitting a letter plate into a new door or replacing one in an old door with a wider one may mean accurate sawing through timber from 32 to 50mm (1¼ to 2in) thick. It is not an easy job, even with a jig saw. Probably the easiest method is to drill a series of holes around the edge of the required slot, then to use a chisel to cut through the thin sections dividing them and to level the sides. Remember to mark the slot on both sides, and to work inwards from each side when trimming to size.

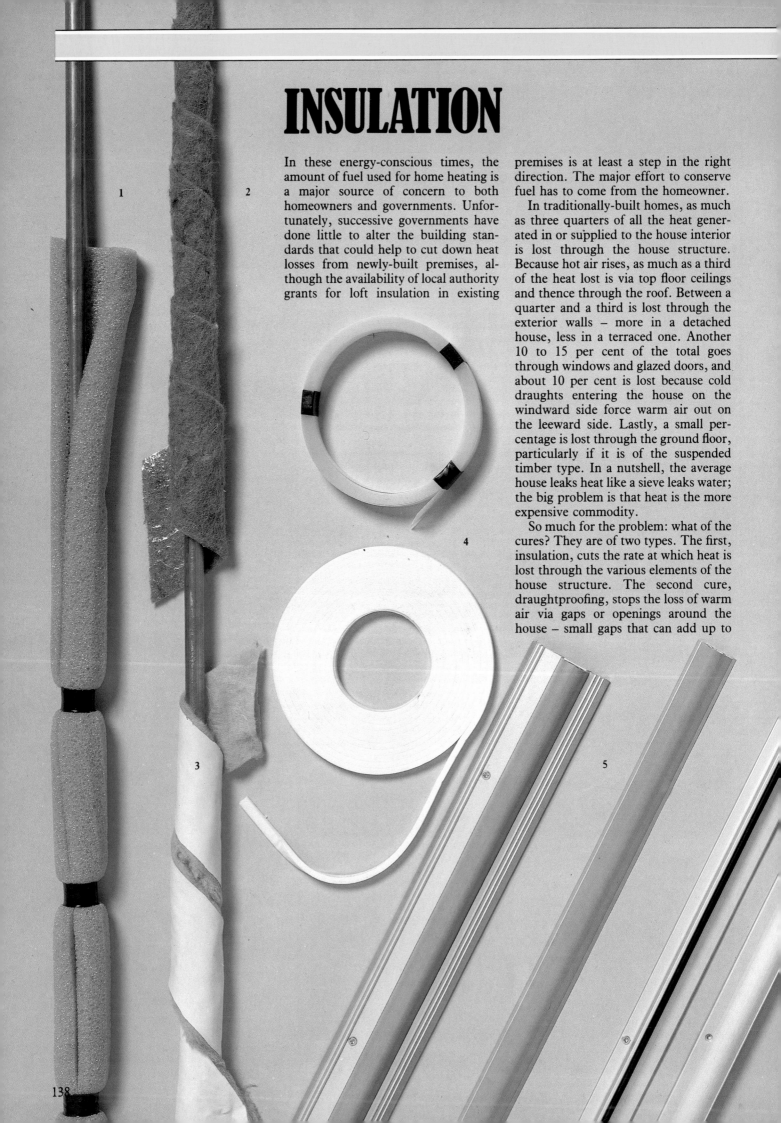

INSULATION

In these energy-conscious times, the amount of fuel used for home heating is a major source of concern to both homeowners and governments. Unfortunately, successive governments have done little to alter the building standards that could help to cut down heat losses from newly-built premises, although the availability of local authority grants for loft insulation in existing premises is at least a step in the right direction. The major effort to conserve fuel has to come from the homeowner.

In traditionally-built homes, as much as three quarters of all the heat generated in or supplied to the house interior is lost through the house structure. Because hot air rises, as much as a third of the heat lost is via top floor ceilings and thence through the roof. Between a quarter and a third is lost through the exterior walls – more in a detached house, less in a terraced one. Another 10 to 15 per cent of the total goes through windows and glazed doors, and about 10 per cent is lost because cold draughts entering the house on the windward side force warm air out on the leeward side. Lastly, a small percentage is lost through the ground floor, particularly if it is of the suspended timber type. In a nutshell, the average house leaks heat like a sieve leaks water; the big problem is that heat is the more expensive commodity.

So much for the problem: what of the cures? They are of two types. The first, insulation, cuts the rate at which heat is lost through the various elements of the house structure. The second cure, draughtproofing, stops the loss of warm air via gaps or openings around the house – small gaps that can add up to the equivalent of a hole in your house wall no less than six bricks wide and four bricks high.

Insulation is effective in four main areas – the underside of the roof slope, the floor of the loft, the outside walls and all glazed areas. The first would be chosen when the loft contains an attic room, and it would involve fitting board or blanket insulation materials to the underside of the roof slope and to the walls of the attic room. In the second area, insulation is laid between the joists to reduce the passage of warm air into the loft through bedroom ceilings.

Insulating exterior walls is comparatively easy if they are of cavity construction; insulation materials can be blown or pumped into the cavity after construction, or built-in during it. If the walls are solid, insulating material has to be added to the inner (or, rarely, the outer) face of the wall, the former resulting in considerable domestic upheaval. Insulating glazed areas involves the installation of double glazing, turning single layers of glass into a glass-air-glass sandwich with far greater resistance to the passage of heat.

Draughtproofing is effective in three main areas – windows, doors and floors. Doors and opening windows must have some clearance within their frames, but these gaps can be plugged without interfering unduly with the opening and shutting action thanks to the development of mechanical draught excluders. These take the form of strips of foam

plastic, rubber, rigid plastic or metal that are compressed to seal the opening more or less effectively when the door or window is closed. Slightly different principles are used to seal the threshold of exterior doors. As far as floors are concerned, only ground floors are worth draughtproofing; in practice modern floorcoverings do a reasonable job both in stopping draughts through suspended timber floors and in insulating solid floors against the transmission of heat through the floor structure.

The one problem with draughtproofing is its effect on the ventilation of the house. People living there need a supply of fresh air – a completely draughtproofed room soon becomes unbearably stuffy – and more importantly, fuel-burning appliances need a good air supply, too, if they are to burn efficiently and safely. Deaths from combustion fumes emitted by boilers, water heaters and the like do occur, and over-zealous draughtproofing is often a cause. A happy medium must be struck.

To judge the effectiveness of the various means of insulating and draughtproofing your home, you need to balance the cost of carrying out the works against the savings they will give. And it must be remembered that better insulation can do one of two things; it can save money by letting you stay as warm as you were before while burning less fuel, or it can save you nothing while keeping you a lot warmer.

The various forms of insulation and

draughtproofing mentioned can be ranked approximately for cost-effectiveness. Draughtproofing of doors and windows is the cheapest measure you can carry out, and will pay for itself in saved fuel in roughly a year. Loft insulation recoups its cost in two to three years, wall insulation in about five years, while double glazing may not pay for itself in fuel savings for up to 20 years if professionally installed, but in a shorter period with a do-it-yourself installation. However, double glazing has other, less quantifiable, benefits. It will lessen draughts through treated windows, and it will eliminate the cold one feels when sitting next to large windows in cold weather. If double glazing is fitted as part of a window replacement programme, it will contribute towards reducing future maintenance and will add to the value of the house.

Draughtproofing
Draughtproofing aims to block the clearance gaps that are necessary if doors and windows are to open without binding, and also to stop air leaving the

Insulating materials and draught-proofers: 1, 2, 3 Split-foam, felt, and bandage pipe insulation; 4 Draught strip for doors and windows; 5 Threshold draught excluder; 6 Interlocking door-bottom and threshold strips; 7 Rise-and-fall excluder; 8 Plastic strip excluder; 9 Bristle strip excluder; 10 Spring bronze draught strip for doors and windows.

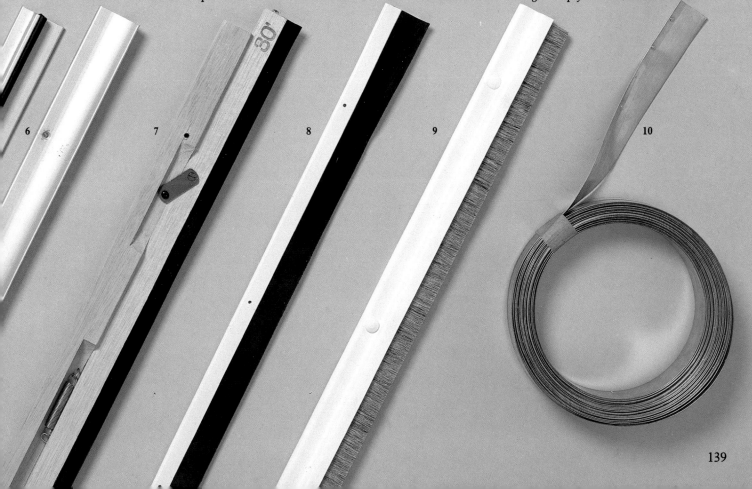

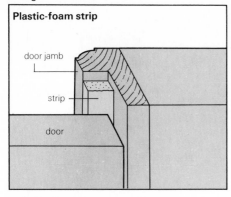

Plastic-foam strip

door jamb
strip
door

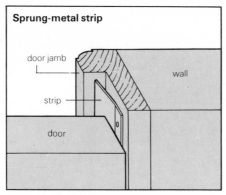

Sprung-metal strip

door jamb
wall
strip
door

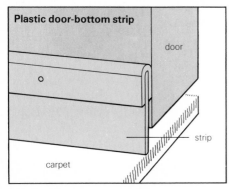

Plastic door-bottom strip

door
strip
carpet

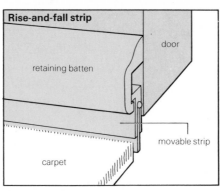

Rise-and-fall strip

door
retaining batten
movable strip
carpet

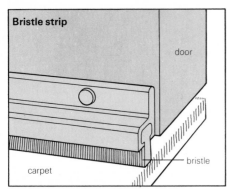

Bristle strip

door
bristle
carpet

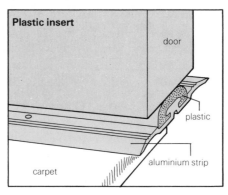

Plastic insert

door
plastic
carpet
aluminium strip

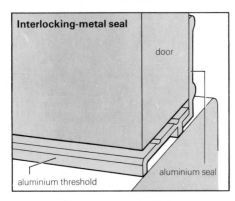

Interlocking-metal seal

door
aluminium seal
aluminium threshold

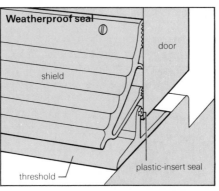

Weatherproof seal

door
shield
threshold
plastic-insert seal

house through other openings such as disused fireplaces and letterboxes.

The cheapest form of draught-proofing and the easiest to fit is self-adhesive foam strip. This is stuck round the rebate into which the door or window closes so that it is compressed to form a virtually air-tight seal. It is certainly effective, but is not very durable – it probably needs replacing every couple of years on doors and most windows. It is suitable for all hinged doors, and for both metal and timber windows except sliding sashes.

Where the gap is larger, a rigid

extrusion incorporating a flexible rubber or plastic tube seal is a more expensive but more effective product to use. The extrusion is pinned to the frame so that when the door or window closes it compresses the tube and forms a seal. It is suitable for timber doors and windows only. A similar product incorporating a brush pile instead of a tube seal is slightly less efficient, but can be used on sliding doors and sliding sash windows. Sprung metal or plastic draught excluders have a flange which presses against the edge of the door or window as it closes. They are durable,

although not as easy to fix accurately as other types. They can, however, be painted over, so do not have to be removed during redecoration. They can also be used on sliding doors and sash windows. Different types are sold for timber and metal windows; the former are pinned into place, while the latter are attached to the frame by small clips.

Under-door draughts require a different approach, since there is no rebate into which a draught excluder can be fitted. The commonest type is fitted to the face of the door at floor level, and incorporates a rubber, plastic, felt or bristle strip that seals the gap between door and floor when the door is closed. Bristle types can also be used for sliding doors. More complex types have a draught strip that is housed in a slot, allowing it to rise over a deep-pile carpet.

There are also threshold strips with a rubber or plastic insert that presses against the underside of the closed door. They are easy to install, but can be a trip hazard.

For exterior doors, a combination excluder is the best choice. Such excluders come in two parts; one is fixed to the threshold, the other to the outer face of the door, so that when it is closed the two are pressed together or interlock to keep draughts out.

It is also worth checking that door and window frames are a tight fit within the masonry that surrounds them. If there are any gaps outside, seal them with a non-setting mastic. Inside, make good gaps, especially beneath window sills, with filler.

Disused fireplaces are a major source of draughts, and are best blocked up – either permanently with brickwork that can be plastered over, or temporarily with a plasterboard or plywood panel. In either case, a ventilator should be built in to allow ventilation of the flue, so preventing damp. If the flue is permanently blocked off it is worth having the chimney stack capped.

Lastly, letterboxes can easily be draught-proofed by fitting a weighted or spring-loaded flap, or a brush-pile excluder over the inside of the opening.

Methods of draughtproofing floors are described.

Insulating roofs

If you have a typical loft, unboarded and used for storage, the simplest way of insulating it is to lay blanket material or loose-fill insulant in the gaps between the joists. These are usually 400mm (16in) apart, although the spacing may be as much as 450mm (18in) or as little as 350mm (14in).

The object of the exercise, as with all

insulation work, is to trap a layer of still air above the bedroom ceilings to discourage the passage of warm air upwards into the loft. Two common types of material are available which do this admirably; they are glass-fibre matting and an expanded mineral product called vermiculite. The former is sold in roll form, usually 400mm wide and about 6m (20ft) long. You may also find mineral fibre matting sold in this form. Vermiculite is a loose-fill insulant, sold in bags. Granulated polystyrene and loose mineral wool are also available, but the former may blow about in draughty lofts, while the latter can be dusty and awkward to lay to a uniform depth.

Blanket insulation is the easier type to lay; most of the loft can be insulated with long strips, while awkward corners can be filled with pieces torn or cut from the roll. It is available in standard thickness – usually 75mm (3in) and 100mm (4in); the latter is essential for homes with no insulation, while the former is ideal for topping-up existing 25 or 50mm (1 or 2in) thick insulation.

Complete the job by insulating the top of the loft trap-door, tacking or tying the insulation in place. Fit foam or sprung-metal draught-excluder around the trap opening.

Insulating attic rooms

Where all or part of the loft space is used, whether as a playroom for children or as part of a full-scale loft conversion, then the insulation should be fixed to the underside of the roof slope and incorporated in the walls of an attic room instead of being laid on the loft floor (which makes a cold attic).

In an open loft, insulation blanket can be held against the roof slope between the rafters. Alternatively, special paper-wrapped insulation, made to match the rafter space and with flanges along the edges, can be tacked to the rafters (see drawing, page 153).

Grants for loft insulation

The Homes Insulation Act 1978 allows local authorities to pay grants to both householders and tenants towards the cost of loft, tank and pipe insulation, provided that certain conditions are met. The most important are that the loft must initially contain no insulation and that installation does not begin until the claim for a grant has been approved. The grant covers two thirds of the cost up to a specified ceiling (1984: £69); elderly people may qualify for up to 90 per cent of the cost (maximum £95), and this can include fees for installation by a contractor rather than by the applicant.

With loose-fill insulation, a thicker layer is needed to get the same degree of insulation as a blanket provides; 150mm (6in) is the recommended requirement, and ceiling joists may be no deeper than this. This type is not so easy to lay, especially into sloping eaves where it tends to disappear down the wall cavities unless the end of each trough between the joists is blocked off near the eaves.

Laying the insulation

After working out how much insulation material you need, the first job is to clear the loft so that you can work easily. If the loft is well-stocked with bric-a-brac, move everything up to one end. Should you for any reason not have access to the roof space, you will have to cut an opening at least 760mm (2ft 6in) long in the ceiling between adjacent joists; this can be made good afterwards, or converted into a proper loft hatch opening by lining it with a timber frame and fitting a trap-door or panel.

Before laying the insulation, check on pipe runs and electricity cables. Pipes can be covered by the loft insulation if they are close to the ceiling; otherwise they must be separately insulated with proprietary pipe lagging to prevent them freezing in what will be a considerably colder loft than before. Electricity cables, which will probably be lying loose across the surface of the ceiling, should either be lifted above the insulation or, if there is enough slack, they can be clipped to the sides of the joists. The object in either case is for them to remain accessible. If the cable is rubber-covered, replace it with new PVC-insulated cable before laying the loft insulation.

Start laying the insulation at one side of the loft, kneeling on a stout board placed across the joists to avoid damaging the ceiling. Use a broom to push

*Upper Blanket-insulation materials are laid between the loft-floor joists. **Lower** Insulating granules are poured between the joists, then levelled flush with them.*

blanket or loose fill material towards the eaves (remember to block the trough first if you are laying loose-fill insulation), but do not cover the eaves completely: a loft needs ventilation to dry off any moisture that penetrates the roof, and to discourage condensation which can soak the insulation, rendering it useless, and can cause rot in the roof timbers. Work across the loft, over-lapping lengths of blanket material and levelling loose-fill material to the required depth with a T-shaped board cut to match the joist spacing. Use blanket off-cuts in awkward corners.

If you were forced to clear one end of the loft at a time, take this opportunity to board over the loft after the insulation to make storage (and retrieval) easier. Use softwood boards or 600mm (2ft) wide strips of chipboard.

With a loft conversion, unused areas of loft should be insulated at floor level as described earlier. Ceilings of loft rooms should incorporate insulation

blanket between the roof slope or dormer roof, while the walls should be insulated with blanket then clad with hardboard on the loft side of the wall framing and plasterboard lining on the room side. Alternatively, the room can be lined with insulating plasterboard instead of the ordinary variety; this is a sandwich material incorporating a layer of insulating foam.

Insulating flat roofs
Flat roofs are difficult to insulate unless access can be gained to the space between the roof covering and the ceiling.

The quickest and most effective solution, possible only if the room is high enough, is to erect a new false ceiling below the existing one by screwing battens to the joists and sandwiching insulating material between the old ceiling and the new. The new ceiling should be of insulating plasterboard to add to the insulation value; polystyrene ceiling tiles are simply not thick enough to make much impact on the rate of heat loss through an uninsulated ceiling.

Insulating walls
Most houses built since the 1920s have outer walls of cavity construction, which means they consist of two 'skins' of brickwork or blockwork 100mm (4in) thick, separated by a cavity about 50mm (2in) wide. The cavity can be filled, via drill holes, with an insulating foam. You must first obtain local authority approval, and the operation should be carried out by a reputable firm specialising in this type of work. The insulation value of a cavity wall can be improved dramatically by filling the gap between the 'leaves' with a suitable insulating material.

Insulating solid walls is a much trickier proposition. One or two enterprising firms have developed systems for insulating solid walls from the exterior, a process that involves covering the walls with metal mesh held away from the walls on battens. The gap between the mesh and the wall is filled with insulating material, and the mesh is covered with a durable surface rendering. Ingenious and effective the system may be; it is also extremely expensive.

The usual method adopted for insulating solid walls is to dry-line them on the inside with insulating material, covered with a new wall lining – a job that means considerable upheaval inside the house. The methods employed vary, but are all within the scope of the competent do-it-yourselfer.

Perhaps the simplest involves lining the inner surface of exterior walls with insulating plasterboard. This can be stuck in place with special adhesive, although if the walls are uneven it may be better to screw the sheets in place, using packing pieces where appropriate to take up any unevenness in the wall surface. Window reveals are generally not insulated; the cut-edges of the boards do, however, need protecting

Solid-wall insulation

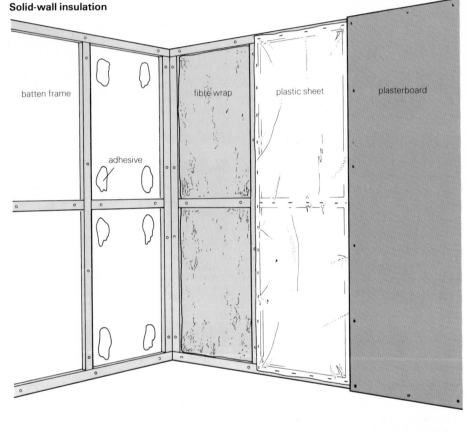

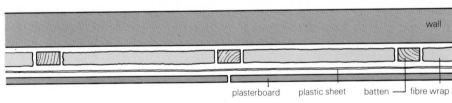

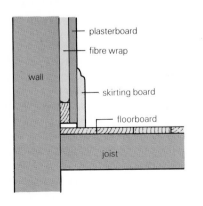

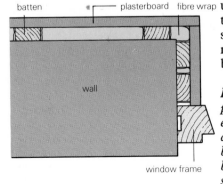

Left above Lining solid walls involves pinning up a framework of battens, filling each panel with an insulating blanket and a vapour barrier, then nailing on a plasterboard panel. *Left below* New skirting boards will be needed; window reveals should also be lined.

with lipping of some sort at the edge of the reveal. At door openings, a new timber lining will be needed, in the form of battens fixed to the existing frame to carry the door architrave level with the new wall surface, unless the door is set in a reveal in the same way as a window frame.

An alternative to this method is to fix vertical timber battens to the wall at spacings that match the width of loft insulation blanket, and to sandwich this material (or the paper-wrapped type mentioned previously – see drawings on page 152) between the original wall surface and the new wall lining, which can be of ordinary or insulating plasterboard nailed to the timber battens. You should also fix horizontal battens at floor and ceiling levels, and approximately one third and two thirds of the way up the wall, to support the plasterboard Use only pre-treated timber.

Fit the boards flush with the ceiling, where the join can be hidden with decorative coving. At skirting-board level the existing skirting-board can be left in place (with battens pinned to it to bring it to the required thickness) and new skirting fitted once the boards are in place. Electrical sockets and plate switches will need remounting flush with the new wall surface.

Whichever method is used, one vital ingredient must always be included; a vapour barrier between the existing wall and the new lining, which prevents water vapour from the wall making the insulation (and the new wall lining) damp. It also prevents condensation from forming behind the wall lining. Insulating plasterboard usually includes a vapour barrier in the sandwich, but if it does not or if other insulating materials are being used, a vapour barrier of heavy-duty polythene or foil-backed building paper must be tacked to the battens behind the wall lining.

Outbuildings, particularly those used as workshops or children's playrooms, will be a lot more comfortable if the walls and roof are insulated and doors and windows draughtproofed. Those with a timber frame faced with timber cladding can be insulated using the technique described for dry-lining solid walls. Buildings with blockwork or pressed concrete panel walls are best insulated simply by lining the walls with insulating plasterboard, held in place by battens at floor and ceiling level (it is difficult to make simple fixings into pressed concrete panels). The roof, which is usually felted and boarded on timber rafters, can be insulated in the same way, or the insulation-blanket-and-hardboard method can be used instead.

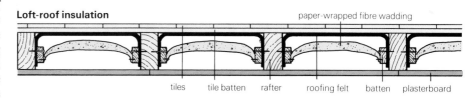

Loft-roof insulation — paper-wrapped fibre wadding — tiles · tile batten · rafter · roofing felt · batten · plasterboard

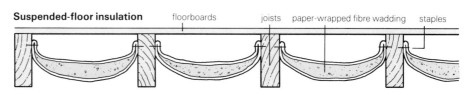

Suspended-floor insulation — floorboards · joists · paper-wrapped fibre wadding · staples

Finally, the concrete floor of an outbuilding can be made much warmer by laying 25mm (1in) thick slabs of expanded polystyrene and covering them with chipboard laid over heavy-duty polythene.

Insulating floors

Ground-level suspended timber floors let out more heat than solid ones and tend to be draughty, too. Insulating them effectively involves lifting the floorboards; loft insulation blanket (the paper-wrapped type is easiest to install) is then laid between the joists with the flanges tacked to their upper edges, then the floor covering is replaced. Another method is to cut 25mm (1in) thick expanded polystyrene slabs to match the joist separation, and to support the slabs with their top surface flush with the joists by driving nails into the sides of the joists at intervals.

With the floorboards raised, take the opportunity to lag any pipework below the floor (whether on the plumbing or the central heating system) and to replace any rubber-insulated electric cable with new PVC-covered cable. When replacing the floor covering, butt the boards tightly together to close draughty gaps, adding a new fillet of wood at the edge if necessary to make up the deficit. Lay stout kraft paper, building paper or hardboard over the boards to eliminate draughts between the boards (and in the case of hardboard, to level an uneven surface ready for laying smooth floorcoverings).

Finish by pinning quadrant beading to the skirting board, its lower edge flush with the floor, to help reduce draughts. If you stick foam draught strip to the underside of the beading first you will eliminate floor-edge draughts almost completely. Remember that timber floors move slightly under load, or as the humidity of the air varies; for this reason the beading is pinned to the skirting board only. The

use of fillers to close this gap is not recommended; floor movement will soon crack it and force it out.

On solid floors, insulation is seldom worth considering. Draughts are nonexistent and the floor will feel cold only if tile or sheet floor covering is used. The only viable method of insulation is to lay slabs of polystyrene foam and to cover them with a new chipboard floor. This will raise the floor level by up to 38mm (1½in), and will mean that doors have to be shortened and adjustments made at the door thresholds between insulated and uninsulated rooms, using wedge-shaped battens as ramps.

Insulating windows and doors

Double glazing offers the only practical way of cutting the heat loss through windows and glazed doors. For thermal insulation, the thickness of the glass makes no difference; it is the size of the air gap between the two panes that matters. A 6mm (¼in) gap offers a substantial improvement over single glazing, and the insulation value rises to its optimum value with an air gap of about 20mm (¾in). In air gaps larger than this, convection currents begin to occur and actually reduce the insulation value by transmitting heat from the warm inner pane to the cold outer one and thence to the exterior.

Glazed areas can be double-glazed in one of two ways. The glass can be replaced by a factory-made sealed unit, or a secondary sash can be fitted. Both methods can be used to double-glaze fixed or opening windows.

Sealed units consist of two panes of glass separated by a glass or metal spacer and sealed hermetically during manufacture. They are the most efficient form of double glazing because air leakage into the gap between the panes cannot occur (unless the seal is damaged). Once installed, it is hard to distinguish them from ordinary single glazing, and because the panes are sealed condensation will not form in the air gap. They can be fitted into existing windows, although if the rebate is not deep enough to take a standard unit, a special stepped unit must be selected.

The units are installed in the same way as ordinary glass, being retained by glazing sprigs covered with putty. A number of standard-sized units are available, but most sealed units are purpose-made to order. They are fitted as a matter of course in patio door and replacement window units, and are the best choice for double-glazing picture windows and other large glazed areas. They are available with one of the panes of patterned, wired, or solar-control glass, and with toughened glass in both panes – vital for safety with glazed doors and windows to ground level.

Secondary sashes usually use the existing window pane as the outer pane of the double glazing and are fitted to the inside of the window frame, to the inner face of opening casements and top lights, or to a subframe mounted within the window reveal. The nearer the secondary pane is to the existing pane the better for thermal insulation.

Whatever type of secondary glazing system is selected, condensation remains a problem. For a start, the existing window must be weatherproof and draughtproof for the system to be an efficient insulator. Yet as soon as the windows are opened for ventilation, moist air enters the air gap and will

form condensation as soon as the windows are closed again. Placing trays containing silica gel in the space between the panes may help to reduce condensation but it must be dried at intervals in a warm oven if it is to remain effective. Drilling small holes at a downward angle through the outer frame will also help in allowing condensed water to run away to the outside; the hole should be fitted with a plug of loose fibre (loft insulation blanket is ideal) to stop insects crawling in.

The simplest type of secondary window is plastic film similar to the type used to wrap food, and this is stretched across the window and held in

place with double-sided adhesive tape. It is not suitable for insulating metal windows, since the resulting air gap would be too small; although it does not look particularly attractive and it is easily damaged, it is inexpensive, easy to fit and to remove in summer, and prevents condensation quite efficiently.

The commonest sort of DIY double glazing involves fixing panes of glass to the window with U-shaped plastic channel or wooden beading, held by clips or screws. It is therefore easy to fit and to take down, and since each section of the window has its own secondary pane, its installation does not interfere with ventilation. However, it does not effectively prevent condensation unless the channel fits tightly against the window frame and incorporates a flexible seal to keep air out.

Sliding double glazing resembles glass cupboard doors; two or more panes of glass are mounted in track fitted round the window reveal. The simplest systems have sheets of glass with polished edges sliding in the track, these are rarely air-tight enough to prevent condensation. More elaborate systems, both DIY and professionally installed, have the glass mounted in rigid frames of plastic or aluminium, which usually incorporate sealing strip to reduce draughts and condensation. With this type, it is vital that the top and bottom tracks are precisely parallel, or the panes will not slide properly.

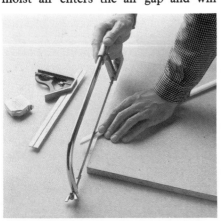

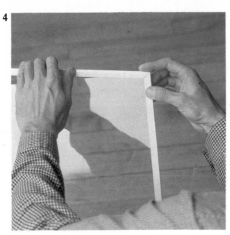

Installing proprietary double-glazing using plastic sheets instead of glass. 1 Mitre-cut the frame sections to length. 2 Score the glazing sheets to size with a sharp knife. 3 Snap the sheet along the score line. 4 Clip the frame sections to the edges of the sheets. 5 Attach the frames to the existing window; fit the locknuts that hold the hinged frames in the closed position. Hinged panels are also available; they are more convenient than fixed ones as they can be swung open for ventilation and window cleaning and can provide a means of escape in an emergency.

The importance of ventilation

As mentioned earlier, adequate ventilation is essential if the occupants of the house are to feel comfortable, and is most important for the safe and efficient functioning of fuel-burning appliances, especially boilers, gas fires, gas water heaters and paraffin heaters. Without the proper level of ventilation, poisonous combustion products can be emitted into the room with potentially lethal results.

Efficient draughtproofing will cut off many of the sources of air on which a heating appliance traditionally relied. It is therefore vital that, after draughtproofing your home, you guarantee an adequate supply to all fuel-burning appliances by fitting a ventilator near to it. This should have a 'free' area of at least twice the cross-section of the flue leading from the appliance; therefore a 100mm (4in) diameter flue needs a vent area of about 1500mm^2 (23¼sq in), a 150mm (6in) flue a vent area of 3500mm^2 (54¼sq in). By fitting the vent near the appliance, draughts are minimised.

Balanced-flue boilers and fires draw the air they need for safe and efficient combustion through the balanced flue, so you do not need to provide extra ventilation.

Draughtproofing will also reduce the speed at which cooking smells clear from a kitchen and steam from a bathroom. Here, controlled ventilation in the form of a cooker hood and a wall- or window-mounted extractor fan will clear the air rapidly, drawing air from the rest of the house into the room to replace that expelled through the duct in the exterior wall. It is important to select the correct size of extractor – it must be powerful enough to give between ten and 20 air changes per hour in a kitchen, or between five and ten air changes in a bathroom, so you should select a fan with a quoted extraction rate which is that number of times the volume of the room. For maximum efficiency, the fan should be sited high on the wall or window, at the opposite side of the room to where air enters the room from the rest of the house. See page 107 for how to wire extractors.

Such an extractor will help greatly to reduce condensation in the room where is is fitted. Since condensation occurs when warm, moist air strikes a cold surface, it makes sense to avoid as many cold surfaces such as ceramic tiles, as possible, and to double-glaze windows. It is also sensible to avoid adding more moisture to the air, by ducting the exhaust from washing machines and tumble driers directly to the outside via a length of flexible hose.

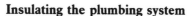

Insulating the plumbing system

It is vitally important to insulate the storage tanks and pipes in an insulated (and therefore cold) loft. The photographs *above* show the use of sheets of expanded polystyrene for insulating a cold-water tank. This material is easy to cut into intricate shapes – around pipes, for instance – and the sides and ends can be stapled or taped together. You can buy kits of this material; or you can use loft-floor insulation blanket. Do *not* insulate the loft floor immediately under the tank; heat rising from the room below will help prevent freezing.

Pipes can be insulated with bandage-type materials (*below, left*) that are wrapped around the pipe and taped at intervals, or with lengths of split foam

tube (*below, right*) that are slipped around the pipe and taped at joints or bends. The latter type is easier to instal on inaccessible pipe runs: it can be 'shunted' into position by succeeding lengths pushed along the pipe behind it.

Pipes to outside taps, and within the house on external walls and under floors, should certainly be insulated against frost. Outdoor piping is most effectively protected by enclosing it in plywood boxing packed with insulation: in frosty weather this piping should be isolated and drained by a stop-tap inside the house, with the outside tap left on.

Insulate the hot-water cylinder (if not pre-lagged) with a jacket conforming to BS5615. Measure the height and diameter of the cylinder before buying.

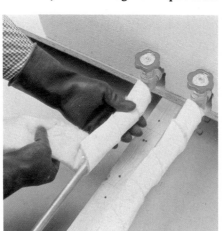

PART 3 INTERIOR DECORATING

More than a straightforward guide to decorating techniques, this thoroughly up-to-date section demonstrates how to use colour, pattern and texture creatively in your home, whether it's to produce a particular atmosphere, to accentuate a favourite feature or to disguise a problem. There are detailed explanations of the latest painting techniques, such as rag-rolling and bag graining, and descriptions of modern floor and wall coverings, plus lots of scope for you to indulge your own artistic talents in home decorating to produce that all-essential individual touch.

Colour 148–149
Equipment 150–151
Painting 152–159
Wallcoverings 160–173
Floor coverings 174–181

COLOUR

Colour in the home

In planning a decorative scheme it is useful to bring together samples of curtaining, carpeting and wallcoverings, as well as paint charts to experiment with different combinations.

Never under-estimate the importance of making the right decision about new colour schemes for the home. Different colours, tones and contrasts can create exciting or calming atmospheres, whichever you desire. Only a handful of people are probably fortunate enough to have the natural ability to blend different colours and textures together successfully and find it an extremely pleasurable activity, too! But for many other people, the prospect of producing a colour scheme that is different and entails experimenting with colour is daunting. In the end they play 'safe' by choosing neutrals which have worked for them in the past even if they have produced rooms that are uninteresting to live in!

Inspiration and confidence can gradually come simply by studying other people's ideas. If you are planning to redecorate in your home, make a point of visiting stores to look at their room sets or window displays, study manufacturers' brochures and paintcharts and obtain swatches of furnishing fabrics. Use a colour board to pin all these different colour references to so that you can judge how colours, patterns and textures blend together.

Often you are limited in the choice of new colour schemes by existing furnishings, like fixed carpets. You have to start a colour scheme somewhere, so pick out a primary colour from the patterned carpet and use this as your base colour. If possible, fix a

small piece of the carpeting onto your colour board so that you can take this around with you when visiting shops to look for paints, wallcoverings and soft furnishings.

An extremely important factor in the choice of colour is the atmosphere you want to create. Bedrooms tend to be thought of as places where you go to rest, and therefore relaxing soft colours have traditionally been used in these situations. However, children's bedrooms are often places which are used as playrooms, too, which indicates that perhaps strong, aggressive colours, like reds and greens, should be introduced to produce a lively atmosphere for active young children.

Bathrooms tend to be thought of as traditionally cool places, not only because of their damp atmospheres, but also because of the use of 'cool-looking' fittings, like ceramic baths, sinks and tiles! The whole atmosphere could be softened and given a 'warm' ambience by the use of earthy browns, complemented by apricot.

The size and shape of rooms should also have a strong influence on the choice of colour. For instance, where there is a particularly large room, it can be given a feeling of intimacy not only by using different shades of one basic colour but also by dividing it into different smaller areas for a variety of activities, for example, television watching, dining or reading. Small rooms generally need light tones or pastels in order to create a feeling of space.

The illustrations on these pages will give some exciting ideas for tricking the eye with the skilful use of colour.

Lighting must also be taken into consideration. Both natural and artificial light can affect a colour scheme, so as a rough guideline you can use cool colour schemes from blues and greens in a bright, sunny south-facing room, but they would create a distinctly chilly atmosphere in a north-facing situation, where the daylight tends to be limited. Here you can introduce warmth by choosing colours from the brown, red and yellow spectrum.

Patterns needs to be introduced with caution into a colour scheme, especially where the rooms are small, as they can cause overpowering atmospheres, especially if used in bright, advancing colours, like red. If you are nervous about introducing pattern into your colour scheme, remember that it can be done in other ways than with wallcoverings or furnishings. Patterns can be used subtly so that they add interest without dominating the room. They can be introduced as borders or friezes onto plain walls, as ceramic tiles used in panels for splash-backs, or as flooring. Pattern can also be obtained from textured surfaces, for example with upholstery fabrics or carpeting, or appear in striking effects on stylish laminated surfaces, used as wallboards in kitchens and bathrooms or for worktops or cupboards.

Aim to use a mixture of textures with different finishes, especially if you are using paints exclusively in one type of finish, for example, matt, silk or gloss. Interesting visual effects are achieved by a mix of both flat and shiny surfaces, so avoid the use of too many shiny textures found in silky furnishings, glass, chrome and laminated surfaces – they can be disturbing on the eye. Equally avoid the use of too many flat finishes found in natural woven fabrics, or wood, for example, that can produce a dull, non-stimulating atmosphere.

In the end it is a matter of experimenting with colours, textures and patterns by introducing a little of each and blending and balancing them to suit your particular needs. By using a selection of samples and swatches on the colour board and moving them around, eventually you should be able to produce a workable colour scheme for the different rooms in the home.

SOLVING PROBLEMS WITH COLOUR AND PATTERN

Problem	Suggested Solution
Rooms seem dark, with little natural light	Use white, cream, or yellow as predominant colour with plenty of bright-colour accents. Use mirrors to make the most of whatever light is available. Keep flooring pale.
Room seems cold; light comes from north or east	Use warm colours from red, orange, or yellow spectrum. Add plenty of 'warm' textures furnishing materials, and some patterns.
Ceiling seems too high	Paint ceiling in a dark, 'advancing' colour eg bright red. Dark *cool* colours (deep blue or green) can also be effective. Continue this colour partly down the walls to picture-rail height, possibly adding a border or frieze. Paint skirting same colour as flooring, which should also be dark. Avoid vertical patterns for the wallcovering.
Ceiling seems too low	Paint ceiling in light colour, eg pale blue, pale green, or blue-grey. Use a wallcovering with a vertical emphasis. Paint skirting same colour as walls. Floor coverings should be pale.
Narrow room	Paint end wall in an advancing, warm colour such as yellow; use a floorcovering with crossways stripe, or choose a plain one and paint the skirting the same colour.
Room seems too small	Use a wallcovering with a small pattern in pale colours, preferably in cool colours, such as greens and blues. Mirrors can give an illusion of more space.
Room has ugly features – mismatched windows or doors, unattractive radiators, pipes	Paint ugly features the same colour as their background or surrounding, and their faults will be less obvious. The all-surface silk-finish, oil-based paints are particularly satisfactory for this method of camouflage.
Ceiling slopes, with lots of awkward shapes	Use wallcovering with small design for both ceilings and walls in order to unify room. Avoid a pronounced pattern match.

Pale colours and large mirrors produce a bright and airy atmosphere.

Bright colours and strong patterns or textures have an advancing effect.

Ceilings with awkward shapes and angles are unified by small patterns.

EQUIPMENT

Tools and materials

Before you start it is important to make sure that you have a comprehensive range of tools and materials. The following items should enable you to tackle most jobs.

Steps Tubular metal steps are more durable than wooden ones, and not so heavy. Choose a pair about 2m (6½ft) high with a platform top.

Dust sheets are essential to protect flooring and furniture. Use old sheets, blankets or curtains.

Putty knife for filling cracks and holes.

Stripping knife A stiff-bladed scraper,

about 75mm (3in) wide, for removing old paint and wallpaper.

Filling knife Like a stripping knife but with a more flexible blade, from 25 to 150mm (1–6in) wide.

Shave hook A triangular tool with curved and flat scraping edges.

Wire brush for rust removal and also for scoring impenetrable wallcoverings.

Abrasives Available in various qualities and grades for different surfaces. Glasspaper is used for general work; 00 is the finest grade, 3 the coarsest. Wet and dry (silicon carbide) paper is best for preparing new wood or used wet for sanding old paint-

work to reduce dust; the finest grade is 400, coarsest 60. Use emery paper for metal preparation. Integrally powered orbital sanders (with dust bags) will cut down sanding time and reduce dust dispersal. Abrasive blocks with different qualities on opposite sides are suitable for curves and corners.

Bucket, sponge, sugar soap or detergent for washing down walls and paintwork.

White spirit for cleaning and preparing greasy areas.

Paint stripper and blowlamp or hot air gun for loosening paint (see page 153).

Primers and sealers for porous surfaces.

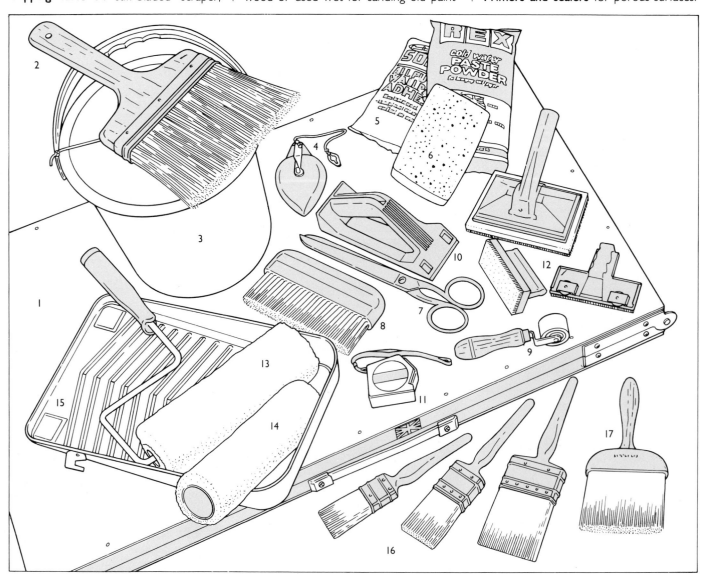

150

Fillers for cracks and holes.

Brushes The best brushes are made from first-grade pure bristle from wild hogs; bristles of poorer grades can also be satisfactory. Cheaper brushes may contain

Interior Decorating Tools and Equipment:
1 Fold-up wallpaper pasting table; 2 Pasting brush; 3 Plastic bucket; 4 Plumb line and bob; 5 Wallcovering adhesives; 6 Sponge; 7 Wallpaper scissors; 8 Wallpaper smoothing brush; 9 Seam roller; 10 Wallpaper scraper; 11 Steel measuring tape; 12 Paint pads; 13 Lambswool roller and head; 14 Mohair roller head; 15 Paint tray; 16 Paint brushes; 17 Large emulsion brush; 18 Scraper with replaceable blade; 19 Shave hook; 20 Stripping knife; 21 Laminate cutter; 22 Impact adhesive; 23 Adhesive spreader; 24 Sheet-vinyl knife; 25 Craft knife and 26 Blades; 27 Tenon saw; 28 Abrasive block; 29 Glasspapers; 30 Block plane; 31 Try-square; 32 Spirit level; 33 Steel straight-edge; 34 Profile gauge; 35 Wire brush; 36 Angled putty knife; 37 Filling knife; 38 Filler; 39 Tile grouts; 40 Tile cement; 41 Artisan's tile cutter; 42 Tile clipper.

other hair, or vegetable or synthetic fibres. Use the widest possible brush when covering large surfaces, as this will considerably cut down the time involved. A 100mm (4in) brush is good for applying emulsion to the walls; a range of brushes between 75mm (3in) and 25mm (1in) will cope with most other situations. Use a 12mm (½in) cutting-in brush with angled bristles for tackling narrow glazing bars.

Rollers For covering large, flat wall and ceiling areas, rollers score on speed and convenience. Foam are cheapest and can be thrown away after a paint job. However, they do tend to splash and produce paint drips – use for emulsion and oil-based paints. Mohair holds the paint well and is also good for emulsion and oil-based paints on smooth or slightly textured surfaces. Sheepskin or lambswool are best for heavily textured surfaces.

Paint pads made from short-pile fibre, are backed with foam and attached to metal or plastic plates with a handle, into which long attachments can be slotted for ceiling work. They are ideal for cutting in round architraves and door frames, and between ceilings and walls.

Paste Cellulose paste allows considerable 'slideability', while the traditional starch pastes are often recommended for certain relief wallcoverings. Heavy-duty pastes containing fungicides must be used for vinyl and the heavier types of wallcoverings to avoid mould growth behind them.

Pasting brush A coarse brush for applying wallcovering adhesives.

Pasting table folds flat for storage. Standard size is 1.8m × 0.6m (6 × 2ft).

Measuring rule Use a folding boxwood rule or a rigid steel tape.

Scissors A long pair of household scissors will suffice, but it pays to invest in large-bladed paperhanger's shears.

Plumb line and bob for drawing a straight upright guide line when wallpapering.

Seam roller A wooden roller is needed for smoothing down butted seams. Don't use on heavily embossed wallcoverings.

Hiring equipment Items like pasting tables, steam strippers (for removing stubborn wallcoverings), tile cutters and scaffold boards can be hired at a reasonable cost from hire shops. Compare prices, check equipment before leaving the shop and always ask for equipment instructions.

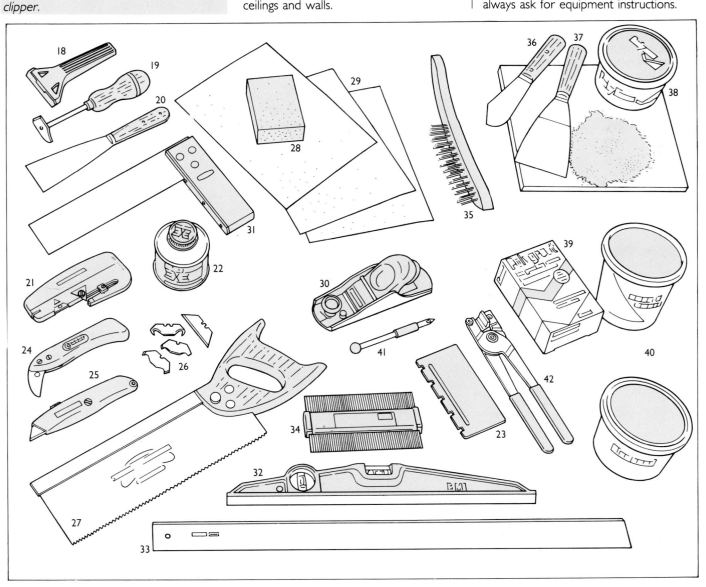

PAINTING

Paint types

A paint finish not only produces dramatic changes in appearance, it is also necessary to protect surfaces, particularly if they are of wood. This is why it is important to know what kinds of paint are available, and where to use each type.

Emulsion
This is a water-based paint that is thinned down with water, if necessary, and is particularly easy to remove from brushes and clothes. It is suitable for use on interior plaster surfaces on both walls and ceilings and also over textured wallcoverings. Emulsions should not be used as top coats on woodwork, where a stronger, more protective finish is required, although they may be used as an undercoat before an oil-based top coat is applied.

It is now possible to buy a solid emulsion which comes in a plastic paint tray. Used with a roller, this type is ideal for ceilings as it reduces the likelihood of runs, drips and mess generally. Only available in white, its coverage is similar to traditional emulsions.

Emulsions are available in various types of finish: matt, eggshell or silk. Matt gives a non-reflective finish, while silk provides a sheen, allowing more light to bounce off the painted surface. While there are no definite rules about where to use these finishes, it is best to use matt on a less than perfect surface, perhaps where a plastered wall has a large number of cracks and holes. Eggshell, with its mid-sheen, is particularly suitable for kitchens and bathrooms where the surfaces are subject to heat, steam and condensation generally.

Many emulsions are now toughened by the addition of synthetic resins like acrylic and vinyl. These are particularly suitable for any surfaces which will need to be regularly sponged or washed down to remove stains, or where condensation is likely to be a persistent problem, in bathrooms or kitchens, for example.

These toughened emulsions are also available in different finishes of matt, silk and eggshell. They tend to dry out more quickly once applied to the surface and their spreading power is slightly less than ordinary emulsion paint.

Oil-based paint
Although usually known as 'gloss' paint, there are matt or semi-matt finishes here, too. Polyurethane is often included to provide extra protection. Oil-based paints are thinned down with white spirit and are particularly suitable for heavy-wear areas such as woodwork, both inside and outside the home. They can also be used on metal surfaces.

The traditional oil-based paint is a liquid gloss and requires a certain degree of skill in application. If the brush is over-loaded with paint, it can easily cause unsightly runs and drips. The alternative for the amateur decorator is the non-drip type, known variously as thixotropic or gel paints. These must not be stirred at all, as this can reduce or completely eliminate their non-drip qualities. The brush is loaded and the paint applied in one even flow. It is not spread out and thinned down as with ordinary liquid gloss paints.

Some types contain alkyd resins that, like polyurethane, give an extra tough finish, which works well in heavy traffic areas, for example for the woodwork in hallways or where there is a young family. When using non-drip types, it is not necessary to apply an undercoat on previously painted woodwork, and normally one coat will be sufficient to give good coverage on a well-prepared surface.

Oil-based finishes range from gloss and semi-gloss, known also as egg-shell, to matt. Choice will depend upon individual taste, although egg-shell is considered to be particularly suitable for bathrooms and kitchens, because of its high resistance to

---

DECORATING SEQUENCE

There is a correct order in which to tackle work in order to prevent a muddle and to avoid subsequent spoiling of completed jobs:

Painting the ceiling and woodwork, papering walls
1 Preparation, including any priming and undercoating
2 Paint ceiling (first coat)
3 Paint woodwork (first coat)
4 Hang lining paper (if necessary)
5 Paint ceiling (second coat)
6 Paint woodwork (second coat)
7 Hang paper

Painting woodwork, papering ceiling and walls
1 Preparation, including any priming and undercoating
2 Paint woodwork (first coat)
3 Hang lining paper on walls (if necesary)
4 Paint woodwork (second coat)
5 Paper ceiling
6 Paper walls

Papering and painting the ceiling, papering and painting walls, painting woodwork
(With this plan, use a white textured paper such as a woodchip, which can be painted over; or simply paint over a lining paper.)
1 Preparation, including any priming and undercoating
2 Paper ceiling
3 Paint woodwork (first coat)
4 Paper walls
5 Paint ceiling (first coat)
6 Paint wallpaper (first coat)
7 Paint ceiling (second coat)
8 Paint walls (second coat)
9 Paint woodwork (second coat)

Painting ceiling, walls, and woodwork
1 Preparation, including any priming and undercoating
2 Paint ceiling (first coat)
3 Paint walls (first coat)
4 Paint woodwork (first coat)
5 Paint ceiling (second coat)
6 Paint walls (second coat)
7 Paint woodwork (second coat)
You may be able to get away with only one coat on some surfaces, but always finish up in the order 'ceiling, walls, woodwork'.

heat, steam and condensation. It can also be washed frequently without reducing its durability and appearance.

Textured paint

It is particularly recommended for surfaces that are uneven, or covered with hair-line cracks, or are just generally in poor condition. Textured paints also bring interesting effects to the walls and ceilings, eliminating the need for wallcoverings. Ready-mixed, textured paints provide a flexible, washable decorative coating, which is obtainable in different thicknesses depending on the state of the surfaces to be covered. Some brands are available in pale pastels, apart from the widely available brilliant white. Textured paints have a certain amount of flexibility, which means they can withstand the normal movement of the house structure.

When applied with a brush, textured paints give a fine finish, whereas a coarse roller produces a much rougher effect, camouflaging imperfect surfaces. In addition, there are different roller heads that can be bought specially for use with these paints to provide different patterns and designs after the paint has been applied. Usually individual manufacturers supply useful leaflets on how to achieve different decorative effects with their product. Before applying, old wallcoverings must be stripped off and bare plaster will need to be primed.

The condensation resistance characteristics of textured paints make them particularly suitable for bathrooms and kitchens.

Special paints

A large variety of special paints is available for particular projects:

Brick and tile paint, available in matt or shiny red, is specially formulated to adhere well to these surfaces.

Bitumen black can be used to protect all exterior metalwork.

Berlin black is an eggshell finish suitable for cookers, stoves and structural ironwork such as railings and gates.

Heatproof stove black, tested to 177°C (350°F) is also available.

Blackboard flat-black paint can, when dry, be written on with chalk. It can be used for renovating scoreboards or to make a message area on any wall.

Scoreboard green is also available for scoreboards and table-tennis tops.

Fluorescent paints give an outstandingly brilliant effect in pink or green, and green *luminous paints*, which shine in the dark, are also available.

Glass paints from craft shops are for applying translucent coloured designs to window panes.

Technique and preparation

Successful decorating starts long before you open a can of paint. It is important to put right, at the outset, any defects outside or inside the room, which might later spoil all your hard work.

Filling holes and cracks

Scores of brands of filler for plaster and other walling materials are available from DIY and decorating shops, and their uses are explained fully on the packaging.

Cellulose general-purpose fillers are available ready-mixed or, more economically, in powder form. Use this type for filling holes in interior walls and in and around woodwork. Large gaps can be plugged with dampened newspaper before filling, but if you are working near a power point, use strips of wood or hardboard instead. When filling dents, cracks, or nail holes in woodwork, make a fairly stiff mix and press well in with a filling knife, leaving the filler slightly proud of the surface. Allow it to harden, then rub it smooth and flush with its surrounding surface with glass-paper. Apply a metal primer or multipurpose primer to nail and screw heads before filling to prevent rust marks.

New multi-purpose ready-mixed fillers are available in tubs and can be used for wood and plaster as described above (although they are more expensive). Many of them dry harder than old-style cellulose fillers and so they can also be used for filling brickwork, metal, and concrete.

Plaster, available in small bags, is cheaper than proprietary fillers for large-scale repairs to defective plaster. There are two extra tools which make large-scale plaster repairs easier: a hawk (a flat square of metal or wood set on a handle, to hold the plaster, and a plasterer's float (a tool with a rectangular blade used to smooth down the wet plaster).

Primers and sealers

Many manufacturers offer universal or multi-purpose primers, which are suitable for applying to virtually any priming job (but always make a point of checking the list of applications on the can).

Painting over new plaster, brick, stone, cement and concrete. All new surfaces should be allowed to dry out for at least six months before painting, owing to the large amounts of water used in building construction. Fresh plaster in an old room is

Burning off old paint with a hot-air gun.

If old paint is unsound it must be removed. There are three main methods:

Burning off. This is the only suitable method for removing oil-based paint from woodwork. You can use a blowlamp which works off bottled gas, or a hot-air gun which is powered by electricity; the latter is more suitable near glass as there is less likelihood of damage. Always remove anything from the work area that might catch fire and wear gloves to protect your hands from flakes of hot paint.

Chemical paint strippers. These are applied either with an old paint brush or with steel wool. After 10 to 15 minutes the paint will bubble and soften and can be stripped off with a paint hook. Again always wear gloves and always follow the manufacturer's instructions.

Dry scraping. This technique may be suitable if the area concerned is small. Use a stripping knife gently to avoid damage.

usually dry enough to paint within five days. You may find white powdery deposits (efflorescence) on the surface; this is caused by salts left behind by the water. Do *not* wet or wipe them with a damp cloth or the wall will simply re-absorb them. Brush them away with a piece of dry, coarse fabric, such as sacking. Fill any holes or cracks, and sand smooth. If you are using emulsion paint there is no need to prime the surface, but thin the first coat as directed on the can; be careful not to over-thin. Allow it to dry completely (on new work this may take 12 hours) before applying a second coat. If you are using oil-based paint (gloss or satin finish) seal the surface first with a primer-sealer or multipurpose primer, applied liberally, and allow it to dry thoroughly.

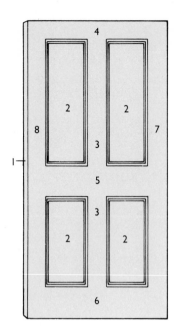

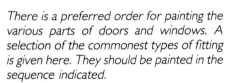

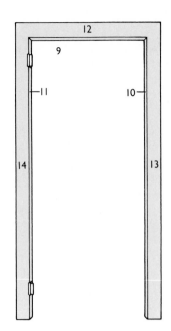

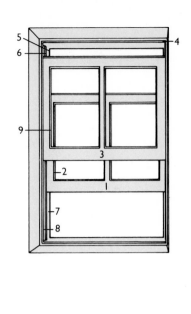

There is a preferred order for painting the various parts of doors and windows. A selection of the commonest types of fitting is given here. They should be painted in the sequence indicated.

Painting over wallboards

Prime any nail heads with metal primer, allow it to dry, and then fill any cracks and sand the surface smooth. If you are using emulsion paint there is usually no need to prime, but the first coat can be thinned as directed on the can. If you are using an oil-based paint, treat the surface first with a coat of primer-sealer or multi-purpose primer. Seal hardboards and other wallboards with multi-purpose primer or a hardboard primer-sealer. For polystyrene ceiling tiles or panels, use only emulsion paint: oil-based paints are a considerable fire risk. Apply two coats, if necessary thinning the first. On asbestos wallboards and tiles you should also use emulsion paint, but seal the surface first with a stabilizing primer.

Painting over old paper

You can paint over many old wallpapers with emulsion provided they are soundly stuck to the wall. Some prominent patterns, particularly those containing gold or silver, have a tendency to bleed through the new paint when it dries. If this proves the case in a test area, seal the whole wall with a coat of primer-sealer and allow it to dry before applying the emulsion paint.

Stripping off old paper

For a good finish it is often necessary to strip off old wallpaper before painting. In older properties it is not unusual for the walls to have several sheets of paper stuck one on top of another. In such cases it is often possible to begin the work of strip-

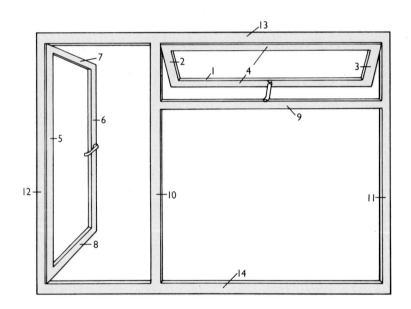

ping by peeling away the paper at any corner where it has begun to lift. When you have removed as much of the old paper as possible by this method, take a bucket filled with hot water to which you have added a few drops of household detergent or a proprietary wallpaper stripping agent. Apply the solution with an old paintbrush or a sponge, repeating the process several times if necessary, until the paper comes away reasonably easily. Use a scraper to lift the paper away from the wall. When you have removed all the old paper, wash down the wall again to get rid of the old paste. Sponge the wall yet again with clean water. Several layers of paper are difficult to remove. Steam strippers are available for hire and are especially useful for softening layers of wallpaper or wallpaper that has been painted.

Repainting walls and ceilings

Wash down the walls with water and household detergent or a proprietary paint cleaner. Work from bottom to top to avoid runs down into the dirty parts, which can create difficult-to-remove marks. Rinse off, again from bottom to top, with clean water. Then wash down the ceiling.

Any projecting nibs of old paint must be scraped or sanded smooth, and holes or cracks then filled. When the walls are dry, use a scraper to remove any loose or flaky areas of paint – but take care not to dig into the surface. Sand the edges of bare patches with a fine grade of silicon-carbide (wet-and-dry) paper used wet. Then, if you are using emulsion, apply paint so as to bring this surface up to the same level as the surrounding area before applying the first all-over coat.

Prime any bare areas of plaster with primer-sealer or with a multi-purpose primer, and allow it to dry before applying an oil-based paint. Flaky surfaces can be treated with primer-sealer before painting with emulsion or oil-based paints. Apply an aluminium sealer (prior to painting) to old stains which might come through the top coats. Areas which have been attacked by mould should be washed down with a solution of fungicidal cleaner and allowed to dry, then coated with a primer before painting.

Stripping off old distemper
Old-fashioned size-bound distemper is still found in some old houses (it is rarely used for modern decorating). Usually applied to ceilings, it comes off as a dry powder when rubbed and softens easily when wet. It must be completely removed, otherwise new paint (or paper) will start to come away after a short time. Using an old paint brush, apply water over an area of about 1m², wetting the surface thoroughly. Dampen a sponge and remove the old coating with a scrubbing motion. Change the water frequently. Thick coatings can be gently scraped off. When completely dry, treat the whole area with a coat of primer-sealer, and allow this to dry thoroughly before applying the first paint coat.

Painting over bare wood
Apply metal primer to any nail or screw heads. Fill any holes and cracks, allow the filler to dry, and then sand the whole surface with glasspaper, finishing off with a fine grade. Seal knots with shellac knotting to prevent resin oozing through and staining the paint at a later date. Prime softwoods with a coat of white or pink wood primer (there is little difference between them but if your undercoat is to be white, a pink primer will help you to apply an even undercoating). Use aluminium primer for hardwoods and for all woods treated with preservative. Allow the primer to dry thoroughly, then apply a thin coat of undercoat and one or two coats of oil-based gloss or silk finish, lightly sanding in between to provide a good key.

Painting over old gloss paintwork
Do not remove old gloss paint unless you have to. This applies even if there are already many coats of paint on the woodwork, and even if you are changing from a dark colour to a light one: a thick coating of sound, old paint helps to protect the wood.

Painting over metal
All traces of grease, dirt, and rust must be removed by rubbing with abrasive paper or a wire brush, using white spirit if necessary. Wash down the surface

thoroughly, allow it to dry, and treat it with metal primer immediately, as corrosion of bare steel and iron can start within an hour. When the primer is dry, apply an oil-based undercoat and allow this to dry, then finish with one or two coats of oil-based gloss or silk paint.

Ceilings
Paint pads are particularly useful for ceilings, as they minimize drips and splashing. If you want to use a roller, choose a mohair type with a long-handled extension. Emulsion paint is generally ideal for ceilings; matt types are probably best as the reflection from silk or satin finishes can be tiring to the eyes in artificial light.

Rig up a comfortable working platform, preferably a scaffold board between two step ladders. Try to paint ceilings in a single operation without a break because joins between old and new work may show. Work backwards from the window wall into the room, otherwise you will be operating in your own shadow. If you are using a brush, cut-in to achieve a straight edge where the ceiling meets the walls, then apply paint in broad strips, about 600mm (2ft) across, and finish off with light, even strokes in the direction of the light. Use a non-drip jelly paint if possible, and never overload the brush.

If you are using a roller, cut-in edges and corners with a brush, then apply the paint, working in strips across the room. Use alternate criss-cross strokes, finishing off with light strokes in the direction from which the light comes.

Walls
Oil-based paint. If using a brush, start in the top right corner if you are right-handed (top left if left-handed). Use the cutting-in

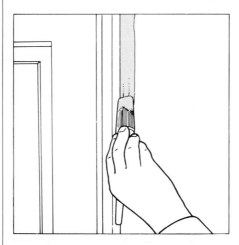

Before painting a wall it is important to run along all the edges with a small paint brush to give a neat clean finish. This is known as cutting in.

technique for the top edges. Paint in squares about 600mm (2ft) wide, working down the wall. Apply the paint in up-and-down strips; then, without reloading, brush out crossways, and finish off with light upward strokes from the wet edge back into the freshly painted area. When one section is completed, start at the top again. Use the largest-size brush you can comfortably handle: 100mm (4in) wide is best for walls.

When using a roller, first cut-in corners and edges with a brush, keeping the strip as narrow as possible to avoid a contrast in finish between the brush and roller strokes. Then apply paint by roller in criss-cross strokes, finishing off with light upward strokes in one direction to achieve the smoothest surface.

Emulsion paint. If using a brush, work in strips of about 200mm (8in) across the room, from right to left. Cut-in the top edge; then, with matt emulsion, apply the paint with criss-cross strokes, and with sheen (silk or satin) emulsion, finish off with light upward strokes for an even finish. If using a roller, work in similar strips, but remember to cut-in all the corners and edges first.

Skirtings
Always use an oil-based paint as these areas need maximum protection. Thorough preparation is essential to remove inevitable dirt and grime and to repair chipped and cracked or flaking areas. Use wide adhesive tape to protect floorings that cannot be taken up for painting; or it may be possible to push a piece of thin card under the skirting. Cut-in along top and bottom edges. Apply the paint with up-and-down strokes, then brush-out horizontally, following the line of the grain.

Radiators, pipes, cisterns
Preparation is particularly important: it is essential to remove all traces of rust. For areas of rust that are particularly difficult to shift, you can buy special chemical treatments from motor-accessory shops. After cleaning back to bare metal, it is vital to prime immediately with a metal primer. Use oil-based paints on metalwork – a radiator brush is useful for getting into awkward corners, particularly on pillar radiators. Always paint radiators when they are cold, otherwise the quality of finish will be impaired. Never use paints containing metal pigment, as they will lessen the amount of heat radiated.

Doors
Oil-based paint is preferable to emulsions, as doors receive a fair amount of wear and

the paintwork should therefore be easy to keep clean. Remove the door handles and finger plates before painting. Leave the spindle in place and keep the handle nearby in case you accidentally shut yourself inside the room. Paint the door edges first. If using different colours for each side of the door, stand so that the door opens away from you and paint the hinge edge the same colour as the side of the door facing you. Paint the opposite (closing) edge the same colour as the other side of the door.

Flush doors

Work in strips across the door, from top to bottom, using as big a brush as feels comfortable. Near the edges, brush outwards to avoid a build-up of paint. If you use a roller, paint in strips the full height of the door, completing the edges and frame with a brush.

Windows

If you find it difficult to paint a straight edge around the glass, use masking tape. Peel off the tape before the paint is completely dry, otherwise you may pull off some of the paint film with it. Alternatively, you can use one of the metal shields available at decorating shops, or a cutting-in brush. There is a correct order for painting windows which makes the job easier and gives a better result. (See page 154.)

Sash windows

Again, tackle the window first and then the frame. Pull down the top (outer) sash so that it is in the middle of the window, and push up the bottom sash slightly further, so that the top sash projects below the bottom sash by a few inches as shown in the illustration (page 154). Paint as much of the window as possible in the order shown. Next put the sashes back into their normal positions, with the sashes almost closed top and bottom. Carry on painting as indicated.

Laying masking tape around the edge of the glass gives a perfectly clean finish. Remove the tape before the paint is dry.

Decorative paint finishes

Paint is one of the cheapest forms of decoration for the home, although on large expanses the results can be fairly bland and therefore uninteresting unless some kind of relief decoration or finish is added.

Before the arrival of wallcoverings, designers and artists added their own individual touches by using a variety of paint finishes, which brought originality to the walls and ceilings. These techniques are still used by interior designers in beautiful old stately homes in order to retain the original character. However, they can equally well be carried out by amateur decorators as they require few tools and no special skills – just plenty of patience while you try to test out the different paint finishes and find the one that suits both you and the room.

In most cases, the paint finishes described here use just a base coat of ordinary emulsion with an additional toning or contrasting emulsion to provide the finish. After the base coat has been applied to the wall and left to dry (in most cases), the second colour is coaxed into subtle patterns and designs by a variety of simple techniques.

Whichever paint finish is chosen, the walls and ceilings must always be properly prepared (see page 153). None of these fine paint finishes will disguise bad workmanship, like unfilled cracks or dirty walls, so be prepared to spend at least the usual amount of time on surface preparation.

The secret of successful paint decoration is to try out all the different paint techniques on odd sheets of white paper or lining paper to check how the imprint or impression works out. You may need, in some cases, to reduce the amount of pressure on the tool you are using, or thin the paint down, or perhaps change the sponge or use just one side of it. If you practise well first, you will soon find the 'knack' of achieving the results you want, so allow plenty of time at the beginning for this part of re-decoration.

When using certain paint finishes, like bag graining, it is helpful to have a second person working with you so that the pattern or design can be worked through before the paint dries.

Before you take a freshly loaded applicator to the wall, always test out the imprint on a spare piece of paper first to make sure it is the right size, depth, etc. Keep a piece of paper handy for this by the side of the paint basin. Dabbing the applicator onto the sheet first will ensure that any excess paint will be removed and none will drip onto the walls.

Rag-rolling

This technique gives a glazed finish that resembles the look of fine taffeta or water silk. It was used to decorate the drawing rooms of fine homes many centuries ago and is still used as a favourite form of decoration today in older houses with character, where the designs are exaggerated to enhance large expanses of wall or ceilings. It is achieved by rolling a piece of creased rag over a 'glazed' surface.

To successfully produce the high glaze associated with rag-rolling, you must use an oil-based eggshell emulsion instead of ordinary water-based emulsion. You will need enough eggshell emulsion to use as the base coat for all the surfaces, plus half this quantity of the rag-rolling colour. Also required are a large brush, white spirit, measuring jugs, a paint kettle, plenty of cotton rags, and sheets of white paper or lining paper for testing the technique.

Technique

Once the walls have been correctly prepared, washing down and filling where necessary, apply the base coat, making sure that it covers the surfaces well. If necessary, apply two coats for good coverage and leave to dry for at least 24 hours.

To prepare the 'glaze', add one part of white spirit to one part of rag-rolling colour and use a spoon to mix well together. Pour this solution into the paint kettle and mix again for even colouring. It is important to have another person helping so that once the 'glaze' has been applied to

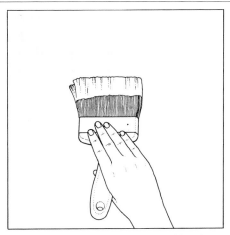

In rag-rolling, a glaze is applied with a large brush over a base colour. The texture is

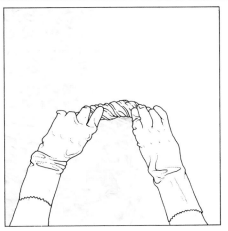

produced by running a rolled-up cotton rag over the glaze when wet.

Without the textured paint finish this beautifully cool green room would be much less attractive; the walls would appear hard and flat and the atmosphere would be harsh and unwelcoming.

the wall, the other person can rag roll immediately.

Begin by working from either a top right- or left-hand corner downwards, using a wide brush to apply the 'glaze' in an area about the width of a piece of average-sized wallpaper. Apply the 'glaze' in long, even, vertical strokes, making sure it doesn't drip. If it does, it has been thinned down too much and a fresh 'glaze' must be prepared.

Immediately the first strip has been applied, the second person should begin to rag roll as follows: wearing rubber gloves, take a piece of fine rag and roll it into a kind of 'sausage' about 10cm (4in) wide. Carefully place this 'sausage' at the bottom of the wall and roll upwards over the

'glaze'. The creases in the rag 'sausage' leave a broken pattern in the 'glaze'. Very soon the edges of the rag will become saturated with paint 'glaze', so re-roll the fabric so that a clean side can be used over the 'glaze'. As the rag becomes coated, you will need to replace it with a new one. Continue rolling upwards, just slightly overlapping one vertical strip with another.

As the first strip is completed, the next width of 'glaze' needs to be applied quickly, ready for rag-rolling. When rag-rolling close to the previous strip, always slightly overlap onto it to avoid join marks when the 'glaze' dries. If the 'glaze' is applied too thickly to the wall, don't attempt to take it off, but instead re-rag this section, which will remove more paint and give the surface an even texture.

It is important not to stop in the middle of a wall, but carry on to completion to avoid obvious joins and overlaps. Never use a new 'glaze' to finish off a wall. It could vary slightly in colour from the old one already used. Instead add the remains of the old to the new and use this mixture to give continuity of colour and tone.

Ragging on

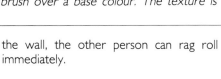

This is a much simpler version of rag-rolling and only requires ordinary emulsion plus rags to give subtle patterns similar to those found on wallcoverings. It is usual to apply a slightly darker colour over a paler base coat, but you can experiment with pale colours over dark backgrounds, or even contrasts to give a modern look to a traditional paint technique. Here, it is worth practising first as the effects can be as subtle or as dramatic as you desire!

You will need a sufficient quantity of emulsion base coat — two coats may be necessary on poor or porous walls — plus one third of this amount of a ragging-on colour in emulsion, pieces of fine cotton, such as ordinary sheeting, plus a bowl and

an old spoon for mixing, and paper for testing the prints.

Technique
It is worth trying pieces of rag of different sizes as they will each produce different patterns. The rag needs to be scrunched up into a ball and then dipped into the ragging-on paint. Where you want to achieve a uniform pattern, just keep dipping the same side of the rag into the paint and dabbing it onto the wall. If you want a random, uneven effect, rearrange the rag frequently when reloading it with paint. It is best to try out the pattern on the paper before applying it to the wall. As before, brush on the base coat and make sure it is completely dry before proceeding with the second colour.

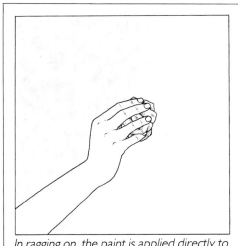

In ragging on, the paint is applied directly to the wall with a rag.

Decant a little of the 'ragging-on' colour into a shallow basin. Scrunch up the rag between the fingers; dip it well into the paint and press onto the wall, applying the same pressure as for your test. Be careful not to slide or skid the rag when taking it off as this can cause smears. If this happens, use a clean rag to gently mop up the excess and then re-rag this spot.

Once you have taken the rag off, change the angle slightly and replace on the wall near the previously ragged area, but leaving a little space to accentuate the design; leave even spaces between each ragging. Don't allow the paint to become too faint on the rag. Keep dipping it into the basin to reload with paint, pressing it down onto a spare piece of paper to take off excess paint. It is always wise to check the density of colour and pattern each time you re-coat the rag as they can change, causing obvious variations in the overall effect on the walls themselves.

When you come to the junctions between walls and ceilings or close up to door frames or woodwork, use just a tiny corner of the rag to apply the colour. If you get any paint onto the surrounding woodwork, rub it off immediately with a clean damp cloth. When the paint has dried out completely, you may discover the odd solid blob of colour. This is easily camouflaged by 'ragging-on' the base colour over the top of the ragging-on paint in delicate amounts.

Sponging

Probably one of the easiest finishes to achieve is sponging. It can be done very quickly once the 'knack' has been acquired. By dipping a sponge into paint then dabbing it on the wall a fine mottled effect is produced rather like a speckled egg. Usually two colours are used. The first, a lighter base colour, is applied in the normal way to the walls and left to dry out, then the second colour is sponged on top. You can add more toning colours on top by sponging, but great care must be taken to use blending tones to obtain pleasing results. This fine decorative finish looks pretty in bedrooms or in 'country style' kitchens.

Sponging produces a beautifully soft mottled appearance and is equally perfect as a foil for the clean-lined furniture as it is for the large-leaved houseplant. It is not a difficult technique.

You will normally need enough base-colour emulsion to cover the surfaces in one coat. If the walls seem to soak up the paint or are in bad condition, apply a second and leave to dry for at least twenty-four hours.

For the sponged patterns, you should only need about one litre of paint of each colour. The ideal sponge for producing the speckled effect is a natural (marine) type that can be bought from good quality chemists. Study it well before purchase. The sponge, which can be cut up into manageable sizes, needs to have a fairly even surface. A largish hole in the middle of groups of smaller holes can create uneven patterns. You may like the irregular features that this can bring – but always make sure by testing first on a spare piece of paper. A shallow bowl is needed to decant the sponge paints so that the right amount is used each time.

Technique

Always make sure the sponge is fully expanded by dipping into water and then squeezing it out thoroughly. At this stage the sponge should be damp but not wet which could noticeably dilute the paint colour.

Decant a few tablespoonfuls of the paint to be sponged into the shallow basin, making sure it just coats the base evenly. Too much paint would make the sponge too wet and result in a splodgy effect. Holding the sponge firmly in your fingertips, dip the flat edge into the paint so that it coats the sponge and is absorbed.

At this stage it is vital to try out the impression the sponge will make, so dab the sponge onto your spare piece of paper, placing the flat, coated edge down firmly. Don't apply too much pressure, but rather adopt a dabbing, 'pecking' action, pulling off quickly and cleanly from the surface so that a crisp pattern is left behind. Any hesitation can result in smears round the edges. If this happens when working on the wall itself, don't attempt to deal with it immediately. Instead, let the paint dry, then dip a clean sponge in base coloured paint and lightly sponge this over the affected spot until it is hidden.

When you are satisfied with the tests, start on the wall itself. Confine yourself to small sections at a time, placing the sponge down firmly and releasing it equally firmly. You can make the speckling as open or as dense as you wish. The character will depend on the size of the sponge holes and the pressure applied.

Eventually all the paint on the sponge will be used, so dip it into the basin again to fill it. Always test the loaded sponge on the spare sheet of paper before going back to

The speckled appearance produced by sponging varies according to the pattern of holes in the sponge. This texture is produced by applying paint directly to the wall over a base colour.

the wall again. This will also take off any potential drips of excess paint.

When you get to the junctions between the walls and ceiling, you will need to take special care that the effect is not spoiled by large blobs of solid colour. In these situations, just use the corner of the sponge to get into these tight spots. It is always useful to have a clean rag handy to quickly wipe off splashes and specklings that become merged together and appear as blobs.

Paint colours usually dry darker, so if your top colour looks close to the base colour and does not give the desired contrast, wait until it dries before doing anything about it. If you feel the sponged-on colour is too dark, you can dilute it with about 50 per cent water and mix well by stirring with a wooden spoon. This should give a paler shade. Obviously all these tests for colour should be done at the testing stage, and not on the walls themselves where mistakes are difficult to rectify.

It is best to complete one wall before finishing for the day. Always wash out the sponge in warm water and rinse in cold.

If you intend to apply a second base coat, always allow the first to dry out for at least 24 hours. Use the second sponge colour to fill in any tiny gaps between the base coat and the first sponging. If you use a smaller sponge, or one with tinier holes with a contrast colour, you will achieve a fine but pronounced speckling.

Bag graining

Bag graining gives a traditional broken-paint finish to the walls using only the simplest of tools – a plastic bag filled with rags. The effect can be beautifully subtle, giving an appearance of crushed velvet, and is highly suitable for living rooms or study areas.

You can 'bag grain' either in a pale colour over a white base coat, or vice versa. Using a slightly deeper tone for graining can produce a lovely faded design. This paint finish is achieved by painting on a base colour followed by a graining colour which is patterned by pulling a rag-filled plastic bag across it. It is therefore advisable to have a second person handy, so that while one is applying the graining paint, the other can follow behind with the plastic bag while the paint is still wet.

For this finish, you need enough base coat to cover the surface, plus half this quantity of the bag-graining colour, a paint kettle, a large brush, clear plastic bags plus rags, clean cloths and some white sheets of paper or lining paper for carrying out tests prior to working on the walls themselves.

Technique
If necessary apply two base coats, and allow the second coat to dry for at least 24 hours. Half-fill the plastic bag with small pieces of rag and secure the top with a small piece of string. The graining paint needs to be thin to be effective, so dilute one part water to one part paint and mix well with a wooden spoon.

Starting from a right- or left-hand corner and, working in sections of about 60cm (2ft), use a wide brush to paint on the graining paint in even vertical strokes. The paint should be thin enough so that it covers the base colour but doesn't run down the wall. When each section has

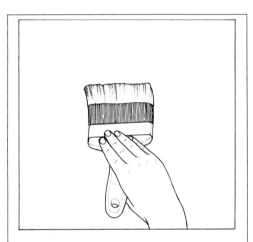

As with rag-rolling, bag graining is carried out on a coat of thin paint.

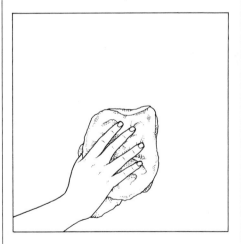

The texture is produced by pressing down and lifting off a rag-filled plastic bag.

been completed with the brush, the second person should follow straight behind using the plastic bag to press down, immediately lifting off and pressing down onto the next spot. This will produce a crinkled effect, which should be left to dry out. Try to overlap each graining slightly.

Make sure you practise this paint finish before starting on the walls – it is quite easy to smudge the graining as you bring the plastic bag away from the surface. To avoid 'bands' where one section finishes and another starts, one person will need to paint in the next 60cm (2ft) section quickly as the graining in the previous section nears completion. Here also never stop in the middle of one wall – it can be very noticeable. Instead, try to complete one wall before you finish for the day. Always make sure you dilute enough graining colour to complete a whole wall. Add any surplus to the next dilution – to ensure that the right colour is achieved.

Decorative paint techniques produce an atmosphere of style and elegance. The walls look best when pictures and other decorations are kept small.

WALLCOVERINGS

What to choose

Although 'wallpaper' is the term in general use, strictly speaking we should talk about wallcoverings, as many of the patterns and textures now sold for walls are made not from paper but from plastic or fabric. Indeed, unless you are familiar with them already, you may well be confused by what is now a bewildering variety of types of wallcovering on the market.

Pulps are the cheapest type of paper available, made from a single thickness of paper with a printed pattern. When pasted, pulps are easily torn.

Duplex papers are made in layers and are therefore stronger and easier to handle during hanging. There is a vast range of designs, often with matching or toning fabrics. Some duplex papers are embossed to create textured effects.

Woodchip papers are relatively cheap papers, which have woodchips bonded to the front surface to give a textured effect; they are available in a range of grades from fine to coarse.

Relief papers have a deeply embossed relief effect, which may be a formal pattern or a simulation of a certain texture, such as rough plaster, brick, or pebble-dash. Anaglypta is the cheapest and most easily available; Supaglypta is more expensive, being thicker and heavier; Lincrusta is expensive and is made from a thick mixture containing linseed oil, which is fused onto a backing paper; expert hanging is essential as, once hung and painted, it is very difficult to strip.

Flocks are expensive wallpapers. They are available in mainly traditional patterns – originally, they were developed to copy Italian velvet wall-hangings. The designs are made from chopped fibres of silk or rayon stuck to a backing to give a raised pile effect. They need expert hanging to avoid crushing or marking the pile.

Ready-pasted wallpapers have dry adhesive on the back. To activate the paste, each length of paper is soaked in a small trough of water and then applied directly to the wall.

Dry-strippable paper is useful when the time comes to redecorate as it can be pulled away dry from the wall, without the need for soaking and scraping.

Washable papers have a coating of clear plastic, which makes them easier to hang. Strictly speaking, however, they should be sponged rather than washed.

Vinyl wallcoverings have patterns printed with vinyl inks onto a layer of vinyl fused to a paper backing. It is reasonably priced and a wide variety of designs is available, including co-ordinated ranges. Textured vinyls are available for a more subtle effects; they are plain coloured but textured to imitate other types of surface. Heavily textured vinyls are also available to imitate tiles and materials such as glasscloth, stone, and brick. Roll lengths of these may be less than standard. There are also flock vinyls with a pile surface, available in rich or pastel colours in a variety of mainly traditional designs. Metallic vinyls are sophisticated and glamorous (but expensive), with shiny areas of gold, silver, bronze, and copper incorporated into the design. Most of the vinyls are dry-strippable and are available ready-pasted or unpasted, the latter usually being cheaper.

Polyethylene, a thick film of foamed plastic, is used for some of the newer wallcoverings which are extremely light in weight and easy to hang. With this type, you paste the wall, not the wallcovering, and roll the paper on, cutting and trimming as you go.

Fabric wallcoverings are available paper-backed, either in rolls the same size as wallpaper or by the yard or metre, so that you can order exactly what you require with no wastage – a distinct advantage, as this type of wallcovering is expensive, but could be used to add a sense of luxury.

Felts are also available paper-backed for walls; they are used to deaden sound, and they also insulate against heat loss to some extent. They come in a wide range of rich colours.

Silks with paper backing are very expensive and luxurious; they require expert hanging. You could use them just for a small recess or alcove, or perhaps behind an area of shelving.

Tweeds and other woollen cloths offer a range of natural colours, plus some brightly dyed effects. Textures range from coarse fibres, laid parallel onto the paper backing, to fine cloths in herringbones and other weaves. Crushed suede and velvet effects are also available.

Grass cloths are becoming more easy to obtain, and some shops sell them by the metre off a roll. Hand-made in the Far East, these wallcoverings have a unique charm.

Cork wallcoverings consist of thin layers of cork in a choice of browns ranging from pale to rich deep brown; they are laminated to a paper backing. Many people use them as a cheap alternative to cork wall tiles.

Lining papers are recommended for use under many types of heavier wallcovering, to conceal wall imperfections, and generally to provide a surface suitable for hanging the top covering.

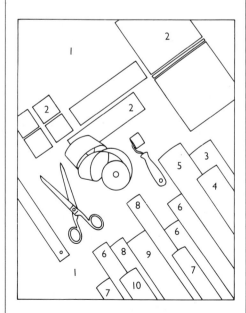

1 Wallboard; 2 Ceramic tiles; 3 Hessian; 4 Washable paper; 5 Cork; 6 Vinyl; 7 Ready-pasted washable paper; 8 Spongeable paper; 9 Woodchip paper; 10 Relief (embossed) paper.

How much paper?

The standard size for wallpaper rolls is (with a small tolerance) 10.05m (11yd) long by 533mm (21in) wide. Some continental papers may be narrower and many American papers are twice as wide. Always check roll sizes carefully when working out costs and quantities.

The type of pattern will affect the amount of wallpaper you require:

Free-matching papers are printed with a non-directional design which does not require pattern matching, and so they involve little wastage.

Set-match papers have motifs that repeat in a straight line across the paper. They, too, can be matched with little wastage, but the overall size of the pattern repeat, which may vary from about 100mm (4in) to 600mm (2ft), will affect the amount of paper required.

Drop-match papers have patterns that repeat in diagonal lines over the surface of the paper, and each new length of paper has to be moved up or down to allow for this. This type of pattern involves more wastage, and your retailer will guide you on how much extra to allow, according to the size of the pattern repeat. Wastage can be minimized by cutting alternate lengths from two rolls.

ROOM SIZE/ROLLS NEEDED CHART FOR WALLPAPERS

WALLS		Measurement around walls, including doors and windows												
Height from skirting		feet	30	34	38	42	46	50	54	58	62	66	70 1	74	78
feet	metres	metres	9.1	10.4	11.6	12.8	14.0	15.2	16.5	17.7	18.9	20.1	21.3	22.6	23.8
7–7½	2.15–2.30		4	5	5	6	6	7	7	8	8	9	10	10	10
7½–8	2.30–2.45	Number of rolls required	5	5	6	6	7	7	8	8	9	9	10	11	11
8–8½	2.45–2.60		5	5	6	7	7	8	9	9	10	10	12	12	12
8½–9	2.60–2.75		5	5	6	7	7	8	9	9	10	10	12	12	12
9–9½	2.75–2.90		6	6	7	7	8	9	9	10	10	11	12	13	13
9½–10	2.90–3.05		6	6	7	8	8	9	10	10	11	12	13	14	14
10–10½	3.05–3.20		6	7	8	8	9	10	10	11	12	13	14	15	15
Number of rolls for ceilings			2	2	2	3	3	4	4	4	5	5	6	7	7

Free – match paper

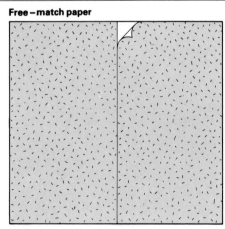

Free-match papers have no regular pattern.

Set pattern

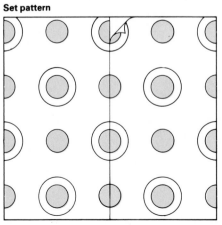

Set-match papers have patterns that repeat straight across the paper.

Drop pattern

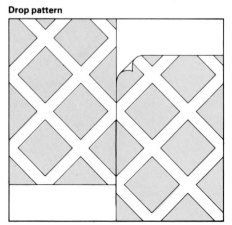

Drop-match papers have patterns that repeat diagonally across the paper.

Technique and preparation

The general principles of wallpaper hanging apply to all wallcoverings that are available on the roll. The following description of techniques refers mainly to wallpapers, but providing the manufacturers instructions are obeyed they can be followed for almost all varieties of materials.

In a typical room with a window on one wall and a door on the wall facing it, start from one side of the window and continue papering around the room until you reach the door. Then come back and start from the other side of the window and work around the room to the other side of the door. If the wallcovering design has a pronounced pattern and your room has a projecting chimney breast, it is better to make this the starting point, so that you can centre the pattern over it. Measure the chimney breast and decide whether a single central width of paper, or two widths with a central join, is the better way to begin to allow sufficient paper to turn the corner.

Guide lines

It is essential to mark vertical guide lines before starting to hang the wallcovering on each wall. The lines of walls, windows, doors, and chimney breasts are seldom 'true' or upright, and joins in the wallcovering would be crooked and the pattern distorted if you relied solely on these features to establish your verticals.

Use a plumb-line to mark the guide lines. From the starting point, measure and mark a point that is the same as the width of your paper, less 12mm (½in). Fix the end of your plumb-line with a small nail at the top of the wall so that the line hangs through the mark you have just made.

Above, left A bright wallcovering with a striking pattern in primary colours has been used for this children's bedroom. It features boldly the colours that one mostly associates with children's toys, but is not simplistic or garish.

Above A small windowless bathroom is given a bright sunny atmosphere by the clever use of golden yellow vinyl wallcovering and mirror doors. The vertical stripes contrast with the patterned towels and chair fabric.

Right A cork finish is an unusual choice of covering for bedroom walls, but here it blends well with the natural wood furniture, basketwork and stripped pine floor.

When the weight stops swinging, mark several points on the wall, from top to bottom, with a pencil along the line. This vertical line serves as the guide against which to hang the edge of the first length of wallcovering.

Cutting

Measure carefully the distance from the top of the wall to the top edge of the skirting board, and add 50mm (2in) for trimming at the top and the same for trimming at the bottom. Taking the position of the pattern into account, cut the first length of paper to this measurement. Before cutting each length you must check back against the previous length to make sure that you are matching the pattern correctly, according to whether it is a set, straight, or drop match. With a drop match, each new length of paper has to be moved up to accommodate the pattern.

Pasting and folding

Straighten out the cut length of paper by rolling it back on itself. Line up the top end of the paper with the right-hand end of the table, as you face it, and turn the paper face downwards; allow the paper to hang over the other end of the table onto the floor. Position the paper carefully so that its back edge lines up with the back edge of the table. Using a pasting brush and generous amount of paste, start pasting outwards from an imaginary line down the middle of the paper. Paste the far half of the paper first, using short strokes out from the middle to the edge, but leave a strip of about 25mm (1in) unpasted along the top right-hand edge of the paper. Next, pull the paper towards you, so that its near edge is in line with the front edge of the table. Paste the near half, again working outwards towards yourself from the imaginary centre line. In this way the surface of the pasting table is kept more or less free of paste.

Hold the pasted section of the paper by its corners (using the strip you left unpasted), lift it up, and fold it back on itself so that the two pasted surfaces meet. Allow the paper to curve over gently; do not press the fold down so that it creases. It is essential to fold the paper in this way so that you can carry it easily; placing the wet surfaces together also stops them from drying out. Slide the other, unpasted, end of the length onto the table, and paste and fold it in the same way as before. The second fold will usually be smaller than the first, so you can identify the top by the size of the fold.

Soaking

Paper must be left for anything between 2 and 15 minutes for the paste to soak in. If it is not soaked sufficiently, the paper may wrinkle and bubble when hung. While one length of paper is soaking, paste the next. The paper is ready to hang when it feels supple.

Hanging

Carry the pasted, folded length of paper carefully to the wall draped over one arm with the large fold that indicates the top of the paper nearest your body. Climb up the steps and, referring to your marked guide line, use both hands gently to position the top pasted edge against the wall. Hold the paper by the unpasted strip. Let the side edge of the paper run against the guide line as you unfold, and position the top section.

Allow 50mm (2in) at the top for trimming, as planned. Use the smoothing brush to ease the paper gently into place, brushing from the middle of the paper outwards to avoid wrinkles and expel air. Come down the steps a little and unfold the bottom length of paper. Smooth it into position with the brush, against the guide line.

Trimming

To trim the top edge of the paper, first run the edge of your closed scissors into the angle of wall and ceiling in order to make a crease across the paper. Pull the paper a little way from the wall, cut along the crease, and then smooth the paper back into position. It is possible to trim vinyls without creasing and pulling away: use a sharp knife, and cut directly into the ceiling angle. Do not attempt this with ordinary papers. Trim the bottom edge along the skirting board in the same way as the top edge. As you go along, pick up the trimmed-off strips, fold them paste sides together, and put them in a plastic bag; if you leave them lying around on the floor you could slip on them.

The next length is butted up to the length already hung; do *not* overlap. Run a seam roller in a diagonal action across the seams. Corners are rarely 'true', so do not wrap the paper around them or the result will be wrinkles. When there is less than a full width between the last length of paper and an internal corner, proceed as follows: measure from the edge of the last piece of paper to the corner in three places (at the top of the wall, the middle, and the bottom). Add 12mm (½in) to the largest of these measurements, and cut the next

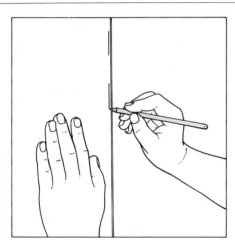

Basic wallpapering techniques Draw a vertical guide line on the wall using a plumb-line and a pencil.

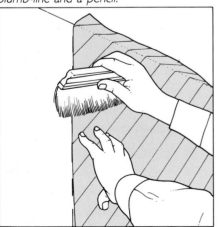

Slide the paper into position and smooth it down with a brush to remove bubbles.

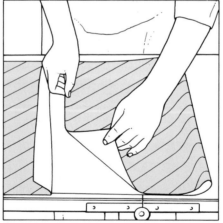

Paste the paper leaving a small strip unpasted. Fold as shown for carrying, with the unpasted strip turned back.

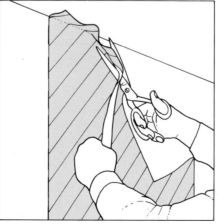

Make a crease into the angle of the ceiling and trim off with paper shears.

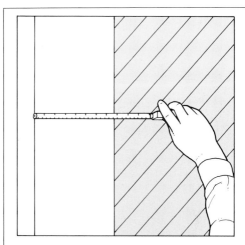

At a corner measure from the last piece of paper into the angle in three places.

Paste down a strip 12mm wider than the largest measurement and smooth round.

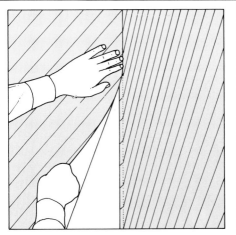

Draw a new vertical and hang the off-cut so that it overlaps the previous piece.

length to this width, taking care to match the pattern as before in the usual way. Now hang this length in the normal fashion, smoothing the extra half-inch neatly around the corner. Measure the width of the off-cut, and make a new vertical guide line the same distance from the corner on the next wall. Hang the off-cut against this guide line: although it overlaps the first piece slightly, the pattern should match.

External corners are the right angles that jut out into the room – at the chimney breast, for example. First use the plumb-line to check whether these are vertical. If they are, you can wrap up to half a width of paper around them. If they are not, cut the paper so that about 75mm (3in) wraps around the corner. Then strike a new plumb-line, and hang the remaining strip.

Papering around doors

If the distance between the edge of the last length and the door frame is just short of the width of a roll, you can proceed in the normal fashion, simply trimming around the frame. But if there is only a narrow strip between the door and the last length, proceed as follows: measure the width of the gap and carefully cut a part-width to fill it. Then continue above the door with the off-cut, trimming at the bottom to the top of the door frame. Hang a further width over the door. This should bring you almost to its other edge. From a complete length, cut a strip which exactly fills the remaining area over the door. Trim away its underneath part along the door frame. Hang the remaining part of this width, which will match the pattern over the door, and fit down alongside the frame.

Papering window recesses

Measure the depth of the recess at the side of the window. Draw a vertical guide line (using a plumb-line as before) on the wall to one side of the window at a distance

equal to the width of the paper minus the depth of the recess. Hang a length of paper against this guide line: it will overlap the window by an amount which is the depth of the window recess.

Cut horizontal lines across the paper at the height of the top and bottom of the recess. Turn the resulting flap into the side wall of the recess. Trim into the window frame. Hang the next length of paper over the top of the recess, matching the pattern as usual, and measure off enough paper at the bottom of the length to turn under neatly to cover the inside top of the recess. You will find there is a small gap in the inside top corner of the recess. Taking care to match any pattern, cut a small piece of

paper to fill this gap neatly, allowing about 50mm (2in) at the top. The extra paper allows you to carry your infill over the angle of the recess onto the face of the wall above the window. Peel away a little of the paper just pasted above the window, tuck the infill in and brush down the top paper.

Continue papering over the recess, matching the pattern and leaving enough extra each time to turn under to cover the top of the recess. When you reach the other side of the recess, with just a part-width left before the window ends, cut a full length of paper and hang this so that it overlaps the side wall of the recess. Make horizontal cuts at the top and bottom of the window and fold in the flap.

Papering around switch plates, electric sockets and ceiling fittings *Always remember to turn off the electricity at the mains before beginning. For square fittings, such as power points, take the paper right over the object and press down lightly to make an impression. Pull away and make four diagonal cuts from the centre outwards. Press the paper back around the fitting and*

mark the outline then pull away again. Loosen the fitting slightly and turn back any excess paper on the outline.
For round fittings, such as ceiling roses, take the paper up and over so that a slight outline is produced, pull the paper away then make a series of star-shaped cuts from the centre to the marked edge, press down, and mark and trim as above.

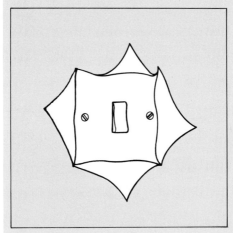

Make diagonal cuts from the centre.

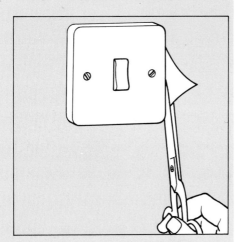

Trim off the excess with scissors.

If the flap is not deep enough to cover the side of the recess, fill in with a small strip of matching paper. You will be left with a small gap at the top inside edge as before, so you must cut a small matching piece of paper to fill it neatly. Fill below the window with matching lengths of paper.

Ceilings

Ceilings should be papered before walls. They are much trickier to handle, and beginners should avoid ceilings until they have built up their confidence with other papering jobs.

It is essential to rig up a safe working platform when working on ceilings. Use a scaffold board supported between two pairs of steps. Your head should be 75 to 225mm (3 to 9in) below the level of your work. Strips of ceiling paper are hung parallel to the window wall; start there and work away from the light. It is, however, satisfactory to work at right angles to the window if this enables you to use shorter strips of paper.

Start by drawing a guide line across the ceiling for the first length of paper. Make this a little less than your first width of paper so that you can trim into the ceiling angle, which is rarely true. At one end of the ceiling measure and mark, outward from the window wall, a distance equal to the width of the paper less 12mm (½in). Repeat at the opposite end of the ceiling. Join these two points with a taut length of

Ceilings Mark a guide-line a little less than the width of the paper away from the window wall with chalked string.

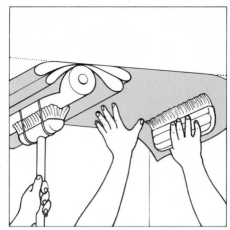

Support the folded paper while offering one end to the ceiling parallel to the guide-line. Smooth down with a brush.

string, coated with chalk and fixed by a small nail at each end. Pull the string away from the ceiling and snap it back to leave a chalk guide line.

Measure the width of the ceiling and cut the paper into strips, allowing 50mm (2in) at each end for trimming and taking care to match any pattern. Paste the paper in the same way as described for walls, but fold it concertina-fashion, making each fold about 300mm (12in) wide. Allow the adhesive to soak in as necessary.

Support the folded paper on a spare part-roll of paper, or on a length of dowel or

broomstick, and carry it over to the scaffold board. Matching the edge against the chalk line, brush the end of the paper firmly into place. Unfold the next section and brush it down firmly. Proceed in this manner, working across the room. You may find it easier to have another person to support the folded paper, leaving you two hands free to work with (see illustration). In this case, your helper can use a clean broom head to support the paper from below. Trim the paper at each end, as for walls. If the last length is less than a full paper width, trim it roughly to size before hanging, and then finish it off with an exact final trim.

Plastic laminates

These are available in various forms and can be used in any situation where a highly decorative finish is required that is extremely hygienic, able to withstand water and easily maintained. Modern coating and printing techniques have now produced a finish that is durable, resistant to scuffs, colourfast, and heat-proof in many cases.

Plastic laminates work well in kitchens, bathrooms, utility rooms, shower cubicles, cloakrooms and as wallboards where the surfaces are in poor condition. They can also be used to re-cover old doors and kitchen units, to cover work-tops, and finish shelving systems. Partition walls are another area where plastic laminates used in natural designs can help to 'marry' the new structure with its surroundings. Used on wallboards, they also give additional insulation and therefore are successful

when used in loft conversions or attics giving both high styling and comfort at the same time.

Laminates offer the same stylish design features as natural materials, such as cork, wood, brick, and stone and can also accurately mimic the characteristics of ceramic tiles with considerably less cost and labour time.

They are available in an enormous range of surface textures, finishes and colours and are ideal for bringing character to a room's interior decoration. Manufacturers are now very much in tune with current fashions in colour and try to produce designs that can be used to complement new ranges of bathroom fittings, and kitchen units. Apart from pretty pastel florals, there are sophisticated plains with stunning black-and-white tile designs or realistic

textured finishes, which have the appearance of leather, linen, velour, marble, etc.

Other 'natural' effects can be achieved using wood-grained laminates in pine, mahogany, teak etc. Bought as wallboards, they can be planked or given tongued-and-grooved finishes to simulate real wood lengths. Apart from lack of texture they can be very difficult to distinguish from the genuine article. At the expensive end of the range, these laminates are available in stunning metallic designs that resemble aluminium, copper or brass.

Laminates are produced in various forms: as sheeting, there is a range of sizes, the standard being 2440 × 1220mm (8 × 4ft). Sheeting must be fixed to a sound, rigid substrate, such as plywood, chipboard, blockboard to avoid bowing after a period of time.

To give pleasing curves instead of sharp edges, with the consequently ugly joints, some companies offer a laminate post-forming service. This means that the laminate is heated, then coaxed into the form required. Post-forming adds interesting design features to the edges of worktops or on internal/external corners of walls. Another plus point of post-forming is that without joints, water and dirt seepage is not a problem as with conventional joints.

A cheaper alternative to the sheeting is decorative wallboards. These are made of hardboard which is painted, printed and lacquered to give an attractive, look-alike finish at lower cost in 2440 × 1220mm (8 × 4ft) panels. However, the range of designs and textures is limited mainly to tile, wood and brick effects.

Because of their rigid backing, decorative wallboards are easier to use than sheeting and can be fixed directly onto sound, flat walls with special wallboard adhesives. If the walls are very uneven, then the wallboards need to be secured onto wooden battens.

It is also possible to obtain smaller wallboards, known as tile panels, in sizes 1830mm (6ft) and 1220mm (4ft) long by 610mm (2ft). They are ideal as splashbacks against kitchen worktops or wash-basins, or round the edges of baths. They can also be used as bath panels. The tile patterns themselves conform to standard tile sizes of 102mm (4in) square and 152mm (6in) square and can successfully take the place of the more expensive ceramic tiles.

Hardboard-based 'door skins' are another example of the innovative applications of laminates. Teak, mahogany and planked oak woodgrains are used to produce look-alike finishes printed onto 1988 × 768mm (6ft 6in × 2ft 6in) panels. These 'skins' will quickly refurbish flush, panelled or glazed doors without the need for special tools or much expertise. They can instantly change the character of a room by bringing a warm wood look that is so popular today.

Right Plastic laminates provide highly durable and easily looked after surfaces. When they are used on both walls and work surfaces they produce a feeling of unity. The severe grey tones are here relieved by brilliant red edging.

Right, above plastic laminates are available post-formed as shown on this wash basin unit. The laminate is tailored to the article it is to cover so that it curves round corners without any ugly joints or hard edges.

Laminate techniques

For measuring up and marking out you need a tape measure, either a soft pencil or a felt-tipped pen, a try-square, and a long straight-edge, preferably made of metal. For cutting, use either a craft knife fitted with a special laminate-cutting blade, a fine-toothed tenon saw, or a proprietary laminate-cutting tool. For trimming, use a plane and a file.

With regard to adhesives, if you intend doing a lot of work in a space that is difficult to ventilate, choose a modern water-based contact adhesive: the fumes are less harmful. A few brands also allow some slippage before they set, which makes accurate positioning easier.

Preparation
It is vital that the surface you want to cover is clean, dry, and free from grease. On new wood, this means sanding it thoroughly, wiping it over with a damp cloth, and leaving it to dry. If you are covering old laminate, rub it down with wire wool, then scrub it with detergent, rinse and dry. The surface must also be stable. In this respect, man-made boards (plywood, blockboard, or chipboard) are better than natural timber. The only preparation the laminate needs is to be stored flat in a warm, dry room for a few days before laying. Un-secured surfaces, such as doors, should have a balancing veneer applied to the reverse side to prevent warping.

Measuring and marking
Plastic laminate costs a lot of money, so mistakes are expensive. To avoid them, mark out as accurately as you can, double checking everything before you get down to the cutting.

To begin with carefully work out how the pieces to be cut can best be arranged to avoid waste. When you are satisfied, begin marking out the shapes accurately. Squares and rectangles are easiest. Just measure the surface to be covered, and, with the aid of a try-square and straight-edge, transfer the dimensions to the pat-terned side of the laminate using a soft pencil or a felt-tipped pen. Allow an extra 3mm (⅛in) all round for final trimming.

Mark out an irregular shape by drawing around the surface itself or make an accurate template from thin card and draw round that; check that it is the right way round before transferring the shape to the laminate surface. Remember, whichever

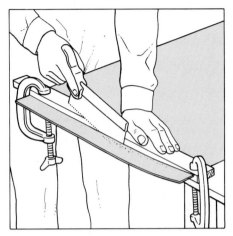

Working with plastic laminates *After marking, the laminates can be sawn with a tenon saw providing it is given support.*

The adhesive must be spread evenly over the back of the laminate and also the surface it is to cover.

Position the laminate accurately before smoothing it into place. Take care not to trap bubbles of air beneath it.

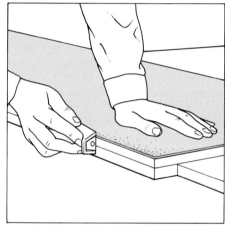

Remove excess laminate with a laminate trimmer and smooth down as shown here with a surform or block plane.

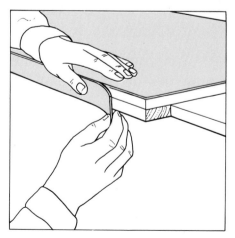

Complete the job by covering the edges with laminate strips and then finish off with a plane to produce neat bevelled corners where the two laminate surfaces meet.

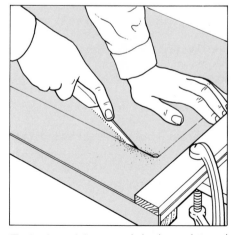

To let in a sink or wash basin, an internal hole in the laminated surface can be cut with a padsaw once the laminate is firmly stuck down. Clamp the edges as a pre-cautionary measure.

method you use, to allow the 3mm (⅛in) trimming allowance.

Cutting

There are three ways to cut plastic laminate. The simplest is to score the patterned side with a sharp knife using a straight-edge as a guide. You then gently but firmly lever the waste *upwards* until the laminate snaps in two. You can then clean up the cut edge with a block plane or a file.

The second way is to use a tenon saw (or any saw with fine teeth). Again working with the laminate pattern-side up, use a knife to score a line where you want to cut.

Now, keeping the saw just on the waste side of this line, and holding it at a very shallow angle, saw away. Give the laminate enough support to prevent it bending. The third way is to make the cut with a proprietary laminate cutter.

Sticking down

Unless you are skilled at laying laminate sheeting, use a contact adhesive with a certain amount of slideability. This allows you to make adjustments when the surfaces are brought together. Smooth laminate into position from the centre outwards. This will make sure that you do not trap any air bubbles.

Finishing

With the laminates firmly in place, remove the trimming allowance. Ideally this should be done with a block plane, but a smoothing plane set to give a very fine cut will do. Working from the ends towards the centre, keep planing until the laminate edge is almost flush with the substrate edge, then finish off by rubbing down with glasspaper of successively finer grades. Finish by fixing a vertical strip of laminate to the edge of the substrate, overlapping the edge of the main piece of laminate. Plane back the excess as before, and finish with a plane to produce neat edges where both pieces of laminate join.

Wallboards

You will need either a fine-toothed saw or a sharp trimming knife, a rigid steel rule for taking accurate measurements, a pencil, a fretsaw or padsaw for producing curves and holes, wallboard adhesive plus a caulking gun with which to apply it, or an impact contact adhesive, acrylic or silicone sealer for making a waterproof bond between wallboards and any potentially wet surface and glasspaper. If the wallboards are to be fitted onto a grid of timber battens, then you will need timber battens in planed softwood, plus masonry nails and hammer.

Preparation and techniques

The walls must be clean, dry and free from dust and grease, so wash down thoroughly with a sugar soap solution first. Rinse off, and leave to dry out thoroughly. Scrape off flaking paint, dig out crumbling plaster and re-fill holes with the appropriate cellulose filler. Any wallcoverings should also be removed, too.

The wallboards themselves must be conditioned with water prior to fixing: lay the boards flat on the floor and sponge or brush three-quarters of a pint of water onto each board, then leave in this position for at least 48 hours. This will ensure that the boards will stay rigid and straight once fixed onto the walls. This treatment is not necessary for tile panels, which are normally factory finished.

Cutting

Support the wallboard well while cutting to size, having marked the cutting line with a soft pencil. Use a fine-toothed saw to cut carefully on the patterned side of the wallboard. Carefully sand the edge to give a neat, clean finish.

Using the caulking gun for easy application, apply the adhesive in ribboned sections, as shown in the illustration, and press onto the wall firmly. Ease the wallboard away and leave it propped upright until the adhesive on both the wall and wallboard is touch-dry. Then smooth the wallboard into position and leave to dry.

If, instead, you use an impact contact adhesive, apply this to the wallboard and wall, leave until touch dry and fix the boards in the same way, pressing well from the centre outwards to eliminate air bubbles. Wipe off any excess adhesive.

Joints

When using woodgrain patterns, butt the edges of the wallboards together very carefully so that they produce a continuous grooved appearance. If the plain boards show their seams, you can either fix special plastic extrusions or wooden strips or leave slight gaps in between and paint these sections when the boards are dry.

Tile boards need slightly different treatment: fix as above, but then grout as you would for normal tiles and, if they are being used as splash-backs for kitchens or bathrooms, make sure the gaps are well sealed by using a silicone or acrylic sealant in the normal way.

In any event, if the wallboards are being used anywhere where they may come into regular contact with water, any gaps between the boards or edges need to be sealed with a waterproof sealant.

If the walls are in particularly bad condition, it is best to fix wooden battens on the walls and mount the boards on this structure.

Make a grid with wooden battens 400mm (16in) apart. At the corners, a batten will be required on each adjacent wall onto which the wallboards can be butted for a neat appearance. Each wallboard can then be fixed onto the battens with a wallboard adhesive.

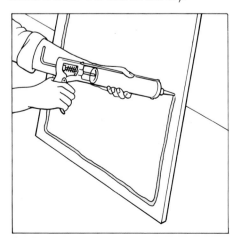

Apply the adhesive with a caulking gun onto each of the 400mm sections.

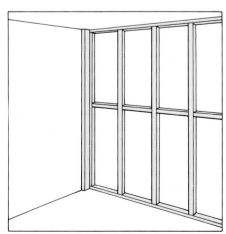

On imperfect surfaces wallboards need to be fixed to a grid of timber battens.

Ceramic tiles

Ceramic tiles have been used for many centuries, not only as an extremely hard-wearing, hygienic and easily maintained wallcovering, but also as a decoration. In the past the majority of the most exciting ceramic tile designs were imported from Spain, Italy and Portugal. They were not always of the highest quality, but were bought because of the lack of interesting colours and designs to be found in England.

Today, however, English manufacturers are producing a variety of patterns and colours that, with imagination on the part of the user, can produce attractive designs to blend with existing bathroom or kitchen fittings and furnishings.

Ceramic tiles are the perfect protection against water penetration, and therefore are extensively used to decorate bathrooms, kitchens, utility rooms and anywhere water is in constant use. These tiles should not only be used in specific areas, like splashbacks against baths, sinks, worktops etc, but also to link these areas into the rest of the room by using them as bath panels or on shelving around the baths themselves to give a more co-ordinated finish.

The size of tile you use will depend upon individual situations. The 152 × 152mm (6 × 6in) size will be suitable for large expanses of wall and will obviously take less time to fix than smaller ones. These are 108 × 108mm (4¼ × 4¼in) and work particularly well in small, poky rooms where the tiles blend in with surrounding fittings to help create an illusion of space. The smaller tiles are easier to cut when it comes to awkward shapes or curves.

Smaller than the two standard sizes, are tiny mosaic tiles, which obviously take much longer to fix into position, but look very attractive as low splashbacks around worktops, giving a cool Continental flavour to a kitchen. Rectangular tiles are now available, too, and can be used to make interesting herring-bone and other traditional brick patterns.

It is also possible to buy very large ceramic tiles. These look best where there are large expanses of wall and ceiling and where dramatic, eye-catching effects are required.

The shape and size of your room are of fundamental importance when choosing the size, colour and design of the tiles. For instance, using small tiles, where a room is small or awkwardly shaped, or tiling both the floor and the walls, around the bath panels, will create an illusion of space. However, note that floor tiles are made to different specifications from wall tiles to stand the higher level of wear and if you are using the same pattern for both walls and floors, make sure that they are of the right grade in each situation.

In planning a tiling job, it is best to use graph paper to pencil down the dimensions of the area to be tiled, using each square to represent a tile. This will not only help to work out quantities accurately and economically, but also allow you to adapt the design to suit the situation.

Before you decide on a particular scheme, spend some time in looking around special tile shops, where there are normally displays of types and patterns, and where you will be given direction on what to use, where. If you already have plenty of pattern or texture in the room itself, perhaps a patterned frieze running round areas of plain or white tiles, or if you prefer, a simple border in complementary colour tones to the main tiles would provide enough additional character. Spend a little time working out the design, which may need to be modified so that you are not left with less than half tiles facing each other in a corner.

Left, below Pale, almost white ceramic tiles have been used on the floor and work surfaces of this bright, clean-lined kitchen. The decorative motif used on shelf and table edges softens the effect and gives a distinct character.

Right These lovely soft-blue tiles help to accentuate the country atmosphere of the bathroom. The border of flower tiles is echoed by the floral prints, and neatly rounds off the decor.

If you have collected old hand-painted tiles, similar to the beautiful vibrantly coloured heat-proof ceramic tiles found around Victorian fireplaces, why not introduce them into the decoration of an old kitchen. A mix of colour and design could be used to provide a charming splashback. They look particularly good against mellowed wood surfaces. Never set these old tiles into a worktop as a cutting block — they won't stand up to rough treatment and will easily crack. The glaze would become cracked and unsightly.

Blue Delft tiles also complement kitchens with a general country look or containing a lot of wooden surfaces. It is now possible to buy the English equivalent in both standard patterns and colours. A mix of plain borders, tiny floral patterns and scenes can be used to create larger scenes or continuous patterns. They harmonize particularly well with white sanitaryware and brass fittings in the bathroom.

Look out, too, for moulded Victorian tiles that were used originally as dado decorations. They exist in a variety of opulent designs, often featuring fruit. These border designs can be used with plain, matching tiles in either traditional dull greens, or in more modern colours.

Don't just think of plain tiles for wall decoration. Why not use two colours to achieve a chequer board or some other plain and patterned effect. Or use plain tiles with tiny mosaic tiles to introduce spots of colour, thus adding visual interest without increasing the cost significantly.

Plain tiles lend themselves to coloured grouting which is available in both bright primary colours and more subtle tones. A contrast grouting can just add a zing of colour where needed, and give a stylish appearance to an area of plain tiling. Pick out a grouting colour that will either contrast or blend with surrounding fittings.

Tiling techniques

To work out how many tiles you need, measure the width and height of the area to be tiled, expressing the dimensions as so many whole tiles and rounding up as necessary. Multiply the two figures together, and add 10 per cent extra tiles to allow for cutting and breakages. Also allow some extra glazed-edge tiles for use in corners and on open edges.

Tools
For tools you will need a tile cutter, a spirit level, a plumb-line (unless the level has a vial that gives verticals), a few long, straight timber battens, a serrated-edge spreader (often supplied with the adhesive), pliers or pincers, a sponge, and a soft cloth. If the tiles have no spacer lugs, you will also need spacers. There are proprietary types but matchsticks will do.

Adhesive and grout
There are several types to choose from; for condensation-prone areas or those subjected to prolonged wetting, for example in showers, use a waterproof grout. Tell your supplier what areas you are tiling and ask for advice.

Preparation
If the tiles are to stick, it is important to make sure that the wall is clean, dry, free from grease, and relatively flat. Old wallpaper must be removed, as should any loose or flaking paint. Rub down sound gloss or semi-gloss paint with medium-grade wet-and-dry abrasive paper used wet. From here on, preparation is exactly the same as for bare plaster, or for a wall that has been painted with emulsion. If the bare plaster is very porous, seal it with thinned emulsion or a stabilising primer.

Covering up existing tiles

Provided the existing tiles are firmly fixed to the wall you can apply the adhesive directly to them, and tile in the normal way. Tap each one with your knuckle. If it sounds hollow, chip it off with a club hammer and cold chisel, and fill the resulting 'dent' and any chipped corners with cellulose filler.

Setting out

Next to preparation, setting out is the most important stage in any tiling job. Mark off a long, straight timber batten in tile widths. If the tiles have built-in spacer lugs, the tile width should include the lugs, otherwise allow a 2mm ($\frac{3}{32}$in) gap between tiles for grouting. Hold this batten upright against the walls, and use it to work out where the rows of tiles will fall, adjusting its position as necessary to avoid narrow cut tiles at the top and bottom. When you are satisfied, draw a horizontal line on the wall with the aid of a spirit level and another batten to mark where the bottom edge of the bottom row of whole tiles will go. Along this line nail a batten to support the tiles until the adhesive sets.

Use the marked-off batten in the same way to find the best arrangement for the tiles in this row. Aim to give the row a symmetrical appearance with cut tiles of a reasonable size at each end. When you have found such an arrangement, draw a vertical line to show where the centre join will go. It is against this line that you will begin tiling, to left and right. In many cases, you will have to make allowances for the shapes of baths, basins, windows, fitted cupboards, and the like.

Basic tiling

Starting against the centre-line on the wall, apply the adhesive for the first square metre. Keep the teeth of the notched spreader pressed against the wall to avoid making the adhesive layer too thick.

Rest the first tile on the support batten, line up its vertical edge with the centre-line, and press it firmly into place. Lay the second tile in the same way, butting it up against the first if it has spacer lugs, otherwise separate the two with spacers, matchsticks or card. Check the surface level of the tiles as you proceed. Continue until all the whole tiles are in position; then move on to the row above, and so on, until only the gaps for cut tiles remain to be filled.

By this time, the adhesive should have set sufficiently for the support batten to be removed. Once it is out of the way, mark up and cut the tiles for the gaps and glue them in place. If you find it difficult to spread the adhesive on the wall, apply it to the backs of the cut tiles instead with a flat-bladed trowel.

Grouting

With the entire wall tiled, allow the adhesive to dry for the recommended length of time (usually about 24 hours) before moving on to the next stage – grouting. Having first removed all the spacers, mix up the grout according to the manufacturer's instructions, and using a sponge press the grout well into the tile joints. Remove the excess grout with a clean damp sponge. For a professional finish draw a round, pointed stick (such as a child's lollypop stick) along the grouting and leave to dry out. Any smears left on the tiles can be removed by polishing the surfaces with a clean dry cloth.

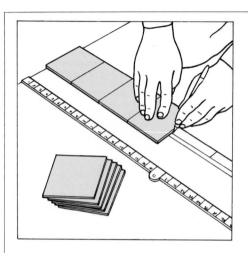

Tiling a wall Mark off a batten in tile widths, leaving space for grouting.

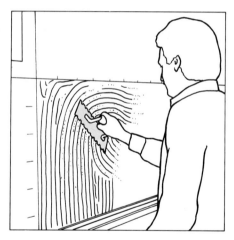

Find the best position for the rows and mark a horizontal line on the wall.

With the batten find the best position for the vertical rows and draw a vertical.

Apply the adhesive with a notched spreader to the first square metre of wall.

With the bottom row temporarily supported by a batten, press the tiles firmly into place.

When the job is complete, apply the grouting with a squeegee, pressing it into the gaps.

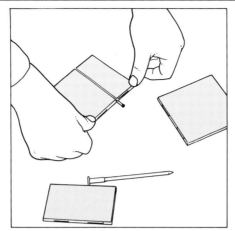

Tile cutting To cut a tile, score a cut-line through the glaze with a tiler's spike or purpose-made tile cutter.

Place matchsticks under the tile along the cut-line and press down on both ends of the tile to snap it cleanly in two.

To cut irregular shapes, score the tile with the spike as before and then nibble away the unwanted portion with pincers.

Cutting tiles

This is the part of the job most first-time tilers dread. In fact, cutting the tile is quite easy. The difficult part is making sure the cut is in the right place: you have to allow for the fact that, while the edge of the last whole tile in the row is absolutely vertical, the same is unlikely to be true of the wall against which the cut tile has to fit.

Measure the gap to be filled at the top and bottom, and transfer these measurements to the tile you want to cut, having first deducted the necessary allowance for grouting – 2mm (3/32in) if you are tiling towards an external corner, and 4mm (3/16in) if towards an internal one. Connect the two marks on the face of the tile with a straight line.

There are several types of tile cutter and each normally comes with a set of instruc-

tions. However, they all work in the same way as an artisan's tile cutter; incidentally an ordinary glass cutter can also be used.

Working with the tile, pattern-side up, and using a straight-edge to keep the spike on course, score a line where you want to make the cut, making sure you go right through the glaze, including any that has strayed onto the edge of the tile. Do not press too hard: you will soon get the feel of the amount of pressure required and be able to score with one smooth stroke. Now lay the tile face up on a flat surface with two matchsticks underneath it, immediately below the score line. Apply firm, even pressure downwards on both halves of the tile, and it should snap cleanly along the score line.

In addition to straight cuts you may occasionally have to cut an L-shaped tile to fit

around an obstacle. Mark out the tile, bearing in mind the points made about marking for a straight cut. Score along the intended cut line with the cutter, again making sure you go right through the glaze. Then, with a pair of pincers, carefully nibble away at the waste up to the cut line. Do *not* take off too much in one go or the tile will break. If necessary, tidy up the cut edges with a file.

If you can arrange for protruding pipes to coincide with the join between two tiles, so much the better. You merely nibble out a semi-circle from each tile in the same way as you remove the waste from an L-shaped cut, then bring the two together to surround the pipe – some trial and error may be involved in getting a good fit. If the pipe emerges from the middle of a tile, cut the tile neatly in two and treat the halves as separate tiles.

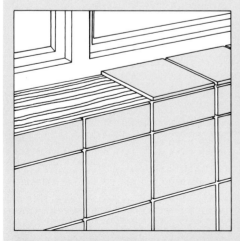

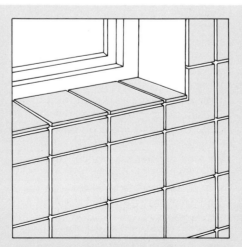

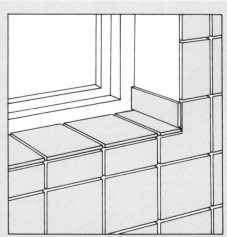

Tiling a recess To produce a neat effect, tiles lining a window recess should overlap those on the wall. The recess tiles should have glazed edges.

Make sure that the tile spacings in the recess match those on the wall. Use cut tiles with glazed edges at either end of the ledge to finish it off.

On the vertical wall of the recess another glazed-edged tile will have to be cut so that the spacing between the horizontal rows on the wall is preserved.

Types

Floor coverings take the hardest wear of any furnishing in the home and therefore need to be considered not only in terms of design but also suitability for the different areas of the home. On the whole it pays to buy the best quality you can afford. Alternatively, if you have reasonably good floor boards, don't cover them up, but instead use them as a base for introducing floor decorations, like stencilling, staining or painting.

Any areas that are subject to water spillage need a hard-wearing waterproof flooring. One hundred per cent wool is not suitable because it is likely to shrink and will deteriorate very quickly. The alternatives are rubber or vinyl floorings, cork which brings additional insulation and warmth, and washable carpet tiles that can be cleaned or removed if they become stained or dirty.

Carpeting

This tends to bring more underfoot comfort to the home than other types of flooring. However, it must be laid on top of good quality underfelts to protect its fibres. There are various grading systems in existence which will enable you to choose the right quality for particular situations. For example, in halls, stairways and landings, always buy a heavy-duty grade. Many more coverings now have a mix of synthetic and natural fibres that give both the good looks and appearance of a pure wool carpet, and also the durability that the synthetic fibres can guarantee.

If you are designing a room scheme from scratch, use the flooring as the basis of the colour scheme, picking out the colours of your furnishings from the pattern of the carpet. If the house is small, it is a good idea to choose one plain colour and continue it throughout all the rooms and adjoining treadways. This scheme opens up the rooms, so creating more space.

Foam-backed carpeting tends to be cheaper than ordinary carpeting, but won't last as long. This type is suitable for use in bathrooms, as the backing will prevent shrinkage. As an alternative you could use 100 per cent synthetic fibre in these situations which won't hold spillages and from which any stains can be cleaned off easily. Foam-backed carpeting does have the advantage that it is reasonably easy to lay. Otherwise, if hou have invested in good quality carpeting, it is preferable to have a professional carpet fitter to lay it, thus ensuring years of good wear.

Carpet tiles

These are available mostly in a stain-resistant polypropylene material, which has a mixed tweedy appearance. They are designed mainly for use in kitchens and bathrooms. In addition, there are now designs with a soft velour pile which are ideal for bedrooms, because of their luxurious appearance. At one time they were produced in rather unexciting colours, but it is now possible to buy carpet tiles in subtle, mottled shades which will harmonise with kitchen and bathroom accessories and won't show the dirt.

Carpet tiles work well in children's rooms, giving the flexibility of being able to change the decor frequently and replace damaged or stained sections.

Sheet vinyl

Here it pays to buy the best. Cheap vinyl sheeting will crack after a time, especially if laid on a poor sub-surface, and has low resistance to scratches, stains and spillages. The variety of designs is enormous: from the traditional, but still very popular, Spanish and Portuguese ceramic-tile patterns, to marbled and textured designs; wood parquet effects; stunning modern designs in blacks, whites and bright primary colours with graph-line effects to finish off a high-tech look in both the kitchen, bathroom, and indeed the living areas, too. The best form of vinyl sheeting is the cushioned type, which has an inner layer of tiny bubbles, giving a particularly soft, warm feeling underfoot, and guaranteeing longer wear.

Vinyl tiles

Provided the centre of the room is correctly located, tiles are generally easier to lay than large pieces of sheeting. Another advantage of tiles is that if localized damage has been caused, such as a cigarette burn or a bad dent, the offending tile can be easily removed and replaced. With many manufacturers' ranges, it is possible to mix and match plain and patterned tiles to produce attractive chequerboard effects. To simulate real wood, there are wood planking tiles. These are available with matching edging strips which complete the perfect impression of a solid wooden floor with a fraction of the expense.

Rubber flooring

Synthetic rubber flooring is a high-fashion alternative to vinyl. It is not only resistant to all normal household spills but is anti-slip, too. It is particularly suitable for high-tech situations, with eye-catching raised designs in bright primary colours and subtle two-tone effects in soft greys, blues, beiges and greens to harmonize with today's kitchen fittings. This material is also available in tile form, too.

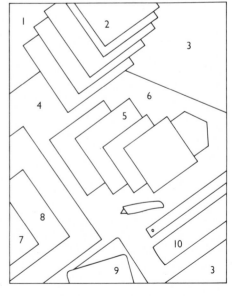

1 Carpet tiles; *2* Vinyl tiles; *3* Coir; *4* Oak strip flooring; *5* Ceramic tiles; *6* Beech strip flooring; *7* Cushion flooring; *8* Cork tiles; *9* Woollen carpet; *10* Sheet vinyl.

Cork

The pale, natural characteristics of cork lend themselves to kitchens and bathrooms or anywhere where the flooring not only needs to be practical and warm but also to be sympathetic to its surroundings. It is not only available in the traditional grainy bark style but it is now possible to buy a white cork tile treated with a white stain that allows the grain to show through. This tile was designed specially to co-ordinate with today's trends for soft, pale colours in the home. You can save yourself time by buying pre-sealed tiles, otherwise all tiles, once layed and cleaned, must be sealed with at least three coats of floor grade polyurethane, lacquer or varnish. Finishes are in matt, silk and gloss and care should be taken in making the choice. A gloss finish looks good in rooms with flat-texture walls or furniture where it produces a contrast.

Cork is also available in sheeting, which cuts down on the laying time. If the natural qualities of cork do not appeal, it is possible to stain or stencil it to bring relief to large areas. Whichever type you use, make sure the quality is right for each situation. When being laid in kitchens and bathrooms, use the heavier floor grade.

Wood veneers

Wood veneers are available as small planks coated with a protective vinyl to protect them. They are laid like 'tiles' and provide the real look of wood flooring without the expense. Laid in dining rooms, hallways or bright sunny rooms, where light hits the floor, they look stunning overlaid with coloured rugs.

Wood flooring

If the floorboards are in good condition, you can strip them back to bare wood and re-seal with polyurethane, lacquer or varnish. Alternatively they can be stained in traditional wood or other colours to bring out the natural grain, or coloured with floor paints. Another way of highlighting a good-looking wooden floor is to sand it, and stencil a border around the floor area and surrounding walls. The same design on both areas would look attractive.

Preparation

Whichever type of flooring you choose, always make sure that the sub-floor is even, clean and that any obstructions or dips are dealt with as these could affect the new floor covering seriously.

Where vinyl or rubber flooring is to be laid, or indeed cork, you must have a completely clean, grease-free surface upon which to lay it. Clean off any polish using wire wool and white spirit, changing the pad frequently to avoid spreading the dirt. Then carefully brush down the floor surface to remove all traces of dust before using the adhesive. If the floors are slightly uneven, it is advisable to lay sheets of hardboard first.

If you suspect any rising damp coming up from solid floors, it must be dealt with before starting. Damp will eventually penetrate through any new flooring, lifting tiles or causing deterioration in soft floor coverings, such as carpet tiles. The damp must be tackled at its source and it may be that you need a new damp-proof membrane. Damp may be tested for by securely taping polythene sheeting to the floor and seeing if condensation collects after a few days.

Levelling timber floors

Re-fix loose floorboards with screws and punch any protruding nails below the surface. If the floor is very uneven, level it off by covering it with 1220mm × 610mm (4ft × 2ft) sheets of hardboard. Brush water into the mesh sides, and leave them stacked back to back in the room in which they will be used for two days before you lay them. Starting in one corner of the room, lay a row of sheets, mesh-side up, along the longest wall, fixing them in place with 20mm (¾in) annular nails – these have ringed shafts for extra grip – driven in at 225mm (9in) intervals across the face of the board, and at 150mm (6in) intervals around the edge. Cut the last sheet in the row to fit, and use the off-cut to begin the next row, on the other side of the room. This ensures that the sheet joins are staggered brick-fashion. There is no need to trim the sheets to hug the wall closely.

White cork tiles provide a striking contrast and being reflective, effectively increase the amount of working light.

Laying cork or vinyl tiles

Open the tile packaging and allow the tiles to stand freely in the room where they are to be laid. It is important to establish the centre of the room before you start. To do this, join up the mid-points of opposite walls with a line to give a cross in the centre of the room. In bathrooms and kitchens, because the units and fittings cover most of the floor area, concentrate on finding the centre of the tiled area, rather than the centre of the room.

Using the cross as a guide, dry lay (do not stick down) two rows of tiles in an L-shape from the middle of the room out towards the walls. From these rows, you can get a clear idea of the size of cut tile needed around the edge of the room. If necessary adjust the L-shape. When you have found the best starting place, re-strike the chalk lines accordingly.

Spread the correct tiling adhesive onto the floor in about a one-metre square. Make sure you press down the centre of the tile first, before smoothing out towards the edges. This prevents air bubbles from being trapped.

Stick down the L-shape of tiles that you set out first, and fill in the rest of the floor until you have laid all the whole tiles you can. Finish off by filling in the gaps around walls with cut tiles.

Each cut tile must be tailored individually to fit. Lay the tile you want to cut over the last whole tile in the row, positioning it very accurately, then lay another whole tile on top of that, this time with its edge butted up against the wall. The other edge of this tile can now be used as a guide for drawing an accurate cut line on the tile below it. The cut is made with a knife, using a straight-edge to stop it wandering off course.

The same technique can easily be adapted to fit tiles around (or into) corners, but it will not do for fitting a tile around a curve or an irregularly shaped obstacle – you will have to use a template instead. There are several ways you can make one, but perhaps the simplest is to take a piece of paper the same size as the tile, and try to lay it. Cut and fold the paper as necessary, until you can accurately draw in the outline of the obstacle. Now cut off the waste paper, and draw round the resulting template to transfer the pattern onto the tile.

Laying sheet vinyl

The planning stage is not so complicated as with tiles, but there are still a few points worth bearing in mind. The first is that in kitchens and bathrooms it is best to use an extra wide vinyl – one 4m (13ft) wide. Unless the room is exceptionally large, this dispenses with the need for joins through which spillages and water might seep. Finally, when working out how much vinyl you need, allow an extra 50mm (2in) all round for trimming, in case the walls are uneven, or out of square. Allow extra, too, for matching patterns at joins.

Below When carefully laid, carpet tiles can look virtually indistinguishable from a fitted carpet. They have the advantage that the tiles can be individually replaced if they become worn or stained.

Bottom Vinyl flooring is available in a wide variety of designs, such as this stylish tile-patterned finish.

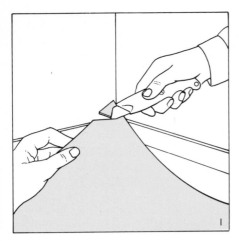
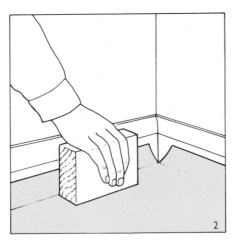
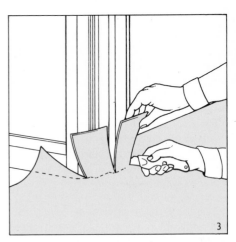
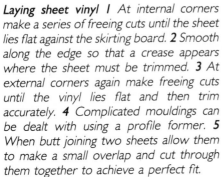
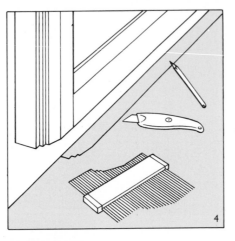
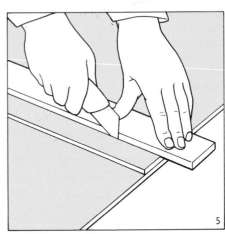
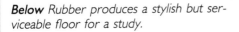

Laying sheet vinyl 1 At internal corners make a series of freeing cuts until the sheet lies flat against the skirting board. **2** Smooth along the edge so that a crease appears where the sheet must be trimmed. **3** At external corners again make freeing cuts until the vinyl lies flat and then trim accurately. **4** Complicated mouldings can be dealt with using a profile former. **5** When butt joining two sheets allow them to make a small overlap and cut through them together to achieve a perfect fit.

Below Rubber produces a stylish but serviceable floor for a study.

Loosen the roll as soon as you get it home, and leave it to stand for a day or two in a warm room. Cut the first length of vinyl roughly 100mm (4in) longer than you need. If it is reasonably thin, position it so that its ends and one side turn up the walls by about 50mm (2in), and press it firmly with a wooden block into the angle between the floor and skirting board; make diagonal cuts at the corners to allow the vinyl to lie flat. The resulting crease gives a fairly accurate line along which to cut, using a sharp knife.

Where awkwardly shaped obstacles such as WC's are concerned, you must make a pattern by using a variation on the scribing technique. Roughly cut out a piece of paper so that it fits round the obstacle, drawing an enlarged version of its outline on the paper. Place this pattern on the vinyl you want to cut, and reverse the process, running the pencil round the inside of the line, to create an outline of the correct size to which you can cut.

With the first length of vinyl in position, lay and trim the remaining lengths needed to cover the floor. But before you trim the second length to fit the room, match its pattern with that on the vinyl already laid. This is straightforward if the pattern goes right to the edge of the sheet, but often the vinyl has a trimming edge which must be removed before laying.

Overlap the two sheets slightly, adjusting their positions until the patterns match, then, with a sharp knife and a straight-edge, cut through the double thickness of vinyl. Peel away the excess and smooth down the two sheets; they should join perfectly.

Although you can loose-lay vinyl, the manufacturers normally recommend that you either stick it down at the edges and at any joins, or that you stick it down all over. Check this when you buy, and make sure you have enough adhesive to do the job. If you are sticking only the edges, lay the vinyl and leave it for a week or so – you can walk on it during this time – to get used to the temperature and humidity of the room before you trim it accurately to fit. You can then stick down the edges.

If you are sticking down the flooring all over, trim it accurately, then lift it again so that you get a clear run to apply the adhesive. Replace the vinyl and smooth it carefully into place, making sure you do not trap any bubbles of air. Avoid this by unrolling the trimmed sheet a little at a time; then, working from the centre out towards the edges, press it into place by dragging something soft and heavy – a sackful of sand is ideal – across it.

Floorboard finishes

Often when old floor coverings are taken up, a potentially attractive wooden floor is discovered. Although a great deal of preparation and finishing is needed to bring the floorboards back to their former glory, it is always rewarding. Finely finished floorboards are a perfect foil for beautiful rugs and small carpets and, when decorated too, become distinctive features in the room.

Having sanded the floorboards using professional floor-sanding equipment, which will provide a clean, even finish, there are a number of floor treatments which will enhance the grain and natural good looks of seasoned timber.

If the wood already has a good, even colour, you can simply seal the surface with polyurethane lacquer or varnish, which will provide a durable, protective finish. Where you require depth of colour or perhaps a more even finish, you should use a traditional wood stain which will bring out the grain. If you want a more modern treatment for the floor, you can now buy stains in many different colours to co-ordinate with the room's furnishings and colours generally. Stencilling on top of stain or straight onto bare, finished wood, not only brings colour and pattern to the floor, but can also help disguise less than perfect surfaces. Where the wooden floors are scratched or filled, or have been painted previously, you can achieve an attractive floor finish for minimal cost by coating with a coloured floor paint.

Sanding
You need a special floor sander for this and a heavy-duty disc sander. Both can be rented from most tool-hire shops.

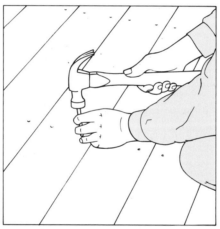

Sanding a timber floor. Punch all nail heads well below the surface of the boards before beginning sanding.

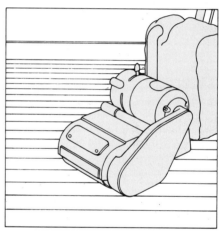

Start by running the sander diagonally across the line of the floor boards. This will flatten down any warped boards.

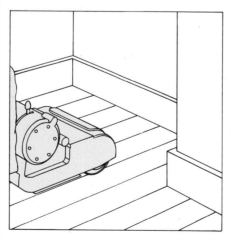

Finish the main part of the floor by running the sander up and down the boards until the surface is even.

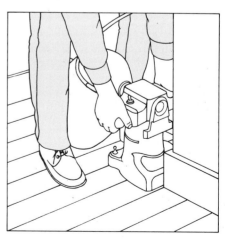

Use a heavy-duty disc sander in inaccessible areas and remove all traces of dust. The floor can now be sealed.

Screw down any loose or squeaking boards, and punch all nail heads about 3mm (⅛in) below the surface. You should also check the floor carefully for carpet tacks or anything that might tear the abrasive paper. Lift them where possible, and fill the hole with a little stopping compound. Otherwise, nip off their heads with pliers, and punch the shafts, well into the wood. Finally, fill any large gaps between boards, otherwise there will be draughts when the floor is finished. Filling the gaps with papier mâché can spoil the appearance of the floor. Instead, tailor fillets of timber to give a tight fit between the boards, and then drive these into place using a mallet.

Although the big floor sander vacuums up most of the dust it produces, there will still be a lot flying about, so wear old clothes and, to prevent breathing in the particles wear a face mask. Protective goggles are also recommended for both comfort and reasons of safety.

Your first job is to flatten off the edges of any warped boards to leave them flush with the surrounding floor. Fit the floor sander with a really coarse grade of abrasive, and run it diagonally across the offending board or boards. Now tackle the main body of the floor, taking care to work in the direction of the wood grain. Never work across the grain, as this will scratch the boards so badly it will take hours of sanding to get them smooth again. Position the sander at one end of the room, making sure it is pointing in the right direction. Switch on and let it run forward under its own steam, restraining it slightly. When you reach the far end of the room, without switching off, drag the sander backwards over the strip you have just covered. It is vital that you make this change of direction as smoothly as possible. If the sander is allowed to stay in one place for too long, it will gouge a rut in the floor.

Continue in this way, smoothing as much of the floor as you can reach with the big sander, then switch to a medium-grade abrasive, followed by a fine-grade one, and repeat the process until the desired finish is achieved. By the time you have finished, you will be left with a narrow strip around the walls where the big sander cannot reach. Tackle this with the heavy-duty disc sander, again working through the various grades of abrasive until the finish matches the rest of the floor. Any small patches you still cannot reach must be sanded down by hand. Remove any marks with white spirit making sure the floor is perfectly free from grease, dirt, and fine dust before applying a new finish.

Floor painting

An exciting alternative to carpeting in a child's bedroom, where a tough, scratch-proof finish is required, is floor paint. The floor could be painted in one solid colour and covered here and there with patterned rugs to add comfort. Alternatively, the floor area could be divided up rather like a football pitch or a hopscotch bed with the squares painted in contrasting colours. A main road could even be drawn out in a striking colour with a pedestrian crossing over it.

The floor must be properly prepared before the floor paint is applied – sanded flat (see above) then dusted and cleaned with white spirit.

If the floor has previously been polished, use medium-grade wire wool and white spirit to take off all residues of wax first. If the floors have already been gloss-painted, they should be 'keyed' to take the new coating. Do this by using a floor sander. Clean off with white spirit and you are ready to start.

Work out how much floor paint you will need: a one-litre can normally covers 10 square metres. For quick, even coverage, use a roller with a long handle, or alternatively a wide 100mm (4in) brush.

If you are painting a bare floor, thin the first coat with 10 per cent white spirit and apply a second, unthinned coating, at least 12

hours later. The timing will depend on climatic conditions and there are no hard and fast rules so check that the first is completely dry before applying any more.

Paintwork is easily cleaned and makes an ideal surface for a child's bedroom floor. A design such as a roadway can be incorporated to stimulate imaginative play.

Start in the opposite corner to the door of the room and back towards the door. Work in strips of four-metre sections. If the design involves sections of colour, mark these sections out on the floor, either in pencil or with sticky tape. Use a roller or brush to take the colour up to the tape and leave to dry. Remove the sticky tape very carefully and paint in the next colour, using a small, fine brush to produce a clean line up against the previously painted section.

Surfaces which have been painted at some time in the past may need two coats. Leave the second coat for at least 12 hours before walking on the floor.

Above The baskets of oranges on the plain sanded boards are delightfully complemented by the frieze stencilled on the table cloth.

Below A boldly stencilled floor has been produced by a repeated geometrical motif.

Stencilling

Stencils can be used as single designs in random fashion over the floor, or linked up to provide a continuous border round the edge of a room. Good art or stationery shops usually have a wide selection of stencils in different designs and sizes. They are made of a waxed stencil board that won't crease while the stencil is being used. You can use coloured stains or oil-based paints. Before beginning, mark out the area you want to stencil, decant the stencil paints into small saucers or containers, and attach strong sticky tape to the corners of the stencil to secure it to the floor area.

A stubby stencil brush is recommended for small designs. This allows you to apply the paint evenly through the stencil holes. Either use a different brush for each colour, or wash the brush out thoroughly when you change colours. When you take the stencil off, remove it very carefully to avoid smudging the design.

When using a stain, apply it with a pad of clean cloth, and dab it well into the holes, taking care that the stain doesn't creep underneath the stencil. When the stencilling has been completed, leave to dry, then immediately protect it with at least two coats of clear polyurethane varnish, preferably in a matt finish. Wipe the stencil clean with either a damp cloth where stain has been used, or with a little white spirit if oil-based paints have been employed.

An alternative to using bought stencils is to make your own. Choose a single motif from existing furnishings, or perhaps from the wallcovering, trace this off and transfer it onto a piece of stencil board, and make a trellis or border or use it as individual motifs on the floor.

Sealing
After sanding, staining or stencilling, all that remains is to seal the surface with a polyurethane varnish. This comes in a range of finishes, from matt to a high gloss. Sweep the floor thoroughly and vacuum it to remove all trace of dust. It is a good idea to leave the room for an hour or two, then clean it again to get rid of any dust that was hanging about in the air. When the floor is as clean as you can get it, wipe it over with white spirit and, when that is dry, brush on the seal. Apply at least three coats to get an attractive and durable finish. Allow each coat to dry completely, then rub it down lightly with fine-grade wire wool before applying the next. To make the polyurethane go as far as possible, it is worth diluting the first coat with a little white spirit, so that it soaks in and seals the wood.

CRIME PREVENTION Consult the Crime Prevention Officer at your local police station.

GENERAL PRECAUTIONS	Insurance	Check that you are well insured for buildings and contents
	At night	Lock and bolt all external and garage doors; locking all accessible windows including upstairs if near drain-pipe or flat roof.
	Every time you go out	Lock all external doors and windows, including vents, and don't leave hidden keys under mats etc.; don't leave doors of empty garage open. Leave on lights in some rooms in evening (*see security lights*).
	Before you go on holiday	Cancel all deliveries – newspapers, milk, etc. Cut lawns, and trim hedges so that house isn't hidden from road. Ask neighbour to clear letterbox of circulars, move mail from doormat, put lid on dustbin, open and close curtains. Beware of careless talk in presence of strangers.
DOOR LOCKS	Final exit door	5-lever mortise deadlock or automatic deadlocking rimlatch; mortise rack bolt or surface bolt at top and bottom; door viewer (if solid door); door chain or limiter.
	Side/back door	5-lever two-bolt mortise deadlock; bolts as for final exit door.
	French doors	Hook-bolt mortise deadlock; rack or flush bolt at top and bottom of first-closing door; hinge bolts if outward-opening.
	Patio door	Cylinder-operated hook-bolt lock; sliding-door lock at top and bottom of fixed frame.
WINDOW LOCKS	General	Drill out screwdriver recesses on all exposed screw heads, or use clutch-head screws, to prevent locks from being unscrewed.
	Pivoting/hinged window	Four basic types: separate lock to secure casement to frame; cockspur handle restraint; locking cockspur handle; restraint for stay. State if for timber or metal window when buying lock.
	Sash/sliding window	Standard sash fastener should be of Fitch or Brighton type. Secure timber types with sliding-bolt lock; dual screw or screw-stop both sides. Secure metal types with small sliding-door lock. Alternative locking positions allow opening for ventilation.
	Louvre window	Secure glass with epoxy adhesive or fit expanding metal grille.
OUTDOOR SECURITY	Shed/ outbuilding	Secure door with hardened steel locking bar, fixed with coach-bolts, and close-shackle 5-lever or 6-pin hardened padlock; lock away tools, and chain and padlock ladder to secure wall-bracket.
	Side gates	Bolt or padlock on inside, barbed wire or carpet-gripper on top.
	Drain-pipes	Coat with anti-climb paint from 2m above ground upwards.
SAFES AND VALUABLES	General	Keep a list of all serial numbers, mark valuables with house number and postcode using security marker (ink invisible in normal light) and take colour photographs of them.
	Wall safe	Mounted in brickwork of wall; may be removed by professional thief.
	Floor safe	Mounted in reinforced concrete under floor; larger and easily concealed; small items may be deposited without unlocking door.
ALARMS AND LIGHTING	Burglar alarms	It is recommended that alarms are installed by a member of the National Supervisory Council for Intruder Alarms (Telephone 0628 37512). Domestic components may include, in addition to alarm and control box, infra-red detector, magnetic-reed door and window sensors, pressure mats (which should not be used alone as system will not operate if wires are cut), door-chain switch and panic buttons. Great care is needed during installation to avoid false alarms.
	Security lights	Plug-in time-switch can operate table-light at selected times; security wall-switch gives varied switching of main light and can 'learn' switching times; outside lights prevent dark corners.

FIRE PREVENTION Consult your local divisional Prevention Officer

GENERAL PRECAUTIONS	Before going to bed	Ensure all occupants know positions of keys to main exit doors at night; close internal doors; unplug TV; check ashtrays.
	Emergency exits	Ensure each room has at least one openable window (not a vent); double-glaze opening sashes and casements separately.
	Dangers in the kitchen	Cooker near door or curtains; unattended chip-pan; flames up side of pan; towels drying over cooker; frayed flex; overloaded socket.
	Dangers in other rooms	Unguarded open fire; upswept chimney; portable fire tripped over or close to furniture or clothing; moving or filling lit oil fire; oil fire not secured to floor or wall; folded or creased electric blanket; smoking in bed.
ALARMS		Fit smoke detector on every level of dwelling and interconnect them. Some burglar alarm systems have fire alarm facility.
EXTINGUISHERS	Fire Blanket	Hang near, but not over, cooker; good for oils, fats and clothes.
	Dry powder	General purpose, including flammable liquids, parafin stoves and electrical fires.
	Halon gas	Leaves no residue; especially suitable for electrical equipment.

GLOSSARY

CEMENT, MORTAR, AND CONCRETE

Aggregate Material that, when mixed with cement and water, makes mortars, concrete, and render. Coarse aggregate consists of gravel, shingle, etc with a minimum particle size of 4.76mm (³⁄₁₆in); fine aggregate consists of sharp (coarse) or fine sand.

Blinding Spreading a smooth, level layer of sand over compacted hardcore (qv) before laying concrete.

Boning rod T-shaped timber sighting tool, three (or more) of which are used to establish levels when laying concrete foundations.

Cement Fine powder, made from burnt limestone and clay, which hardens when mixed with water. The 'glue' in concrete, mortar, and render.

Datum peg A peg, hammered into the ground, whose top is at a known level and from which all other levels at a site are determined.

Expansion joint Softwood plank 9mm (³⁄₈in) thick inserted between adjacent bays of concrete newly placed in formwork; prevents the hardened concrete from cracking when it expands.

Formwork Frame of timber that acts as a mould for concrete.

Hardcore Broken pieces of brick, rubble, or stone which, after compaction, form a base on which to place concrete.

Mortar General term for various mixtures of sand and cement and/or lime used for binding bricks, blocks, etc together.

Profile boards Timber boards to which two parallel lengths of string are attached, used to set out the line and width of strip foundation trenches for, eg, walls.

Punner Tool for compacting newly placed concrete in restricted space. *See also* Tamping beam.

Render Mortar applied as a protective and decorative screed to external brick or block walls. Typically a 1:4 mix of cement and sharp and soft sand.

Tamping beam A plank used on edge to compact newly placed concrete.

BRICK- AND BLOCKLAYING

Air-brick Perforated brick included in a wall to aid ventilation.

Batt Quarter, half, or threequarters of a brick; batts are made by cutting at right angles to a brick's longer sides. *See also* Closer.

Bolster chisel A cold chisel with a blade about 100mm (4in) wide, used with club hammer (qv) for cutting bricks, blocks, paving slabs, etc.

Bond The way in which successive courses of bricks are laid to ensure that vertical joints are staggered.

Builder's square Timber triangle, the length of whose sides is in ratio of 3, 4, and 5; used to determine right angles in bricklaying.

Cavity wall A wall consisting of outer and inner 'leaves' separated by a gap or cavity about 50mm (2in) wide.

Closer A brick divided lengthways so as to give one uncut stretcher (qv) face.

Club hammer Hammer with club-shaped head, used with bolster (qv) and other cold chisels.

Coping Topmost course of brick, block, or stone wall; designed to throw off or resist penetration by moisture and so protect the wall as a whole.

Course A horizontal layer of bricks.

Damp-proof course (DPC) A water-impermeable layer built into a wall to bar the upward movement of ground moisture. A DPC is commonly laid over the second brick course above ground level; it is usually made of bituminous felt, but slate and other materials are also used.

Efflorescence A harmless, fluffy, white deposit on brickwork, caused by water-soluble salts being drawn to the surface.

Frog The depression (often V-section) in the surface of a standard brick.

Gauge rod A straight piece of timber, up to 1.5mm (5ft) long and 50–75mm (2–3in) wide, with saw marks every 75mm (the height of a brick plus its mortar bed). Used to ensure the courses of a brick wall rise evenly.

Hawk Square plywood or metal plate on short handle for holding small quantity of mortar close to wall in patching and pointing work.

Header A brick laid with its end faces parallel with the line of the wall.

Pebbledash A wall surface made of fine gravel thrown onto soft mortar.

Perpend A vertical mortar joint; also called cross joint.

Pier Bonded-in reinforcement for brick or block wall to increase its vertical stability.

Pilaster block In screen-block walls, a purpose-made pier with a groove on either side into which screen blocks are slotted.

Pointing A decorative finish to mortar joints.

Quoin External corner of a wall.

Spalling Frost-induced crumbling of brick.

Spotboard Flat board, about 1m (3¼ft) square, for mixing mortar or bringing it close to work. Usually made of plywood supported by battens.

Stretcher	Brick laid with its long sides parallel with the line of the wall.	**Slater's ripper**	Tool for cutting through nails when damaged slates are replaced.
Stop end	End of a wall where courses finish flush.	**Soaker**	Lead, zinc, or felt waterproofing fitted under tiles and into angle of roof and chimney. *See also* Flashing.
Stucco	Coat of fine plaster on brickwork; used also to coat internal walls and ceilings.	**Soffit board**	Horizontal timber planking hung between fascia board (qv) and wall.
		Tile gauge	Straight piece of timber marked with tile and tile-and-a-half widths to ensure correct bond when tiling.

PAVING, PATIOS & STEPS

Going	Distance from front to back of a tread (qv).	**Valley**	Internal angle formed by junction of two pitches.
Plate vibrator	Machine for bedding-in paving blocks.	**Verge**	Edge of tiling projecting over a gable (qv); usually mortared.
Riser	The vertical component of a step.	**Wall plate**	Timber beam, laid on top of brick or block wall, to which ends of joists or rafters are fixed.
Screed	A level bed of concrete, mortar, or sand onto which bricks, blocks, slabs, or interior flooring materials are laid.		
Tread	The horizontal component of a step.		

ROOF AND ASSOCIATED STRUCTURES

Bargeboard	Decorative board mounted under the verge at the gable (qv) end of a pitched roof.
Batten, roof	Horizontal batten, nailed to rafters, to support tiles and fix roofing felt.
Delamination	Breakdown of the structure of roofing slates into flaky pieces.
Dormer	Vertical window built into the slope of a pitched roof.
Eaves	Bottom edge of a pitched roof overhanging the walls.
Fascia board	Timber planking, hung on edge from the end of rafters at the eaves (qv), to which gutter is fixed.
Flashing	Lead, zinc, or felt waterproofing of the angle made by abutting vertical and pitched or horizontal surfaces on a roof. *See also* Soaker.
Flaunching	Mortar or concrete bed on a chimney stack into which chimney pots are set.
Gable	House wall supporting ends of a pitched roof.
Hip	Sloping ridge formed by junction of a roof slope and hip end (qv).
Hip end	Tiled, sloping end to a pitched roof.
Joist	Timber or steel beam supporting a floor or ceiling.
Nibs	Projections on clay tile for hooking over roof batten.
Pantile	High-profiled roof tile that interlocks with its neighbours on either side.
Purlin	Horizontal roof timber supporting the rafters (qv).
Rafter	One of the beams forming the framework of a pitched roof.
Ridge	Junction of two slopes at top of a pitched roof.
Ridge board	Timber board to which upper ends of rafters are fixed.
Ridge tile	Square- or round-profile tile that covers the ridge.

PLUMBING & CENTRAL HEATING

Crowsfoot wrench	Plumber's spanner.
Elbow	Pipe fitting for connecting two lengths of pipe at a given angle to each other.
Gland	Sealing ring around the stem of tap, valve, and other fittings to prevent leaks.
Gravity circulation	Circulation of water in a system that depends on the property of hot water to rise above cold. In such a system, heat is applied at a low point in the circuit.
Gully	Opening to a drainage system.
Immersion heater	Metal-sheathed electrical element inserted into hot-water cylinder or tank to heat the water.
Inspection chamber	Often called a manhole; a point of access to an underground drainage system.
Joint, capillary	Method of joining copper pipe in which, when heat is applied, solder is conducted by capillary action between the pipe and a special fitting.
Joint, compression	Joint in which two olives (qv) are held in place by nuts.
Lagging	Protection of water tanks and pipes by insulation wrapping.
Olive	Brass or copper compression ring that acts as a seal in a compression joint (qv).
PTFE	Tape or paste waterproofing compound containing polytetrafluorethylene used for sealing joints in pipes and other fittings.
Rising main	Pipe that brings water into house from the Water Board's system.
Stopcock	Hand-operated on/off valve permitting water flow in only one direction. *See also* Valve, gate.
Tail	On a tap, the threaded section that connects to the supply pipe.
Trap	Water-filled fitting below a sink, bath, gully, or WC to prevent smells rising from drains.
Valve, ball	Used to control level of water in a cistern.

Valve, bleed	Used, with a key, to evacuate air trapped in a system.
Valve, gate	Hand-operated on/off valve permitting water to flow in either direction. *See also* Stopcock.
Valve, lockshield	Used to balance each part of a heating system; fitted to return side of central-heating radiators.
Valve, safety	Operated by pressure; opens when pressure exceeds a pre-selected level.
Valve, thermostatic	Opens and closes at pre-selected temperature levels. A thermostatic radiator valve (TRV), which replaces a lockshield valve, opens and closes in response to air temperature.
Valve, wheel-head	Hand-operated, on/off valve connected to the flow side of a radiator.

ELECTRICITY

Ampere (amp; A)	Unit of electric current expressing volume of flow.
Cable	Used for circuit wiring. *See* Flex.
Cartridge fuse	Small fuse used in plugs and fused connectors: 13amp (brown) for appliances with load of 750W and over; 3amp (red) for appliances and lamp with less than 750W.
Circuit breaker	Switch that automatically breaks contact in the event of overloading or a short circuit. Miniature circuit breaker (MCB) is alternative to a fuse (qv).
Consumer unit	Consumer's fuse board, usually with an on/off switch.
Current	Movement or flow of electricity, expressed in amps (qv).
Double-pole switch	Switch in which circuit is broken at both live and neutral poles.
Earth	Conductor enabling electricity to pass into the earth.
Flex	Used for connecting up appliances. *See* Cable.
Fuse	Intentionally weak link in a circuit, designed to fail or break contact if system is overloaded. *See also* Circuit breaker.
Fused connection unit	Used on a ring main or spur to connect an appliance without using a plug.
Insulator	Non-conducting material used for isolating a conductor.
Loop-in method	Connects up a lighting circuit to each ceiling rose in turn.
Ohm	Unit of electrical resistance (the resistance of wiring to passage of electricity).
Radial circuit	System in which circuit cables radiate from a consumer unit.
Ring circuit	System arranged in form of a ring starting from and returning to the same sub-circuit fuse or circuit-breakers.
Short circuit	Connection (usually accidental) between two sides of a circuit.

Spur	Branch cable attached to a ring circuit.
Switchfuse unit	Unit that controls an individual circuit; it is connected to the main switch unit.
Terminal	That part of an appliance, socket, plug, or switch to which electrical conductors are fixed.
Volt (v)	Unit of the pressure that causes an electric current to flow in a circuit.
Watt (W)	Unit of power: 1 watt equals the work represented by a current of 1 amp under a pressure of 1 volt. The kilowatt (kW) is a unit equal to 1,000 watts; it is the unit by which the power (and electrical consumption) of most domestic electrical appliances is defined.

INTERNAL WALLS

Head plate	Horizontal member of partition framework, fixed to ceiling.
Load-bearing wall	Wall carrying the weight of a superstructure such as a roof or second storey.
Nogging	Horizontal member of the timber framework of a partition wall.
Padstone	Block of concrete or stone surmounting a pier or column to support a load-bearing beam, lintel, or joist.
Partition	Non-load-bearing internal wall.
Sole plate	Horizontal member of partition framework, fixed to floor.
Stud	Vertical member of the timber framework of a partition wall.

TIMBER AND CARPENTRY

Architrave	Moulding above a door or window.
Beading	Small timber or plastic moulding used as decoration.
Bevel	Angled edge.
Blockboard	Board made of thin outer single or double veneers sandwiching a core of softwood strips bonded edge to edge. Standard thicknesses of 12–32mm (½–1¼in) are available.
Carcase	The basic, box-like structure of, eg, a cupboard or wardrobe.
Chamfer	A corner or bevel with the edge cut into one or more faces.
Chipboard	Board made by bonding resin-coated chips of wood under heat and pressure; often has veneered or laminated surface. Made in various thicknesses and grades of hardness.
Cladding	Decorative timber (or PVC) boards, usually interlocking, for exterior house walls.
Cramp	Tool for gripping wood for sawing, drilling, etc, or for holding parts together after glueing.
Dowel	Headless, cylinder-shaped peg used (with glue) to join pieces of wood; available in standard diameters of 3–50mm (⅛–2in).

Gauge, wood	Tool for scoring a line parallel to a face or edge of timber. A mortise gauge scores two parallel lines a variable distance apart.
Hardboard	Board made from heated and compressed wood pulp; single- and double-faced types are available, also perforated boards for decorative use. Medium hardboard, much thicker and softer, is used in partitions.
Hardwood	Timber from broad-leaved trees.
Jamb	Vertical face of a door- or window-opening.
Kerf	Cut made by a saw.
Moulding	Decorative, shaped strip or edge of wood or plaster.
Nominal size	Standard 'as-sawn' dimensions of a piece of timber before being planed down. *See also* PAR.
PAR	Planed all round: machine-smoothed timber in which width and depth are commonly 3mm (⅛in) less than the nominal size.
Plane, block	Standard metal bench plane suitable for small work and end-grain trimming.
Plane, moulding	Small, narrow-bladed plane for forming shaped edges to timber.
Plane, plough	Plane for cutting a groove or rebate.
Plane, router	Two-handed plane for cutting clean grooves across the grain.
Plane, shoulder	Narrow-bladed plane for cleaning up the surfaces of joint shoulders, mortises, and tenons.
Rail	(1) Horizontal timber of a door. (2) Horizontal timber from which vertical boards of a fence or pales of a gate are hung.
Sliding bevel	Essentially a try square with a movable blade pivoted about one end of the stock. For marking complex angles.
Softwood	Timber from coniferous trees.
Spur post	Concrete or timber replacement for rotted lower portion of fence post.
Stile	Vertical member of a gate, door, or window-frame.
Winding	A twist in timber boards caused by faulty seasoning.

DECORATING: EXTERIOR & INTERIOR

Brushing out	Spreading out paint to an even thickness on surface.
Grout	Waterproof filler used between ceramic tiles and mosaics.
Knotting	Shellac-based solution for sealing knots in wood.
Laying off	Final, light brush strokes in painting to give a perfectly smooth surface.
Medium	In paint, the liquid vehicle, such as oil or water, in which the pigment (qv) is suspended.
Parquet	Hardwood flooring blocks laid in symmetrical patterns.
Pigment	Finely ground substance that provides the colour in paint.
PVA	Polyvinyl acetate, the basis of various types of adhesives and paints.
Primer	The first coat of paint on a surface. Different types are used for different surfaces (wood, steel, non-ferrous metals, and so on) to provide good protection and achieve maximum adhesion.
Size	Thinned adhesive used to seal a surface before hanging wallcovering.
Tiler's spike	Sharp-pointed tool for scoring through the glaze of ceramic tiles prior to cutting them.
Undercoat	Paint applied after the primer to provide a key for the top coat(s).

INDEX

Number in *italics* refer to captions.

Abrasives 150, *151*
Adhesives:
  for ceramic tiles 171
  for fixings to walls 121
  for plastic laminates 169
  neoprene-based 121
  types 125, 126
  using 126
  working times 126
Admixtures for concrete 11
Aggregate 11
  storing 16
Aggregate wall finish,
  painting 69
Air thermostat 92
  checking 94
  position of 92
Airlocks in pipes 87

All-surface primer 69
Aluminium, concrete stains on 15
Aluminium primer 69
Angle grinder *129*, 130
Angle iron,
  supporting fence posts 64
Architrave,
  running cable behind 104
Architrave box, 111, *111*
Armoured cable 108, *108*
Arris rail, repairing 67
Asbestos-cement roof 55
  repairing cracks in 55
Asphalt roof, repairing 55
Attic room, insulating 141
Auger 64
Auger bits *125*

Backsaw 126–7, *127*
Bag graining 159, *159*
Bagging-in blockwork 73
  rendering 33
Balanced flue 91, 154
Ball valve, fitting 87
  replacing washer in 89, *89*
Bandage pipe insulation *139*, 145
Bar cramp *125*, 126
Bargeboard *56*, 56

cutting new 59
deterioration of 56
repairing rotten 59
replacing 59
treating 57
Basket-weave bond *39*
Baths, removing blockages in 88
  sealing gap against wall 87
Bath trap 78, 83
Bathroom ventilation 145
Batt (brick) *26*, 28
Beech 122
Bell push, fitting 136
Bench grinder 129–30, *129*
Bench plane 124–5, *125*
Bending spring, using 82, *83*
Berlin black paint 153
Birdsmouth joint 62, *63*
Bitumen black paint 153
Bituminous felt, repairing 55
  replacing *55*
Blanket insulation,
  fitting in roof 141–2, *141*
  fitting to walls 142
Blanking-off plate 106
Bleed valve 93, *94*
Bleeding radiator 94, *94*, 95
Block, concrete: *see* Concrete

Block cutter *38*, 39
Block plane 124, *125*
Blockwork:
  bagging-in 73
  painting 73
  pointing 31
  rendering 33
  See also Concrete block
Blowlamp, use of *82*, 153
Blue Delft tiles 171
Board, fence: *see* Fence
Board, roof: *see* Roof
Boiler 91, *94*
  maintenance 92
  safety valve 94
  thermostat 92
Bolts (screw) 133
Bonding bricks 26, *26*
  brick paviors *39*
  concrete blocks 28
Boning rods, making 13
  using 18, *19*
Bottle trap 78, 83
Box eaves 56
Brace (drill),
  types, 125–6, *125*
Brick:
  bonding 26, *26*

buying 24
calcium-silicate 22, 23
choosing 22–3, 24
clay 22
cleaning 27
common 22, 23
concrete 22, 23
cutting 28, 30
engineering 22
estimating quantity 24, 29
facing 22
fletton 22
interior quality 22
joint profiles 29, 30, *30*, 32
jointing 30, *30*
laying, 28–9
mixing 24
modular 23
ordinary quality 23
piers 29
second-hand 24
sizes 23
special quality 23, 29
special shaped 24
stacking 24, *24*
stock 22
storing 24
traditional 23
types 22–3, *23*
uses 22–3
wire-cut 22
See also Bricklaying; Brickwork
Brick Advisory Centre 24
Brick-cutting gauge,
    making 30, *30*
Bricklaying *27, 28, 28, 29, 29*
Bricklaying tools 25, *25*
    home-made 13, 30, *30*
Brick paviors, bonding *39*
    laying 39
    types 39
Brickwork:
    efflorescence on 24, 29
    openings in 29
    paint for 153
    painting 153
    pointing 30, *30*
    removing 115
    repairing 72
    replacing 72
    repointing 30, 32, *32*
    weatherproofing 69
Brush, paint: *see* Paint brush
Brush draught-excluder 140, *140*
Buckets for concrete 13
Builder's square, home-made 13
Building Authority byelaws 78
Building Regulations:
    for internal wall 114
    for lean-to 62
    for shed 64
Burst pipe, repairing 89
    repairing lead 89
Butt hinge *137*
    letting-in 136, *136*
Byelaws, plumbing 78

Cable 100
    armoured 108, *108*
    colour-coding 97
    replacing in loft 141
    running 104
    sizes 100
    types 97
Calcium plumbate primer 69
Canopy, construction of 62, *63*
Capillary fittings 78, *79*
Capillary joint, making 82, *82*
Carpet 175
Carpet tiles 175, *175*
Carport, construction of 62, *63*
Casement windows,
    painting 71, *154*

repairing joints 59
Cavity walls,
    insulating 139, 142
    mounting-boxes in 104–5
    running cable down 104
Cedar, western red 122
    restoring colour of 68
Ceiling, erecting false 142
    fixing to 121
    painting 154, 155
    papering 166, *166*
Ceiling fixings 165, *165*
Ceiling rose 100, 101
    fitting 105
    rewiring 103, *103*
    wiring loop-in 110
Ceiling switch 101, *101*
    repairing 111
    wiring 109, *109*
Ceiling tiles 142
Cellulose filler 153
Cement:
    coloured 10–11
    masonry 11
    painting 153
    Portland 10
    rapid-hardening 10
    skin-sensitivity to 11
    storing 16
    sulphate-resisting 10
    white 10–11
Cement paint 69, 72–3
Central heating,
    effect on humidity of 122
Central-heating systems:
    blockages in 95
    controls *90–1*, 92–3, *93*
    corrosion in 95
    drain valves 93–4
    draining 94, 95
    expansion pipe 94
    feed-and-expansion tank 91–2,
        94
    flushing out 95
    gravity feed 92
    layout *90*, 91–2
    maintenance 92–5, *95*
    microbore 91
    pipework 91
    pipework sizes 91
    vent pipe 94
Ceramic tiles:
    adhesives for 171
    cutting 130, 173
    drilling 129, 130
    grout for 171, 172
    laying 171–173, *172, 173*
    varieties and styles 170–171
Chestnut (timber) 122
Chimney, capping pots 51, 140
    repairing 51
    replacing flaunching 51, *51*
    replacing pots 51
Chipboard,
    marking 126
    treating edge 135
Chisels, sharpening 125, *125*
    types 125, *125*
Chuck, care of power-drill 129
Circular saw *129*, 130
Circular saw attachment 130
Cisterns, painting 155
    replacing valve washer 89, *89*
    See also Cold-water storage tank;
        Feed/expansion tank
Cladding (PVC extrusion) 60
Cladding (timber) 56, 57, *57*
    deterioration of 57
    for shed walls 64, *66*
    repairing rotten 60
    replacing 60, *60*
    replacing battens of 60, *60*
    treating 57

Clamp: *see* Cramp
Clench nailing 130
Closer (brick) 28
Coach screw 133
Coarse stuff (mortar) 27, 28
Cold-water storage tank 78
    cutting holes in 86, 87
    draining 84
    installing 86
    insulating 141, *145*
    replacing 87
    replacing valve washer 89, *89*
Colour and colour schemes 148–9
Compression fitting 79, *79*
    making joints with 82, *82*
Concrete:
    admixtures for 11
    buying 10
    compacting 17, *19*
    curing 17
    drilling 120
    dry-mix 10, 15
    edges, repairing 21, *21*
    estimating quantity 14
    expansion joints in 18, *19*
    finishing 17, *20*
    ingredients 10–11, *11*
        buying 15
        estimating 14–15, *15*
        storing 16
    laying (placing) 17–21, *19, 20, 21*
    mixes 14–15, *15*
        testing 15
    mixing 10, 14–16, *16*
        hand 16, *16*
        power 16
    painting 153
    path, laying 18–20, *18–20*
    ready-mixed 10, 14, *14*
        suppliers of 14
    repairing 21, *21*
    slab, laying 17
        laying damp-proof *21*
Concrete block:
    bonding 28
    breezeblock, drilling 120
    choosing 24
    cutting 30
    laying 28
    laying screen-wall 28
    pier 26, 28, 31, *31*
    pilaster 31, *31*
    sizes 24
    stacking 24
    storing 24
    types 24
    See also Blockwork
Concrete-block paviors:
    cutting 38, 39
    laying 38, *38*
    types 38, *38*
Concrete mixers 16
Concrete paving slabs:
    buying 37
    cast 37
    colours 38
    cutting 38–9
    filling joints 36
    hydraulically pressed 37
    laying 36, *36–7*
    levelling 36, *41*
    sizes 38
    spacing 36, *36*
Concrete spur fence post 64
Concrete walling units *40–1*
Concreting tools 12–13, *13*
    cleaning 15
Condensation, cause of 145
    in double glazing 144
Conductor (electrical) 97
    earth-continuity 97
    live 98
    neutral 98

Consumer unit 96, *96*, 97
Cooker, wiring free-standing 106
    wiring split-level 106
Cooker control unit 100–1, *101*
    distance from cooker 106
    wiring 106
Cooker terminal box 106
Coping, wall 29, 31, *31*
Coping saw (joinery) 127, *127*
Cord-operated switch 101, *101*
    repairing 111
    wiring 109, *109*
Cork flooring 176
    laying floor tiles 177, *177*
Cork wallcovering 160, *161, 163*
Corrosion inhibitor 95
Corrugated roofs 55
    repairing 55
Corrugated sheet, cutting 55
    fixing 55
    flashing strip for 62
    repairing cracks in 55
    replacing 55
Countersink bit 126
Countersunk screws 131, *131*
Coving, for plasterboard 120
Cramp *125*, 126
Crazy paving, buying 39
    laying 39
Creosote 57
Crime prevention 182
Crosscut saw 126, *127*
Crowsfoot wrench 84
Cylinder, hot water 91
Cylinder lock, fitting 137

Damp, rising: *see* Rising damp
Damp-proof course, felt 62
    fitting 73
    linking lean-to to house 62
Damp-proof membrane 21
Danish oil 134
Datum point for paving 35
Decorating: *see* Exterior
        Decorating; Interior
        Decorating
Decorating tools 150–1, *150–1*
    hiring 71
Decorative paint finishes 156–9,
    157–9
Dentil slips 48
Dimmer switch, fitting 111
    minimum rating 111
Dining room:
    joining with kitchen 114
    joining with living room 113
Disc sander 181
Dishwasher, water supply to 84
Distemper, stripping 155
Door:
    colour of edges 156
    draughtproofing 139, 140, *140*
    fitting new 60
    hanging 136, *136*, 137
    heat loss through glazed 138
    internal 117
    painting *154*, 155–6
    painting external 60, *69*, 71
    painting glazed 71
    shed, construction 64, *66*
    sticking in frame 60
    wallpapering round 165
    warping of 60
Door frame:
    deterioration 57
    fixing in stud partition 120
    painting *154*
    repairing external 60
    sealing in masonry 140
Door sill:
    deterioration 57
    fitting 60
    replacing 60

securing 60
Double glazing:
  cost effectiveness 139
  optimum gap 143
  sealed unit 143–4
    installing 144
  secondary sash 143, 144
    condensation in 144
    installing 144, 144
  types 144
Double-pole switch 98
Dovetail gauge, making 133, 133
Dovetail joint 133, 133
Dovetail saw 127, 127
Dowel bit 126
Dowel jig 137
Dowel joint, drilling holes for
  125–6
Downpipes, clearing 52
DPC: see Damp-proof course
Drain, removing blockage in 88
Drain rods 88
Drain valves 93–4
Drainage:
  from concrete 17
  from patio 36
  from paving 36
Draught, heat loss by 138
Draught excluders 139, 139
  fitting 140, 140
  types 139, 139, 140, 140
Draughtproofing 138, 139–40
  cost effectiveness 139
Drill, electric: see Power drill
  push type 136
Drill bits:
  for masonry 120
  for timber 125, 126
  screwdriver 125
Drill stand, vertical 129, 129
Drives, repairing edges of 21, 21
Dry-dash: see Pebbledash
Duplex rebate plane 124, 125
Duplex wallpaper 160
Dust sheets 150

Earth-continuity conductor 97
  insulating on cable 100
Earth-leakage circuit breaker
  (ELCB) 98, 99
Earthing 97
Earthing rod 97–8
Eaves, box 56
Edging cramp 125, 126
Efflorescence:
  on brick 24, 29
  on plaster 153
ELCB: see Earth-leakage circuit
  breaker
Electric tools: see Power tools
Electrical accessories 100–1, 100–1
  replacing 103–4
Electrical appliances,
  double-insulated 109
  rating 99
  replacing flex 103
Electrical circuit:
  labelling 98
  lighting 98, 99–100, 99
  radial 99
  ring main 97, 99
Electricity:
  safety rules 96
  tools for 102, 102
  understanding 96–8
Electricity Board service fuse 96, 96
Electricity meter 96, 96
Emery paper 150
Emulsion paint 152
  applying 155
  exterior grade 69, 73
Emulsion preservative 57
Engineering bricks 22

English bond 26, 26
English garden wall bond 26
Expansion joint 18, 19
Extension cable 102
Exterior decorating:
  following the sun 71
  four-year cycle 68
  frequency 68
  hiring equipment 71
  optimum conditions 68
  preparing metal 70–1
  preparing walls 72
  preparing wood 70
Extinguishers, fire 182
Extractor fan, size of 145
  wiring 107

Fabric wallcoverings 160
Facing bricks 22
Fascia boards 56, 56
  deterioration 56
  mitring ends 59
  protecting 58
  repairing rotten 58
  replacing 58
  treating 57
  water penetration 57
Feather-edged boards 67
Feed/expansion tank 91–2, 94
  maintenance 94
  overflow pipe 94
  replacing valve washer 89, 89
Felt roofs:
  repairing 55, 55
  sealing to house wall 62
  shed, construction 64, 66
Felt slates 55
Fence:
  close-boarded 67
  open-boarded 67
  repairing 64, 67
Fence boards, types 67
Fence panels, erecting 64
  securing loose 67
Fence posts:
  capping 67
  concrete spur 64
  fixing loose 64
  replacing timber 64
  treating 67
Fillers 153
Fire prevention 182
Fireplace, blocking up 116, 116
  draughtproofing 140
  removing 116, 116
Firmer bevel-edge (FBE) chisel
  125, 125
Firmer chisel 125
Flashing:
  cutting stepped 50
  fitting self-adhesive 50, 50
  fitting stepped 50
  fitting to lean-to 62
  repairing cracks in 50
  replacing straight 50
  repointing 50
Flat bits (joinery) 125
Flat roof, insulating 142
  repairing 55, 55
Flaunching, replacing 51, 51
Flemish bond 26, 26
Flemish garden wall bond 26
Flex, colour coding 97
  replacing on appliance 103
  stripping 102–3, 103
  types 97, 101
Flexible cord: see Flex
Float, plasterer's 153
Flock wallpaper 160
Floor:
  draughtproofing 139, 143
  filling gaps in 180
  heat loss through 138

laying concrete 21, 21
levelling with hardboard
  143
outbuilding, insulating 143
running cable under 104
sanding 182
shed, construction 64, 65, 66
solid, insulating 143
  levelling 179
timber, insulating 143, 143
  levelling 177
Floor coverings 174–81 see also
  Carpeting, carpet tiles, cork,
  rubber flooring, vinyl sheet
  flooring, vinyl tiles, wood
  flooring
  preparing surface for 177
Floor painting 180
Floor sander 179, 179
Floor tiles:
  cutting 177
  fitting round obstacles 177
  laying 177
  setting out 177
  See also Carpet; Cork; Vinyl
Floorboard finishes 179–81 see also
  Floor painting, Stencilling
Floorboards, lifting 106
  replacing 143
Flue, balanced 91, 155
  ventilating blocked 116, 116
Fluorescent tube 101
Flush joint in brickwork 30
  making 30, 32
Foam draught excluder 140, 140
Footlifter 119, 119
Formwork:
  curved 21
  for drives 17, 17
  for paths 17, 17, 18, 18–19
  for repairing edges 21, 21
  for slabs 17
  for steps 40
Foundations:
  compacting 18, 19, 20
  excavating 18, 18, 20, 20
  for path 18, 18
  for patio 36
  laying 20, 20
  marking out 20
  sizes 20
  stepped 17, 20, 40
  strip 17
Frame cramp 126
French polish 134
Frenchman (pointing) 32
Frog (in brick) 23
Frozen pipe, thawing 89
Fuse:
  cartridge 98–9
  circuit 96, 98–9
  colour coding 99
  mending rewirable 102
  plug 101
  rating 98
  reasons for blowing 98
  service 96, 96
  testing cartridge 102
  understanding 98
Fusebox 96, 96
  See also Consumer unit;
    Switchfuse
Fused connection unit 101, 108
  wiring 108

G-cramp 125, 126
Galvanised post, boxing in 62
Garage door, repairing 58
Garden path, laying 18–20, 18–20
Garden shed, building 64, 65–6
Garden wall, building 29
Gate, repairing 67
  securing posts 67

Gate valve, fitting 87
Gauge (woodworking) types 126,
  127, 133, 133
Gauge rod, making 25
Gland nut (in tap) 88
Glass doors, heat loss 138
  painting 71
Glass fibre insulation,
  fitting in loft 141, 141
  fitting to walls 143
Glass-fibre-polyester roof 55
Glass roof, sealing 62
Glasspaper 150, 151
Glazing, stained wood frame 72
  varnished wood frame 72
Glazing bars, repairing 62
  repairing greenhouse 62, 64
Glazing bead 72
Gloss paint 69, 152
  painting over 155
Grain, filling 70, 135
Grant for loft insulation 141
Grass cloths 160
Gravel board, replacing 67
Greenhouse, repairing glazing
  bars 62, 64
Gerinders 129–30, 129
Grouting 173
Guide holes, drilling 129
Gulley (waste system) 78
  clearing 88
Gutter:
  clearing 52
  cutting 52
  fitting PVC 52, 53
  fixing brackets 53
  painting 52
  removing 58
  removing brackets 58
  repairing valley 49
  replacing cast iron 52
  replacing valley 49
  sealing joints 52
  support brackets 56
  types 52, 52

Hacking knife, glazier's 59
Hall, joining with living room
  113–4
Hammer, types 125, 125
Hammer drill 128
Handsaw 126, 127
Hardboard, levelling floor with 177
Hardcore, compacting 12, 19
Hardware for timber 136–7
  lay-on positioning 136
Hardwood:
  buying 123
  characteristics 122
  staining 69
  varnishing 69
Harling: see Roughcast
Hawk, plasterer's 153
Header (brick) 26
Hearth, constructional 116
  superimposed 116
  removing 116
Heat loss through house 138
Heat-proof paint 153
Herringbone bond 39
Hinge, letting-in 136, 136
  replacing gate 67
  types 137
Hip, repairing 48, 49
Hip iron, fixing 48
Hip tiles, replacing 48
Hole saw, using 86
Hopper (waste system) 78
Hot-water cylinder 91

Immersion heater switch 107
  wiring 107
Insulation (electrical) 97

Insulation (thermal) 138
  cost effectiveness 139
  fitting 139, 140–5, *141–5*
Interior decorating, tools for 150–1, *150–1*
  order of work 152
Internal walls:
  building 112, 116–20, *117–20*
  definition 112
  hollow 112–3
    fixing to 121, *121*
  load bearing 112
    removing 112, 115, *115*
  non-load-bearing 112
    removing 116
  partition 112
    removing 116
  removing 112, 113–6, *113–5*
  safety rules 113
  solid 112–3
    fixing to 120–1, *121*
  sound insulation 117
  See also Stud partition
Iroko (timber) 122

Jigsaw *129*, 130
  blades for *129*, 130
    using worn 130
Joint box: *see* Junction box
Joint profiles in brickwork *30*
  making 30
  recessed 29
Jointing brickwork 30, *30*
Jointing timber *132–3*, 133
Joists, locating 117, 121
  running cable parallel to 104
  running cable through 104
Junction box *100*
  inserting in ring cable 105, *106*

Kitchen, joining with dining room 114
  ventilation in 144–5
Kitchen sink. *See* Sink
Knocking pipes 87
Knots (timber), sealing 70, 155

Lacquer:
  applying to floor 181
  coloured, for timber 134–5
  thinning 135
  types for timber 134–5
  See also Varnish
Ladder:
  choosing 44
  extending 44
  painting from 71
  roof, *44*, 46
  securing 44, *44*, 46
  using 44
Ladder stay 44
Lambswool paint roller *150*, 151
Laminate: *see* Plastic laminate
Lamp: *see* Light bulb
Lampholder *101*
  wiring 103, *103*
Lath-and-plaster 113
  removing 116
Lean-to *62*, 63
  building *62*, *63*
  sealing to house walls 62
Lean-to roof 55
  access to 62
  building shed 64, *65*, *66*
Letter plate, fitting 138
Letterbox, draughtproofing 140
Levels, establishing 13
Light bulb 101
Light switches *100*, 101, *110–11*
  converting one- to two-way *110*, 111
  two-way 111
Lighting circuits:

extending 109–10, *110*
  in outbuilding 108
  junction box *98*, 99–100, *99*
  loop-in *98*, 99–100, *99*
  number of points 100
Lining paper 166
Linked timber, 62, *63*
  galvanised posts for 62
  replacing support posts 62
Living room, joining with dining room 113
  joining with hall 113–4
Lock, fitting mortise 137, *137*
Locks, security 182
Lockshield valve 93
  adjusting 95
Loft, boarding over 142
  insulating floor 139, 140–1, *141*, 142
  ventilation in 142
Loft conversion, insulating 142
Loft insulation:
  blanket 141
  cost effectiveness 139
  grant for 141
  handling materials 141
  laying 141–2, *141*
  loose fill 141, *141*
Loft opening, making 141

Mains water pressure 87
Man-made boards *123*
  cutting 130
  stacking *123*
Marking gauge 126, *127 See also* Mortise gauge
Masonry, paints for 69
  See also Brick; Brickwork
Masonry bolt, expanding 121
Masonry paint 69
Masonry pins 121
MCB: *see* Miniature circuit breaker
Metal:
  cutting 130
  fitting 71
  paint for 69
  painting 68, 69, 71, 162
  preparing 70–1
  priming 70–1
Meter, electricity 96, *96*
Miniature circuit breaker (MCB) 98, 99
  restoring power with 102
Mitre square 126, *127*
Mixer tap, fitting 84, *84*
Mixing board, making 25
Mixing platform, making 13
Mohair paint roller 159
Mortar dry-mix 28
  for bricks 28
  for concrete blocks 28
  matching 30, 32
  mixes 28
Mortise, cutting 132, *132*, 133, 142
  cutting for lock 137, *137*
Mortise and tenon joint 132, *132*, 133
Mortise chisel 125, *125*
Mortise gauge, 126, *127*
Mortise lock, fitting 137, *137*
Mounting boxes *100*, *101*, 104
  fitting flush 104, *105*
  fitting surface 104, *107*
  for wall lights 111, *111*

Nail, starting short 131
  types 130, *131*
Nail punch *125*
Nailing, principle of 130
Nogging (timber) 113
  fitting 117

Oak 122

special finishes 135
Oil, for finishing timber 134
Oil-based paint, for walls 152
Olive oil, as timber finish 134
Orbital sander *129*, 130
  removing heavy stock 135
Organic-solvent preservative 57
Outbuilding, insulating 143
Outbuilding (timber):
  maintenance 62
  raising from ground 62
  repairing roof 62
  treating walls 64

Paint:
  acrylic-based 73
  applying metal primer 70–1
  applying wood primer 70
  Berlin black 153
  bitumen black 153
  blackboard 153
  brick 153
  burning off 153, *153*
  cement 69, 72–3
  chlorinated rubber 73
  dry-scraping 153
  exterior emulsion 69, 73
  for masonry 69
  for metal 69
  for wood 69
  gloss 69
  heatproof 153
  resin-based 73
  scoreboard green 153
  stone 69
  textured 153
Paint brushes 151, *151*
Paint pads 151, *151*
Paint rollers 151, *151*
Paint stripper, using 72, 153
Painting:
  aggregate wall finish 69
  blockwork 73
  casement windows 71
  ceilings 154, *155*
  cisterns 155
  doors *154*, 155–6
  door frames *154*
  exterior doors *69*, 71
  exterior walls 72
  from ladders 71, *71*
  from scaffold tower 72
  glass doors 71
  metal 68, 69, 71, 162
  pebbledash 73
  pipes 155
  porous walls 72
  preparing wood for 70
  radiators 155
  rendering 69, 73
  skirtings 155
  softwood 68
  undercoating 71
  walls 155, *155*
  windows 71, *154*, 156
  with brush 72–3
  with roller 72–3
  with spraygun 73
  wood 71
Paintwork:
  causes of cracking 57, 60
  deterioration of 57
  dusting 71
  filling 70
  removing flaked 70
  removing blistered 70
  sticky-tape test 70
  stripping 70, *70*
Paper-wrapped insulation 141
  installing 143, *143*
Papering wall: *see* Wallpapering
PAR. *See under* Timber
Partition. *See under* Internal wall

Paste, wallpaper 151, *151*
Pasting brush 151, *151*
Pasting table 151, *151*
Path:
  laying concrete 18–20, *18–20*
  marking out 18
  marking out curve 18, *19*
  planning 34–5
  repairing edges 21, *21*
Patio:
  laying 36, *36*
  marking out 36, *36*
  planning 34, 35
  siting 34
Paving, choosing materials 35
  datum point for 35
Paving slabs: *see* Concrete; Stone
Paviors: *see* Brick; Concrete
Pebbledash rendering 32
  painting 73
  repairing bald patch 73
Pendant light, wiring 103, *103*
Philips screw and driver 131
Pier, brick 29
  concrete block 26, 28, 31, *31*
Pilaster block 31, *31*
Pillar tap *88*
Pilot hole 131
Pipe, pipework:
  airlocks in 87
  bendable 84
  bending 82, *83*
  burst 89
  connecting to cistern 87
  copper 79
  copper-iron adaptor 82
  cutting copper 81, *81*
  frozen 89
  imperial sizes 79
  imperial-metric adaptor 79
  joining copper to iron 82–3
  knocking in 87
  lead 78–9
  metric sizes 79
  outdoor, insulating 145
  painting 155
  sizes 79
  supporting 79, 84, 87
  waste. *See* Waste pipe
Pipe cutter, using 81, *81*
Pipe fittings, capillary 78, 79
  compression 79, *79*
  soldered 78, 79
Pipe insulation 139, 141, 145, *145*
Pitched roof, for shed 64, *65–6*
  repairing 42–3, 46–9, *47–50*
Planes 124–5, *125*
  power *129*, 130
  sharpening blade 124
Planking, repairing rotten 58
Planning permission,
  for lean-to 64
  for shed 64
Plaster 153
  burying cable in 104
  painting new 153
Plasterboard:
  cutting 116, *117*
  cutting hole in 116
  fixing 116
  insulating 142
    fixing to walls 142–3
  joins, hiding 119–20, *120*
  removing 116
  sizes 116
  tapered edge 116
  tools for 116, 119
Plastic laminate:
  adhesive 169
  cutting *168*, 169
  edging strip, fixing *168*, 169
  marking out 168
  preparing surface 168

styles 166–7
sticking down *169*, 169
trimming *168*, 169
uses 166–7
Plastic wood, using 135
Plate vibrator, using 38, *38*
Plough plane 124, *125*
Plug (electrical) 101
wiring 102–3, *103*
Plug (timber), cutting 129
Plumbing, tools for 81, *81*
Plumbing fittings *78–9*
Pointing blockwork 31
brickwork 30, *30*
Polyethylene wallcovering 160
Polystyrene (expanded):
ceiling tiles 142
tank insulation 145
Polyurethane lacquer 134–5
applying to floor 181
Post, fence, replacing 67
gate, securing 67
Post-and-rail fences 67
Post-hole borer 64
Power centre *129*, 130
Power drills 129–30, *129*
attachments 129, 130
chuck, care of 129
electronic control 128–9
hammer action 128
micro-chip control 129
Power tools 128–30, *129*
Pozidriv screw and driver 131
Preservatives for timber 57
Primer 161
applying 70
choosing 69
types 69
Profile-cutting saw 127, *127*
Profile gauge 126, *127*
Profiled joint (brickwork) *30*
making 30
Programmer (central heating) 93
Prop, adjustable steel 115, *115*
PTFE tape 83
Pulp wallpaper 160
Pump (central heating) 92, 93
bleeding 94–5
removing sludge 95
replacing 95, *95*
Punner, making 13, *13*
Purlins, for lean-to 62, *63*
Push-drill 136
Putty, bedding-in new 59
defective 57
raking out 59
sealing to glass 59
Putty knife 150, *151*
PVC corrugated roof 55
PVC rainwater system 52, *53*

Quarter bond (blockwork) 28

Radial circuit 99
Radiator 93
balancing 93, 95
bleed valve 93, *94*
automatic 94
bleeding 94, *94*, 95
lockshield valve 93
painting 165
panel *94*
thermostatic valve 93, *93*
types 91
Rafters, for lean-to 62, *63*
repairing rotten end 58
Rag-rolling 156–7, *157*
Ragging on 157–8, *157*
Rainwater drainage:
from concrete 17, 18
from patio 36
from paving 36
Raised-head screws 131, *131*

Rammer, home-made 12–13
Ranch fences 67
Rebate plane, duplex 124, *125*
Recessed joint (brickwork) 29
Relief wallpaper 160
Rendering:
applying to blockwork 33
painting 69, 73
pebbledash 32
repairing 32–3, *33*, 73, *73*
roughcast 32
stucco 32
Tyrolean 32
Repointing brickwork 30, 32, *32*
Resistance (electrical) 97
Retaining wall 10
Rewiring 99
Ridge, repairing 47–8, *48*
Ridge tiles, replacing 47–8, *48*
Ring circuit 97, 99
number of sockets 99
Ripsaw 126, *127*
Rising damp 73
Rising main 78
Rolled steel joist (RSJ) 115
concealing 115
installing *114*, 115, *115*
Roller, paint: *see* Paint
Roof, roof covering:
access to lean-to 62
access to loft 44
corrugated 55, 62
felt 55, 62
flat 55, *55*
glazed 62
heat loss through 138
insulating loft floor 139, 140–1,
141, 142
insulating slope 139
lean-to 55, 62
lean-to shed 64, *65, 66*   .
pitched 42–3, *46*, 47–50, *47, 48,
49*
pitched shed 64, *65, 66*
renewing 43–4
repairing corrugated 55
repairing flat 55, *55*
repairing pitched 42–3, *46*,
47–50, *47, 48, 49*
shed, construction 65, *65–6*
slate 42, 43, *46*, 47
structure *42–3*
surface coating 43
symptoms of condition 43
tile 47–8, *47, 48, 49*
See also Loft
Roof boards 56, *56*
deterioration of 56–7
repairing 58–9
replacing 58–9
treating 57
water penetration 57
Roof covering. *See* Roof
Roof ladder *44*, 46
Roof tiles:
clay 42
removing 47, *47*
replacing 47, *47*
water penetration 42–3
colours 44
concrete 42, 44
hip: *see* Hip tiles
ridge: *see* Ridge tiles
spalling 43
underburnt clay 43
Roofing felt:
repairing bituminous 55
replacing bituminous 55, *55*
underfelt, fitting 48–9, *49*
Rooms, joining 113–4
partitioning 116
Room thermostat 92
checking 94

position of 92
Rot in timber:
causes 56–7, 59, 60, 62, 122
preventing 57, 58–9, 60, 62, 64,
67, 68
Roughcast rendering 32
Round-head screw 131, *131*
Router, power *129*, 130
Router plane 125
RSJ: *see* Rolled steel joist
Rubber flooring 174
Rule (measuring) 126, *127, 151*
Rust, removing extensive 71
removing surface 70
Rust-neutralising agent 71

Safety valve 94
Sand 11
storing 16
Sanders *129*, 130
for floor 179–80, *179*
Sash window, insulating 144
painting *154*, 156
Saw:
circular: *see* Circular saw
hand, types 126–7, *127*
jig: *see* Jigsaw
Saw teeth, number per inch 126
set of 126
Sawing, square to timber 126
Scaffold tower *44*, 46
attachments for *44*, 46
painting wall from 72
Screen-block wall 31, *31*
Screen-wall blocks, laying 28
Screw:
coach 133
gauge of 130–1
guide holes for 131
head types 131, *131*
types *131*
withdrawing with power drill 129
Screw-anchor, metal 121, *121*
plastics 121, *121*
Screw bolt 133
Screw drilling 129
Screwdrivers 125, *125*, 131
drill bit 125
Screwing:
principle of 130
without guide holes 131
Sealant, silicone 69
silicone rubber 87
Sealer (paint) 153
Seam roller 151, *151*
Security locks and lights 182
Service connector box 109
Set-match wallpaper 162, *162*
Shave hook 150, *151*
Shaver unit:
bathroom supply unit *101*, 107
socket outlet *101*, 107
wiring 107
Shed, building 64, *65–6*
recovering flat roof 55, *55*
recovering pitched roof 55
Sheepskin paint roller 151
Shelves, support spacings 123
Shiplap boards 67
Shooting board 124
Shower:
fitting curtain 87
fitting mixer tap 87
fitting screen 87
installing 87
installing instantaneous electric
109, *109*
Shrouded-head tap *88*
Silicon carbide paper 150
Silicone rubber bath sealant 87
Silicone sealant 69
Silk wallcoverings 160
Sills, repairing 58, 59, 60

Sink:
fitting double bowl 84, *84–5*
removing blockage 88
waste system *85*
Sink plunger, using 88
Skew-nailing 119, *119*, 130
Skirting, fixing 120
painting 155
running cable behind 104
Slater's ripper, using 46, 47
Slates 42, 43
felt 55
fixing *46*, 47
removing *46*, 47
replacing *46*, 47
Sliding bevel 126, *127*
Smoothing brush *151*
Socket outlets 99, 100, *100*
adding *105*
converting single to double 107,
107
wiring spur 105–6, *106*
Soffit boards 56, *56*
mitring ends 59
protecting 58
repairing rotten 58, 59
repairing bearers 58
replacing 58, 59
Softwood 122
painting 68
pickling 135
priming 162
special finishing 135
Soil, compacting 12
types 20
Soldered joint, making 82, *82*
Soldered pipe-fittings *78*, 79
Soldier course 29
Spalling, of bricks 22
of roof tiles 43
Spirit level, 126
Sponging 158–9, *158*
Spot board, making 25
Spraygun, using 73
Sprung metal draught excluder
140, *140*
Spur (concrete) 64
Spur (electrical) 99
wiring 105–6, *106*
Square, carpenter's 126, *127*
making builder's 13
Square-edged boards 67
Stabilising primer 69
Stack bond (blockwork) 28
Stain for wood 69
Staining hardwoods 69
wood 71
Stencilling 181
Steps, building *40–1*, 41
for decorating 150
Stone, painting 153
Stone paint 69
Stone paving slabs, cutting 37
laying 37
second-hand 37
Stopcock:
fitting 84
identifying 79
position in rising main 84
replacing washer 85
rising main 78
Water Authority's 78
Straight-edge 126
Stretcher (brick) 26
Stretcher bond:
in blockwork 28
in brick paving *39*
in brickwork 26, *26*
Stripping knife *151*
Struck joint (brickwork) *30*
making 30, 32
Stucco rendering 32
Stud (timber) 113

Stud partition:
building 116–20, *117–20*
constructing framework 117, *118–9*
fixing ceiling plate 117, *118*, 119
fixing nogging 119, *119*
fixing plasterboard 119, *119*
fixing soleplate 117, *118*
fixing studs 119, *119*
running cable down 104
Sulphates, in brick 10
in soil 10
Supadriv screw and driver 131
Supatap *88*
replacing washer 88
Switch. *See under types*
Switchfuse 96
fitting 108, *108*, 109
Sycamore 122

Tampling beam, making 13, *13*
using *19*
Tap:
fitting shower mixer 87
fitting sink mixer 84, *84*
leaking 88
removing old 87
replacing shield 85
replacing washer 84–5, 88
types 88, *88*
Tap connector, fitting 84
Tap converter 85
Tap-in screw 121
Tar-oil preservative 57
Teak 122
Teak oil 134
Tenon, cutting 132, *132*, 133, 142
Tenon saw 127, *127*
Terminal block, 3-way 106, *108*
Thermostat 92–3
Thermostatic radiator valve (TRV), fitting 93, *93*
Third bond (blockwork) 28
Threshold strip 140, *140*
Tiles, floor: *see* Floor tiles
roof: *see* Roof tiles
wall: *see* Ceramic tiles
Tile-hung walls 54, *54*
Tile roof, repairing 47–8, *47–9*
Tile slips 48
Tiling walls:
grouting 172, *172*
preparing surface 171
round pipes 173
setting out 172, *172*
spacing 172
tools for 171
Timber:
buying 122–3
causes of rot in 122
faults in *123*
filling grain 70, 135
joining 130–3, *131–3*
joints in 62, *63*, *132–3*, 133
kiln-dried 122
marking *132*
moisture content 122
paint for 69
painting 71
painting unprimed 155
planed all round (PAR) 122
preparing for painting 70
priming 70
removing paint from 153, *153*
sawn 122
sealing 134
sealing knots 70
seasoned 122
size of section 122–3
stacking *123*
stain for 69
staining 71
stripping stain 71–2

stripping varnish 71–2
tools for 124–30, *125*, *127*, *129*
types 122, *123*
varnish for 69
varnishing 71
water-resistant 122
weather-resistant 122
See also Hardwood; Man-made boards; Softwood
Timber (external):
constructing 57
deterioration of 56–7
factory-treated 57
features *56*
fixings for 58
jointing 57
linked to house: *see* Linked timber
moisture content of 60
preserving 57
protecting 57
repairing rotten 58
sealing 57
shrinking of 60
swelling of 60
tools for 58, *58–9*
treating 57
Timber cladding *56*, 57, *57*
deterioration of 57
for shed walls 64, *66*
repairing 60
replacing battens 60, *60*
treating 57
Timber finishes 134–5, *134–5*
Timber preservatives 57
Timber primer 69
aluminium 69
Time clock 93
Toggle fastener 121, *121*
Tools:
cleaning concrete from 15
for bricklaying 25, *25*
for concreting 12–13, *13*
for electricity 102, *102*
for exterior timber 58, *58–9*
for decorating 150–1, *150–1*
for internal walls 116, 119
for plasterboard 116, 119
for plaster 153
for plumbing 81, *81*
for tiling walls 171
for timber 124–30, *125*, *127*, *129*
sharpening *125*, 130
Town & Country Planning Act 62
Trowel, bricklayer's 25
Trunking, running cable in 104
TRV: *see* Thermostatic radiator valve
Trysquare 126, *127*
Tube draught excluder 140, *140*
Twist bits *125*
Tyrolean rendering 32, *33*
applying 33
finishing 33
mixing 33

U-trap *78*, 83

Valley gutter, repairing 49
replacing 49
Vapour barrier for walls 143
Varnish for wood 69
See also Lacquer
Varnishing hardwoods 69
wood 71
Vaseline, as timber finish 134
Ventilation, effect of draughtproofing on 139
for fuel-burning appliance 145
Ventilator, fitting 145
free area of 145
Verges, repairing cracked 48
repointing 48

Vermiculite, laying 141, *141*
Vinyl sheet flooring 174
laying 177–8, *178*
Vinyl tiles 174, *174*
laying 177
Vinyl wallpaper 160
Voltage 96

Wall:
brick, building 28, 29, *29*
marking out 20, 29, *29*
external, definition 112
heat loss through 138
insulating 139
free-standing 10, 29
garden 29
hollow, fixing to 121, *121*
insulating 152
internal. *See* Internal walls
painting 154, 155
painting exterior 72
from scaffold tower 72
painting porous 72
painting over old paint 155
preparing 72
retaining 10
screen, building 31, *31*
shed, construction 64, *65–6*
solid, dry-lining 142–3, *142*
fixing to 120–1, *121*
insulating 139
insulating exterior of 142
insulating interior of 142–3, *142*
tile-hung, re-covering 54, *54*
tiling 171–3, *172*, *173*
timber, treating 64
Wall cladding:
PVC extrusions 60
timber *56*, 57, *57*
deterioration of 57
repairing rotten 60
replacing 60, *60*
replacing battens 60, *60*
treating 57
Wall-coverings 166, *167*
See also Wallpaper, Wallboards
Wall fixings 120–1, *121*
for exterior timber 58
Wall lights, fitting 111, *111*
Wall plate, fixing 62, *63*
for lean-to 62, *63*
Wall plugs 120–1, *121*
holes for 121
lubricating 121
securing loose 121
Wall tiles: *see* Ceramic tiles
Wallboards 166, 167, 169, *169*
painting over 153
Wallpaper:
dry-strippable 160
estimating quantity 162, *162*
hanging 164: *see also* Wallpapering
painting over 154
ready-pasted 160, *160*
types 160, *160*
washable 160, *160*
stripping 154
Woodchip 160
Wallpaper paste 151, *151*
Wallpapering 163–6, *164–6*
matching pattern 162, *162*
pasting and folding paper 164, *164*
trimming paper 164–5
Wash basin, removing blockages from 88
Washing machine, water supply for 84
Waste fittings *78–9*
Waste outlet 83
fitting 84, *85*

Waste pipe, cutting 83–4, *83*
expansion allowance 83, 84
joining 83, 84
Waste systems 83
for double sink 85
push-fit plastics 83
removing blockages 88
single stack 78, *80*
solvent-welded PVC 83, *83*
two-pipe 78
Waste trap:
bath *78*, 83
bottle *78*, 83
clearing 88
fitting U-trap 84, *85*
U-trap *78*, 83
Water, for mixing concrete 11
Water Authority byelaws 78
Water-borne preservatives 57
Water supply *80*
cutting off 84
for dishwasher 84
for shower 87, 109
for washing machine 84
Waxing timber 135
WC, removing blockage 88
Weatherboard, replacing 60
Weatherproofing brickwork 69
Web cramp 126
Wet-and-dry paper 150
Wet dash: *see* Roughcast
Wheelbarrow for concrete 13
Window, window frame:
deterioration of 57
draughtproofing 139, 140
glazing 72
stained-timber 72
varnished timber 72
heat loss through 138
insulating 139, 143–5, *144*
See also Double Glazing
painting 59, 71, 164, *165*
casement 154
repairing casement 59
repairing timber 59
replacing timber 59
shed, constructing 64, *66*
water penetration 57
Window recess, papering *165*
Window sill, deterioration 57
painting drip channel 71
repairing 59
Wire brush 150, *151*
Wiring, outside 108, *108*
Wood: *see* Timber
Wood flooring *174*, 176
Woodchip wallpaper 160
Woodworking tools 124–30, *125*, *127*, *129*
Worktop, laying floor slab 21

Yorkshire fittings 78, 79

Zinc chromate primer 69
Zinc phosphate primer 69
Zinc sheet for roof valleys 49

ACKNOWLEDGEMENTS

SPECIAL PHOTOGRAPHY
Most of the photographs in this book were specially commissioned from the following, to whom the publishers extend their thanks:

Theo Bergstrom 161, 175; **Jon Bouchier** 110 below; **John Cook** 148; **Simon de Courcy Wheeler** half title, title, 81 inset, 82–94 above, 95, 103–111, 132, 133, 136, 137, 144, 145; **Chris Linton** 12, 16–20, 21 below, 27–30 left, 32, 33, 38, 60, 61, 70, 71, 117–20; **Reg Perkes** 10–11, 22–3, 25, 58–9, 78–9, 81, 96–7, 98–9, 100–103, 122–129, 131, 134, 135, 138–9.

TOOLS, EQUIPMENT & FACILITIES
The publishers are grateful to the many organizations and individuals who supplied materials, tools, and other equipment or who provided locations and/or facilities for specially commissioned photography. Thanks are due especially to the following:

Tools
BLACK & DECKER LTD, Maidenhead (Mr David Whitcroft): power tools and Workmate
GEORGE BUCK LTD, Goodge Street, London, W1)Mr Quentin Russell and Mr Bill Brett): hand and power tools
KANGO WOLF LTD, London) Mr David Budge): power tools
STANLEY TOOLS LTD, Sheffield (Mr Paul Wright): carpentry toolkit

Concrete and Concrete Products
CEMENT AND CONCRETE ASSOCIATION (Mr David Helsden, Publicity Manager, and Mrs Hildegard Mahoney, Photographs Librarian, at Grosvenor Gardens, London, SW1; Mr Don Creasy at Fulmer Grange, Bucks): location, materials, technical advice
DAWSON & CO LTD, Falcon Lane, London, SW11: concrete blocks
MR WILLIAM EDWARDS: timber tools
JACKSON & CO (BARKING) LTD, Erkenwald Road, Barking: concreting tools

Bricks and Bricklaying
MR R. J. BALDWIN (Building Crafts Department, Willesden College of Technology, London, NW2): bricklaying technique and materials
DAWSON & CO LTD, Falcon Lane, London, SW11: bricks
IBSTOCK BRICKWORK DESIGN CENTRE, Crawford Street, London, W1: bricks and blocks
REDLAND LTD, Reigate: bricks, tiles, and technical advice

Plumbing and Central Heating
ASTON-MATTHEWS LTD, Essex Road, London, N1: sink unit
CLAPTON BUILDERS' MERCHANTS LTD, Upper Clapton Road, London, E5: pipe fittings and tools
GENERAL WOODWORK SUPPLIES LTD, Stoke Newington High Street, London, N16: taps and sink unit
OBC (Southern Region), Mowlem Trading Estate, Leeside Road, London, N17; central-heating controls, pump, and panel radiator

Electricity
BICC COMPONENTS LTD, Runcorn: exterior wiring glands
CITY ELECTRICAL FACTORS LTD, Kelvin Road, London N16: electrical fittings and tools
MK ELECTRIC LTD, London: electrical fittings

Internal Walls
BRITISH GYPSUM LTD, Ruddington (Notts): location for and erection of Gyproc plasterboard partition

Carpentry and Joinery
MR HUGH A. F. ALLEN: wood joints and surface treatments of timber
GENERAL WOODWORK SUPPLIES LTD, Stoke Newington High Street, London, N16: timber
W. H. NEWSON & SONS LTD, Pimlico Road, London, SW1 (Mr Dennis Sainsbury-Brown): joinery for photo-studio room set

Insulation
LUMITE DOUBLE GLAZING LTD, Slough (Mr K. Kermode): double-glazing kits

Interior Decorating
AMTICO, St. George Street, London W1
INTERFACE FLOORING SYSTEMS LTD
JUNCKERS (LONDON) LTD
MARLEY FLOORS LTD
NAIRN FLOORS
W. H. NEWSON, Pimlico Road, London SW1
SANDERSON, Berners Street, London W1
TILE MART LTD, Great Portland Street, London W1

OTHER PHOTOGRAPHS
The publishers thank the following organizations and individuals for their permission to reproduce the photographs in this book:

David Allen 21 above, 72, 73, 115; Black and Decker 130 above and middle; Bosch 130 below; Camera Press 76–7, 149 right, 162, 163 below; Cement and Concrete Association 14, 31, 36, 37, 40, 41; Cristal Tile Advisory Service 170, Coverplus (available exclusively at Woolworth) 149 left, 149 middle, 177 below; Dupre Vermiculite Ltd 141 below; Greg Evans Picture Library 8–9; Fibreglass Ltd 141 above; Good Housekeeping (David Brittain) 163 above, (William Douglas) 171, (Dennis Stone) 176; Jerry Harpur 34 (designer Geoff Kaye), 34–5 (designer Rodney Slatford); Heuga UK Ltd 177 above; House of Mayfair 149 left and middle, 177 below; ICI Paints Division 57, 69; Bill Mason 30 right, 49 above, 50; Nairn Floors 177 below; Potterton International/Donnely Burns Nicklin 94 below; Redland Ltd 39, 46–8, 49 below, 51, 54; Elizabeth Whiting and Associates 146–7, 157, 158, 159, 178, 181.

ARTWORK
Hayward & Martin Ltd 13, 17, 19, 24, 26, 30, 36, 39, 40, 42, 45, 46–7, 48, 50, 55, 56, 62–3, 64–5, 66–7, 68, 80, 85, 88, 90, 92, 121, 136–7, 140–1, 142–3, 150–1, 153–60, 162, 164–6, 168–9, 172–4, 178–9 **Ed Roberts/Jillian Burgess** 112–13, 114, 116; **David Salariya/Jillian Burgess** 122–3; **Ralph Stobart/Jillian Burgess** 96–7, 98–9, 106, 108–9; **Technical Art Services** 15, 52–3, 133.

Artwork Visualizer Mike Trier